THE SECOND
Touring Guide
to Britain

THE SECOND
Touring Guide
to Britain

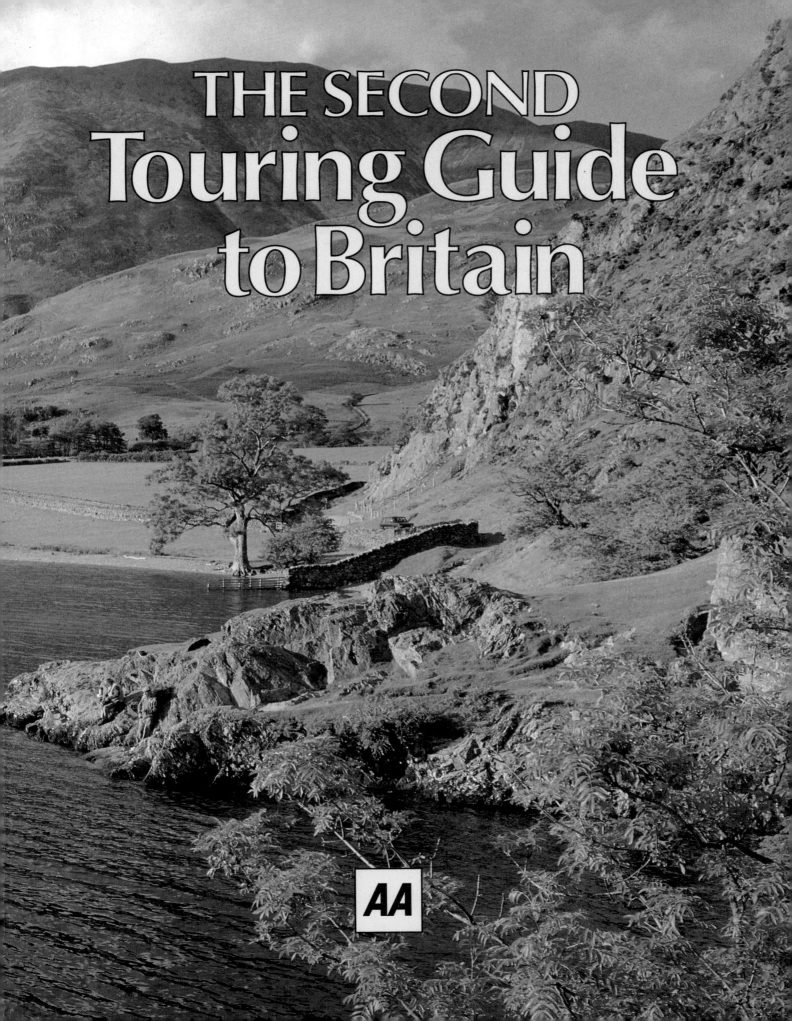

AA

Gloucester Cathedral, tour 32

Produced by the Publishing Division of the Automobile Association
Editor Rebecca Snelling
Art Editor P M Davies
Assistant Editor Richard Powell
Editorial contributors Barbara Littlewood, Michael Cady

Tours compiled and driven by the Publications Research Unit of
The Automobile Association

Photographs by Martyn J Adelman, Barnabys Picture Library, Biofotos, Martin
Boddy, British Tourist Authority, J Allan Cash Ltd, Richard Corbett, David
Cripps, Joy Hunter, Jarrold & Sons Ltd, Bob Johnson, S & O Mathews, Colin
Molyneux, Geoffrey Player, Alan Rutter, Scottish Tourist Board, Spectrum,
The Revd Jon Sumner, Richard Surman, The National Trust, Trevor Wood,
John Wyand, Yorks & Humb Tourist Board

Maps produced by the Cartographic Unit of
The Automobile Association
Based on the Ordnance Survey Maps, with the permission of the Controller
of HM Stationery Office Crown Copyright Reserved

The contents of this book are believed correct at the time of printing
Nevertheless, the Publisher cannot accept any responsibility for errors or
omissions or for changes in details given

This edition produced for Dolphin Publications, Bridge Mills Business
Park, Langley Road South, Pendleton, Salford M6 6EL

Reprinted 1990 , 1992
Reprinted with amendments 1986
Reprinted with amendments 1984
Reprinted 1983
First edition 1981

Filmset by Senator Graphics, Great Suffolk St, London SE1

Printed and bound by New Interlitho SPA, Milan, Italy

Published by The Automobile Association, Fanum House, Basingstoke,
Hampshire RG21 2EA

ISBN 0 86145 377 8

AA Ref 59501

INTRODUCTION

Britain is a land of rich heritage — the legacy of a long and crowded history — and is often described as the most varied and the most beautiful country in the world. Wherever you are, there is a place of unique interest and beauty nearby and the carefully planned motoring tours in this book provide an ideal way to discover these treasures. Each self-contained tour, which is circular and can be completed in a day, includes easy-to-read maps of the route, detailed route directions, concise text describing the most interesting places on the tour and stunning full-colour photographs which give you a foretaste of what is to come.

Top: Blickling Hall, tour 56
Above right: Pembridge, tour 40
Above: near Solva, tour 34
Right: Cromer, tour 56

ABBREVIATIONS & SYMBOLS

MAPS

Main Tour Route	
Detour/Diversion from Main Tour Route	
Motorway	
Motorway Access	
Motorway Service Area	
Motorway and Junction Under Construction	
A-class Road	A68
B-class Road	B700
Unclassified Road	unclass
Dual Carriageway	A70
Road Under Construction	====
Airport	
Battlefield	
Bridge	
Castle	
Church as Route Landmark	
Ferry	
Folly/Tower	
Gazetteer Placename	Zoo /Lydstep
Industrial Site (Old & New)	
Level Crossing	LC
Lighthouse	
Marshland	
Memorial/Monument	m
Miscellaneous Places of Interest & Route Landmarks	
National Boundary	
National Trust Property	NT
National Trust for Scotland Property	NTS
Non-gazetteer Placenames	Thames /Astwood
Notable Religious Site	
Picnic Site	PS
Prehistoric Site	
Racecourse	
Radio/TV Mast	
Railway (BR) with Station	
Railway (Special) with Station	
River & Lake	
Woodland Area	
Seaside Resort	
Stately Home	
Summit/Spot Height	KNOWE HILL 209▲
Viewpoint	

TEXT

AM	Ancient Monument
c	circa
NT	National Trust
NTS	National Trust for Scotland
OACT	Open at Certain Times
PH	Public House
SP	Signpost (s) (ed)

SCOTLAND

THE NORTH COUNTRY

CENTRAL AND EASTERN ENGLAND

WALES AND THE MARCHER LANDS

SOUTH AND SOUTH EAST ENGLAND

THE WEST COUNTRY

The book is divided into six geographical regions shown on the key maps and every tour can be located on these by its key number. Each tour occupies two pages and has a clear map accompanying the text. All the places described in the text are shown as black type on the tour maps and the route directions are set in italic type. If buildings and places of interest are open to the public at certain times only (on the date of publication) they are labelled OACT. Properties labelled NT, NTS, or AM are run by the National Trust, the National Trust for Scotland or are Ancient Monuments. These organisations should be consulted for opening details. All museums are open at certain times. It is advisable to check the opening times of any place before planning a stop there.

CONTENTS

THE WEST COUNTRY
PAGES 10-37

Opening picture: The coast near Polperro, Cornwall

SOUTH AND SOUTH EAST ENGLAND
PAGES 38-79

Opening picture: The seafront at Hastings, E Sussex

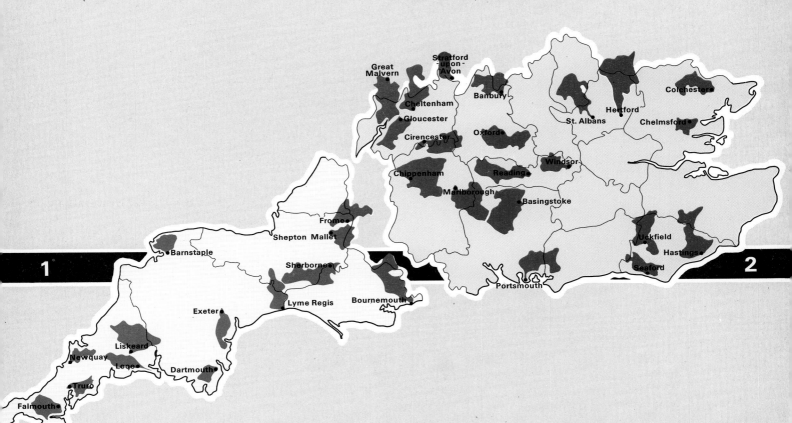

7

CONTENTS

WALES AND THE MARCHER LANDS
PAGES 80-107

Opening picture: The Black Mountains, Powys

CENTRAL AND EASTERN ENGLAND
PAGES 108-129

Opening picture: The Moot Hall at Aldeburgh, Suffolk

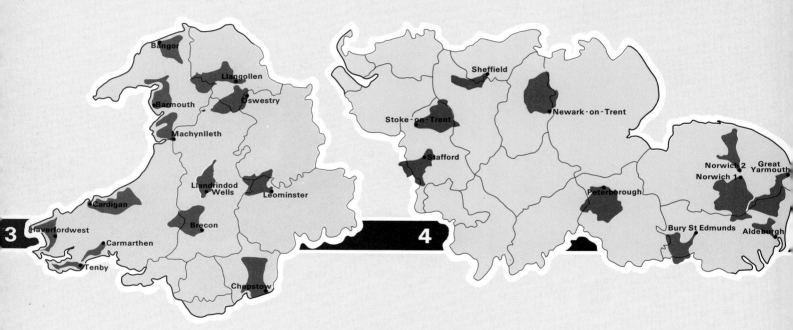

8

THE NORTH COUNTRY
PAGES 130-153

Opening picture: The village of Goathland, Yorkshire

SCOTLAND
PAGES 154-189

Opening picture: The Talla Reservoir, Borders

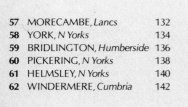

The West Country

COAST TO COAST

From Falmouth and the gentle southern coast where land and sea interlace in a maze of wooded waterways; inland to Redruth, onetime centre of tin mining and still Cornwall's industrial pulse; then northwards to jagged cliffs constantly struggling with the fierce Atlantic.

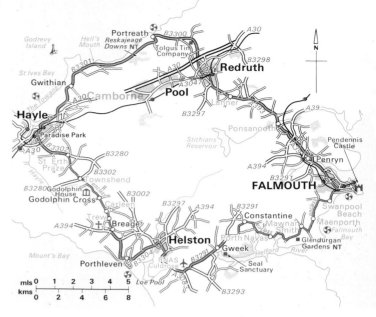

FALMOUTH, Cornwall

Falmouth has 2 distinct roles — holiday resort and port — and although tourism is more prosperous now than shipping, the harbour and docks remain busy. The town stands at the entrance to the Carrick Roads, a beautiful stretch of water formed by the merging of 7 river estuaries, and has a huge natural harbour on one side and sandy beaches and gardens on the other. The port really began to develop in the 17th century when Falmouth was made a Mail Packet Station, reaching its heyday in the 19th century. At this time it served as the hub of communications for the British Empire, and 39 ships were despatching letters all over the world. Unfortunately for Falmouth the packet service was later transferred to Southampton and prosperity declined. However, Falmouth's second role as a resort developed rapidly when the railway reached Cornwall and the exceptionally mild climate assured it year-round popularity. The long main street of the town runs beside the River Fal up from the harbour and here the older, more attractive, buildings are to be found. The twin castles of Pendennis (OACT) and St Mawes (opposite Falmouth) once stood stern guard over the entrance to the Carrick Roads. They were built by Henry VIII and Pendennis was the last Royalist stronghold to fall during the Civil War, having valiantly withstood Cromwellian armies for 5 months.

Follow SP 'Beaches' and 'Helford Passage', then 'Maenporth' and 'Mawnan'. Pass Swanpool Beach and in ½ mile at the T-junction turn left to Maenporth. In 1¼ miles turn right for Mawnan Smith. At the Red Lion Inn turn left, SP 'Helford Passage', and in ¾ mile pass (left) Glendurgan Gardens.

GLENDURGAN GARDENS, Cornwall

A small, almost secret valley descending to the Helford Passage has been turned into an oasis of exotic trees, flowers and shrubs. The gardens (NT), including a laurel maze, were originally planted on these slopes in 1833 by Alfred Fox. Three successive generations continued to cultivate the gardens which thrive in southern Cornwall's almost sub-tropical climate.

Continue for nearly ½ mile then turn right, SP 'Constantine'. After 1¼ miles turn left across a bridge, continue to Porth Navas, and in 1½ miles turn left to Constantine.

CONSTANTINE, Cornwall

The village of Constantine climbs up a long, winding street and its cottages, built of locally quarried stone, are nearly all fronted with neat, pretty gardens. Just to the north, opposite Trewardrera Manor, is an underground passage imaginatively called Piskie Hall (not open). It was part of a prehistoric fortified enclosure and is known as a fogou, the Cornish word for cave.

Continue through the village and turn left, SP 'Gweek'. In 1 mile turn right, then ½ mile farther join the B3291 to reach Gweek.

GWEEK, Cornwall

The tranquil banks of the Helford River at Gweek have become a sanctuary (OACT) for seals and birds that have been washed up around the Cornish coastline. Five large open-air pools house the animals in varying stages of recovery and the seals in particular are very appealing.

Cross the Helford River and in 1¾ miles turn right on to the B3293, then in ½ mile turn right again to join the A3083, pass the Culdrose Royal Naval Air Station and, in another 1¾ miles turn left, SP 'Penzance', for Helston.

Seals well on their way to recovery at Gweek Seal Sanctuary after being rescued from Cornish beaches where they were found orphaned or injured

HELSTON, Cornwall

At one time Helston, like most of its neighbours, was a port. However, when the Cober River silted up in the 13th century the town became landlocked and its sea trading days ended. It was not until the 18th century that Helston gained importance once more, this time as one of Cornwall's 4 official stannary towns, to which all the smelted tin in the area had to be taken for quality testing and taxing. A stannary was a mining district in Devon and Cornwall at that time. Now this pleasant market town is probably most famous for its annual festival called the Furry Dance, or Floral Dance. In early May there is continual dancing in the streets and many people dress up in top hats for the occasion. Folklore claims the dance is a celebration of the fact that no harm was done when a dragon dropped a boulder down on the town. Whatever its origins, the custom certainly stretches back thousands of years. Among Helston's hilly streets and grey stone houses is the Old Butter Market, now serving as the town museum. The small but interesting collection here covers all aspects of local history and includes an old cider mill. Also of interest is the Cornwall Aero Park and Flambards Victorian Village, an all weather family leisure park. South-west of Helston is Loe Pool, which, with a circumference of 7 miles, is Cornwall's largest lake. It was formed about 600 years ago when the Loe Bar cut the Cober off from the sea. It is possible to walk right round the lake (NT), but the less energetic might content themselves with a stroll through the beautiful woodlands on the lake's west side.

Leave Helston on the A394 Penzance Road and then turn left on to the B3304, SP 'Porthleven'.

A creek of the Helford Passage

PORTHLEVEN, Cornwall
The sweep of Mount's Bay lies at the foot of this small rocky village perched above its harbour, which at one time sheltered many sea-going vessels. Now, ship-building yards are the mainstay of the village's economy.

At the harbour turn right then right again, SP 'Penzance'. In 1¼ miles turn left on to the A394 and 1 mile farther turn right, SP 'Carleen and Godolphin', to enter Breage.

BREAGE, Cornwall
Breage's church of St Breaca is of unusual interest. Built entirely of granite and dating originally from the 15th century, it contains wall paintings on the north wall depicting, amongst others, St Christopher and the Warning to the Sabbath-Breakers. Although as old as the church itself, these were not discovered until 1891. The churchyard has a sandstone 4-holed wheel cross with Saxon decoration.

At the T-junction in Breage turn left and continue through Trew and Carleen to Godolphin Cross.

GODOLPHIN CROSS, Cornwall
A Cornish family of diverse interests gave this tiny hamlet its name, and they occupied Godolphin House (OACT) from the 15th to late 18th century. Francis Godolphin was one of the first local landowners to finance tin mining; Sidney Godolphin was Queen Anne's 1st Minister for 7 years; and the 2nd Earl of Godolphin owned one of the 3 imported Arab stallions from which all British thoroughbred horses descend. The house itself is mainly 16th century and looks most impressive from the north side with its heavy colonnade. Of particular interest inside are the

Jacobean range with its fireplace and a painting of the famous Godolphin Arabian stallion.

At Godolphin Cross go over the crossroads and after ¾ mile pass Godolphin House on the left. In ½ mile bear right over the bridge and at Townshead cross the main road, SP 'Hayle'. In another 1¾ miles turn left on to the B3302 for St Erth Praze. Before entering Hayle a side road (left) may be taken to Paradise Park.

PARADISE PARK, Cornwall
Aviaries full of richly-coloured foreign birds such as the Hyacinthine Macaw and Great African Wattled Crane are the main attractions of this complex; others include a zoo for children, a miniature steam railway and a craft village.

Continue into Hayle.

HAYLE, Cornwall
During the 18th century, Cornish copper miners had to send ore to South Wales for smelting and Hayle developed as a port for this trade. Now it is mainly a light industrial town but there is a good bathing beach beyond the nearby sand dunes called The Towans.

At Hayle join the B3301 Redruth road, then in 1½ miles turn left SP 'Portreath'. Pass grass-covered sand dunes and continue to Gwithian.

GWITHIAN, Cornwall
There is no visible evidence of it in sea-facing Gwithian, but buried beneath the sands lies a small chapel, possibly dating back to Celtic Christianity when nearby Hayle was an arrival point for Irish saints. The chapel was uncovered during excavations in the last century but has sunk into oblivion once again through neglect. The present church was built in 1886.

From Gwithian the B3301 runs parallel with the coast to Portreath. There are several good viewpoints to the left within short walking distance of the road.

PORTREATH, Cornwall
At the bottom of bleak windswept cliffs nestles the small port and holiday resort of Portreath, consisting of a cluster of tiny harbour cottages around an 18th-century pier. The views from Reskajeage Downs (NT) above are spectacular.

From Portreath follow the B3300 Redruth road. After 2 miles, on the right, is the Tolgus Tin Company.

TOLGUS TIN COMPANY, Cornwall
A small part of 18th-century industrial Cornwall can still be seen at the Tolgus Tin Mill where the ancient practice of streaming — a process which involves washing the deposits of tin from the stream bed — has been carried out for generations. The

machinery which sifts and washes the extracted deposits includes the only Cornish stamps in commercial use. These heavy stamps, powered by the water mill, crush the ore so the tin can be separated from the waste.
A small shop and visitor centre are open to the public.

Continue into Redruth.

REDRUTH, Cornwall
Camborne and Redruth have practically merged into one town and between them support the largest concentration of population in Cornwall. Redruth has always been at the centre of the mining industry and the town has remained primarily an industrial centre. Probably the most interesting aspects of this tradition are the engines displayed at nearby Pool. One of these is an 1887 winding engine which used to wind men as well as materials several hundred feet up and down copper and tin mine shafts. The other is an 1892 pumping engine, with a 52-ton beam used to pump water.

In Redruth turn left with the one-way traffic, then turn right and follow SP 'Falmouth' on the A393. Continue through Lanner to Ponsanooth, then in 1¾ miles go forward on to the A39 and skirt Penryn.

PENRYN, Cornwall
Almost everything that could be is built of granite here, and huge blocks of it from the Penryn quarries lie on the docks waiting to be shipped out of Cornwall. Penryn lies around the headland from Falmouth on another finger of the Carrick Roads, enjoying the same mild climate and luxuriant vegetation.

Return to Falmouth on the A39.

Hundreds of ships, including the *Nile* that cost many lives, were wrecked before Godrevy Lighthouse was built off Godrevy Point in 1859

13

TRURO, Cornwall

Although it lies on the River Truro — a finger of the Fal estuary — and its history belongs to the sea, Truro serves its county now as administrative capital and cathedral city. During the Middle Ages it was important in the export of mineral ore and from the 13th to 18th centuries was one of the 4 Cornish stannary towns that controlled the quality of tin. The city's 18th-century popularity with wealthy sea merchants left a legacy of fine Georgian architecture to rival that of Bath. Truro became a fashionable focal point of society and the old theatre and assembly rooms next to the cathedral were particularly popular meeting places. However, it is in Lemon Street and Walsingham Place that the finest buildings can be seen from this elegant era. The cathedral is a relatively recent feature of Truro. For 800 years the See of Cornwall was shared with Devon, but when it was reconstituted in 1897 a new cathedral was begun. Built in early English style, it incorporated the old Church of St Mary and was completed in 1910. Inside, the main features are the baptistry, a massive Jacobean monument and the wall of the north choir. For a comprehensive picture of Cornwall's history visit the County Museum in River Street. Here too is an excellent array of Cornish minerals, together with unusual collections of porcelain and pottery. There is a small art gallery as well, containing paintings, engravings and drawings.

Leave Truro on the A39, SP 'Bodmin'. Continue through wooded country to Tresillian, situated on the creek of the Tresillian River. Cross the bridge and in 1 mile keep forward on the A390, SP 'St Austell', to Probus.

PROBUS, Cornwall

This tiny village boasts the tallest church tower in Cornwall, rising in 3 tiers to 126ft. Built during the 16th century of granite, it is richly decorated with figures, heads, animals and tracery, and lichen has given it all a pleasant greenish hue. It is strange to find this lofty tower here because the style resembles that of Somerset's churches and this ranks among the best examples.

Beyond the village pass on the right the County Demonstration Garden.

COUNTY DEMONSTRATION GARDEN AND ARBORETUM, Cornwall

Keen gardeners will find this place fascinating. Detailed displays show all aspects of gardening, including layout, the selection of plants and flowers to suit particular requirements and the effect of different weather conditions on gardens. Attractive exhibitions of fruit, herbs, flowers and vegetables

CATHEDRAL CITY BY THE SEA

In all her Georgian elegance, Truro lies demurely between shady creeks of woodland and water and the strange white moonscape of St Austell's hills of china clay. Away from these the tour runs through hidden fishing villages by way of twisting lanes, high-banked and narrow.

Truro Cathedral, although built in the 20th century, harmonises well with the town's Georgian architecture

illustrate a wealth of information and interest for those either with or without a garden.

Continue on the St Austell road and in ½ mile pass the entrance to Trewithen House and Gardens.

TREWITHEN HOUSE AND GARDENS, Cornwall

This simple, elegant manor house (OACT) of Pentewan stone was built for the Hawkins family in 1723. The interior is mainly Palladian yet each room has its own individuality: the oak room is panelled with oak, the dining room is decorated in grey-green and white and the drawing room is embellished with Chinese fretwork. The surrounding gardens are typical of Cornwall — huge banks of rhododendrons and magnolias ornament landscaped woodland affording frequent glimpses of sweeping parkland.

Remain on the A390 and continue through Grampound and Sticker to St Austell.

ST AUSTELL, Cornwall

White, unnatural peaks rise up to the north of St Austell, giving the moors an almost lunar appearance. They are the great spoil-heaps of white china clay which forms the basis of the town's main industry. Before the discovery of this valuable natural resource in 1775 by William Cookworthy, St Austell was just another small tin-mining town. Clay pits were opened soon after this date and today the clay is one of Britain's major export materials. The town itself has more the appearance of a market town than an industrial one, and numbering among its pleasant buildings are the town hall, the Quaker Meeting House, the White Hart Hotel and Holy Trinity Church.

Leave St Austell on the B3273 and continue to Mevagissey.

MEVAGISSEY, Cornwall

Narrow streets wind up from the harbour of Mevagissey and colour-washed cottages cover the cliffsides haphazardly. Like many Cornish coastal villages, fishing has always provided Mevagissey with a livelihood and pilchard fishing in particular brought wealth to the village in the 18th and 19th centuries, although smuggling contributed substantially to the riches too. Besides frequent shark and mackerel fishing trips, other attractions in the village include a folk museum and a model railway. The former occupies an 18th-century boatbuilder's workshop and concentrates on local crafts, mining and agricultural equipment and seafaring relics. The latter runs through varied model terrain which includes an Alpine ski resort and a china clay pit.

Return along the B3273 and in 1 mile turn left on to an unclassified road, SP 'Gorran'. After another 1¼ miles turn left again and continue to Gorran. Beyond the village keep left, SP 'Gorran Haven', then take the next turning right and bear right again to reach Gorran Haven.

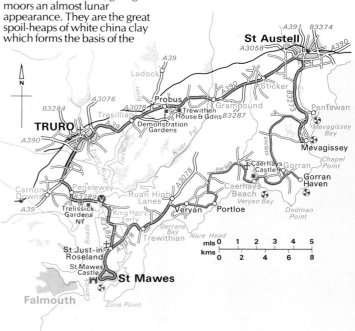

GORRAN HAVEN, Cornwall
This tiny, remote village rivalled Mevagissey in the heyday of pilchard fishing. It is a charmingly unspoilt resort now, with one village street and a pebbly beach.

Return for 1 mile to the T-junction and turn left, then in 250 yards turn left again, SP 'Caerhays'. Touch the coast again at the attractive Caerhays Beach where to the right stands Caerhays Castle.

CAERHAYS CASTLE, Cornwall
Perched above a bay, this castellated mansion (not open) looks like a fairy castle when seen from the cliff road. It was built by John Nash in 1808 for J.B. Trevannion — whose family had owned the estate since the 14th century.

A steep climb leads to St Michael's Caerhays Church. In ¾ mile take the 2nd turning left, SP 'St Mawes and Veryan', then keep left. After 1¼ miles keep left again then turn left, SP 'Veryan' and 'Portholland'. In ¾ mile turn left and nearly ½ mile farther left again, SP 'Portloe'. In just over ¼ mile bear right then descend to Portloe.

PORTLOE, Cornwall
A stream flows through this minute fishing village down to the sea. Between the steep cliffs there is a small rocky beach which is good for swimming. Traditional south Cornish beach boats work here full time, each handling about 100 crab pots.

Beyond the village ascend, then in 1 mile go over the crossroads and continue to Veryan.

VERYAN, Cornwall
Hidden in a wooded valley is the delightful inland village of Veryan. Its most distinguishing feature is its 5 Round Houses. These, placed 2 at each end of the village and 1 in the middle, are round, white-washed cottages with conical thatched roofs. A local story has it that a parson built them for his 5 daughters and he made them round so that the devil would have no corners to hide in.

Turn left, then right on to the St Mawes road. In ½ mile turn left on to the A3078. Pass through Trewithian to reach St Just in Roseland.

ST JUST IN ROSELAND, Cornwall
Tucked away up a creek of the Carrick Roads lies a tiny hamlet that more than lives up to its picturesque name; St Just was believed to be a 6th-century Celtic saint. There is little more to this place than the church, the rectory and a cottage or two, but it has one of the most beautiful churchyards in the country and it is this which has made St Just in Roseland so famous. The church lies at the bottom of a steeply wooded combe descending from the road. Enter it through a lychgate and at this point you can look down on the church tower. The way down passes through luxuriant trees and shrubs — many

familiar such as rhododendrons, hydrangeas and camelias; many not so well known — such as the Chilean myrtle, bamboos and the African strawberry tree. On either side of the path stand granite blocks inscribed with biblical verses and quotations. Another lychgate at the bottom (with an unusual granite cattle grid) leads out of the churchyard. This glorious garden is largely due to One Revd C.W. Carlyon (church rector) who began planting the shrubs in the mid-19th century.

Continue on the A3078 and in 1 mile turn right into Upper Castle Road, SP 'St Mawes via Castle'. Pass St Mawes Castle to enter the resort of St Mawes.

ST MAWES, Cornwall
St Mawes commands a fine view over the Carrick Roads and it was this strategic position which provided such an ideal site for Henry VIII's defensive castle (AM) built in the early 1540s at the

Both fishing boats and pleasure craft share Mevagissey's lively harbour

southernmost tip of the town. In fact the castle saw very little action and its great tower and battlements still stand today in excellent repair. The resort itself is smart and relatively unspoilt by tourism, backing up steeply behind the quay which was busy with sea trade in the Middle Ages.

Follow the road around the harbour and return to St Just in Roseland. Here, branch left on to the B3289 and later descend to the King Harry Ferry. On the far side climb steeply and pass Trelissick Gardens on the left.

TRELISSICK GARDENS, Cornwall
Although a house (not open) has stood here since the mid-18th century, it was not until the late 19th century that the grounds (NT) were landscaped. The Copelands, who inherited the house in 1937, continued to improve them and gave the gardens their present shape. Smooth expanses of lawn enclosed by dense shrubs and woods pierced by winding walks characterise Trelissick. Two specialities here are a collection of over 130 species of hydrangea and a dell full of giant cedar and cypress trees.

The tour continues on the B3289 and after ½ mile, at the crossroads, turn right, SP 'Truro'. Beyond Penelewey turn right again on to the A39 for the return to Truro.

CORNWALL'S STERNEST COAST

Great Atlantic rollers forever pound the towering cliffs of north Cornwall, spilling their energy in roaring white surf along the wide sandy beaches which have made Newquay and Padstow such popular resorts. The calm of antiquity is reflected inland, however, where a rolling landscape gently laps the rugged edge of stark Bodmin Moor.

NEWQUAY, Cornwall

Newquay's popularity as a holiday resort stems chiefly from its magnificent sandy beaches and the superb surfing which is probably the best in Cornwall. The most attractive area of the town itself is the 17th-century harbour. Here, some of the pilot gigs which used to guide in the cargo schooners during the 19th century have been preserved. On the headland west of the harbour is another relic from Newquay's past — the Huer's Hut. In the days when pilchards provided the town with a living, a man called a huer kept watch for shoals of pilchards entering the bay. When he saw the water reddening from the mass of fish, he alerted the town by shouting. To the west lies Trenance Park and Cornwall's only full-size zoo. Eight acres of landscaped grounds effectively display wild animals, tropical birds, wildfowl, reptiles, seals and penguins and there is a pets' corner to keep children happy.

Leave Newquay on the A392, SP 'Bodmin'. In ¾ mile, turn left on to the B3276, SP 'Padstow'. Continue to Mawgan Porth.

MAWGAN PORTH, Cornwall

The small safe bay at Mawgan Porth lies at the entrance to the lovely Lanherne Valley leading up to St Mawgan. There is a wooden monument shaped like a boat in this village which commemorates the lives of 10 seamen who were shipwrecked and swept ashore at Mawgan Porth. Remains of a settlement (AM) that supported a small community of fishermen and cattle breeders from the 9th to the 11th centuries are visible near the beach and the foundations of their courtyard houses and outline of the cemetery can be discerned.

From Mawgan Porth climb to Trenance. After another mile, on the left, is the track which leads to Bedruthan Steps.

BEDRUTHAN STEPS, Cornwall

Huge lumps of granite march along this beautiful, rugged beach. The rocks were, allegedly, named Bedruthan Steps because they were thought to be the stepping stones of the giant Bedruthan. This stretch of coast (NT) is one of the most spectacular in Cornwall and the great sands are usually deserted because a steep scramble down the cliff is the only access.

Continue on the B3276 and in 1¼ miles at the T-junction turn left, then ½ mile farther turn left again for the descent to Porthcothan.

The great crags of Bedruthan Steps rise up some 200ft from the deserted sands

PORTHCOTHAN, Cornwall

The sea reaches almost to the road at Porthcothan and the great cliffs on either side are more than a match for the angry attacks of the relentless Atlantic ocean. The shelter of the rocks obviously well suited smugglers because an underground passage emerges further up the valley, and it was along here that the daredevil smugglers hid their spoils and hauled up their luggers.

Turn inland from Porthcothan and after 1 mile turn left and continue to St Merryn.

ST MERRYN, Cornwall

A newer village has developed a little way from the old church and its protective cluster of cottages. The interior pillars of the church and font are made of locally cliff-quarried Catacleuse slate. This handsome dark blue-grey stone was the only slate that could be carved easily, which is why nearly all the carved work in Cornish churches is out of this slate. Old village stocks are kept in the church porch.

At the Farmers' Arms PH in St Merryn turn left SP 'Harlyn'. In 1 mile turn right for Harlyn Bay.

Most of Newquay, north Cornwall's largest resort, has been built along the cliffs above its large, sandy beaches

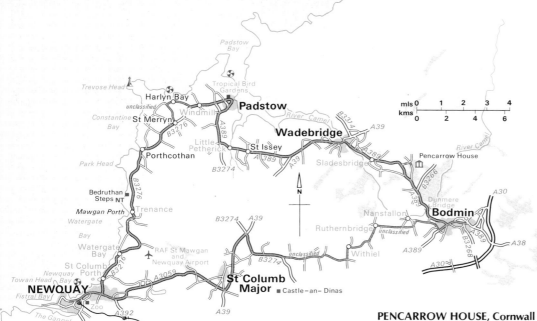

into steep granite tors, the highest being Rough Tor and Brown Willy, yet there is also a gentler aspect to the moor, of fields and wild flowers. St Petroc founded a monastery in Bodmin and his name lives on in the parish church, St Petroc's, which is the largest in Cornwall. At one time the town was renowned for its holy wells which cured eye complaints. One such well, St Guron's, stands near the church inscribed with the date 1700 and an advertisement extolling the well's powers.

Follow SP 'Redruth (A30)' and at the end of the town go forward. In ½ mile turn right, SP 'Wadebridge and Nanstallon'. In nearly another ½ mile keep left still SP 'Nanstallon'. In ¾ mile bear left, SP 'Ruthern', and go forward at the crossroads to Ruthernbridge. Here, turn left, SP 'Withiel', then in ¾ mile turn right and continue to Withiel. Here turn left, SP 'Roche', and at the church turn left again and in ½ mile turn right, SP 'St Wenn'. In 1¾ miles keep forward, SP 'St Columb', then in another mile join the B3274. In 2¼ miles turn left on to the A39 SP 'Truro', and continue along the St Columb Major bypass. From this road a detour may be made to St Columb Major.

ST COLUMB MAJOR, Cornwall
One of the chief churches in Cornwall belongs to St Columb Major. St Columba stands in a commanding position in a large churchyard and the tower has the unusual feature of 4 tiers. The good 16th-17th-century brasses inside are dedicated to the Arundell family who lived at Lanherne. Every Shrove Tuesday a local adaptation of the handball game of hurling takes place in the town's streets, using a traditional, applewood ball covered with silver. Two and a half miles south-east of St Columb Major is Castle an Dinas — an Iron-Age fort which still has 3 ramparts visible.

From the southern end of the St Columb Major Bypass the tour follows the A3059 Newquay road. In 5½ miles turn right on to the A392 for the return to Newquay.

HARLYN BAY, Cornwall
For thousands of years an Iron-Age cemetery lay hidden beneath the sands near Harlyn Bay. In 1900 it was accidentally discovered and proved to have once been the site of over 100 graves. Five of the slate slabs have been preserved on the site and a small museum nearby contains the various other finds such as brooches, tools and combs which were buried with those far-off peoples.

Cross the river bridge and in 1 mile turn left to rejoin the B3276, SP 'Padstow'. Pass through Windmill and in ¾ mile keep left, then nearly ½ mile farther turn left again for Padstow.

PADSTOW, Cornwall
Padstow is one of north Cornwall's oldest and most charming fishing towns. However, its days as a fishing and export port ended in the mid-19th century when the Camel estuary silted up, and the picturesque harbour and crooked streets now throng with holiday-makers. An annual highlight in Padstow is May Day when the Hobby Horse Dance Festival takes place. The ritual of a masked man and a bizarre hobby horse dancing through the streets welcomes summer and is supposed to be the oldest dance festival in Europe. St Petroc's Church is a reminder of the early Christianity in Padstow, dating from the 6th century when St Petroc came here from Ireland to found a monastery. (Padstow is a derivation of Petrocstowe.) The original monastic site may have been the one now occupied by Prideaux Place (not open) just above the church. This is a handsome Elizabethan house — home of the Prideaux family for several hundred years — and a monument to the Prideaux lies in

the church. Another interesting feature of Padstow is its tropical bird and butterfly gardens. A walk-in tropical house with free-flying birds and a butterfly exhibition where butterflies fly free in the summer, shows off these creatures in ideal conditions.

From the one-way system in Padstow follow SP 'Wadebridge' and ascend and at the top turn left on to the A398. In 2 miles turn left, continue through Little Petherick, and climb to St Issey.

ST ISSEY, Cornwall
About 20 figures placed in niches of Cataclewse stone stand inside St Issey's church. They were probably part of a tombchest at one time, but form part of the altar canopy now. The church tower collapsed in the last century but was rebuilt in 1873. A photograph from 1869 shows the tower falling and a policeman in a top hat looking helplessly on.

Remain on the A389 and in 2 miles turn left on to the A39 and continue to Wadebridge.

WADEBRIDGE, Cornwall
The centrepiece of this small market town is a fine medieval bridge crossing over the River Camel to Egloshayle. It was built by the vicar of Egloshayle, (the mother church of Wadebridge), because he deemed the ferry crossing to be too dangerous for his parishioners. The bridge, 320ft long, the longest in Cornwall, originally had 17 arches but 1 has since been blocked up. The foundations beneath the pillars are believed to have been based on packs of wool.

Cross the River Camel and on the far side turn right on to the A389, SP 'Bodmin'. A pleasant road then passes through Sladesbridge and after 2¼ miles a turning on the left leads to Pencarrow House.

PENCARROW HOUSE, Cornwall
Dense woods and rhododendrons cover an estate of 35 acres and in the middle hides modest, 18th-century Pencarrow House (OACT). The approach is mysterious; along a winding wooded drive and past an Iron-Age encampment ringed by dwarf oaks. Sir John Molesworth began the house in the 1700s and his descendants live there now. A great deal of the contents have been accumulated through prosperous marriages and the interior has been tastefully adapted to show the beautiful treasures off to maximum advantage.

Continue on the Bodmin road and recross the River Camel at Dunmere Bridge. A short climb then brings the tour into Bodmin.

BODMIN, Cornwall
Bodmin lies on the steep south-west edge of Bodmin Moor, equidistant between Cornwall's north and south coasts, which makes it an ideal touring base. Approximately 12 miles square make up Bodmin Moor and very few roads cross its bleak face. The boulder-strewn slopes break out

The beach at Harlyn Bay, satellite of Newquay, is a popular bathing spot

LOOE, Cornwall

Now one resort, until 1883 West and East Looe were separate towns facing each other over the Looe River. Large beaches provide good bathing, surfing and angling, and Looe is Cornwall's main centre for shark fishing. The British International Sea Angling Festival is held here every autumn, and the captured sharks are subsequently chopped up and used as crab and lobster bait. West Looe has an attractive quay, and its focal point is the 19th-century church of St Nicholas, which was built mainly from the timber of wrecked ships. The tower of the church was effectively used at one time as a cage for scolding women. Nearby a 16th-century inn is renowned as a onetime haunt of smugglers. East Looe's museum is housed on the upper floor of the 16th-century guildhall (once used as a gaol), and downstairs the old town stocks and pillory can be seen. The narrow winding main street has little alleys and courts on one side leading to the quays. Near the Victorian warehouses is an aquarium which also has a stuffed shark and an old boat-building shed.

Leave on the A387 SP 'Plymouth via Torpoint'. In ½ mile branch right on to the B3253. In 3¾ miles rejoin the A387 and at Hessenford turn right on to the B3247, SP 'Seaton'. From Seaton an unclassified road on the right may be taken to the Woolly Monkey Sanctuary at Murrayton.

WOOLLY MONKEY SANCTUARY, Cornwall

South American woolly monkeys, Chinese geese, donkeys and rabbits live in this haven where there are no cages. Part of the wooded valley at Murrayton has been turned into a free-roaming sanctuary where visitors can observe these animals at close quarters (OACT).

From Seaton the main tour continues through Downderry and in 1¼ miles bears right. At Crafthole continue on the Millbrook road then in 2 miles turn right SP 'Whitsand Bay'. After 3 miles veer inland to reach the outskirts of Cawsand and Kingsand.

CAWSAND AND KINGSAND, Cornwall

As the streets of these twin villages run into each other it is hard to distinguish between them. Before the Plymouth breakwater was built, Cawsand Bay was an ideal place for the Royal Naval fleet to anchor in the 18th century and the wealth that they bought accounts for the many fine houses in the villages. The pubs too date from these prosperous times and Lord Nelson and Lady Hamilton used to stay at the Ship Inn.

SOUTH-EASTERN CORNWALL

Between Bodmin Moor and the Channel lies the high tableland of south-east Cornwall, its surface cut by deep wooded valleys branching into the sea. Two former capitals of the ancient royal Duchy lie within this peaceful region: the tiny cathedral 'city' of St Germans and the old stannary town of Lostwithiel.

Keep left and in ½ mile turn left, SP 'Millbrook'. At the top of the ascent turn left again on to the B3247. Alternatively, turn right to visit Mount Edgcumbe House and Country Park.

View from the long-distance coastal path, near Polperro

MOUNT EDGCUMBE HOUSE AND COUNTRY PARK, Cornwall

Facing Plymouth across the Sound is Mount Edgcumbe House. First built in the 16th century, it was a victim of the 1941 Plymouth Blitz and afterwards was restored as a Tudor mansion. The house, home of the Earl of Mount Edgcumbe, has fine Hepplewhite furniture, much of which came from the Edgcumbe family's original home, Cotehele. Most of the large estate has been turned into a country park and it provides scenic walks along 10 miles of beautiful coastline.

The main tour continues to Millbrook. Here turn left, SP 'Torpoint', then bear right. In 2¾ miles turn right and later descend to Antony. From here another detour can be made by turning right on to the A374 Torpoint road to Antony House.

ANTONY HOUSE, Cornwall

This dignified, silvery-grey Queen Anne mansion (NT) overlooks the Lynher River Estuary just over the water from Plymouth. The house is well known for its associations with the Cornish Carew family who played an active and often dangerous part in political affairs. Richard Carew wrote *Survey of Cornwall* in 1602, and it provides a unique record of the county during those days. The house is currently lived in by the Carew descendants and with its small, panelled rooms has more the air of a country home than a showplace.

From Antony follow the A374 Liskeard road, and continue through Sheviock to Polbathic. Here turn right on to the B3249, SP 'St Germans'. In 1 mile bear left, SP 'Saltash', to enter St Germans.

ST GERMANS, Cornwall

Until 1043 when the Cornish Bishopric merged with Exeter, this little village was Cornwall's cathedral 'city'. During the following century St Germans was recognised as an Augustinian priory and the existing church was consecrated in 1261. Much of this building has survived and stands as one of Cornwall's best examples of Norman architecture. The turreted house (not open) quite separate from the church, has been the home of the Earls of St Germans, the Eliots, since 1655. It was rebuilt about 1804 although the grounds were laid out 10 years

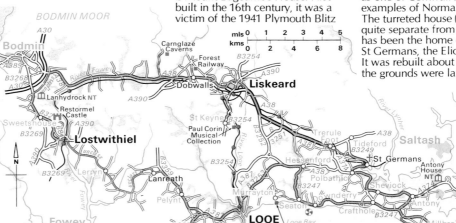

One of the Forest Railway's locos

earlier by the famous landscape gardener Humphry Repton. Of particular interest in the village itself are 6 gabled almshouses. The projecting gables stand on tall stone piers, forming a balcony which may be reached by an outside flight of steps.

At the far end of the village branch left, SP 'Liskeard'. In 1 mile go over the crossroads and in another ¾ mile turn right on to the A374. At the roundabout take the 2nd exit to join the A38. Follow this trunk road for 5½ miles before branching left on to the A390 to reach Liskeard.

LISKEARD, Cornwall

Liskeard's site across a valley accounts for its steep, narrow streets. It is a pleasant market town with a large monthly cattle fair and was one of Cornwall's 4 stannary towns. Among Liskeard's (pronounced Liscard) attractive buildings is Stuart House, where Charles I slept for a week during 1644. Well Lane is so named because a spring there, Pipe Well, was supposed to have healing properties in medieval days. Four pipes from an arched grotto produce a continual flow of water.

A 2½ mile diversion south of Liskeard leads to the Paul Corin Musical Collection at St Keyne Station. The best approach is via the B3254 and an unclassified road, SP 'St Keyne'.

PAUL CORIN MUSICAL COLLECTION, Cornwall

This fascinating collection of mechanical musical instruments founded by Paul Corin at St Keyne is housed in an old mill. Examples from all over Europe can be seen here, including fairground organs, cafe and street organs and pianos. The exhibits are all played daily, and there are European cafe orchestrations and piano performances of famous pianists to be heard.

From Liskeard the main tour follows SP 'Bodmin' and then rejoins the A38 to Dobwalls.

DOBWALLS, Cornwall

Just north of the village run 2 miles of elaborate miniature railway line. This is the Forest Railway and it is based on the steam era of the American railroad and the corresponding landscape includes lakes, forests, tunnels and canyons. In addition, the Park has an indoor railway museum, a railway walk, and play and picnic areas. Next door, in a large converted barn, is a different source of interest — the Thorburn Museum and Gallery. Here are the works of Archibald Thorburn, one of Britain's greatest bird painters (1860-1935), as well as sketches, books, letters and photographs which make up a permanent memorial exhibition to the artist.

Remain on the Bodmin road and descend into the Fowey valley. After crossing the River Fowey a road on the right, SP 'St Neot', leads to Carnglaze Slate Caverns.

CARNGLAZE SLATE CAVERNS, Cornwall

Slate has been quarried from these caves (OACT) since the 14th century and it has been traditionally used as a roofing material; now it is used more widely for all types of building. One of the caverns is 300ft high and the original tramway built to haul the stone to the surface can be seen here. Deeper into the quarry is a clear greenish-blue underground lake and lichen on the surrounding rocks reflects the light.

Continue on the A38 for 5 miles before recrossing the River Fowey. After 1½ miles, at the crossroads, turn left, SP 'Lostwithiel'. In another 1½ miles turn left again on to the B3268 passing, on the left, the entrance to Lanhydrock.

LANHYDROCK, Cornwall

Lanhydrock (NT) suffered badly from a fire in 1881 so there is little of the original building left, although the house was rebuilt to the same plan. However, the charming 2-storeyed gatehouse and north wing did survive and the long gallery, 116ft long, in the latter is particularly splendid with its ceiling of intricately carved plasterwork depicting biblical scenes. The estate is approached down a long avenue of beech and sycamore, some 4 centuries old. Formal gardens lie close to the house featuring rose-beds, yew hedges and some bronze vases by Ballin, goldsmith to Louis XIV.

Remain on the B3268 Lostwithiel road and at the hamlet of Sweetshouse keep left and continue to Lostwithiel.

LOSTWITHIEL, Cornwall

Lostwithiel, with Helston, Truro and Liskeard, is another of Cornwall's 4 stannary towns, and was also the county capital in the 13th century. The former stannary offices and county treasury in Quay Street occupied a great hall and there are still remains of this 13th-century building. Overlooking the Fowey valley a mile away is Restormel Castle (OACT), where Edmund, Earl of Cornwall, ruled the county. It has been a ruin since it was abandoned in the 16th century, having been used for a time by Parliamentarian forces.

From the centre of Lostwithiel turn right into Fore Street (one-way) and at the end turn right across the River Fowey and go over the level crossing. In ¼ mile, at the crossroads, turn right for Lerryn. At the Post Office keep left, then take the next turning left, 'SP 'Polperro'. In ¾ mile go over the crossroads and follow this narrow byroad for another 1½ miles where, at the T-junction, turn left. In 2 miles turn right to enter Lanreath.

LANREATH, Cornwall

There is an extremely interesting farm museum (OACT) in Lanreath featuring farm machinery from the past. Vintage tractors, engines and old farm implements, such as a turnip and cattle cake cutter and grappling irons, are just some of the things to see and sometimes there are demonstrations of traditional rural crafts including spinning and the making of corn dollies.

At the church keep left and then turn right on to the B3359 for Pelynt. In 1½ miles turn right, SP 'Polperro', then right again on to the A387 for Polperro.

POLPERRO, Cornwall

All Polperro's tiny streets and alleyways lead down to the harbour tucked into a fold in the cliffs, well protected by timber and masonry from the savage onslaught of Atlantic winter storms. Lime-washed cottages seem to grow out of the rock one on top of another, understandably attracting artists wishing to capture the true flavour of Cornwall. The Land of Legend and Model Village (OACT) gives a fascinating glimpse of old Cornwall all through the medium of animated models.

Return along the A387 to complete the tour at Looe.

Polperro, smuggling haven during the 18th century

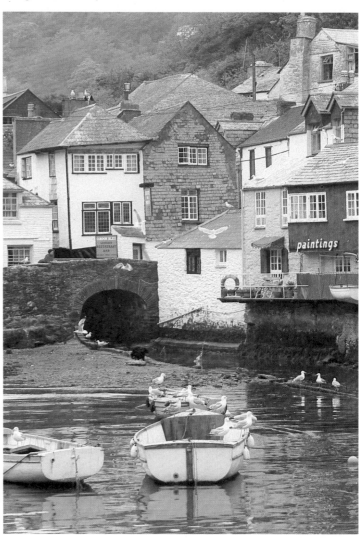

CORNWALL'S INTERIOR

Wild moorland once ridden over by highwaymen and
trodden by smugglers: a landscape interrupted only by the
ruins of an ancient past and lonely, forgotten mine
workings: a landscape sometimes as savage or as moody as
the better known coast.

LISKEARD, Cornwall
This small, busy town with several
Georgian and Victorian buildings
is well placed in east Cornwall as
an agricultural and industrial
centre. See tour 4.

*Leave Liskeard on the A390, SP
'Tavistock', and continue through
Merrymeet to St Ive.*

ST IVE, Cornwall
Eight centuries ago the Knights
Templar built a hostel in St Ive and
Trebeigh manor house (not open)
now marks the site. They also
founded the church, although the
present building dates mainly from
the 14th century.

*Continue on the A390 then in 2¾
miles cross the River Lynher and
continue to Callington. In 1½
miles pass the turning on the left to
Kit Hill (toll).*

KIT HILL, Cornwall
To the north of Callington is a
magnificent 1,094ft viewpoint
called Kit Hill. Its summit is
marked by a modern radio mast
and, in contrast, the old chimney
stack of a derelict tin mine. Spread
out below in a breathtaking
panorama is the valley of the
Tamar and the waters of Plymouth
Sound.

*There are more fine views from the
A390 before reaching St Ann's
Chapel. From here an unclassified
road on the right leads to Cotehele
House.*

COTEHELE HOUSE, Cornwall
Cotehele (NT) is all a romantic,
medieval house should be, and it
seems suspended in that distant
time. Its grey, granite walls
surrounding 3 courtyards have
scarcely changed since they were
built between 1485 and 1627 by
the Edgcumbes, nor have the
furniture, tapestries and armour
which grace the rooms altered.
Colourful gardens of terraces,
ponds and walls slope gently
down to the Tamar and merge
with the thick natural woodland of
the valley. Cotehele Mill, the
manorial water mill used for
grinding corn, is here in full
working order and Cotehele Quay
on the banks of the river has some
attractive 18th-and 19th-century
boathouses.

*Continue into Gunnislake. Beyond
the town cross the River Tamar into
Devon and climb out of the valley.
In 1½ miles turn right on to an
unclassified road and follow SP
'Morwellham'.*

MORWELLHAM, Devon
At one time Morwellham was the
busiest inland port west of Exeter
and its active life spanning 900
years continued until the
beginning of this century. The
quays and docks on the River
Tamar handled copper from
nearby mines, which was then
shipped to Tavistock. Now the
area is preserved as an open-air
industrial musuem (OACT) and an
underground canal built to reach
the ancient productive copper
mine is just one of the fascinating
things to see here amid lime kilns,
waterwheels, riverside and
woodland walks.

*Return along the unclassified road
and follow SP 'Tavistock'. On
reaching the A390 turn right and
continue to Tavistock.*

TAVISTOCK, Devon
Tavistock's long industrial history
began in the 14th century and
today light industrial and timber
firms keep the tradition going.
Before the Dissolution, Tavistock's
10th-century Benedictine abbey
was one of the richest in Devon,
but little remains as evidence of
this now. The town was granted to

The ancient borough of Liskeard is well-
known for its monthly cattle fair

the Russell family (Dukes of
Bedford), and they owned it until
1911. Of its 3 phases of industry
— tin, cloth and copper — the
latter had the most impact on
Tavistock, although the 15th-
century church was built with
Devon serge profits. During the
19th-century boom the Dukes of
Bedford virtually rebuilt the
castellated town centre around
Bedford Square and the result was
a pleasant combination of
architecture. With its weekly cattle
and pannier market Tavistock is an
attractive market town which
makes an ideal touring base. Sir
Francis Drake was born south of
the town and a statue (of which a
replica stands on Plymouth Hoe)
commemorates him.

*Leave Tavistock on the A384, SP
'Liskeard', and later pass the edge
of Lamerton.*

LAMERTON, Devon
A shady avenue of trees leads to
the village church, the priest's
house and the vicarage. The
original church was practically
destroyed by fire and the priest's
house, now the church hall, was
rebuilt in the 15th century. Two
impressive monuments were saved
from the church; one to the
Tremaynes and one to the
Fortescues. The Tremayne's home
was Collacombe Manor (not open)
— a lovely Elizabethan farmhouse
just off the Launceston Road.

Continue to Milton Abbot.

Strange outcrops of granite, such as
this one on Rough Tor, are scattered
all over Bodmin Moor's bleak face

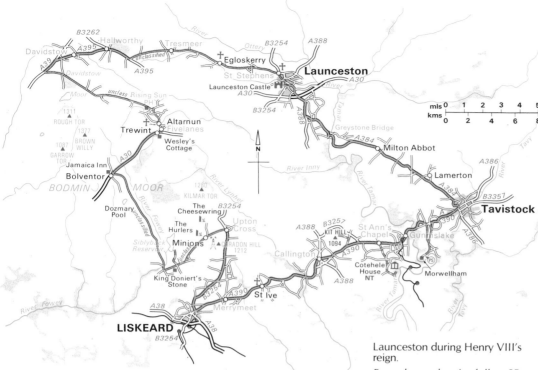

Continue to Fivelanes then turn right, SP 'Bodmin', and join the A30 to skirt the hamlet of Trewint.

TREWINT, Cornwall
John Wesley, founder of Methodism, spent some time in a small cottage here between 1744 and 1762. The cottage, restored in 1950, has been turned into a shrine to his memory and a Wesley Day Service is held here annually.

Remain on the A30 to Bolventor.

BOLVENTOR, Cornwall
On the outskirts of this tiny hamlet lies the inn made famous by Daphne du Maurier's novel *Jamaica Inn*. The lonely hostelry on the main highway across Bodmin Moor provided an ideal meeting point for smugglers in Cornwall's lawless past.

DOZMARY POOL, Cornwall
High up on Bodmin Moor, Dozmary Pool lends itself well to the many romantic legends associated with it. One of the most famous says that Sir Bedivere threw King Arthur's sword, Excalibur, into the pool at the King's request.

By the nearside of Jamaica Inn at Bolventor, turn left SP 'St Cleer'. Follow the Fowey River for 6½ miles then, at the crossroads, turn left. In ½ mile pass, on the right, King Doniert's Stone.

KING DONIERT'S STONE, Cornwall
A cross standing just off the main road bears a Latin inscription stating that 'Doniert ordered this cross for the good of his soul'. This may have been Dungarth, King of Cornwall in 875. Another Saxon cross stands next to it.

Continue on the unclassified road then in ¾ mile bear left to the village of Minions.

MINIONS, Cornwall
Near Minions, 3 stone circles make up a prehistoric monument (AM) known as the Hurlers. In the 15th century local people thought the stones were men who had been turned to stone as a punishment for hurling a ball on the Sabbath. Whatever their mysterious origin and purpose, the tops of the stones apparently needed to be on the same level. They were placed in pits of varying depths to achieve this and held in place with small granite boulders. Not more than a mile from the Hurlers on Stowe's Hill is a natural phenomenon called the Cheesewring. Encircling the summit of this strange stack of rocks is a stone rampart which once formed part of a fort — possibly Bronze Age.

Beyond Minions the tour passes a TV transmitting mast on Caradon Hill before descending to Upton Cross. Here turn right on to the B3254 for the return to Liskeard.

MILTON ABBOT, Cornwall
Tavistock Abbey used to own the village, but, like Tavistock, Milton Abbot was granted to the Russell family after the Dissolution. Similarities to the 19th-century architecture of Tavistock can be seen in the village which reflects the Russell's prosperity from copper and lead mining. Milton Green (just south) in particular has several attractive Gothic buildings, notably a Poor School and Schoolmaster's House which was a freehouse for the estate labourers' children. Endsleigh Cottage above the Tamar (now a hotel) is the romantically ornate house built in 1810 for the Dowager Duchess of Bedford.

Remain on the A384 and cross the River Tamar at Greystone Bridge to re-enter Cornwall. In 2 miles, turn right on to the A388. After crossing the Launceston Bypass go forward over the crossroads and enter Launceston.

13th-century ruins of Launceston Castle

LAUNCESTON, Cornwall
Arguably Cornwall's most appealing town, Launceston was the county capital until 1838. There was early settlement here because of the advantages offered by this elevated site, and the castle ruins (AM) show it to have been a Norman stronghold. The castle, erstwhile seat of William the Conqueror's brother, still has its huge round keep and from its walls great tracts of Cornish and Devonshire landscape can be surveyed. The grass below was a public execution site until 1821. Ancient, narrow streets surround the town's main square and among the many interesting Georgian buildings is Lawrence House (NT) in Castle Street. The rooms have been turned into a museum of local history now, but at one time the house was a well-known rendezvous for French prisoners on parole during the Napoleonic Wars. Narrow South Gate is the only evidence left of the town walls which encircled Launceston during Henry VIII's reign.

From the castle ruins follow SP 'Bude (B3254)'. At the bottom of the hill cross the river bridge and at the mini-roundabout go forward. At St Stephen's Church turn left SP 'Egloskerry'.

EGLOSKERRY, Cornwall
Cottages cluster around the little church which has been the village centre since Norman times. Much of the building has since been rebuilt, but the font has survived intact. On the walls hang memorials to the Specott family who lived a mile away at the large manor house called Penheale (not open) during the 17th century.

Continue along the unclassified road to Tresmeer and go forward with the Hallworthy road. In 2 miles turn right on to the A395 to reach the hamlet of Hallworthy. In 2¾ miles turn left on to the A39, then in another mile turn left again, SP 'Altarnun'. This byroad crosses Davidstow Moor with occasional views of Bodmin Moor to the right. In 5 miles, at the Rising Sun PH, bear left, then take the next turning right for Altarnun.

ALTARNUN, Cornwall
This, Cornwall's second largest parish, lies in a hollow on the edge of Bodmin Moor. Two little streams, crossed by a ford and a narrow bridge, flow through the village past the uneven stone walls of Altarnun's cottages. The church, nicknamed Cathedral of the Cornish Moors because of its size, is mainly 15th century. One of its best features is the collection of 16th-century carved bench ends depicting Tudor men and women, a piper, a jester, dancers, sheep and sheaves of corn.

DARTMOUTH, Devon

Naval tradition in Dartmouth goes back to medieval times when the port was one of the busiest in England. The ships of the 2nd and 3rd Crusades anchored here on their way to the Holy Land, and in peacetime Dartmouth grew rich on the proceeds of the wine trade with France. In wartime, the town's formidable 15th-century castle could rake the estuary with cannon shot and close off the river mouth with a massive chain running across to Kingwear Castle on the opposite shore. Today the town is dominated by the Royal Naval College, designed by Sir Aston Webb and opened in 1905. Dartmouth's streets, climbing the steep wooded slope of the Dart Estuary, are intriguing to explore. Of the many ancient buildings scattered throughout the town, 14th-century Agincourt House contains a small museum, and there is another museum with a fine collection of model ships in the Butterwalk, a picturesque 17th-century market arcade. In the gardens on the quay stands what may be the world's oldest steam pumping engine, designed in 1725 by Thomas Newcomen, a native of Dartmouth. The 14th-century church of St Saviour, whose building was mainly financed by Sir John Hawley, 7 times mayor of the town, is worth a visit. The interior is richly decorated and contains an elaborate brass to Hawley and his 2 wives. Although the church door bears the date 1631, the ironwork depicting prancing leopards on the branches of a great tree belongs to the 14th century. Dartmouth has a carnival every year in July and its famous regatta is held on the Dart during late August.

Leave Dartmouth on the A379, SP 'Kingsbridge', and climb past the grounds of the Naval College. At the top turn left, SP 'Stoke Fleming' and 'Strete', and continue with occasional coastal views to Stoke Fleming.

STOKE FLEMING, Devon

Perched on the cliffs 300ft above the sea, the pretty streets of Stoke Fleming overlook a Mediterranean seascape; the white shingle of Blackpool Sands sweeping away to the south, framed by shelving headlands wooded with dark green pines. The tower of the 14th-century church served for centuries as a daymark for shipping; inside are two brasses, one, almost lifesize, to John Corp and his little grandaughter Elyenor, and one to Elias Newcomen, a 17th-century rector and ancestor of the Dartmouth born inventor, Thomas Newcomen. From the cliff path there is a fine view over Redlap Cove to the awesome Dancing Beggar rocks.

The tour skirts the cove of Blackpool Sands before ascending to Strete.

DARTMOUTH AND THE SOUTH HAMS

The scenery of the South Hams is a landscape of rounded hills and quiet valleys, of greens and browns. In contrast are the greys and blues of the slate cliffs and the rocky outline of the coast and it is the lure of the sea which leaves the working countryside free from bustling tourism.

The sheltered naval town of Dartmouth

STRETE, Devon

Old stone houses set in a pleasant sheltered valley stand in peaceful contrast to the wild slate cliffs of Pilchard's Cove. Down in this cove once lived a community of fishermen, but now only the placename survives; the houses long since destroyed by the sea.

Continue on the A379 and later descend to reach Slapton Sands.

SLAPTON SANDS & SLAPTON LEY, Devon

The simple obelisk on the edge of Slapton Sands was erected to commemorate the United States troops who used this area in World War II as a training ground to practise for the Normandy landings in 1944. The long stretch of shingle beach is a good hunting ground for collectors of shells and pretty pebbles, but bathing can sometimes be dangerous. A 3-mile sandbar, carrying the road, protects the freshwater lagoon of Slapton Ley from contamination by the sea. The lake and its surrounding reedbeds are now a nature reserve for birdlife, particularly waterfowl and reed warblers.

From Slapton Sands a turning to the right may be taken to Slapton.

SLAPTON, Devon

The village lies inland from the coast road, along the steep side of the valley. Many houses in its twisting streets have had their walls rendered to hide shell damage. During the last war, villagers had to evacuate their homes when the US Army took the place over for manoeuvres. The ruined tower is all that remains of a 14th-century collegiate chantry founded by Sir Guy de Brien, one of the first Knights of the Garter and Standardbearer to Edward III.

The main tour continues with the coast road to Torcross.

TORCROSS, Devon

Pleasant old houses line the seafront along Start Bay at Torcross. Until the pilchard shoals disappeared from the south-west coast, Torcross was the most easterly fishing village to engage in this trade. The fishermen kept Newfoundland dogs who were trained to swim out to the returning boats and carry back ropes to those waiting on the shore, who hauled the laden craft to safety.

From Torcross bear right and continue inland to Stokenham.

STOKENHAM, Devon

In earlier centuries it was the duty of the inhabitants of this large hillside village to maintain a watch on the coast for shoals of fish. The fishing industry has declined, but the local fishermen still put out their pots for lobster and crab.

Turn left at Stokenham and at the next crossroads, turn left again, SP 'Start Point'. In ½ mile bear right and in just over another ½ mile pass the turning on the left to Beesands. Continue for nearly ¾ mile then bear left, and in 1 mile pass the road which leads to North Hallsands.

BEESANDS & NORTH HALLSANDS, Devon

Steep, narrow lanes lead to the two little hamlets of Beesands and North Hallsands at the southern end of Start Bay. The fierce and treacherous storms that periodically assault this part of the coast have, in the past, brought tragedy in their wake. In 1917 a former village of Hallsands, sited to the south of the present one, was completely destroyed in a storm because the Admiralty had allowed the excavation of its shingle bank. Remains of some of its houses still stand as an eerie memorial.

The main tour continues to Start Point.

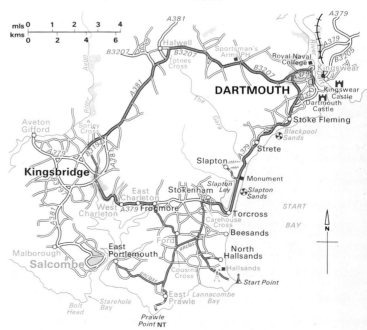

START POINT, Devon

The jagged ridge of Start Point overlooks the whole sweep of the South Hams coast and is an excellent vantage point for birdwatchers. Early migrants from the Continent alight here, and there are many native breeding colonies of seabirds. More seriously, the clifftop lighthouse warns of the Blackstone Rock on which many a ship has foundered. In 1581, a pirate was hanged in chains here as a warning to other outlaws of the ocean.

Return towards Stokenham and after 2¼ miles turn sharp left, SP 'East Prawle' and 'East Portlemouth'. In 1 mile at Cousin's Cross, bear left, then in 1¾ miles turn right. Alternatively, keep forward for the village of East Prawle and the road to Prawle Point.

PRAWLE POINT, Devon

Prawle Point (NT) is the extreme southern tip of Devon, looking west towards the Eddystone Lighthouse and east across Lannacombe Bay to Start Point. 'Prawle' comes from an old English word meaning 'look-out hill', and no name could better fit the lonely, sombre cliffs of this immemorial watching place.

The main tour continues to East Portlemouth.

Above: lobster-pots at Beesands

Right: The freshwater lagoon of Slapton Ley is separated from the sea by a shingle bar.

EAST PORTLEMOUTH, Devon

This small clifftop village looks across the Kingsbridge estuary to the lovely town of Salcombe, where pines, cypresses and palms flourish in almost Mediterranean profusion. Magnolia and fuchsia thrive here and there is an astonishing variety of wild flowers. The estuary is so sheltered that most plants bloom early and fruit ripens early. There are fine views up the many-branched estuary to Kingsbridge and beyond to the bleak expanse of Dartmoor. To the south, paths along the cliffs (NT) lead past sandy coves and weathered rocks as far as Prawle Point.

Return along the unclassified road, SP 'Kingsbridge'. In 2½ miles, at the T-junction, turn left, then in 1¾ miles go over the crossroads, SP 'Frogmore' and 'Kingsbridge'. In ½ mile descend to the hamlet of Ford and turn sharp left and in ¾ mile, at the T-junction, turn right. At the head of Frogmore Creek bear left across the bridge, then turn left on to the A379 for Frogmore.

FROGMORE, Devon

All over the South Hams district slate was used for building, both for important structures such as Dartmouth Castle and for farms and cottages. There were quarries at Frogmore and the nearby village of Molescombe, and traces of old workings, some dating back to medieval times, can be seen along Frogmore Creek.

Continue on the A379 and pass through East and West Charleton before reaching Kingsbridge.

KINGSBRIDGE, Devon

Kingsbridge, an attractive little place at the head of the estuary, offers a sheltered harbour for yachting and is also the market centre for the area. Its town hall boasts an unusual, slate hung ball clock of 1875 and the 16th-century market arcade, the Shambles, restored in the 18th century, is particularly appealing. The miniature railway on the quay carries passengers on a ½ mile trip, and the Cookworthy Museum in Fore Street commemorates William Cookworthy. Born here in 1705, he discovered china clay in Cornwall and made the first true English porcelain.

Leave by the unclassified road SP 'Totnes'. At Sorley Green Cross turn right on to the B3194 and in just over 1 mile turn left on to the A381. After 4¼ miles turn right on to the B3207, SP 'Dartmouth'. In another 4 miles, at the Sportsman's Arms PH, bear right and continue with the B3207 which later joins the A379 for Dartmouth.

DEVON'S ANCIENT CAPITAL AND THE SOUTHERN COAST

From Exeter, 2,000-year-old capital of Devon, the tour follows the contours of the southern coastline from Starcross down to colourful, Italianate Torquay. Turning inland to the wooded slopes of the Haldon Hills, it finally descends to a chequerboard farmland and back to Exeter.

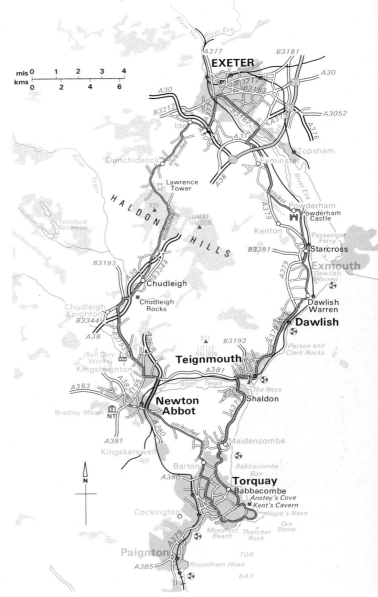

EXETER, Devon

Parts of the massive red walls of the old Roman city can still be seen, but, sadly, much of medieval Exeter was destroyed in World War II. The cathedral, with its 300ft nave, the longest span of Gothic vaulting in the world, was spared, as were the attractive old houses round the Close. The Guildhall in the High Street claims to be the oldest municipal building in England; inside, the hall is roofed with gilded beams supported by figures of bears holding staves. In Princesshay stands the entrance to a network of underground tunnels (OACT), constructed in the 13th century to carry fresh spring water around the city. Exeter's maritime traditions are well represented in the marvellous Maritime Museum on the quay which contains over 100 historic ships, from Arab dhows and Fijian outriggers to Portuguese craft and early steamships. Some are afloat on the canal and several can be boarded and explored. The handsome museum buildings have featured in the BBC television series 'The Onedin Line'.

Follow SP 'Exmouth' (A376) and at the Countess Wear roundabout, take the 3rd exit, SP 'Plymouth' (A38). Shortly cross the River Exe and the Exeter Canal, and at the next roundabout take the 1st exit on the A379, SP 'Dawlish'. Bypass Exminster and after 2½ miles turn left, SP 'Powderham Castle', and continue with views of the Exe estuary to the entrance to Powderham Castle.

POWDERHAM CASTLE, Devon

The castle (OACT), seat of the Earls of Devon, is a grand medieval fortified mansion, extended and altered in the 18th and 19th centuries but with a core some 400 years older. The somewhat flamboyantly decorated rooms are beautifully furnished and well worth a visit. Powderham sits in a magnificent deer park divided by grand avenues of cedar and ilex trees.

At the castle entrance turn left, then at the church turn right. After 1¼ miles turn left on to the A379 and continue to Starcross.

STARCROSS, Devon

Starcross, with its pretty little harbour, has kept much of its quiet village character. In the red tower of an old pumping house it preserves a relic of Brunel's short-lived atmospheric railway which ran through the village just before 1820. The engines were designed to work on the vacuum principle, using atmospheric pressure to drive the pistons, but the leather valves (there was no rubber then) leaked, and so, although trains between Exeter and Newton Abbot reached an incredible 70 mph for short stretches, the experiment failed.

Remain on the A379 for ½ mile then at the crossroads turn left on to an unclassified road, then turn left again for Dawlish Warren.

Teignmouth, seen from Shaldon across the busy estuary that separates them

DAWLISH WARREN, Devon

This promontory of sand and dune was created when a breakwater was built to protect the railway line. It has a fine golf course. On a spithead, the Warren Nature Reserve protects the vegetation, animal and birdlife in an area of just over 500 acres. It is the site of one of the estuary's high-tide wader roosts, which can be viewed from a large hide looking back up the estuary. The most exciting time for birds here is winter.

Turn right at the T-junction. In ½ mile turn left then in ¾ mile turn left again to rejoin the A379 for Dawlish.

DAWLISH, Devon

A charming 18th-century resort, Dawlish has a sandy beach framed by rocky cliffs and the main railway line from London to Penzance runs right along the sands. Through the centre of the town runs Dawlish Water, on whose banks the Lawn, a lovely miniature garden complete with cascading waterfalls and decorative black Australian swans, was created in the 19th century.

Follow SP 'Teignmouth'.

TEIGNMOUTH, Devon

A golfcourse overlooking the town from a height of 800ft, a safe sandy beach with a sheltered harbour and a pleasant promenade, combine to make Teignmouth a perennially popular resort. To the north the bay is guarded by the Parson and Clerk stack rocks, and to the south by a small lonely lighthouse. A number of twisty old lanes wind down to New Quay, built in the 19th century for the purpose of shipping Dartmoor granite to London to rebuild London Bridge — itself replaced in 1968 and shipped to the USA. A ferry runs across the estuary to Shaldon.

Follow SP 'Torbay' and in ¾ mile, at the traffic signals, turn left and cross the River Teign for Shaldon.

Two tiers of kings, queens, saints and angels are carved into the west front of Exeter Cathedral. Inset: the nave

SHALDON, Devon

The French set fire to Shaldon in 1690 and burned about 100 houses and its pretty streets now are lined with Regency buildings. Narrow lanes and alleys converge at Crown Square, the old centre, and among them the traditional Devon cottages of whitewashed cob (clay mixed with chopped straw) and thatch can be seen. Shaldon has 2 beaches; one, otherwise cut off at high tide, is reached by a 'smugglers' tunnel.

Turn right with the main road and continue with some good coastal views. In 4 miles, at the Palk Arms PH, turn left into Hartop Road (one-way), SP 'Babbacombe' and 'St Marychurch'. At the end turn left then at the mini-roundabout turn right. At the next traffic signals turn left into Babbacombe.

BABBACOMBE, Devon

A model village, set in 4 acres of perfectly landscaped miniature gardens, is the main attraction at Babbacombe. There are over 400 model buildings, each beautifully made and detailed, and over 1,200ft of model railway track. Babbacombe also has a pleasant pebbly beach.

Continue along Babbacombe Road and in just over ¾ mile turn left, SP 'Anstey's Cove', into a narrow, one-way road. Shortly pass the car park for Anstey's Cove.

ANSTEY'S COVE & KENT'S CAVERN, Devon

On the heights above Anstey's Cove is Kent's Cavern (AM), a Palaeolithic cave dwelling. There are 2 main caves, containing stalagmites and stalactites and numerous flint and bone implements and weapons, such as harpoons, have been found in them, as well as traces of prehistoric animals including the mammoth and woolly rhinoceros.

From the car park descend to Ilsham Road. (From here turn right to visit Kent's Cavern.) The main tour turns left and almost immediately left again into Ilsham Marine Drive. At the foot of the hill turn sharp left, SP 'The Town'. In ¾ mile, at the crossroads, turn left into Parkhill Road and continue to Torquay.

TORQUAY, Devon

Its white-painted villas, sub-tropical plants and shady gardens set among the limestone crags of the hillside overlooking the bay, have earned Torquay its title of queen of the Devon coast. From Marine Drive, which skirts the headland, there are superb views out across Tor Bay and inland to the town. Torquay is the creation of Sir Robert Palk, a governor of Madras, who made his own fortune in India and was left another by a friend, General Stinger Lawrence, which included the hamlet of Tor Quay. He appreciated the beauty of the site and exploited it during the Napoleonic Wars when the Continent was closed to holidaymakers: Torquay has never looked back. Among its attractions are Aqualand on Beacon Quay, the largest aquarium in the West Country, specialising in tropical marine fish; Torre Abbey Gardens, and the Torquay Museum in Babbacombe Road exhibits finds from Kent's Cavern and other south Devon caves.

Follow SP 'Teignmouth' A379 and at the mini-roundabout turn left into Hele Road. At the next roundabout take the 3rd exit into Barton Hill Road, SP 'Barton'. Ascend through Barton and near the top bear right, SP 'Newton'. Continue with views of Dartmoor ahead and at the T-junction turn left. At the next roundabout take the 3rd exit on to the A380, SP 'Exeter'. Alternatively, take the 2nd exit for Newton Abbot.

NEWTON ABBOT, Devon

A railway town with extensive marshalling yards, Newton Abbot's steep streets are lined with stepped terraces of workmen's cottages. All that remains of its church is the 14th-century tower at the town centre. Charles I once stayed at Forde House and so, later, did William of Orange after he had landed at Torbay when he came to rule England with Mary II. Wednesday is market day, when the town springs to life as people crowd in from the surrounding region. South-west of Newton Abbot, set in the deep valley of the River Lemon, lies Bradley Manor (NT), a charming 15th-century house with a gabled front and pleasingly irregular windows. It is considered to be one of the best examples of a medieval Gothic house in the West Country.

The main tour following the bypass crosses the River Teign then branch left SP 'Kingsteignton', and at the roundabout take the B3193 to Kingsteignton. Here at the Kings Arms PH, turn right, SP 'Exeter', then in just over ¼ mile turn left on to the B3193 SP 'Chudleigh'. In 3 miles cross the A38 and the River Teign. Shortly bear right to join the B3344, then ½ mile farther bear right again and continue to Chudleigh.

CHUDLEIGH, Devon

This pleasant little hillside town is much visited for the sake of its Rocks, a picturesque and romantic limestone outcrop just south of the village. There is a pretty waterfall here and a cavern called the Pixie's Hole. This has a distinctive stalagmite called the Pope's Head. On the walls, among countless less famous initials, are carved those of the poet Samuel Taylor Coleridge and his brother.

At the war memorial in Chudleigh branch left into Old Exeter Street. In 1 mile go forward, SP 'Exeter', and climb on to the Haldon Hills.

THE HALDON HILLS, Devon

The moorland slopes and woods of the Haldon Hills mark the start of the switchback landscapes of east Devon, where hill and valley alternate in a constant upheaval. From the tops of the hills there are wide views of the rich red farmland around Exeter and the patchwork effect of the small fields and hedges so typical of Devon. A landmark on the hills is Lawrence Tower, built by Sir Robert Palk in 1788 in memory of General Stringer Lawrence (see Torquay).

At the crossroads turn left, SP 'Dunchideock' and 'Ide', to follow a high ridge. After a mile, on the right, is Lawrence Tower and in ½ mile bear right. A long descent then leads to Ide. At the T-junction at the end of the village turn right, SP 'Exeter'. At the next roundabout, take the A377 for Exeter.

THE COMBES AND GOLDEN BAYS OF NORTH DEVON

Delightful combes tumble down to the Atlantic, bold headlands guarded by lonely lighthouses jut out between sweeps of sandy beaches and everywhere in this sea-bound corner of Devon echoes with the cries of wheeling seagulls.

Combe Martin Bay

BARNSTAPLE, Devon
Onetime harbour on the estuary of the River Taw and an ancient trading centre, Barnstaple thrives now as north Devon's major market town. The wool trade brought prosperity to Barnstaple in the 18th century and its predominantly Georgian architecture reflects this period of growth. One good example is the attractive colonnaded Exchange by the river, called Queen Anne's walk. Here stands the Tome Stone where any verbal bargains struck were considered binding. Barnstaple's pleasant narrow streets are always busy, but there is an oasis of quiet at the centre. Here the large church, St Anne's Chapel and Horwood's Almshouses and School stand in the leafy churchyard. Within the Chapel is a museum of local history (OACT). On Tuesdays and Fridays the Victorian Pannier Market off the High Street bustles with traders selling delicious Devonshire produce under its high glass roof and fine wrought iron pillars.

Follow SP 'Ilfracombe A361' along the Taw estuary to Braunton.

BRAUNTON, Devon
Practically a small town, but alleged to be the largest village in England, Braunton is certainly of ancient origin. The first church was built by the Irish saint, Brannock, when a dream decreed that he must build a church wherever he first met a sow and her piglets — Braunton fitted the bill. This legend is substantiated by a carving of a sow and her litter on the church roof above the font. The church interior is high and spacious, elaborately Jacobean

with much gilt decoration. To the left of the road to Saunton lie Braunton Burrows — about 3-4 square miles of sand dunes that have been turned into a nature reserve. A nature trail runs through the dunes and a great variety of wild flowers flourish here. Backing on to the Burrows on the seaward side is Saunton Sands, where vast expanses of sand are exposed when the tide goes out.

At the traffic signals in Braunton turn left on to the B3231, SP 'Croyde', and continue through Saunton, round the headland of Saunton Down to Croyde.

CROYDE, Devon
There is a unique museum of local gems and shells at the edge of the village, and in the craft workshop demonstrations of gem cutting and polishing can be seen. To the west of the village the National Trust cliffland of Baggy Point shelters the northern side of Croyde Bay, a magnificent bathing and surfing beach lying round the corner from Saunton Sands.

From Croyde village continue on the Woolacombe road to Georgeham.

GEORGEHAM, Devon
Several old thatched cottages and a stream flowing near the church make a pleasing picture in Georgeham. The church has suffered a great many changes since its first construction in the 13th century, but the Victorians were the last to tamper with it and they attempted to restore its medieval character. Interesting monuments inside include one presumed to represent Manger St

Aubyn — a 13th-century knight who fought in the 1st Crusade.

Remain on the B3231 and in 1¾ miles turn left on to an unclassified road, SP 'Woolacombe Steep Hill', then descend to Woolacombe and follow the Esplanade, SP 'Mortehoe', and continue to Mortehoe.

MORTEHOE, Devon
Rocky terrain characterises Mortehoe — the granite beneath emerging erratically by the roadsides. One of Thomas à Becket's murderers is reputed to have lived here prior to the bloody crime in 1170. Whether or not this is true, a relative of the murderer, Sir William de Tracy, was certainly vicar of the parish in the 14th century and he lies in a tomb-chest in the south chapel. A path from the village leads to the grassy promontory of Morte Point (NT) from where Lundy Island can be seen lying out to sea.

Continue on the unclassified road and in 2 miles join the B3343, SP 'Ilfracombe', then cross the bridge for Turnpike Cross. Here bear left, then take the next turning left B3231 SP 'Lee'. After 1½ miles pass the unclassified road on the left, which leads to Lee.

LEE, Devon
A picture-postcard combe opens on to Lee Bay where the rocks are veined with marble. The tiny hamlet has pretty cottages and gardens overflowing with red and purple fuchsias, but best loved is Three Old Maids Cottage — a white, thatched 17th-century 'show' cottage (not open). It was

This trinket at Arlington Court came from Barbados in the 19th century when shellwork was a flourishing export

the prototype of the many dwellings that sprang up in the 1800s as show cottages belonging to the rich.

The main tour continues to Ilfracombe.

ILFRACOMBE, Devon
In 1874 the railway came to Ilfracombe and the town's future as a holiday resort was established. It subsequently grew rapidly around the harbour and continued to straggle out to become north Devon's largest holiday town. The conical rock called Lantern Hill at the mouth of the harbour is a reminder of Ilfracombe's long history as a port. St Nicholas' Chapel has perched on top of it since the 13th century, with a light burning from its window to guide in ships.

Leave Ilfracombe on the A399 Combe Martin road and later pass the unclassified road, on the right, to Chambercombe Manor.

CHAMBERCOMBE MANOR, Devon
Set in a pretty, sheltered combe, Chambercombe (OACT), with its cobbled courtyard and uneven roofs, resembles a rambling farm building and informal romantic gardens, including a water garden, surround the house.
Much of the furniture is 17th-century and there is a tiny chapel, just 10ft long, that has not been changed since it was licensed in 1404. Well in keeping with the atmosphere of the house is the tale of a corpse walled up in a secret chamber whose spirit still haunts the manor.

Continue on the A399 and in ½ mile pass Hele Mill.

The Boudoir, Arlington Court, was used by the lady of the house as a study

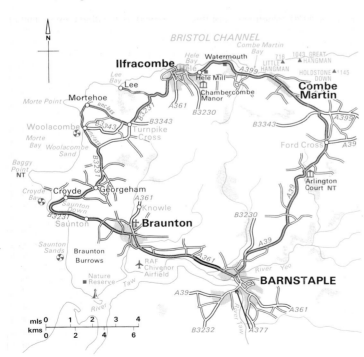

HELE MILL, Devon

Having stood derelict for over 30 years, 16th-century Hele Mill (OACT) has been restored to working order and its 18ft wheel again powers the production of wholemeal flour. Inside several items of mill machinery are on display.

Remain on the coast road and later pass Watermouth (left).

WATERMOUTH, Devon

Greatly commercialised yet still lovely is the inlet at Watermouth where yachts and small pleasure craft ride at anchor. Watermouth Castle (OACT) offers a wide range of family entertainments.

Continue into Combe Martin.

COMBE MARTIN, Devon

Combe Martin derived its name from Martin de Turribus — an adventurer who came over with William the Conqueror and won this piece of land. The village straggles along the main road running through an old mining valley, flanked by abandoned silver and lead mine workings up on the hillsides. Along the main street stands the Pack of Cards Inn, a curious place built in the 18th century by a gambling man.

The inn looks like a house of cards with its curious sloping roofs.

Continue on the A399 and after 2 miles turn right on to the B3229, SP 'Kentisbury Ford'. At Ford Cross (Kentisbury Ford) go forward on to the A39, SP 'Barnstaple'. In 1 ¼ miles pass, on the left, the road to Arlington Court.

ARLINGTON COURT, Devon

The Chichester family owned the estate from 1384 until 1949, when Miss Rosalie Chichester died and left it to the National Trust. This great lady spent her entire life in the house, and her tastes and personality are reflected in practically every item. She was an avid collector — not necessarily of things of any great value — but of objects that caught her fancy. Consequently the rooms are filled with fascinating treasures such as model ships, seashells from the 7 oceans of the world, birds, butterflies, fans, jewels and trinkets. All her possessions were lovingly arranged with the furniture she inherited and the Trust has sensitively preserved the individuality of her home.

Continue on the A39 which climbs to high ground before the long, gradual descent to Barnstaple.

LYME REGIS, Dorset

Beautiful Lyme Regis, set in lovely scenery with the River Lym running swiftly through the town, was one of the first seaside towns on the south-west coast to become a popular resort in the 18th century. Its history as a port goes back much further, however, to medieval times when the picturesque old harbour round the Cobb was first built. Lyme Regis saw the first battle of the Armada in 1588 when local ships joined Drake's fleet in a skirmish with some of the Spanish galleons. Among the town's distinguished visitors in the 18th century was Jane Austen, who loved Lyme Regis and set part of her last novel, *Persuasion*, in the old port. Shingly Lyme Bay is sheltered by cliffs rising to the magnificent Golden Cap, the highest cliff on the south coast. The area is noted for fossils and there is a fine collection in Lyme Regis museum.

Leave on the A3070 Axminster road and ascend to Uplyme.

UPLYME, Devon

Old stone cottages set in a fold of the hills behind Lyme Regis form a pleasant village street overlooked by the church, built on a hilltop from where there are glorious views westwards of the Devon landscape. In the church, near the Jacobean pulpit, is an engraved glass memorial to 2 children by the modern artist Lawrence Whistler.

In 2¼ miles turn left on to the A35 and continue to Axminster.

AXMINSTER, Devon

Some of the finest British carpets come from this delightful, busy, market town which lies on a rise of ground above the River Axe. The Axminster carpet industry was founded in 1755 by Thomas Whitty, who had made a thorough study of Turkish craftsmanship and built his factory in the town centre. Many luxurious carpets were specially woven for the great stately homes of England and the business flourished for 80 years, rivalling Wilton for its superb creations. In 1835, however, the Axminster factory went bankrupt and was bought out by a Wilton weaver. Not until 1937 was the business revived in new premises, where visitors are welcome. Bow-fronted Georgian and early Victorian houses lend charm to Axminster's bustling streets leading up to a shady green where the church looks out over the attractive town centre with its many coaching inns.

Leave on the A358 Chard road and in 3¼ miles pass through Tytherleigh and ½ mile farther turn right on to the B3167, SP 'Crewkerne'. After another 1½ miles, at the end of Perry Street, an unclassified road on the right may be taken to visit Forde Abbey.

SOMERSET TOWNS AND DEVON VILLAGES

Where the south coast cliffs sweep down to the sea around Lyme Bay and the charming seaside resort of Lyme Regis, and the ever changing vista of hills and vales reveals a pageant of historic towns and delightful villages.

The harbour at Lyme Regis

FORDE ABBEY, Dorset

Cromwell's Attorney General Sir Edmund Prideaux acquired this lovely 12th-century Cistercian monastery in 1649 and transformed it into a country house. Among its many treasures are the 5 Mortlake tapestries woven in the early 18th century to fit the walls of the saloon. The tapestries represent Raphael cartoons now in the Victoria and Albert Museum in London. Water and rock gardens are a special feature of the extensive grounds.

The main tour continues on the B3167 and in 3 miles turns right on to the A30 for Cricket St Thomas.

CRICKET ST THOMAS, Somerset

Llamas, camels, bison and wallabies roam incongruously in the landscaped parkland of a Georgian mansion, set in a secluded valley sheltered beneath the aptly named Windwhistle Ridge. Gardens and terraces lead down to a sequence of 9 lakes where flamingoes wade and black swans glide gracefully among a colourful variety of waterfowl. Cricket St Thomas is the home of the National Heavy Horse Centre and a small zoo, aviary and dairy farm add to the interest of the estate, which once belonged to the Bridport family who were connected by marriage to Lord Nelson.

Remain on the A30 for 2½ miles, then turn left on to an unclassified road, SP 'Ilminster'. After 3¼ miles, at the hamlet of Kingstone, bear right. Alternatively keep forward, then take the next turning left to visit Dowlish Wake.

DOWLISH WAKE, Somerset

Standing in the middle of the village is a thatched 16th-century barn (OACT) which belongs to Perry Bros., the famous cider producers. Here the past is recalled by a collection of farm machinery, wagons, cider presses, etc., now, sadly, replaced by more modern equipment. Cider is made on the premises during the autumn after the harvest of locally grown apples and is traditionally matured in wooden barrels under a watchful expert eye. It is for sale in the shop, together with numerous interesting gift items such as stone cider jars, corn dollies and ovenware.

The main tour continues to Ilminster. Join the A303, then branch left for the town centre.

ILMINSTER, Somerset

From the top of Beacon Hill it is said that 30 church towers and spires can be seen. That of Ilminster church, modelled on the central tower of Wells Cathedral, must be among the loveliest. Ilminster, nestling at the foot of the Black Down Hills, hides its prettiest streets away from the main roads and thatched cottages lead to a square built around a pillared market house.

Leave on the A3037 Chard road, then in 2 miles turn left on to the A358. After 1¼ miles, on the right, is Hornsbury Mill Museum.

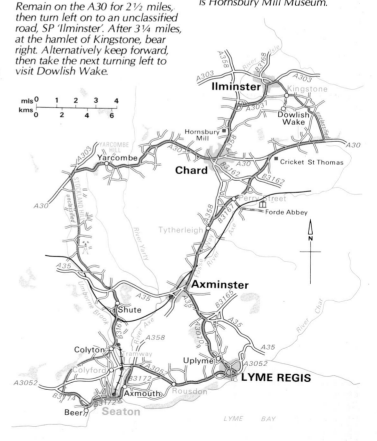

The 1,000-acre estate around Cricket House has been turned into a magnificent wildlife park

HORNSBURY MILL MUSEUM, Somerset
A splendid water wheel 18ft high dominates this 19th-century corn mill (OACT) which is kept in immaculate working order. The mill stands in attractive grounds and has a small museum of country bygones, a craft shop, and cream teas are available.

Continue on the A358 to Chard.

CHARD, Somerset
The long main street of Somerset's highest town is bordered by 2 streams, one flowing north to the Bristol Channel, the other south to the English Channel. The handsome Guildhall faces a charming Elizabethan building, once the town's manor house, where the old court room on the 1st floor can be visited. Here the infamous Judge Jeffries presided during the Bloody Assizes that followed the Duke of Monmouth's rebellion.

Leave on the A30, SP 'Exeter', and follow an undulating road to Yarcombe.

YARCOMBE, Devon
The lovely scenery of the Yarty Valley provides the setting for this graceful village. In the 15th-century church is a rare Breeches Bible (see Aylesham tour 56) and the carving on the bench ends is particularly fine. Almost within the churchyard, the charming village inn may well once have been the Church House.

SHUTE, Devon
A castellated 16th-century gatehouse forms the entrance to the medieval manor house of Shute Barton (NT) of which 2 wings remain. In the kitchen, the enormous hearth holds a spit large enough to roast 2 oxen. The house was once owned by Henry Grey, Duke of Suffolk and father of Lady Jane Grey, the tragic Nine Days Queen whose reign lasted from July 9 to 19 1553. She was condemned for treason and executed by order of Mary I in February 1554.

Continue on the B3161 to Colyton.

COLYTON, Devon
Pretty houses and cottages, mostly of the 17th and 18th centuries, line the narrow streets that wind up the slopes of the hillside where Colyton was founded by the Saxons in AD 700. The vicarage, the grammar school and the fine Great House, with its chequerboard frontage, all date from the Tudor period, when the manor of Colyton was bought by local inhabitants from Henry VIII. They called themselves the Chamber of Feoffees and this name has been preserved by the town authorities ever since.

At the town hall keep left, then turn right into Queen Street. Shortly turn left again on to the unclassified Sidmouth road. Nearly 3 miles farther (at Stafford Cross) go over the staggered crossroads, then at the next crossroads turn left on to the B3174, SP 'Beer', and continue to Beer.

Continue on the A30 and in 2 miles, at the A303 junction, keep left, then take the next turning left, SP 'Axminster'. Later pass the TV mast on Stockland Hill and at the A35 junction turn right, then immediately left on to the B3161 and continue to Shute.

BEER, Devon
Up on the slopes behind the seaside village of Beer runs Beer Heights Light Railway. This steam-operated passenger line travels through the Peco Modelrama park and fine views are to be had of the bay below along the way. There is even a full-size replica railway station with refreshments. Nine separate model railways are on permanent show around the house and gardens and there are souvenir and model shops to browse around.

The main tour turns left on to the B3172 to Seaton. On entering the town follow SP Sea Front. At the end of the Sea Front turn left, then turn right on to the B3172 and cross the River Axe. Follow the Axe estuary to Axmouth.

AXMOUTH, Devon
Thatched, colour-washed cottages and an old inn, grouped around the church, make up the unspoilt village scene at Axmouth. Once a busy port, situated at the point where the Roman Fosse Way crossed the river, Axmouth has seen the Axe estuary gradually silt up, today allowing passage for yachts and pleasure boats only. In 1877 the first concrete bridge in England was built across the Axe.

In 1 mile, at Boshill Cross, turn right on to the A3052 for the return to Lyme Regis.

Much of Forde Abbey's original medieval stonework can be identified in the present Tudor mansion

COUNTIES OF GOLDEN HAM STONE

Dorset, a maze of country lanes; Somerset, the land of the 'summer-farm dwellers'. Both counties a blend of patchwork fields and timeless villages, each with a glorious church built of golden Ham stone once patronised by the lords of the magnificent manor houses.

SHERBORNE, Dorset

There is a great wealth of medieval buildings in Sherborne; a legacy of its ecclesiastical importance seeded in Anglo-Saxon times when St Aldhelm was first bishop of the cathedral. From 864 to 1539 this was a monastery, and during that time Sherborne became a great centre of learning. The monks rebuilt the abbey church in the 12th and 15th centuries, the latter project producing the Ham stone roofing for which it is famous. In the abbey lie 2 Anglo-Saxon kings, Ethelbad and Ethelbert, brothers of Alfred the Great. Sherborne School, founded in 1550, took over many of the abbey buildings after the Dissolution; its chapel is the Abbot's Hall, the Abbot's Lodging has been converted into studies, and also preserved as part of the school are the library and the Abbot's kitchen. One other part of the old monastery still surviving is the monks' washhouse, now the conduit in the main shopping centre, Cheap Street. Outside the town stand Sherborne's 2 castles. The first was built by Bishop Roger in the early 12th century, but was destroyed in the Civil War by Cromwell and remains a ruin in the parkland of the other (OACT). This was built by Sir Walter Raleigh in about 1594, who found the old castle unsuitable for conversion. It is set in gardens with lakeside lawns, a cascade and an orangery in grounds landscaped by Capability Brown. Also in the garden is the seat in which it is said the thoughtful Sir Walter was sitting, quietly smoking the newly discovered tobacco, when a servant doused him with a flagon of ale thinking he was on fire.

Leave Sherborne on the A30, SP 'Yeovil'. In 2½ miles pass, on the right, Worldwide Butterflies.

WORLDWIDE BUTTERFLIES, Somerset

Compton House (OACT), an Elizabethan mansion, is the rather unlikely home of a unique butterfly farm where species from around the world are bred. These entrancing insects can be studied in all stages of their development and there is a tropical jungle where particularly exotic butterflies live. The Palm House is another oasis of luxuriant vegetation and resembles an equatorial rain forest. The Lullingstone Silk Farm also occupies Compton House and the silk from here was used for Queen Elizabeth II's wedding dress.

Continue on the A30 to Yeovil.

YEOVIL, Somerset

This is a thriving town with a definite 20th-century flavour. It suffered disastrous fires in 1499, 1623 and 1640, and air raids in World War II which destroyed many old buildings. One long-standing spectator of the town's fortunes is the Ham stone church built at the end of the 14th century. Its simplicity and size make it impressive, and its greatest possession, a 15th-century brass lectern, is also refreshingly plain. The museum in Hendford Manor displays local archaeology and history, including Roman finds and a good collection of firearms.

Leave on the A37 SP 'Bristol'. In 1 mile branch left on to an unclassified road, SP 'Tintinhull'. Later pass the edge of Chilthorne Domer to reach Tintinhull.

TINTINHULL HOUSE, Somerset

Tintinhull House (NT) stands near the village green of Tintinhull. It dates from about 1600 when it was an unassuming farmhouse, but it was suddenly given architectural distinction by the addition of the west front in 1700. The interior remains plain, the carved staircase and some fine panelling being the only notable decorative features, both dating from the early 18th century. The garden, however, is for many the chief attraction. It consists of several hedged gardens and a sunken garden cunningly designed to give the impression of many varying levels. On the north side of the house there is a large lawn, shaded by a huge cedar tree, and on the west side a forecourt, another lawn and a memorial pavilion overlook a pond.

Leave Tintinhull on the Montacute road and follow this winding lane for 2 miles. At the T-junction turn left to enter Montacute for Montacute House.

MONTACUTE HOUSE, Somerset

Edward Phelips, who became Master of the Rolls, commenced the building of Montacute House (NT) in 1588, the year of the Armada. Built to impress — houses of that period reflected the power and position of the owner — Montacute is an almost magical building, liberally endowed with gables and turrets fashioned in a rich golden stone. The Phelips family faded from power in the mid-17th century, and the house became a quiet country house in a rural backwater for almost 300 years. The great hall has splendid 16th-century panelling, heraldic glass, plaster decoration and an elaborate stone screen and the 189ft gallery is the longest of the period. The house was empty when it came to the National Trust in 1931, but has since been filled with many valuable furnishings.

After passing the house and village square turn right into Townsend. Climb through pleasant woodland before turning right. Continue to Ham Hill Country Park and descend into Stoke-Sub-Hamdon.

STOKE-SUB-HAMDON, Somerset

Churches and houses all over Somerset and Devon are built from the golden stone quarried from Ham Hill up above Stoke village. Since Roman times stone has been hewn from this hill and its summit is much ridged and terraced by the earthworks of prehistoric peoples who built their forts here. Most of the houses of the village date back to the 17th century, and are built of Ham stone with mullioned windows and charming gables. The Priory (NT) was begun in the 14th century, but only the great hall (OACT) and the screens passage remain.

At the T-junction turn left, then turn right into North Street, SP 'Martock'. Later cross the A303 and in 1 mile turn right on to the B3165 and enter Martock.

Stoke-Sub-Hamdon Priory was built in the 14th and 15th centuries of Ham stone for the priests of St Nicolas' chantry

The 16th-century heraldic stained glass in the library of Montacute depicts coats of arms of the Phelips family

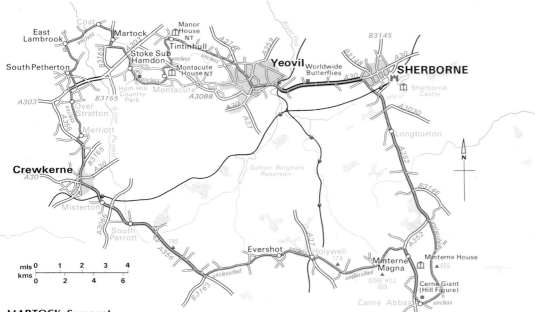

MARTOCK, Somerset
This is a charming little town enhanced by many old stone and thatched houses. The church, mainly 15th century, boasts the finest roof in the county. Virtually every inch of the tie-beam roof erected in 1513 is beautifully carved. Opposite the church is the old 14th-century manor house, one of 3 built here. The one from the 15th century lies ruined in a moated field nearby, while one from the 17th century stands close to the Georgian Market House at the end of the main street.

At the far end of the village (by the Bakers Arms PH) turn left on to an unclassified road, SP 'Coat'. At Coat turn left with the Kingsbury road, then in ¾ mile cross the river bridge and continue to East Lambrook.

EAST LAMBROOK, Somerset
In the village is East Lambrook Manor (OACT), a pretty little Tudor house with fine panelling, best known however for its gardens. These specialise in the growing of rare plants, and are laid out cottage-style as a memorial to the well-known gardener Margery Fish, as was the nursery for the propagation of rare species.

On entering the village turn left on to the South Petherton road. In 1 mile turn right for South Petherton.

SOUTH PETHERTON, Somerset
Tudor cottages, shops and villas, and a church with a roll call of vicars dating back to 1080 belong to South Petherton. Within the church walls lies the effigy of a curly-headed knight in chain mail, brought here after it was discovered by workmen digging a pit for a petrol storage tank. Also here is an extract from the diary of Richard Symonds, a Royalist soldier who stayed here in 1644, and whose writings provide a valuable insight of his contemporary world.

Branch left SP 'Illminster', and in just over ½ mile turn right on to the A303, then take the next turning left, SP 'Over Stratton'. At the far end of Over Stratton turn right then keep left and follow a pleasant byroad to Merriott. At the T-junction turn right (no sign), then at the A356 turn left and continue to Crewkerne.

CREWKERNE, Somerset
Crewkerne is a town of proud and ancient traditions, dating back to Anglo-Saxon times when it had the right of minting coins. In more recent times the town was famous for sail-making; it made sails for Nelson's *Victory*, and now does so for Americas Cup competitors. The Ham stone 15th-century church is the best building in Crewkerne, with a west front of cathedral-like proportions and glorious stained glass. An unsolved mystery are the 2 roofed-over buttresses of the south transept; theories designate it either as a shrine or as a hermit's shelter. In September the town celebrates a 2-day fair, a custom centuries old and happily upheld.

Leave on the A356, SP 'Dorchester'. Pass through Misterton and South Perrott, then gradually ascend on to high ground. At the top follow an almost level road for 2 miles, then turn left on to an unclassified road for Evershot.

EVERSHOT, Dorset
This place among the hills is rather curious; it is a village yet its main street has raised pavements and old yellow and grey-stone houses, fitted with bow-fronted windows in the manner of a small town. George Crabbe, the poet, was rector of the little church here which has a rare silver Elizabethan chalice.

At the end of the village bear right. In 1¼ miles turn right then immediately left across the A37, SP 'Minterne Magna', and continue along the edge of Batcombe Hill. On reaching the A352, turn right for the hamlet of Minterne Magna.

MINTERNE MAGNA
Minterne House was built of Ham stone for Lord Digby between 1904 and 1906 by Leonard Stokes. Only the grounds are open, but, set in a lovely valley, they form a tapestry of rich colour made up of banks of rhododendrons, azaleas and magnolias.

Continue on the A352 towards Cerne Abbas. In 1¾ miles pass the Cerne Giant chalk figure (on the left), and turn left on to an unclassified road for the village centre. At the New Inn turn left, SP 'Buckland Newton'. Ascend on to high ground and at the top turn left, SP 'Sherborne'. In 3½ miles join the A352 for the return to Sherborne.

BOURNEMOUTH, Dorset

Queen of the South Coast resorts, Bournemouth has grown into one of the largest and most popular seaside towns in the country. Its 6 miles of superb sandy beach backed by spectacular cliffs first became popular about the middle of the last century when Dr Granville recommended its mild sunny climate to invalids. Attractive parks and gardens, theatres and the world famous symphony orchestra offer a wide range of entertainment. The town also has 2 notable museums. In the Russell Coates Museum is the Henry Irving theatrical collection, a magnificent display of butterflies and moths, oriental art and a freshwater aquarium. Its geological terrace has exhibits covering 2,600 million years. Finally, the Big Four Railway Museum houses a working model railway and a large collection of nameplates and other relics.

Leave the town centre on the A338, SP 'Ringwood'. In 2¾ miles, at the roundabout, take the 3rd exit on to the A3060, SP 'Christchurch'. At the next roundabout, take the 2nd exit, SP 'Tuckton'. At the end turn left, then at the roundabout turn left again and cross the River Stour to pass Tucktonia.

TUCKTONIA, Dorset

Tucktonia (OACT) is a Britain in Miniature, containing over 200 scale models of historic buildings, all linked by a network of model railways, roads, rivers and canals. Among the models are Hadrian's Wall, London's most famous sights and a typical Cornish fishing village complete with boats.

At the next traffic signals turn right on to the A35, SP 'Lyndhurst', and at the next roundabout take the B3059 into Christchurch.

CHRISTCHURCH, Dorset

According to legend, Christ himself gave the town its name by his miraculous intervention in the building of the great Norman priory in the 12th century. Until then it had been called Twynham,

CRANBORNE CHASE AND THE AVON VALLEY

The well-wooded slopes of the lovely Avon Valley lead up to the spacious chalklands of the rolling Wiltshire Downs and on to the scattered beech woods of Cranborne Chase, a centuries-old forest where King John loved to hunt fallow deer and where, later, smugglers and poachers found refuge from the law.

Harvest time above Cranborne

an old word meaning the meeting place of 2 rivers. Near the priory, on the banks of the mill stream, stand the ruins of the Norman castle and hall, built of rough blocks of local Purbeck marble. The Red House Museum has an interesting collection of Iron-Age finds, mostly from nearby Hengistbury Head.

At the end of Christchurch High Street keep left and cross the River Avon, then at the mini-roundabout turn left B3347 into Stony Lane. At the next roundabout take the 2nd exit on to the Sopley road. Continue along the valley of the Avon to Ringwood.

RINGWOOD, Hants

The attractive, tree-clad valley of the River Avon leads to Ringwood, an old market town lying just inside the Hampshire border between 2 ancient tracts of woodland, the New Forest and the

Forest of Ringwood. Among the many old houses is one called the Monmouth House (not open), where the ill-fated Duke, illegitimate son of Charles II, stayed during his rebellion against James II.

Leave on the A338 Salisbury Road. To the right of the road, beyond Blashford, is Moyles Court.

MOYLES COURT, Hants

Today a school is housed in this attractive 17th-century manor (open by appointment) with a tragic history. Two of Monmouth's rebels, fugitives from the Battle of Sedgemoor, were sheltered here by the 70-year-old lady of the manor, Dame Alicia Lisle. The bloodthirsty Judge Jeffries condemned her to be burned alive, but the sentence was commuted to the more merciful

one of beheading and her execution took place at Winchester, in September 1685.

Continue on the A338 and at Ibsley turn left SP 'Alderholt'. In ½ mile pass Harbridge church and turn left and in another ¾ mile turn right, SP 'Fordingbridge'. In 1 mile turn left on to the wooded Cranbourne road. At the edge of Alderholt bear left, and later join the Verwood road. In 1 mile turn left into Batterby Drove and continue to Verwood. Here turn right on to the B3081. In 1½ miles, turn left with the Wimborne St Giles road, and in 1¾ miles turn left again on to the B3078, SP 'Wimborne Minster'. After 1½ miles turn right SP 'Wimborne St Giles', and pass on the right Knowlton Church ruins and Knowlton Rings.

KNOWLTON RINGS, Dorset

In the quiet, wooded countryside lies a mysterious pagan site dating back to Neolithic times. Knowlton Rings consists of a number of circles and henge monuments, guarded by banks and ditches. Two of the rings can be seen clearly from the road: the Central Circle (AM) in the middle of which stand the lonely ruins of a Norman church; and to the east, the so-called Great Barrow, a 20ft mound crowned by a circle of trees.

Continue, over the River Allen, then at the T-junction turn right for Wimborne St Giles. From the village follow SP 'Cranborne' and later keep forward on to the B3081. In ½ mile turn right on to an unclassified road then in ¾ mile turn left on to the B3078 for Cranborne.

CRANBORNE, Dorset

Brick and timber houses scattered round a green, a 13th-century church with medieval wall paintings and a stone manor house make Cranborne a picturesque sight. Formerly it was the busy market centre of the Chase, to which it gave its name, and the place where the Chase Court sat. The medieval manor, Cranborne House, was rebuilt by the 1st Earl of Salisbury, who turned it into a charming Jacobean house. The lovely gardens (OACT) were laid out at the same time and there is also a garden centre.

In Cranborne turn left on to the Martin road, then in ¼ mile bear right to Boveridge. Nearly 2 miles beyond the Hampshire border at the T-junction, turn left for Martin.

MARTIN, Hants

The thatched cottages of Martin cluster in the valley of the Allen Water at the foot of the downs. To the south-west of the village, 2 ancient boundaries can be seen crossing Martin Down. The oldest

Christchurch stands between the Avon and Stour, which meet in the town's harbour

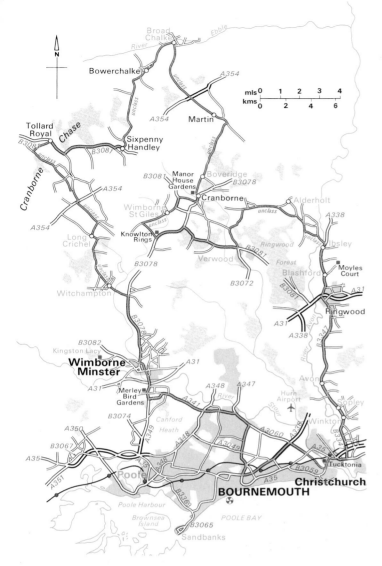

century the inn was the headquarters of a notorious smuggler, Isaac Gulliver, who had married the landlord's daughter. He and his band of 50 men successfully ran contraband from the deep chines of the Dorset coast. Deer poachers also felt safe in Sixpenny Handley and used one of the tombstones in the churchyard with impunity as a hiding place for their stolen carcases.

At Sixpenny Handley turn right on to the B3081 and continue to Tollard Royal.

TOLLARD ROYAL, Wilts
Tollard, hidden in a hollow of the downs, within the old hunting preserve of Cranborne Chase, was designated 'royal' in the 12th century by King John. His house, a lofty medieval stone building on the site of the royal hunting lodge was restored by General Sir Pitt Rivers, whose family had acquired the estate. He also laid out a charming pleasure garden, Larmer Gardens, ornamented with statues and little temples. 'Larmer' means wych elm; until 1894 there was an elm tree here which was reputed to be the place where King John's huntsmen gathered, but it has now been replaced by an oak.

At the telephone kiosk turn left, SP '13th-century church', then immediately bear right and climb on to Cranborne Chase.

CRANBORNE CHASE, Dorset & Wilts
Once a vast area of unbroken woodland, Cranborne Chase stretched across the downs from Shaftesbury in Dorset to Salisbury in Wiltshire. The Chase has long since disappeared, but many fine beech trees survive, to remind one of the vanished forest. It was a royal hunting ground even before the Normans, but it is most strongly associated with King John, who jealously guarded his right to hunt the fallow deer by stringent laws. As royalty became less addicted to hunting deer, these laws allowed the Chase to become the unsavoury haven of all kinds

of smugglers, poachers and wrongdoers, until, in 1830, Parliament put a stop to it all by a special Act.

After 1 mile, at the T-junction, turn left and re-enter Dorset. In another mile bear right and, at the next T-junction, turn right. Reach the A354, turn right then immediately left on to the Moor Crichel road. In 1½ miles, turn right for the village of Long Crichel. Here turn left, SP 'Witchampton', and at the next T-junction, turn left then immediately right, then right again for Witchampton. Later turn right on to the B3078 to Wimborne Minster.

WIMBORNE MINSTER, Dorset
The minster or 'mission' church at the centre of this old market town on the River Stour was built by the Normans on the site of a Saxon nunnery founded by St Cuthberga, sister of King Ine of Wessex. High on the outside wall of the 15th-century west tower a quarter-jack, in the form of a gaily painted Grenadier Guard, strikes the quarter hours. He is part of a 14th-century astronomical clock which can be seen inside the tower. The 16th-century Priest's House near the minster has been converted into an interesting museum of local history. To the north west is Kingston Lacy House (NT) a fine classical structure set in formal gardens and surrounded by 254 acres of parkland.

Follow signs Bournemouth A349, and cross the River Stour. After passing the Willett Arms PH the Merley Bird Gardens lie to the right of the road.

MERLEY BIRD GARDENS, Dorset
Exotic birds are housed in spacious aviaries set in the secluded walled gardens here. The house was built in the 18th century for Ralph Willett, a man who had made his fortune in the West Indies.

After another ½ mile, turn left on to the A341, SP 'Bournemouth'. In 3 miles, at the roundabout, take the 2nd exit and follow SP 'Bournemouth Town Centre'.

of these is part of Grim's Ditch, marking the southern edge of a Bronze and Iron-Age cattle ranch. More prominent is the 6ft rampart of Bokerley Dyke, a Romano-British defence against the invading Saxons.

Continue on the unclassified road and in 1½ miles cross the main road, SP 'Broad Chalke'. After entering Wiltshire climb to over 600ft, with fine downland views, then descend to Broad Chalke and follow SP 'Bowerchalke'.

BOWERCHALKE, Wilts
Watercress beds, rich emerald-green, continually fed by little trickling streams, line the approaches to this tiny downland village, tucked away on a tributary of the River Ebble. The views from here and from the road to Sixpenny Handley of the rolling downs and their belts of beech wood are particularly lovely.

Continue on the road, SP '6d Handley', to Sixpenny Handley.

One of the many monuments in Wimborne's minster: this, to Anthony Etricke, lies in the south choir aisle

SIXPENNY HANDLEY, Dorset
The famous abbreviated signpost 'To 6d Handley' conjures up an idyllic picture that the village scarcely lives up to, perhaps because it was almost totally rebuilt during 1892 in the aftermath of a disastrous fire. It is set in the lovely countryside of Cranborne Chase, however, and its history is colourful. In the 18th

SHEPTON MALLET, Somerset

Shepton is short for the Saxon name Sheeptown, and Mallet was the Norman name of the lord of the manor. The wool trade brought wealth to the village in the 15th century and the magnificent church, with its high, fine tower, was built with the profits. Inside, the oak roof is lavishly decorated with 350 carved panels and about 300 carved bosses — all of different designs. In the market square stands the ornate market cross. Rebuilt in 1841, this has been the social and commercial centre of the village for 5 centuries; at one time even wives were put up for sale here, as well as more usual market goods. There is also a museum in the square where Roman relics and finds from the Mendip caves can be seen. Nearby are the medieval Shambles; these wooden market-benches were not slaughter houses (the usual meaning of Shambles) but market stalls.

Leave on the A371, SP 'Castle Cary'. After 1¾ miles turn right on to the A37, then ¼ mile farther take the A371.
Go through Prestleigh and opposite the Royal Bath and West showground, branch left on to the B3081 for Evercreech.

EVERCREECH, Somerset

Of all Somerset's beautiful Perpendicular church towers, this is perhaps the finest. An impression of great height is achieved by the tiers of tall pinnacles and bell-openings. The nave roof has 16 angels painted on its ceiling and gilded bosses. St Peter's overlooks a pleasant square with old cottages, almshouses and the village cross raised on well-worn steps.

At the crossroads turn left, SP 'Stoney Stratton', and 'Batcombe'. At the T-junction ½ mile later, turn right into Stoney Stratton, then in ¼ mile turn left, SP 'Batcombe'. After 1¾ miles bear left, then turn right, and at the next crossroads turn right again. In Batcombe, by the church, turn right on to the Bruton road and later join the B3081 for Bruton.

Superb landscaping at Stourhead

WEST SOMERSET AND THE WILTSHIRE BORDERS

The graceful spires of the great wool churches pierce the skies above the green, undulating landscape of West Somerset, and the glory of Stourhead's beautiful gardens and the excitements of Longleat's Safari Park draw visitors over the border into Wiltshire.

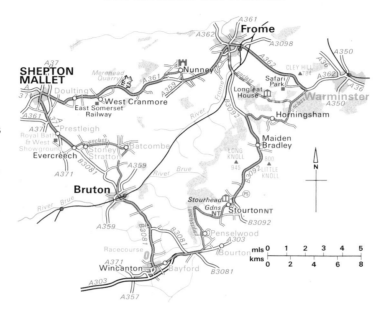

BRUTON, Somerset

Bruton was another of the chief textile towns in Somerset, and in 1290 one of the very first fulling mills in England was built on the banks of a nearby stream. The River Brue flows through the village and crossing it is the ancient packhorse bridge over which men and horses have trudged for centuries. A good view of the town is to be had from here, and several historic buildings hide among the narrow streets. There is, for instance, the 17th-century Hugh Sexey's Hospital, bequeathed to the town by a local stable boy who later found fame in London as auditor to Elizabeth I. Also of note is 16th-century King's Grammar

Most famous of Frome's ancient lanes is Cheap Street, complete with water course

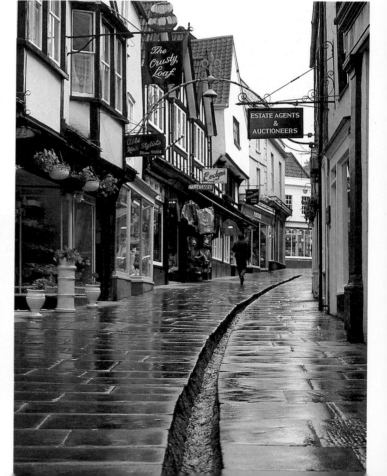

School which was founded by Edward VI. One of its most famous scholars was R. D. Blackmore, author of *Lorna Doone*. Bruton had a priory in the 12th century but all that remains of that now is a dovecot (NT) and part of the wall which both lie in a field behind the town.

From the one-way system in Bruton follow the B3081, SP 'Wincanton'. Continue through hilly countryside and after 4 miles pass Wincanton Racecourse before reaching Wincanton.

WINCANTON, Somerset

The town's medieval name, Wyndcaleton, came from the River Cale on which it stands on the edge of the Blackmoor Vale. Unfortunately a fire in the early 18th century destroyed most of Wincanton's buildings and left little of interest, apart from the church which has a 15th-century tower. Nevertheless it is a pleasant place with steep streets and makes an ideal base for touring the dairy hills of southern Somerset.

Turn left into Wincanton main street, SP 'Andover', and at the far end of the neighbouring village of Bayford turn left on to the A303. In 1½ miles turn left SP 'Penselwood', and in ½ mile turn left again. Later the tour bears left, SP 'Stourton', and the road gradually reaches 793ft. On the way down, after ¼ mile, turn sharp right (still SP 'Stourton'), and in 1½ miles by the ornamental lake, bear left and continue to Stourton.

STOURTON, Wilts
Lovely Stourton (NT) lies on the edge of the Stourhead estate overlooking the lake and gardens. The village consists of an extremely pleasing group of whitewashed 18th-century cottages facing St Peter's Church standing on its smooth open lawn, an inn and the graceful medieval Bristol High Cross — brought here in 1780. Inside the church are several monuments to the Hoare family, the famous bankers and creators of Stourhead.

Continue through the village, past the entrance to Stourhead Gardens.

STOURHEAD HOUSE AND GARDENS, Wilts
During the 18th-century the Hoares built the present Palladian mansion and dammed a nearby valley to form the beautiful lake in the gardens below. The original concept of the gardens was based on 4 ingredients — water, temples, trees and green grass. It was inspired by Henry Hoare's travels through Italy and the whole is a masterpiece of landscape gardening with the lake as a glittering centrepiece. Whatever the season there is always a heady profusion of colour at Stourhead, set against the timeless backdrop of ancient beech trees, rippling water and stone temples.

Leave the gardens and in ¼ mile turn left off on to the B3092, SP 'Frome', for Maiden Bradley.

MAIDEN BRADLEY, Wilts
Bradley House, home of the Dukes of Somerset, once stood on the edge of this neat and leafy village, but apart from 1 wing, this was demolished at the beginning of the last century. At Priory Farm lie the scant remains of a former leper hospital, founded in the 12th-century for the care of female patients, and later turned into an Augustinian Priory.

2 miles beyond Maiden Bradley turn right, SP 'Horningsham' and 'Longleat', and continue to Horningsham.

HORNINGSHAM, Wilts
At the heart of the village outside The Bath Arms, huddle a group of lime trees so intertwined that their branches form a close-weave canopy overhead. There are 12 of them and are thus locally known as the Apostles. Horningsham lies under the shadow of its famous neighbour, Longleat, and its valley borders the park. Possibly it is because of Longleat that Horningsham has what could be the oldest Non-conformist chapel in England. Many think that this small, thatched meeting house was built by Sir John Thynne, builder of Longleat, for his Scottish labour force.

Remain on the Longleat road and after ¾ mile pass Horningsham Church, then in ¼ mile turn left (still SP 'Longleat'). Follow this road through attractive woodland and after 1½ miles, pass the entrance to Longleat House on the left. (Access to the Longleat estate is via a toll road. If taken, leave the grounds by following SP 'Frome' and 'The West'. Later join the B3092 and enter Frome from the south to rejoin the main tour).

LONGLEAT, Wilts
Lions have made Longleat famous, but the hub of this huge estate belonging to the Marquess of Bath, the house, deserves its own notoriety. Builder Sir John Thynne originally transformed the Augustinian priory into a comfortable house, but sadly this suffered considerable fire damage in 1567 and the existing Elizabethan mansion is mostly Robert Smythson's work. The splendid exterior is more than matched by the inside: rich tapestries, Genoese velvet and ancient Spanish leather clothe the

walls, while Italianate painted ceilings and marble fireplaces ornament the state rooms. Much of the beautiful parkland, landscaped by Capability Brown and Humphry Repton, is occupied by the Safari Park. In the drive-through open reserves many wild animals, besides the lions, roam freely. The ornamental lake is the home of sealions and hippos and in the middle lies Ape Island. A narrow-gauge railway, an adventure playground and a pets' corner are just a few of the many other attractions at Longleat.

The main tour turns left on to the A362, SP 'Frome'. (After ½ mile note the turning on the left for Longleat Safari Park). Continue on the A362 to Frome.

FROME, Somerset
The old wool town of Frome, which takes its name from the river, is a busy, thriving place whose attractive character survives the summer traffic jams. Around its market place there is a network of old narrow streets to

be explored; paved Cheap Street, with its central water conduit, leads picturesquely to the church, where Gentle Street winds up in steps towards the top of the town. The bridge over the Frome incorporates an 18th-century lock-up and nearby stand the Bluecoat School and Blue House, an attractive almshouse, built in 1726 and recently restored.

Leave on the A361 Glastonbury road. In 3¼ miles turn right onto an unclassified road, SP 'Nunney' and continue to Nunney.

NUNNEY, Somerset
Grey-stone, red-roofed cottages cluster round Nunney Castle (AM) — the tall, grey centrepiece of the village. Really a fortified manor house built in 1373, it is a fine sight with its 4 round towers and beautiful moat. Although the castle withstood Roundhead attacks well during the Civil War, it was eventually slighted by Cromwell. A footbridge over the moat and stream leads to the village church where there are a number of elaborate stone monuments to the de la Mares, owners of the castle.

In Nunney turn left, SP 'Shepton Mallet', cross the river bridge then turn left again. A mile later, at the T-junction, turn left, then at the main road turn right on to the A361. Continue for 4¼ miles and at the crossroads turn left for West Cranmore.

WEST CRANMORE, Somerset
Near the village the East Somerset Railway Centre can be found. A new engine house has been built here by artist and railway enthusiast David Shepherd, to house his 2 locomotives — *Black Prince* and *Green Knight*.

Return to the A361 and turn left, then continue through Doulting to complete the tour at Shepton Mallet.

WOOL, WEAVING AND WATER

The old wool towns and villages of Somerset and Wiltshire stud the valleys of the Rivers Frome and Avon. Blending harmoniously with the landscape is the warm-toned stone that takes its name from Bath, where it was used so effectively in the Georgian streets and squares that characterise the town.

FROME, Somerset
See tour 12 for a description of this ancient wool town.

Leave Frome on the A361 Trowbridge road and continue to Beckington. Here join the A36, SP 'Bath', and continue to Woolverton. Beyond the Red Lion Inn, turn right and after ½ mile pass the Rode Tropical Bird Gardens.

RODE TROPICAL BIRD GARDENS, Somerset
Seventeen acres of trees, shrubs and lakes provide a setting for over 180 species of exotic birds. These include flamingoes, pelicans, cranes, vultures and cockatoos.

Continue and shortly pass the edge of Rode. At the crossroads turn right on to the B3109, SP Beckington, and in ¼ mile turn right again on to the A361. Pass Rode church and in just over ¼ mile turn left, SP 'Rudge' and 'Brokerswood'. In ½ mile at the T-junction, turn left. At the Full Moon PH in Rudge turn left and shortly turn left again. In ¼ mile, at the crossroads, turn right, SP 'Dilton' and 'Westbury'. Alternatively, continue with the North Bradley road to visit the Woodland Heritage Museum and Woodland Park.

WOODLAND HERITAGE MUSEUM AND WOODLAND PARK, Wilts
A lake alive with wildfowl lies in natural woodland which has been well laid out with nature walks. The natural history museum here, which includes a good forestry exhibition, provides interesting information about the park.

The main tour continues on the Westbury road and after 2 miles turn left on to the B3099, and shortly left again on to the A3098 for Westbury. Leave Westbury on the B3098, SP 'Bratton'. To the right is the Westbury White Horse.

WESTBURY WHITE HORSE, Wilts
Gleaming white on its hillside, the famous horse, carved into the chalk of Westbury Hill, dominates the landscape between Westbury and Bratton. The oldest of several in Wiltshire, this one is thought to commemorate King Alfred's victory over the Danes in AD 878. The elegant shape we see today, however, is an 18th-century remodelling of the original figure.

On the approach to Bratton turn left on to the unclassified Steeple Ashton road. After a mile, go over the crossroads and in a further ½ mile, at the T-junction, turn left and continue to Steeple Ashton.

STEEPLE ASHTON, Wilts
In medieval times, the village once had an important cloth market, and its name was originally Staple Ashton — taken from the wool staple (fibre). The market cross on the green stands next to an octagonal lock-up, where offenders were temporarily detained in the 18th and 19th centuries.

1 mile beyond the village turn left, SP 'Trowbridge', and later cross the A350 for Hilperton. Here turn left on to the A361, then take the next turning right on to the B3105. In 1¼ miles bear right and cross the Kennet and Avon Canal. Beyond Staverton turn left on to the B3107 for Bradford-on-Avon.

BRADFORD-ON-AVON, Wilts
Old houses of honey-coloured Bath stone line Bradford's steep, winding streets. The buildings range in style from late medieval to the elegant Georgian mansions erected by the wealthy cloth merchants. On the arched stone Town Bridge stands a chapel that for generations served as the town lock-up and near the river, in Barton Farm Country Park, stands a monumental 14th-century tithe barn (AM).

From Bradford follow SP 'Frome', across the River Avon, then turn right on to the B3109. Cross the Kennet and Avon Canal, then in ½ mile branch right, SP 'Westwood'. In another ½ mile turn right to reach the edge of Westwood. At the New Inn PH turn left and to the right is Westwood Manor.

WESTWOOD MANOR, Wilts
Thomas Horton, a wealthy clothier, built the attractive stone manor house (NT) at the edge of the village in the 15th century. It contains a medieval great hall and the aptly named King's Room, whose panels are decorated with the portraits of 22 sovereigns up to Charles I. The outstanding feature of the gardens is the topiary work; one of the bushes is shaped like a cottage, and even has a doorway.

The White Horse of Westbury

Continue along this narrow byroad for 1 mile, then turn right on to the A366, SP 'Frome', and continue to Farleigh Castle.

FARLEIGH CASTLE, Somerset
Only ruins remain of the castle (AM) built by Sir Thomas Hungerford in 1370. A later descendant, it is said, cruelly incarcerated his wife in the tower for 4 years and was himself executed for treason and 'unnatural vice' in 1540. A collection of armour and weapons is displayed in the chapel, including about 100 painted shields, a crusader's sword, and a scimitar.

Continue along the A366 and after 1 mile turn left then immediately right, SP 'Radstock', to reach Norton St Phillip.

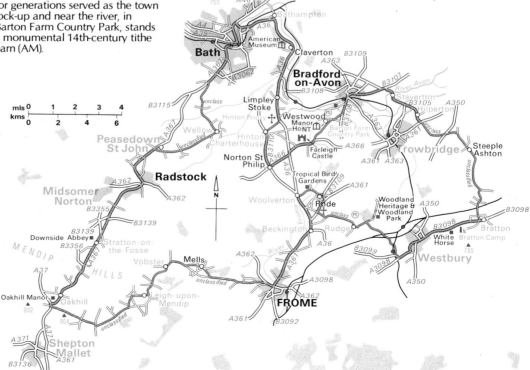

During the 19th century it was a custom in rural America for a group of friends of a bride-to-be to weave a quilt for her trousseau. This one at Claverton Manor was made in Baltimore in 1845

NORTON ST PHILIP, Somerset
The George is one of the best preserved medieval inns in the country. Founded in the 13th century as a guesthouse for Hinton Priory, its half-timbered upper storey was added in the 15th century. The ruined priory nearby, founded in 1232, is the second oldest Carthusian house in England. Among the famous guests were the diarist Samuel Pepys, the rebel Duke of Monmouth and 'hanging' Judge Jeffreys who sentenced so many of the Duke of Monmouth's followers to death in the Bloody Assize of 1685.

At the George Inn turn on to the B3110 Bath road, and continue to Hinton Charterhouse. Here, at the 2nd crossroads, turn right (no sign). In ¾ mile, at the T-junction, turn left on to the A36 and continue to Limpley Stoke.

LIMPLEY STOKE, Wilts
The impressive arches of John Rennie's Dundas Aqueduct carry the Kennet and Avon canal across the river at Limpley Stoke. Rennie designed the canal and many of its bridges and aqueducts in the early 19th century.

Remain on the A36 and after 2 miles pass, on the left, the turning for Claverton.

CLAVERTON, Somerset
Claverton Manor (OACT), built in 1820, now houses an American museum. Period rooms and furnishings give a convincing picture of American domestic life from the 17th to the 19th century, and other exhibits include Shaker and Red Indian art.

The main tour continues along the valley of the River Avon to Bath.

BATH, Avon
Aquae Sulis to the Romans, Bath's warm, healing waters have been famous for more than 2,000 years. Parts of the original Roman baths can still be seen and the nearby museum displays a fascinating collection of Roman remains. The splendid abbey dates from the 15th century, but there has been a church here since Saxon times. Bath's heyday came in the 18th century when the dandy Beau Nash made the place fashionable. Wealthy citizens flocked to take the waters at the Pump Room and attend evening parties at the Assembly Rooms. From this period date the elegant squares, crescents and terraces that have made Bath the finest Georgian city in the country. Ralph Allen, who owned the quarries at Combe Down which provided the warm-toned Bath stone, commissioned a father and son, both named John Wood, to design Queen Square, the Circus and Royal Crescent. Later architects, including Robert Adam, who built Pulteney Bridge, completed the transformation of the city. No. 1 Royal Crescent, furnished in period, is open to the public. The Costume Museum in the Assembly Rooms displays an unrivalled collection and the Holburne of Menstrie Museum in Sydney Gardens has fine examples of china and glass.

Leave Bath on the A367, SP 'Exeter', and begin a long climb out of the city. At the roundabout at the top take the 2nd exit. In ½ mile turn left onto an unclassified road SP 'Wellow' and continue to Wellow. Turn right into the main street, SP 'Radstock', and after 3 miles turn left on to the A367 and later reach Radstock.

RADSTOCK, Somerset
This small, industrial town on a hilly site was a centre of coal-mining from the 18th to the early 20th century; the last pit closed in 1973. All that now remains of the industry are the neat rows of miners' cottages, and traces of disused railway lines and canals.

Leave on the A367 Shepton Mallet road and continue to Stratton-on-Fosse passing, on the right, Downside Abbey.

DOWNSIDE ABBEY, Somerset
The abbey was a Benedictine foundation and is now one of the leading Roman Catholic boys' public schools in England. A group of English monks, who had settled in France but were driven out during the French Revolution, founded it in 1814.

Continue on the Shepton Mallet/Yeovil road to Oakhill passing on the right Oakhill Manor.

OAKHILL MANOR, Somerset
Eight acres of attractive gardens, nestling in the Mendip Hills around Oakhill Manor (OACT), provide the setting for a magnificent miniature railway that covers ¾ mile. There is a museum here as well with numerous models of various modes of transport, all well displayed in an imaginative setting.

Remain on the A367 and in just over ½ mile turn left on to the A37, then almost immediately turn left again, SP 'Frome'. After 2 miles turn right then immediately left. In another 2 miles turn left again, SP 'Leigh-upon-Mendip'. In ½ mile, at the T-junction, turn right for Leigh-upon-Mendip. Here, bear left with the Coleford/Radstock road, then keep forward, SP 'Vobster'. Enter Vobster and turn right on to the Mells road and follow SP 'Mells'.

MELLS, Somerset
Mells, with its well-kept cottage gardens, ranks as one of the prettiest villages in Somerset. The Elizabethan manor house (not open) once belonged to Abbot Selwood of Glastonbury, who, hoping to save the abbey from the Dissolution, sent the title deeds of the manor, concealed in a pie, to Henry VIII. John Horner is said to have stolen them and thus has been identified with Jack Horner of nursery-rhyme fame.

Follow SP 'Frome' and in 1¾ miles turn left. In 1 mile turn right on to the A362 for the return to the town centre.

Pulteney Bridge, Bath

South and
South East England

PORTSMOUTH, Hants

Naval tradition is everywhere in Portsmouth. The docks, founded by Richard the Lionheart at the end of the 12th century, now cover more than 300 acres. Here the most famous ship in British history, HMS *Victory*, Nelson's flagship at the Battle of Trafalgar in 1805, lies peacefully at anchor. It has been restored and fitted out to show what conditions on board ship were like. Nearby, the Royal Navy Museum has a fascinating display of model ships and figureheads, and a huge and impressive panorama representing the Battle of Trafalgar. Also in the dockyard is the Mary Rose, Henry VIII's flagship, which was raised from the seabed after a famous rescue mission. A major exhibition accompanies the restored ship. In old Commercial Road is the birthplace of Charles Dickens, which is now a museum of his life and times (OACT).

From Portsmouth city centre follow SP 'Southsea' to the seafront, then turn left along the Esplanade to Southsea.

SOUTHSEA, Hants

Henry VIII built a castle (OACT) at Southsea in 1539 to defend Portsmouth harbour. Now it houses a naval museum and archaeological exhibits. Southsea is well off for museums: Cumberland House in Easter Parade, has local natural history displays and an aquarium; the Eastney Beam-Engine House is the hub of an industrial archaeology museum and the Royal Marines Museum is to be found in Eastney Barracks.

From Southsea follow South Parade and in ¾ mile turn left into St George's Road. Pass Eastney Barracks (right) and at the roundabout, take the 2nd exit. At the next roundabout, take the A2030, SP 'Out of City'. The tour then runs alongside Langstone Harbour and in 2 miles at the roundabout, take the A27, SP 'Chichester' and continue to Emsworth.

EMSWORTH, Hants

Emsworth, tucked away between 2 of the many small creeks of Chichester Harbour, is an ancient port, famed for its oyster fisheries. Yacht building is the traditional occupation here and yachts jostle in the small, picturesque harbour. On the jetty is a majestic old tide mill.

At Emsworth turn left on to the B2148 Horndean road, pass under a railway bridge then bear left. In 1 mile turn right into Emsworth Common Road and enter Southleigh Forest. Continue to Funtington and join the B2146. In 1 mile turn right, SP 'Bosham', and pass through West Ashling. At the roundabout junction with the A27 a diversion can be made by taking the 2nd exit for Bosham.

ROYAL NAVAL BASE BENEATH THE SUSSEX DOWNS

Portsmouth, historic seat of the Royal Navy, opens the way to the hidden creeks and harbours of the Hampshire and West Sussex coasts sheltered beneath the magnificent beech hangers that cloak the South Downs.

BOSHAM, W Sussex

The village green leading from the waterfront up to the fine old church, the brick and tile-hung cottages along the strand and the sheltered harbour, all create a scene that appeals to painters and yachtsmen alike. Inhabitants of Bosham claim that it was here, and not at Southampton, that King Cnut unsuccessfully challenged the waves to withdraw. As evidence they point to the tomb that was discovered in the church about 100 years ago and said to belong to Cnut's daughter.

The main tour joins the A27 Chichester road and continues to Fishbourne.

FISHBOURNE, W Sussex

The little Sussex village of Fishbourne is outshone by the splendid Roman palace built here c AD 75. Archaeologists have unearthed a 6-acre site, the largest Roman building yet found in Britain. The north wing, with the famous 'boy on a dolphin' mosaic floor, is open, and parts of the original hypocaust (underground central heating system) and baths can also be seen. Outside, archaeologists have reconstructed the gardens as they might have been in Roman-times.

Beyond Fishbourne turn left on to the A259 and follow SP 'City Centre' into Chichester.

CHICHESTER, W Sussex

The county town of West Sussex is a delightful criss-cross of old streets, lined with handsome Georgian houses and shops. The city was founded by the Romans in AD 43, and the old Roman street plan can still be traced in North, South, East and West Streets. These divide the town in 4, meeting at the splendid octagonal market cross built in the 15th century by Bishop Story. The prettiest of the old streets are The Pallants and Little London, where an 18th-century Corn Store has been converted to the City Museum and the museum of the Royal Sussex Regiment. Chichester's great Norman cathedral contains 2 outstanding works of modern art: a dazzling tapestry by John Piper and a painting by Graham Sutherland.

From the Ring Road in Chichester follow SP 'Worthing' to the Chichester Motel Roundabout. Here follow SP 'Goodwood' and in ½ mile, at the T-junction, turn left. Later, on the right, is the entrance to Goodwood Park and House.

The cottages crowded along Bosham's quayside all have steps to their front doors to protect them from the frequent flooding of the harbour at high tide

North Street — typical of Chichester

GOODWOOD HOUSE, W Sussex

Seat of the Dukes of Richmond and Gordon, Goodwood House (OACT) was built during the late 18th century in Sussex flint. It is a treasuretrove of fine pictures, notably Vandyck's portraits and George Stubbs' paintings of racehorses; furniture; tapestries and Sèvres porcelain. Wooded parkland surrounds the house and high above on the downs is Goodwood Racecourse — once part of the estate. The glorious scenery of the downs provides a superb setting and the views are quite breathtaking.

Climb on to the South Downs to reach Goodwood Racecourse. Here turn left and later pass the entrance, on the left, to the Weald and Downland Open Air Museum just before Singleton village.

THE WEALD AND DOWNLAND OPEN AIR MUSEUM, W Sussex

All types of buildings from southern and south-eastern England have been accumulated at this open-air museum (OACT), the first of its kind to be established in this country. Here you can see, for example, a Wealden farmhouse, a charcoal burner's hut, a forge, a pottery and a smithy — just a few of the many old rural buildings from England's past.

Continue to the A286 and turn right, SP 'Midhurst', into Singleton. Continue through Cocking to Midhurst.

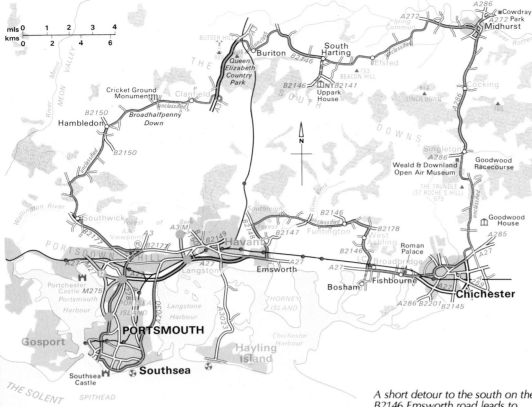

MIDHURST, W Sussex

The little town of Midhurst sits snugly in the Rother valley to the north of the downs. The quaintly named Knockhundred Row leads from North Street to Red Lion Street, where the old timbered market house stands. Of the many picturesque buildings, the half-timbered Spread Eagle Inn, dating back to medieval times, is perhaps the finest. A curfew is still rung in the church every evening at 8 p.m. in memory of a traveller who, lost in the forest long ago, followed the sound of the church bells and so was saved.

To the east of the town is Cowdray Park.

COWDRAY PARK, W Sussex

Viscount Cowdray of Midhurst bought the estate earlier this century and preserved the ruined house (OACT), once the seat of the Earls of Southampton which was destroyed by fire in 1793. The superb parkland forms an appropriate setting for the aristocratic sport of polo which was imported into England from India in the last century.

Leave Midhurst on the A272, SP 'Petersfield'. In 2½ miles turn left SP 'Elsted' and 'Harting'. Cross Iping Common, and continue through Elsted to South Harting.

SOUTH HARTING, W Sussex

The slender church spire rises out of the wooded farmland surrounding this attractive village, whose main street is lined with old houses, some of brick, some tile-hung and some of Sussex clunch — a local soft limestone. It was at Harting Grange (not open) that the 19th-century novelist Anthony Trollope spent the last 2 years of his life.

A short detour to the south on the B2146 Emsworth road leads to Uppark.

UPPARK HOUSE, W Sussex

A magnificent house in a magnificent setting on the downs, Uppark (NT) was the home of Lord Grey, 1st Earl of Tankerville, in about 1690. A later owner, Sir Matthew Fetherstonhaugh (pronounced Fanshawe) furnished it with exquisite furniture and rare carpets. His wife Sarah brought with her a wonderful Queen Anne dolls' house, complete with furniture, glass and silverware. Their extravagant and highly sociable son, Sir Harry, inherited Uppark and brought to the house a beautiful 15-year-old girl, Emma Hart, who later became Lord Nelson's Lady Hamilton. Sir Harry married his 20-year-old dairymaid when he was 70 and left her the

Bayleaf House, built in Kent between 1420 and 1480, was reconstructed at the Weald and Downland Museum in the 1970s

entire estate. The young lady spent the rest of her life conserving Uppark and it remained largely unchanged throughout the 19th century. The novelist H. G. Wells spent much of his youth here, for his mother was housekeeper.

From the Ship Inn at South Harting, follow SP 'Petersfield' along the B2146. After 2 miles re-enter Hampshire, then in just over ½ mile turn left for Buriton.

BURITON, Hants

Glorious beech hangers drop down into Buriton, whose traditional green with its duck pond is surrounded by attractive cottages, an old church, a rectory and a stone manor house. The latter was the home of famous historian Edward Gibbon, best remembered for his mammoth work, *The Decline and Fall of the Roman Empire.*

Continue through the village and in about a mile turn left on to the A3, SP 'Portsmouth'. In 2 miles, on the left, is the entrance to the Queen Elizabeth Country Park.

QUEEN ELIZABETH COUNTRY PARK, Hants

The wooded downland south of Buriton was opened by the Forestry Commission in Jubilee Year (1977) as the Queen Elizabeth Country Park (OACT). Marked trails wind through the park and there is a reconstruction of an Iron-Age settlement to be seen, as well as a craft centre displaying items used to farm the hills for the past several hundred years.

In 1 mile turn left SP 'Clanfield' then left again. At the roundabout take the 1st exit. From Clanfield cross Broad Halfpenny Down to Hambledon.

HAMBLEDON, Hants

On Broadhalfpenny Down near Hambledon, opposite the Bat and Ball Inn, stands a monument commemorating the beginning of cricket. The Hambledon Cricket Club were the first, in 1760, to play the game in an organised manner. To the west of the attractive village, on a south-facing slope, lies one of England's few successful vineyards (open by appointment), producing a white wine similar to German hock.

In Hambledon turn left on to the B2150, then in ¾ mile branch right SP 'Fareham'. After 2½ miles, at the T-junction, turn left, SP 'Southwick', at the next T-junction turn left for Southwick. Here follow SP 'Portsmouth' to join the B2177. At the roundabout at the top of Ports Down Hill take the 1st exit, SP 'Havant'. Nearly 1 mile further is an AA Viewpoint. Continue on the B2177, then shortly, turn right, SP 'Portsmouth', to join the A3. Descend to Cosham and return to Portsmouth city centre via the A3, or the M275.

LEWES AND THE SOUTH DOWNS

Two lovely river valleys cut through the downs on their way to the sea with its high white cliffs. In between, low-lying water meadows and wooded lanes hide dignified manor houses and medieval hamlets with historic Lewes at their heart.

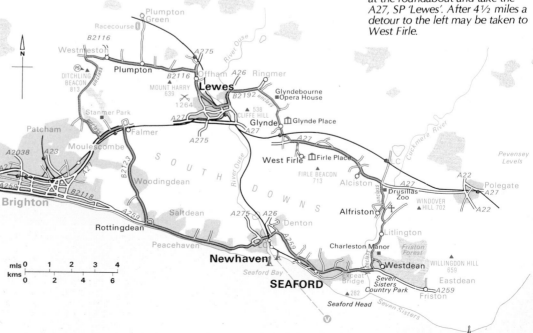

By the 1800s Alfriston's Clergy House was being used as labourers' cottages

SEAFORD, E Sussex

A flat, exposed stretch of land — once wild and empty but now covered with buildings — separates Seaford from the sea. The port lost its importance as long ago as the 16th century when the River Ouse changed its course after a particularly violent storm and flowed into the sea at Newhaven instead. East of Seaford, high white cliffs of chalk stretch away from Seaford Head to Beachy Head. On the promontory of Seaford Head, beside the clifftop path to Cuckmere Haven, lie remains of an Iron-Age hill fort. During excavations broken flint axes, saws and arrowheads were found buried in 2 small pits; they were probably religious offerings.

From Seaford, follow the A259 Eastbourne road. Cross the Cuckmere River by the Exceat bridge, then in ¼ mile turn left on to the unclassified Litlington road. To the right of the A259 at this junction is the Seven Sisters Country Park.

SEVEN SISTERS COUNTRY PARK, E Sussex

Nearly 700 acres of downland and marshland have been turned into the Seven Sisters Country Park. Nature trails wind through the countryside and fishing is available along the Cuckmere valley. An old barn at Exceat houses the park information centre, and here there are interesting permanent displays of local history and temporary exhibitions.

Continue on the Litlington road and after nearly ½ mile pass the turning for Westdean (right).

WESTDEAN, E Sussex

Westdean village sits peacefully at the end of a No Through Road and seems remote from the hectic 20th century. Its cottages, mostly flint, cluster round a pond, a dovecot (AM) and the ruins of the medieval manor house (AM). Inside the Church of All Saints is a Jacob Epstein bronze bust of Lord Waverley, Home Secretary during World War II. It is possible that the site of this little village may be where Alfred the Great first met Asser, the monk who later became Bishop of Sherborne and wrote an account of the king's life.

Continue on the Litlington road and after another ½ mile, pass Charleston Manor on the right.

CHARLESTON MANOR, E Sussex

Only the grounds of this part-Norman, part-Tudor and part-Georgian manor house are open. However, the romantic gardens, full of bulbs and flowering shrubs contained by yew hedges and flint walls, are exceptionally pretty. Particularly interesting are the huge restored tithe barns, one thatched, the other tiled, and the medieval dovecot with its conical roof and revolving ladder.

Continue through Litlington and after ¾ mile turn left, SP 'Alfriston'. In another ¾ mile, turn left to recross the Cuckmere River. At the next T-junction, turn left for Alfriston.

ALFRISTON, E Sussex

The High Street of this tiny market town runs south from its square. Here stands the old market cross, shaded by the branches of a massive chestnut tree. On either side of the High Street are timbered buildings, some hung with tiles, some with weather-boarding, but virtually all are pre-18th century. Among the finest buildings are the 3 inns: The George, The Market Cross and The Star. The latter is most famous, both for its external carvings and the brightly coloured ship's figurehead which stands outside, and for its associations with smugglers. Alfriston was a well-known hideout for these outlaws in the early 19th century as it was on their route up the Cuckmere valley from the sea 3 miles away. Behind the High Street, overlooking the river and a large green known as the Tye, is Alfriston's church. Named Cathedral of the Downs because of its size, the cruciform church is particularly lovely and has some of the best flintwork in the country. On the edge of the green is the Clergy House (NT). This 14th-century building was, in 1896, the first to be bought by the newly formed National Trust.

Return along the unclassified Dicker road and after 1 mile pass Drusillas Zoo Park on the right.

DRUSILLAS ZOO PARK, E Sussex

Hiding in the heart of the Cuckmere's low-lying water meadows and sleepy villages is Drusillas Zoo Park. Apart from the zoo itself, there are a great variety of different attractions here. These include a butterfly house, a farm, an adventure playground, a bakery selling its own freshly baked bread and a railway to take passengers on a round trip through the park.

On reaching the main road turn left at the roundabout and take the A27, SP 'Lewes'. After 4½ miles a detour to the left may be taken to West Firle.

mls 0 1 2 3 4
kms 0 2 4 6

Anne of Cleves House, 16th-century, stands in Southover High Street, Lewes

WEST FIRLE, E Sussex

Such is the feudal atmosphere of West Firle (curiously there is no East Firle) that it still seems to be part of the estate attached to Firle Place (OACT). The village hides on the edge of the parkland and the Gage family crest over the inn confirms its connection with the great house. The Gages have owned Firle Place ever since the 15th century, and the main part of the house dates from that time. No alterations of any consequence were made to it until 1774, when the front was rebuilt to incorporate a gallery for the 1st Viscount's splendid art collection. Half an hour's walk away from the village is Firle Beacon, a magnificent viewpoint with distant views of the sea.

Continue on the A27 and in ½ mile turn right on to an unclassified road for Glynde.

GLYNDE, E Sussex

Like Firle, the small village of Glynde has a great house on its doorstep, Glynde Place (OACT). The present Elizabethan manor was built of flint and Caen stone in 1569, but the impressive stable block was added in the 18th century. The stable buildings surround a delightful courtyard of smooth lawn, roses and climbing plants. Bronzes, needlework and a pottery can be seen at Glynde Place, but one of its most prized possessions is a drawing by Rubens. This was a study for the painted ceiling of the Banqueting House at Whitehall.

At the far end of the village pass Glynde Place, and in ¾ mile bear left, SP 'Ringmer'. After 1 mile pass Glyndebourne Opera House.

Although sheep still graze the chalky slopes of the South Downs, many acres are now being used for arable farming instead

GLYNDEBOURNE, E Sussex

When John Christie, onetime science master at Eton, inherited his ancestral home at Glyndebourne, he decided to indulge his great love of opera and build an opera house in the grounds of his Tudor mansion. Since opening in 1934, Glyndebourne has become internationally famous for its opera festivals performed from May to August. The idyllic setting, the elaborate champagne picnics on the beautiful lawns and the elegance of evening dress, combine to produce a magical atmosphere at Glyndebourne that is unforgettable.

Continue, and on reaching the B2192 turn left, SP 'Lewes'. At the A26 turn left to reach Lewes.

LEWES, E Sussex

With the downs rising up around it and the River Ouse flowing through it, Lewes was an ideal site on which to build a defensive fort and the Normans made full use of it. William de Warenne, husband of William the Conqueror's daughter Gundrada, originally built his castle of wood on 2 artificial mounds. Later a stone keep was built but little except this and the gateway remain, however, because in 1620 the castle was demolished and the stone sold off as building material for 4d a load. The imposing outer gatehouse, called Barbican House, is 14th century and a museum of Sussex archaeology is kept here now. Wide views from the top of the keep encompass Offham Hill. It was there that Henry III unsuccessfully fought Simon de Montfort in 1264 at the Battle of Lewes. East Sussex's charming country town of steep streets, little alleyways and neat, red-roofed Georgian houses covers no more than a square mile. Nearly every building is of interest; Anne of Cleves House — so called because it was one of the properties Henry VIII gave Anne as payment for divorcing him — is open as a folk museum. There is another museum in Regency House and this is devoted to military heritage and includes a short history of the British army. Traditionally, every November 5 the streets throng with torch-lit processions and bonfires blaze in celebration of Guy Fawkes.

Leave the town centre on the A275, SP 'East Grinstead'. Pass through Offham then in almost ½ mile turn left on to the B2116, SP 'Hassocks'. Continue along the foot of the South Downs to Plumpton.

PLUMPTON, E Sussex

A church, a post office, an inn, an old rectory and Plumpton Place make up the old village of Plumpton; the modern village, 2 miles away, is called Plumpton Green and lies handy to Plumpton Racecourse. Plumpton Place (not open) a half-timbered, E-shaped house, was restored by Sir Edwin Lutyens after World War II. Above the village a V-shaped group of fir trees commemorate Queen Victoria's Golden Jubilee.

Continue to Westmeston. Here, turn left on to an unclassified road, SP 'Underhill Lane'. At the next crossroads turn left and climb to the summit of Ditchling Beacon (813 ft) — one of the highest points on the South Downs. 2½ miles later, turn left, SP 'Moulsecombe'. In another 1¼ miles turn left on to the A27 and pass Stanmer Park (the site of the University of Sussex). Branch left then turn right on to the B2123, SP 'Rottingdean', and pass through Woodingdean to reach Rottingdean.

ROTTINGDEAN, E Sussex

Flint and brick cottages brighten up the High Street of this onetime smuggling town which has the salty flavour of the sea. Rudyard Kipling, author of *Jungle Book*, stayed here as a boy with his uncle, the painter Sir Edward Burne-Jones. Some of Burne-Jones' glasswork can be seen in the church, which overlooks a green with a pond — a particularly attractive corner of the town. A Georgian house, remodelled by Sir Edwin Lutyens, contains the library, an art gallery and a museum with some Kipling exhibits and a good toy collection.

At Rottingdean turn left on to the A259, SP 'Newhaven', and continue along the coast road through Saltdean and Peacehaven to Newhaven.

NEWHAVEN, E Sussex

Well-known as a cross-channel departure point to France, Newhaven teems with passengers both coming and going to the Continent. The town was called Meeching until the 1560s, when the Ouse changed its course (see Seaford) and Newhaven seemed more appropriate.

From Newhaven follow SP 'Eastbourne' and remain on the A259 for the return stretch to Seaford.

UCKFIELD, E Sussex

Standing on a hillside above the valley of the River Ouse, Uckfield looks towards the great sweep of the downs. Traditional Sussex houses, brick and tile-hung, or weather-boarded, line its attractive main street.

Leave Uckfield on the Eastbourne Road. In 2½ miles cross the A22, SP 'Isfield', and 1¼ miles farther keep left on the Ringmer road to shortly pass the entrance to Bentley Wildfowl Gardens.

BENTLEY WILDFOWL GARDENS, E Sussex

A succession of ponds, surrounded by luxurious belts of trees and bushes, create an ideal habitat for many varieties of interesting wildfowl; spectacular flocks of rose-coloured flamingoes, black swans and ornamental pheasants bring a blaze of exotic colour to the Sussex countryside.

At the T-junction 2 miles later, turn left on to the B2192, SP 'Halland', then in 1½ miles turn right on to an unclassified road for Laughton.

LAUGHTON, E Sussex

Between wooded countryside to the north and the flat marshlands of Glynde Level to the south, stands the little village of Laughton. A curious buckle emblem can be seen on the church tower, on the ruined tower of Laughton Place south of the village, and on several buildings round the area. This was the badge of the Pelhams and dates back to the Battle of Poitiers in 1356, when Sir John Pelham captured the French King and was awarded the Badge of the Buckle of the King's Swordbelt by a grateful Edward III.

Turn left on to the B2124, SP 'Hailsham'. On reaching the A22 turn right then take the next turning left, SP 'Chiddingly'. In ¾ mile turn left again for Chiddingly.

CHIDDINGLY, E Sussex

The tall church spire soars above the cottages of this small, quiet village. From the church, you can see for miles over the downs, and on a clear day it is possible to pick out the chalky outline of the Long Man of Wilmington — a giant figure cut out of the turf above Wilmington. Inside the church is an outsize monument to members of the Jefferay family, with 2 large standing figures in elaborate Elizabethan dress.

Turn left in the village, SP 'Whitesmith', and in 1 mile at the T-junction, turn right, SP 'Waldron'. Continue for 2 miles, then turn right and immediately left on to the Heathfield road. In 1½ miles, at the crossroads, turn left SP 'Blackboys'. On reaching the main road turn left then immediately right, SP 'Buxted'. After 1¾ miles turn left and continue to Buxted.

ASHDOWN FOREST AND THE FOREST WEALD

Never far from the quietly civilised villages of East Sussex and the Kent borders are the woods and heathlands of Ashdown Forest — a tame fragment of the vast primeval wilderness that covered much of south-east England in ancient times.

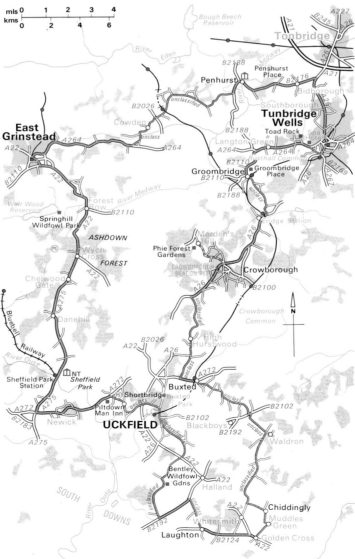

BUXTED, E Sussex

Hogge House, a 16th-century black and white timbered building at the gates of Buxted Park, was the home of Ralph Hogge, a local iron-master, the first man to cast an iron cannon in 1543. The old village that he knew was allowed to fall into ruins during the 19th century because Lord Liverpool, the owner of Buxted Park (not open) wanted to improve the view from his mansion. Consequently Liverpool moved the village to its present site near the station. The parish church still stands in the park. It is dedicated to St Margaret of Scotland and her emblem, the marguerite, is carved around the pulpit and embossed on the ceiling.

At Buxted turn left on to the A272 and skirt the grounds of Buxted Park. After ¾ mile turn right on to an unclassified road and continue to High Hurstwood. Bear left into the village, then ascend to skirt part of the Ashdown Forest. On reaching the A26 turn right, passing over Crowborough Beacon (792ft), and enter Crowborough.

Weather-boarding, typical of Kentish cottages, like these in Groombridge, was added to give extra protection

CROWBOROUGH, E Sussex

Crowborough has grown up around a triangular green, and climbs up over the slopes of the 796ft Beacon Hill from where there are superb views. A relatively modern town — its oldest house dates from the 19th century — it owes its charm to its position on the eastern edge of Ashdown Forest. Nearby the Phie Forest Gardens are a favourite place for country walks and picnics.

Remain on the A26 and in 3 miles pass Eridge Station, then immediately turn left on to an unclassified road for Groombridge.

GROOMBRIDGE, E Sussex/Kent

Groombridge spans the county border between East Sussex and Kent. The old part of the village, in Kent, is exceptionally pretty, with 18th-century brick and tile-hung cottages grouped around a triangular green which leads to the gates of Groombridge Place, (not open) a delightful Jacobean moated manor house set in lovely gardens (open by appointment).

In Groombridge turn right on to the B2110, SP 'Tunbridge Wells'. Pass the grounds of Groombridge Park (right), then in 1¼ miles turn right, on to the A264. Continue through Langton Green and after crossing Rusthall Common, a side road on the left may be taken to visit the curious Toad Rock, so called because of its distinctive shape. Continue on the A246 and in ¼ mile at the Spa Hotel, turn right, SP 'Brighton'. On the far side of the common turn left on to the A26 to enter Tunbridge Wells.

TUNBRIDGE WELLS, Kent

This delightful town owes its existence to Lord North who, in 1606, discovered the medicinal springs in what was then a sandstone outcrop in the Forest of Ashdown. Many of its houses date from the late 17th and 18th centuries, by which time it had become a fashionable spa. The famous Pantiles, an elegant colonnaded walk lined with fashionable shops and shaded by trees, takes its name from the large roofing tiles, 15 of which survive, laid to appease Queen Anne who had protested at the muddy state of the ground. The town museum contains a fascinating collection of Tunbridge Ware — small boxes and trinkets decorated with a mosaic of tiny pieces of wood — and Victorian paintings, toys and dolls.

Leave Tunbridge Wells on the A26, SP 'Tonbridge' and 'London'. Pass through Southborough, then in 1 mile turn left on to the B2176, SP 'Penshurst'. Continue through Bidborough to Penshurst.

PENSHURST, Kent

The pretty village of Penshurst lies between the Rivers Medway and Eden. Around the approach to the churchyard is a charming group of timbered cottages, the central one raised up on pillars to form an archway. Penshurst Place (OACT) was the home of the gallant Elizabethan soldier-poet Sir Philip Sidney who, when dying after the Battle of Zutphen, gave the water offered to him to an enemy soldier, saying: 'Thy necessity is greater than mine'. The manor house, set in lovely 17th-century gardens, was originally built in the 15th century by Sir John de Pulteney, 4 times Lord Mayor of London, and his magnificent medieval great hall survives. Descendants of Sidney, the de L'Isle family, still live at Penshurst.

Branch left on to the B2188, and in ¾ mile turn right, SP 'Chiddingstone'. After 1½ miles, at the T-junction, turn right, and ¾ mile farther keep left, SP 'Cowden'. In another mile turn left, then in 1½ miles cross the main road to reach Cowden. Go through the village and turn right on to the East Grinstead road. On reaching the A264 turn right for East Grinstead.

EAST GRINSTEAD, W Sussex

The old centre of East Grinstead, originally a small market town, remains unspoilt, and in the main street are many Tudor half-timbered buildings. The most attractive group is Sackville College (OACT): gabled, 17th-century almshouses built around a quiet courtyard with the dignified air of an Oxford college.

Leave on the A22 and continue to Forest Row. Springhill Wildfowl Park lies 1½ miles to the west.

SPRINGHILL WILDFOWL PARK, E Sussex

Rare varieties of ducks and wild geese, flamboyant peacocks, graceful swans, flamingoes and cranes inhabit this 10-acre forest garden that surrounds an attractive 15th-century farmhouse on the borders of Ashdown Forest.

Continue on the Eastbourne road into part of the Ashdown Forest.

ASHDOWN FOREST, E Sussex

Ashdown Forest, lying between the North and South Downs, covers more than 14,000 acres. Extensive though it is, Ashdown is merely a remnant of the vast primeval Forest of Anderida which cut Sussex off from the rest of the country. It remained a wild and dangerous area until Elizabethan times when the great trees were felled to provide fuel for the forges of the Wealden iron industry.

A collection of toys and games can be seen in the stable block of Penshurst Place

At Wych Cross turn right on to the A275, SP 'Lewes'. Continue through Chelwood Gate and Danehill to Sheffield Park.

SHEFFIELD PARK, E Sussex

The gardens (NT) of the elegant 18th-century house (OACT) built by Wyatt for the Earl of Sheffield, are one of the great showplaces of Sussex. The original landscape design, featuring broad, curving lakes was carried out by Capability Brown and his pupil Humphry Repton. Two more lakes were added later, and around the

Careful planting at Sheffield Park ensures a blaze of colour all year round

4 stretches of water A. G. Soames, who bought the property in 1909, created gardens and walks of rhododendrons, azaleas, maples, birches and other trees.

THE BLUEBELL RAILWAY, E Sussex

At Sheffield Park station you can take a step back into the past by travelling on the famous Bluebell line, where vintage steam trains trundle along the old East Grinstead to Lewes track, through 5 miles of glorious Sussex countryside to Horsted Keynes.

Continue on the A275 and 2 miles later turn left on to the A272. Pass through Newick to reach Piltdown.

PILTDOWN, E Sussex

Between Newick and Uckfield stands an inn called the Piltdown Man. Its name and the inn sign which depicts on one side an apelike skull and on the other a club-wielding caveman, commemorate one of the greatest archaeological hoaxes of all time. In 1912 a respectable young lawyer called Charles Dawson caused a sensation by announcing his discovery of the skull of a creature that was joyfully hailed as evidence of the 'missing link' between *homo sapiens* and the great apes. Piltdown Man remained a 'fact' for more than 40 years, until scientific dating techniques established in 1953 that the skull had been cobbled together from the jaw of an orangutan and the deformed cranium of a medieval skeleton.

After passing the Piltdown Man Inn turn right, SP 'Shortbridge'. At Shortbridge, cross the river and turn left for the return to Uckfield.

HASTINGS, E Sussex

William the Conqueror ensured Hastings a firm place in English history when he assembled his army here in 1066, although the battle of Hastings actually took place at nearby Battle. His stone Norman castle now lies in ruins overlooking the town and can be reached via a cliff lift. During the Middle Ages Hastings was an important Cinque Port; until the end of the 15th century these south-east defence ports were duty-bound to supply ships and men in the event of invasion. However, when Hastings harbour silted up, the town turned to fishing for its livelihood. The Old Town to the east is the picturesque fishermen's quarter and the heart of the ancient town. Weather-boarded houses crowd down alleys to the shingle beach and the shops mostly sell sailors' bric-a-brac. Curious 3-storeyed square structures made of tarred wood stand on the beach; they are fishing net lofts and were originally built high to keep ground rent to a minimum. Fishermens' Museum which used to be the local chapel, is now packed with seafaring treasures.

Leave Hastings on the A259, SP 'Brighton', along the seafront. Pass through the neighbouring resort of St Leonards to Bexhill.

BEXHILL, E Sussex

In 1880, Lord de la Warr, member of an old Sussex family, developed this little town into a holiday resort. The rather ugly de la Warr Pavilion sitting on the sea front forms the focal point of the traditional range of seaside entertainments — concert halls, theatres, restaurants and sun lounges. Rather more attractive is the old village behind the coast line.

At Bexhill follow the A269, SP 'London', and pass through Sidley to Ninfield. Here turn right on to the Battle road and continue to Catsfield. At the end of the village turn right on to the B2095, SP 'Battle Station'. Later turn left on to the A2100 and enter Battle.

Above: Cranbrook's smock mill

Below: the cottage garden at Sissinghurst Castle

THE KENTISH WEALD TO THE CINQUE PORTS

From Hastings, where English history was made in 1066 to Rye, a smugglers' paradise in the 18th century: both vital Cinque Ports. Inland, towards the Weald, the tour passes the windmills, weather-boarding and hop fields which characterise Kent.

BATTLE, E Sussex

The Battle of Hastings took place just outside Battle, which is how the town got its name. King Harold II lost, and it was this defeat which gave the town an abbey, because William the Conqueror vowed beforehand that if he was the victor he would build one by way of thanks to God. When St Martin's Abbey was built, the high altar was placed on the spot where Harold fell. The abbey remains (OACT), actually of later buildings than William's, include a fine gateway, the monks' sleeping quarters and the cellars. In Langton House the history of Battle from Neolithic times to the present day is vividly illustrated and there are many pieces of Sussex iron from the industry which flourished over a 1,000 years ago. There is also a copy (1821) of the Bayeux Tapestry.

Remain on the A2100, SP 'London', then in 3 miles turn left on to the A21 and continue through Robertsbridge to Hurst Green. Beyond the village turn right on to the A265 and enter Kent before reaching Hawkhurst.

HAWKHURST, Kent

Hawkhurst was a onetime stronghold of the notorious Hawkhurst Gang — a group of smugglers who terrorised much of Kent and Sussex in the early 18th century. Now some way between village and town in size, the older part lies around a triangular green known as the Moor. Among the brick and weather-boarded houses around the green stands the church. Its 15th-century window tracery is particularly fine, as is the 14th-century east window.

Follow the A268, SP 'Flimwell/ Tonbridge'. A gradual climb passes through woodland into Sussex again at Flimwell. Here, at the crossroads, turn right to rejoin the A21. In 1 mile turn right on to the B2079 to reach Goudhurst.

GOUDHURST, Kent

Between the duck pond at the bottom of the hill and the church at the top, typical Kentish houses jostle each other up the main street. Goudhurst stands on a steep ridge of land and its church tower, 500ft above sea level, was used as a lookout post in both World War I and II. The church is 14th century, but the stocky tower dates from 1638, when a storm destroyed the original. Wooden painted figures inside represent Sir Alexander Colepeper and his wife and are the best of the church's many monuments.

At Goudhurst turn right on to the A262, SP 'Ashford', and in 1½ miles turn right again on to the B2085, SP 'Hawkhurst'. In 2 miles turn left, SP 'Cranbrook'. On reaching the A229 turn left, then take the next turning right on to the B2189 and enter Cranbrook.

CRANBROOK, Kent

Cranbrook was built from the profits of the cloth trade. With the streams to power fulling mills, oak trees to use as building material and fullers' earth to clean the cloth, it was an ideal centre for the industry. On the edge of the village stands one of the country's most splendid smock mills — their name supposedly coming from the resemblance to a man dressed in a smock. Built in the 18th century, its sails stretch up to nearly 100ft above the ground.

Remain on the B2189, SP 'Staplehurst', and later turn right on to the A229. In ¼ mile turn right again on to the A262, SP 'Ashford', and pass through Sissinghurst. ½ mile beyond the village a turning on the left leads to Sissinghurst Castle.

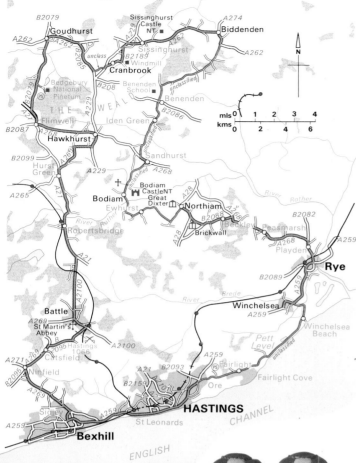

BODIAM, E Sussex

Bodiam Castle (NT) outshines its village by far. The fortress was built in the 14th century to guard this vital crossing point on the River Rother, which was a potential route inland for French invaders. Although it was not attacked at that time, the castle met its fate during the Civil War when Cromwellian armies destroyed it. Now it stands serenely as an empty shell, clearly reflected in its wide lily-covered moat.

At Bodiam turn left on to the Ewhurst road and pass the castle (left). Cross the River Rother and in ½ mile turn left, SP 'Ewhurst Green'. Pass through Ewhurst Green and follow SP 'Northiam'.

NORTHIAM, E Sussex

The gnarled old oak tree on Northiam's village green is famous because Elizabeth I dined under it in 1573. During the occasion she took her shoes off, and let the villagers keep them when she left. They are now kept at Brickwall, so named because of its high surrounding walls. Brickwall was the home of the Frewen family for 400 years and is now a boys' school. At the opposite end of Northiam is Great Dixter (OACT). Nathaniel Lloyd, architectural historian, bought the house in 1911 and commissioned Sir Edwin Lutyens to enlarge and restore it, which he did to good effect. Curiously-clipped yews are the most striking feature of the gardens.

At Northiam turn right on to the A28 Hastings road and on leaving the village branch left on to the B2088, SP 'Rye'. Pass Brickwall House (right) and continue to Beckley. At the far end turn right on to the A268 and continue to Rye.

RYE, E Sussex

Ancient, timbered and Georgian buildings, the romance of a seafaring and smuggling past in every twisting cobbled street and its perch high up on a bluff within sight and smell of the sea, give Rye its considerable charm. When the sea lapped the town walls in the 14th century, Rye was one of the most prosperous ancient ports in Sussex. However, repeated, relentless attacks and burnings by the French, together with the silting up of the harbour, were the town's undoing. One of the buildings to survive the French deflagrations was Ypres Tower — the 13th-century town fort. It is put to good use now as the town museum, containing a fascinating variety of curios from bygone days. Rye so enchanted novelist Henry James that he made his home in the Lamb House (NT) until just before he died.

Leave Rye on the A259 Hastings road. Continue for 2 miles, then cross the river bridge and bear right, then turn sharp left for Winchelsea.

WINCHELSEA, E Sussex

Like Rye, Winchelsea was also a prosperous seaport and a member of the Cinque Ports, but nevertheless the sea has always been its enemy — firstly by completely submerging the old town in the late 13th century, and then by receding and taking with it the prosperity the port bestowed. Court Hall (OACT) is one of the oldest buildings and houses a museum of the town and surrounding area.

Return down the hill and turn right, then turn right again on to the unclassified road for Winchelsea Beach. Continue to Fairlight and later turn left on to the A259 for the return to Hastings.

SISSINGHURST CASTLE, Kent

Vita Sackville-West and her husband Harold Nicolson transformed a few derelict buildings and a near wilderness into an imaginative and beautiful series of gardens, with the Tudor tower and 2 cottages as a centre-piece (NT). Each garden has an individuality of its own. There is the famous white garden (where only white or grey plants grow), the herb garden, the rose garden and many more. Redbrick walls and thick hedges divide the romantic gardens which lead naturally and enchantingly one to another. Vita Sackville-West's study — a glory-hole full of books, letters, diaries, photographs and personal mementoes — is in the tower.

The main tour continues on the A262 to Biddenden.

BIDDENDEN, Kent

Antique shops, tea shops, pubs and restaurants fill most of Biddenden's half-timbered buildings, for it is one of Kent's most popular villages. The quaint village sign depicts the 2 Maids of Biddenden — Eliza and Mary Chulkhurst. They were Siamese twins, said to be born in the 12th century although their dress on the sign is Elizabethan.

A carving of the Biddenden Maids who were joined at the hip and shoulder

At Biddenden turn right and continue on the Ashford Road, then in ¾ mile branch right, SP 'Benenden'. After 3¾ miles, at the T-junction, turn left passing Benenden School (right) and continue to Benenden. Cross the main road here and continue to Iden Green. In 2 miles turn left on to the A268 into Sandhurst, then turn right, SP 'Bodiam', to re-enter Sussex before reaching Bodiam.

These huts at Hastings, dating from the 16th century, are still used by fishermen to dry out their nets

THE CREEKS AND ESTUARIES OF THE ESSEX COAST

Beautiful, unspoilt scenery surrounds the Crouch and Blackwater estuaries — sheltered waterways haunted by wildfowl and seabirds and beloved by yachtsmen. The old riverports of Burnham-on-Crouch and Maldon are redolent of the salty character of the wild and lovely Essex coast, with its deserted creeks and lonely mudflats.

Low tide at the quay in Burnham-on-Crouch, well-known for its local oyster beds

CHELMSFORD, Essex
Roman workmen cut their great road linking London with Colchester straight through Chelmsford and built a fort here, *Caesaromagus*, at the junction of the Rivers Chelmer and Cann. The town has always been an important market centre and is now the bustling modern county town of Essex. The Marconi Company, pioneers in the manufacture of wireless equipment, set up the first radio company in the world here in 1899. Exhibits of the early days of wireless can be seen in the Chelmsford and Essex Museum in

Oaklands Park, as can interesting displays of Roman remains and local history.

Leave Chelmsford town centre on the A130 Southend road. At the bypass roundabout, take the 3rd exit onto the B1009. After ½ mile, turn right at the Beehive PH in Great Baddow, and at Galleywood turn left onto the B1007 before crossing Galleywood Common to reach Stock.

STOCK, Essex
A fine old tower windmill and a delightful church with a traditional Essex-style wooden belfry and spire lend character to this pleasant village of well-kept houses. Some of the timbers in the church belfry are said to have come from Spanish galleons, wrecked in the aftermath of Sir Francis Drake's defeat of the Armada.

On entering Stock turn left onto the Wickford road. (Stock Church lies ahead on the B1007). Pass the windmill on the left before reaching a T-junction. Turn right here, then after ½ mile turn left before reaching the shores of Hanningfield Reservoir. In 1 mile turn left on to the Hanningfields road and continue to South Hanningfield.

SOUTH HANNINGFIELD, Essex
The placid waters of the reservoir that has been created by damming Sandford Brook transform the scattered rural settlement of South Hanningfield into a lakeside village. Standing by the shores of the lake is the 12th-century village church whose graceful belfry is a local landmark in the flat Essex countryside.

In 1½ miles turn right on to the A130, SP 'Southend', and 2 miles farther, at the Rettendon Turnpike roundabout, take the 1st exit on to the B1012. Later skirt South Woodham Ferrers.

SOUTH WOODHAM FERRERS, Essex
The desolate marshland overlooking the sheltered creeks of the Crouch estuary, a yachtsman's paradise, was chosen by Essex County Council as the site for one of its most attractive new town schemes. At the centre is a traditional market square surrounded by pleasant arcades and terraces built in the old Essex style with brick, tile and weatherboard.

Continue through Mayland back to Latchingdon. At the end of the village turn right on to the B1010, SP 'Maldon'. In 1 mile turn right again on to the B1018 and continue to Maldon.

MALDON, Essex
Just outside the fascinating old town of Maldon lies the site of one of the great decisive battles of England's early history. The Battle of Maldon was fought and lost in 991 when the English leader, Byrthnoth, was killed by the invading Danes after a fierce 3-day battle. As a result of this defeat, the English king, Ethelred the Unready, was obliged to pay an annual tribute of Danegeld to the conquerors; eventually the Danes overthrew him and Cnut became king. Maldon itself is a charming town, famous for its sea salt, produced for generations as a result of evaporating sea water. One of its churches, All Saints, has a unique triangular tower, and there are many intriguing shops and welcoming inns in its steep winding streets.

Leave Maldon on the A414 Chelmsford road and in 3¼ miles, at the roundabout, take the 3rd exit and continue to Danbury.

DANBURY, Essex
It is said that this village, crowning a high, wooded hill, takes its name from the Danes who invaded this part of the country in the Dark Ages. Remains of an ancient earthwork defence, thought to be Danish, can still be seen around the site of the church, which contains 3 beautifully carved wooden figures of knights dating from around 1300. To the south is Danbury Common (NT) where acres of gorse flower in a blaze of golden colour for much of the year; to the west, Danbury Country Park offers another pleasant stretch of open country.

At the end of the village turn left into Wells Lane. At the next T-junction turn right, SP 'Country Park'. Continue past Danbury Country Park to Sandon.

SANDON, Essex
The village green of Sandon has produced a notable oak tree, remarkable not so much for its height as for the tremendous horizontal spread of its branches. Around the green have been built the fine church and a number of attractive old houses, some dating back to the 16th century when Henry VIII's Lord Chancellor, Cardinal Wolsey, was Lord of the Manor of Sandon.

At Sandon bear left then immediately right, and at the end turn right. At the next T-junction turn left on to the A414, then at the roundabout go forward across the road bridge and turn right to join the A130 for the return to Chelmsford.

Continue on the B1012, through Stow Maries and Cold Norton to Latchingdon. Here keep forward on to the B1010, then at the church turn right. After 1½ miles turn right again and continue through Althorne. At the T-junction turn left and follow a winding road to the edge of Burham-on-Crouch. Turn right on to the B1021 for the town centre.

BURNHAM-ON-CROUCH, Essex
From the gaily-coloured cottages along the quay, the town climbs up the slopes above the seashore, its streets lined with an assortment of old cottages, Georgian and Victorian houses and shops. This is the yachting centre of Essex. In Tudor times sailing barges thronged the estuary where now yachts tack jauntily to and fro. Yachtsmen and holiday-makers come ashore to buy provisions, following a tradition that dates back to the medieval era when Burnham was the market centre for the isolated farmsteads of Wallasea and Foulness Islands and the inhibitants travelled in by ferry. The whole area was, and is to this day, famous for its oyster beds.

Return along the B1021 and at the end of the town keep forward on to the Southminster road. Continue northwards across the Dengie Peninsula.

DENGIE PENINSULA, Essex
The salty tang of sea air, brought inland by the east-coast winds, gives an exhilarating flavour to the marshlands of the Dengie Peninsula. Like the Cambridgeshire and Lincolnshire fens, the once waterlogged coastal region of this remote corner of Essex was reclaimed from the sea by 17th-century Dutch engineers. The views across the marshes encompass great sweeps of countryside, inhabited by wildfowl, seabirds and cattle grazing on the saltings. The old market town of Southminster and

the marshland villages of Asheldham and Tillingham rise prominently from the flat expanse of the landscape.

In Southminster turn right at the church, then turn left on to the Bradwell road and at the next T-junction turn right. A winding road then passes through Asheldham to Tillingham. After another 1½ miles, at the Queens Head PH, turn right to reach Bradwell Waterside.

BRADWELL WATERSIDE AND BRADWELL-ON-SEA, Essex
Overshadowing the small coastal resort of Bradwell Waterside on the estuary of the Blackwater River, the massive bulk of Bradwell Nuclear Power Station stands as an incongruous 20th-century intrusion on this remote coastline. Bradwell-on-Sea, a village now a mile or so inland from the coast, is a cluster of attractive cottages set about a green leading to the church. Bradwell Lodge (open by appointment) a beautiful part-Tudor, part-Georgian manor house, has an unusually charming

Many of Tillingham's old cottages were built by the Church

summer house. During the 18th century the portrait painter Thomas Gainsborough was a frequent visitor. Not far away, on the coast, stands the tiny 7th-century Saxon church of St Peter-at-the-Wall. It is one of the most ancient churches in England and is built across the line of the west wall of *Othona*, a great 3rd-century Roman fort.

From Bradwell Waterside return along the B1021 and in ¾ mile turn left for Bradwell-on-Sea village, then in 1 mile rejoin the B1021. At the Queens Head PH continue on to the unclassified Latchingdon road with occasional views of the Blackwater estuary, before reaching Steeple.

STEEPLE, Essex
This small village of thatched and weather-board cottages stands on the south bank of the Blackwater estuary, where brightly coloured yachts and the occasional stately sailing barge can be seen. Around the village stretches a rich green countryside of fertile meadows, patterned by lanes bordered with banks of trees.

COLCHESTER, Essex

During the 1st century, Colchester was the capital of the south-east and an obvious target for Roman invasion. The walls of their city can still be traced around the old part of the town and the huge Balkerne Gate is magnificent to this day. By the time the Normans arrived, Colchester (the name coined by the Saxons) was an important borough and they built their tremendous castle on the foundations of the Roman temple of Claudius. All that remains is part of the lofty keep — the largest ever built in Europe — and the museum it now houses provides a fine record of Roman Colchester. Profits from cloth-making, which began in the 13th century, left a substantial legacy of churches and monastic buildings to Colchester and by the 15th century there were 15 parish churches in all. Most have long since been altered and restored and some, like All Saints' housing a natural history museum and St Martin's used as a public hall, have abandoned their rightful purpose altogether. Of St John's Abbey only its 15th-century gatehouse is left, but the stone from the older abbey went into the building of Bourne Mill (NT), a Dutch-gabled fishing lodge on the banks of Bourne Pond. There are several attractive and interesting corners of Colchester with buildings spanning 6 centuries. The Minories, a Georgian house, has an art gallery, period furniture, pictures, china and silver. Another Georgian house, Hollytrees, has 18th- and 19th-century costumes and domestic craft exhibits. Aptly named Siege House bears evidence of Civil War conflict as its timbers are riddled with bullet holes. Much of Colchester's notoriety comes from its oysters and roses. Reminders of a less industrialised past are the annual oyster feast — a civic banquet worthy of royal patronage — and the annual Colchester Rose Show. Both commodities flourish today as they have done since the 18th century.

Leave Colchester on the A134, SP 'Sudbury', and at the roundabout beyond the station take the 2nd exit. Pass through Great Horkesley and gradually descend into the Stour valley.

STOUR VALLEY, Essex/Suffolk

The River Stour forms a natural boundary between Essex and Suffolk, and picturesque bridges along its route join the 2 counties. Landscape artist John Constable immortalised the valley in his famous paintings, capturing to perfection the flat water meadows, willow-lined ditches, locks and watermills.

After crossing the river into Suffolk turn left on to the unclassified Bures road. A mile later pass the turning, on the left, to Wissington.

THE STOUR VALLEY AND THE RIVER COLNE

From the ancient Roman capital of Colchester, the tour circles round the most beautiful tracts of the Essex countryside; along the Stour valley celebrated in the paintings of Constable, to the old market town of Sudbury, birthplace of Gainsborough, and across the peaceful scenery of the Colne valley.

Market day at Sudbury

WISSINGTON, Suffolk

A Norman church with a later white weather-boarded bellcote, a few thatched farm buildings and a handsome redbrick house form an attractive group in this tiny hamlet. Inside the church are fragments of some interesting 13th-century wall-paintings which depicted stories from Christ's childhood and the lives of St Margaret and St Nicholas. Wiston Hall (not open) was built in 1791 for Samuel Beechcroft — a director of the Bank of England — by architect Sir John Soane.

Continue on the unclassified road following the Stour valley to Bures.

BURES, Suffolk

In AD 855 St Edmund, East Anglian king and martyr, was crowned in a chapel above this tiny town. Below, the town full of fine half-timbered buildings, steps across both sides of the river and the boundary. An ancient thatched building called Chapel Barn once belonged to Earls Colne Priory (no longer in existence).

At the main road in Bures, turn right on to the B1508, SP 'Sudbury'. Continue along the valley and later pass through Great Cornard to reach Sudbury.

SUDBURY, Suffolk

Thomas Gainsborough, portrait painter and landscape artist, was born in Sudbury during 1727. The house, 46 Gainsborough Street (then Sepulchre Street) is now a pleasant museum and art gallery devoted to him. A bronze statue of Gainsborough, complete with brush and palette, stands in the market place. This teems with life on market days, but otherwise is only gladdened by the splendid 19th-century Corn Exchange and St Peter's Church surveying the square. The church has a piece of embroidery 5 centuries old which is still used at aldermen's funerals. Sudbury was the largest of Suffolk's wool towns and has more the stamp of a manufacturing town than most of the others. Due to the Act of Parliament passed for improving the Stour's navigation, Sudbury became an important river port. However, the railway ended the era of the flat-bottomed Stour Barge, and the last one was sold by the Canal Company in 1913.

Leave Sudbury on the A131, SP 'Chelmsford'. At Bulmer Tye turn right on to the B1058 and continue to Castle Hedingham.

CASTLE HEDINGHAM, Essex

The castle (OACT), from which the village takes its name, was one of England's strongest fortresses in the 11th century. It belonged to the powerful de Veres, the Earls of Oxford, one of whom was among the barons who forced King John to accept the Magna Carta. Some idea of the castle's great size can be gained from the impressive stone keep which remains. Although not complete, 2 of its 4 round towers and its walls, 12ft thick, rise up to over 100ft. A brick Tudor bridge leads to it over the moat which has long since

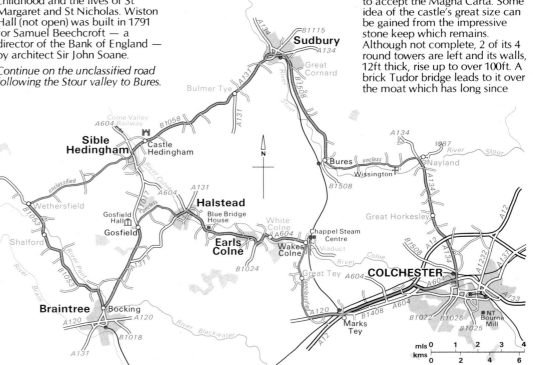

dried up. The village lying in the castle's shadow is a maze of narrow streets radiating from Falcon Square, which takes its name from the half-timbered Falcon Inn. Georgian and 15th-century houses mingle compatibly and the church, St Nicholas's, was built by the de Veres and is virtually completely Norman.

Continue on the B1058 then in ¾ mile turn left on to the A604 and enter Sible Hedingham.

SIBLE HEDINGHAM, Essex
Sir John Hawkwood was born here during the 14th century. He was one of the most famous soldiers of fortune during his time, and led mercenaries to Italy where he was eventually paid to defend Florence, where he died. There is a monument to him in the village church, decorated with hawks and various other beasts.

In Sible Hedingham turn right on to the unclassified Wethersfield road. Shortly turn right again, pass the church then turn left and continue to Wethersfield. In the village turn left on to the B1053 and follow the shallow valley of the River Pant. Pass through Shalford and after 5½ miles bear right to enter Bocking, which is combined with Braintree.

BRAINTREE AND BOCKING, Essex
Braintree was one of those ancient settlements that sprang up at the crossing point of 2 cross-country routes. Subsequent Roman occupation and development is evident from the many coins which have been found in the area. Braintree and Bocking have merged into a single town and they share the textile industry which has prospered here since the 14th century. Wool gave way to more exotic materials in the early 19th century, when the Courtauld family began the production of silk and this has been the main manufacture ever since. The other important industry here, dating from 1884, is the production of metal windows.

Courtauld's weather-boarded mill, which straddles the River Colne at Halstead

Leave on the A131 Halstead road. In 2¼ miles branch left on to the A1017, SP 'Cambridge', and continue to Gosfield.

GOSFIELD, Essex
A large lake built on the edge of Gosfield in the 18th century has been turned into a recreation centre. A paddling area has been roped off from the water-skiing area and rowing boats are available for hire. The lake and the village are all part of the Gosfield Hall (OACT) estate. It is not known for sure exactly when the Hall was built, or by whom, but it was Samuel Courtauld's (the silk manufacturing magnate) home for a time. A long Tudor gallery and some secret rooms are among the house's best features.

Tombs of 3 of the Earls of Oxford in Chapel Barn, Bures

At the far end of the village pass Hall Drive on the left (which leads to Gosfield Hall), then turn right on to the unclassified Halstead road. In 2 miles turn left on to the A131 and enter Halstead.

HALSTEAD, Essex
Through-traffic pounds along Halstead's High Street which drops down from the top of the hill to the River Colne. Here the Courtauld family established a silk factory in 1826 and it is one of the best sights in the town. The river flows beneath the mill, a low, white, weather-boarded building with rows of windows along its sides. Outside the town lies Blue Bridge House with lovely 18th-century ironwork and red and blue brickwork.

Leave Halstead on the A604 Colchester road. After 1 mile, on the left, is the Blue Bridge House. Follow the valley of the River Colne to reach Earls Colne.

EARLS COLNE, Essex
The de Veres, Earls of Oxford, and the River Colne gave the village its name. Aubrey de Vere founded a Benedictine priory here in the 12th century and both he and his wife — William the Conqueror's sister — were buried there. A redbrick Gothic mansion marks the site now. A nucleus of timbered cottages preserves the village atmosphere, although modern housing is spreading fast. Nearby Chalkney Wood, running down to the Colne, is an outstanding beauty spot.

Continue on the A604 to Wakes Colne.

WAKES COLNE, Essex
A working steam centre has been opened at Chappel and Wakes Colne station and every aspect of steam locomotion can be studied here. Locos and items of rolling stock are on display and steam hauled rides are available on some weekends.

At the crossroads on the nearside of the railway viaduct turn right on to the unclassified Great Tey road. Climb out of the valley to reach Great Tey. Continue to the A120 and turn left for Marks Tey.

MARKS TEY, Essex
Norman inhabitants gave the village its name when they came over from Marck, near Calais. The church is distinctive with its oakboarded tower, but its chief treasure is its 15th-century font. This too is made of oak and has 8 intricately carved panelled sides.

At the roundabout take the 2nd exit, SP 'Colchester', and join the A12. Later join the A604 for the return to Colchester.

TOUR 20   *88 MILES*

FAMOUS COLLEGES AND HIDDEN VILLAGES

Unspoilt villages embodying the spirit of rural England
speckle the open rolling fields that separate Hertford from
Cambridge. Yet it is the city of colleges and courtyards, of
beauty and learning, that reigns supreme.

HERTFORD, Herts

Old houses from Jacobean to the
Georgian periods mingle well with
new buildings in this old county
town where 3 rivers, the Lea, the
Beane and the Rib meet. Little
remains of the old Norman castle
except for the charming 15th-
century gatehouse, one of the
childhood homes of Elizabeth I,
standing in pleasant parkland. At
the heart of the town are the
famous old buildings of Christ's
Hospital School, founded by the
governors of the Bluecoat School
in London. Several appealing
figures of Bluecoat children stand
on the walls and above the
entrance. Lombard House (not
open), a lovely Jacobean building,
was the home of the judge Sir
Henry Chauncy who presided over
the last trial for witchcraft ever
held in England (see Walkern).

The delicate vaulted
ceiling of King's
College Chapel,
Cambridge, completed
in 1515, and its
lovely windows which
depict Biblical tales

*Leave Hertford on the B158, SP
'Wadesmill'. After 1 mile turn left,
SP 'Sacombe', bear right at the fork
and after 2¾ miles turn left, SP
'Watton', to join the B1001. In ½
mile turn right on to an unclassified
road and continue through
Sacombe to Dane End. Keep
straight on and in ½ mile bear
right, then keep left. In another 1¾
miles go over the crossroads, SP
'Westmill', then ¾ mile farther
bear right to reach Westmill.*

WESTMILL, Herts

Near to this exceptionally pretty
village, complete with green and
rows of tall-chimneyed cottages
surrounding the church, stands
one bought by the 19th-century
essayist Charles Lamb. He is best
know today for *Lamb's Tales from
Shakespeare*, which he wrote with

his sister, Mary. Button Snap is the
evocative name of this thatched
17th-century cottage with tiny
latticed windows, and it now
belongs to the Lamb Society who
have preserved and restored it (not
open).

*At the village green turn right, SP
'Puckeridge', and on reaching the
A10 turn left for Buntingford.*

BUNTINGFORD, Herts
The old Roman road of Ermine Street runs through this busy village. There is a fine range of almshouses, built in 1684 by Seth Ward who first became a distinguished scholar at Oxford, then Bishop of Exeter and finally of Salisbury.

By the nearside of the town centre turn right on to the B1038 for Hare Street. Here, turn left on to the B1368, and follow an undulating road through Barkway to Barley.

BARLEY, Herts
For more than 300 years the Fox and Hounds Inn has looked down from its hillside on the old cottages of Barley. The famous inn sign stretches right over the road; across the beam, huntsmen and hounds pursue a fox, which appears to be craftily disappearing into a hole in the roof of the inn.

Branch right, SP 'Great Chishill', to pass under the inn sign, and shortly to join the B1039. Cross into Cambridgeshire before reaching Great Chishill.

GREAT CHISHILL, Cambs
Great Chishill looks out peacefully over one of the quietest corners of Cambridgeshire. The showpiece of the village is the lofty 18th-century post mill, with white-painted timbers and a graceful fantail that turns the mill so that the sails always face into the wind.

Continue on the Saffron Walden road and after 3¼ miles turn left on to an unclassified road for Elmdon. In the village turn right on to the Ickleton road. In 3 miles, by the nearside of Ickleton village, turn left for Duxford.

DUXFORD, Cambs
Duxford's old watermill, listed in the Domesday Book, has attracted several famous visitors in the past, including Charles Kingsley, author of *The Water Babies*. Near the village, on the Battle of Britain airfield where World War II hero Douglas Bader served, is the Imperial War Museum's collection of military aircraft and armoured fighting vehicles; more than 60 historic aircraft are on view. The Duxford Aviation Society's collection of civil aircraft, including Concorde 01, is also open.

At Duxford turn right, then at the church turn left and after ¾ mile reach the junction with the A505. From here a detour can be made by turning left to visit Duxford Airfield. The main tour crosses the main road and continues to Whittlesford.

WHITTLESFORD, Cambs
The early 16th-century Guildhall, its overhanging upper storey supported on carved wooden posts, is only one of many attractive buildings around the village green. In the churchyard lies the graves of many brave young airmen who served at Duxford in World War II and fought and died in the Battle of Britain.

Continue on the unclassified road and in 2½ miles, at the T-junction, turn right for Great Shelford.

GREAT SHELFORD, Cambs
Great Shelford looks out towards the gently rolling Gog Magog Hills which lie just south of Cambridge. The hills take their name from a Romano-British giant who appears in legend, sometimes as 1 person, Gogmagog, sometimes as 2, Gog and Magog. By tradition dating back to at least the 11th century, the outline of 2 gigantic figures was carved on the hillside here at Wandlebury Camp, an Iron-Age fort.

On reaching the A1301 turn left towards Cambridge. At Trumpington turn right at the traffic signals on to the A1309 and continue into Cambridge.

CAMBRIDGE, Cambs
The distinguished and beautiful architecture of Cambridge's great colleges has stamped its personality on the heart of the city even more powerfully than at Oxford. The secluded college courtyards and gardens are usually open to the public, as are the many fine college chapels. The most lovely of these is without doubt King's College Chapel, with its graceful and intricate web of fan-vaulting. Visitors can stroll peacefully along the Backs, a green, sunlit sweep of lawns leading down from St John's, Trinity, Clare, King's and Queens' colleges to the river, where in spring and summer unhurried punts drift up and down. Peterhouse is the oldest college — founded in 1284 by the Bishop of Ely — but students had settled here from Oxford in individual groups attached to monastic schools as early as the previous century. The prettiest of the colleges is held to be Queens'. Its

Westmill village green, complete with water pump

Mathematical bridge leading from Cloister Court to the gardens is an interesting curiosity; it was designed in 1749 on mathematical principles and originally stood without nails or similar fixings. Even more famous is the Bridge of Sighs at St John's College, so-called from the one at Venice of which it is a copy. Cambridge, as might be expected, has several interesting museums. The Fitzwilliam contains an unrivalled collection of antiquities, paintings, manuscripts and rare objects. The University Botanic Gardens, rated second only to Kew, are best visited in the afternoons when the glasshouses are open.

From the south west side of the city centre follow the A603, SP 'Sandy'. After 2 miles cross the M11 then in ½ mile turn right on to the B1046, SP 'Comberton' and 'Toft', and enter Barton. Continue, SP 'St Neots', through Comberton to Toft. In 3½ miles, at the Fox Inn, turn right and immediately left across the main road for Longstowe. In another 3 miles turn left on to an unclassified road and continue to Gamlingay.

GAMLINGAY, Cambs
The cosy row of mellow redbrick almshouses that are the focus of this appealing village were built in 1665, the year of the Great Plague. Much of the village had been destroyed by fire in 1600, but fortunately the medieval church, a fine stone building, survived.

At the crossroads in Gamlingay turn left on to the B1040 and continue to Potton. Bear right then left through the square, and at the end turn left, SP 'Biggleswade'. In 1 mile, at the crossroads, turn left on to an unclassified road for Sutton — here cross a ford by the side of the old packhorse bridge. At the end of the village go over the crossroads, SP 'Ashwell'. In 1¾ miles, at the Ongley Arms PH, turn right and ½ mile later turn left, SP 'Ashwell'. After 4½ miles, at the war memorial, turn right into Ashwell.

ASHWELL, Herts
Ash trees around the River Rhee have given this lovely village its name. It stands amid open fields, its church tower rising 176ft above the surrounding countryside. Among the many timber-framed houses scattered about its streets, the pargeted and oak-beamed cottages attached to the 17th-century Guildhall form the most charming group. The old Tythe House (AM), which was once the office of the abbots of Westminster, has been restored and preserved as the village museum, where there is a fascinating collection of village history and rural life.

In Ashwell pass the Three Tuns PH and turn left, SP 'Bygrave' and 'Baldock', then go over the crossroads, SP 'Walkern'. In 2 miles cross the main road and 4½ miles farther join the A507, then keep forward on to an unclassified road to Cromer. Here, join the B1037 for Walkern.

WALKERN, Herts
In 1712, the last trial for witchcraft ever held in England took place in Walkern. A woman called Jane Wenham was accused by a local farmer of witchcraft and was tried and sentenced to death by Sir Henry Chauncy. Queen Anne granted her a pardon and as a result of her case the barbaric laws against witchcraft were repealed in 1736.

At the end of the village go forward on to an unclassified road, SP 'Watton'. After 4 miles turn left SP 'Hertford', and enter Watton-at-Stone

WATTON-AT-STONE, Herts
The elegant, canopied, cast-iron pump, dating from the early 19th century, and Watton Hall (not open), a house of overhanging gables, together form a traditional village group. The flint-built church, containing a wealth of medieval brasses, completes the picture.

At the roundabout take the 3rd exit on to the A602 for the return to Hertford.

EXOTIC ANIMALS IN THE CHILTERNS

Just a stone's throw from Hertfordshire's densely populated towns lie unsuspected areas of wooded countryside hiding Whipsnade's and Woburn's free-roaming wild animals — creatures as much at home here in the Chilterns as in their far-off native lands.

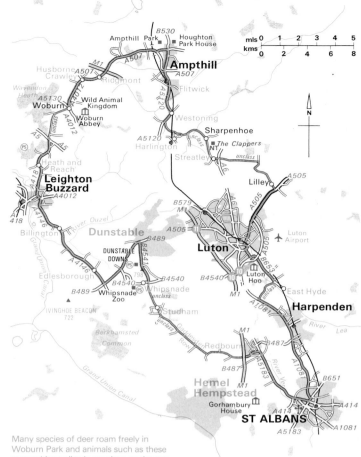

ST ALBANS, Herts

The remains of *Verulamium,* once the most important Roman town in Britain, lie across the River Ver to the west of the present city of St Albans. Here stand the ruins of the great amphitheatre and part of a hypocaust (underground heating system). The Verulamium Museum contains some spectacular mosaic pavements and many other fascinating relics. Modern St Albans takes its name from the first Christian martyr in Britain, Alban, a Roman convert who lived in *Verulamium.* The mighty abbey was founded in 793 on the hill where he is thought to have been killed, and contains his shrine. Made of Purbeck marble, the shrine was lost for years; it was discovered in the last century, shattered into fragments, and restored by Sir Giles Gilbert Scott. The only English Pope to date, Nicholas Breakspear, was a native of St Albans, son of an abbey tenant. He was elected in 1154 and took the name of Adrian IV. Several old streets meander around the town centre where the 15th-century curfew tower rises 77ft high, and there are a number of historic houses to be found. The Old Fighting Cocks Inn claims to be one of Britain's oldest pubs, and on the site of the Fleur de Lys Inn, in French Row, the King of France was held prisoner after the Battle of Poitiers in 1356. Other places of interest are the Kingsbury Watermill Museum, where the 'Handmeade' is preserved — a working watermill of the 16th century; the Organ Museum; the City Museum which houses part of the Salaman Collection of craft implements, and the beautiful gardens of the National Rose Society where more than 1,650 sorts of roses bloom.

Leave St Albans on the A1081, SP 'Harpenden'.

Many species of deer roam freely in Woburn Park and animals such as these pygmy hippos live in spacious enclosures

HARPENDEN, Herts
Harpenden means 'spring or valley of the harpers', and this pleasant small town set in lovely, wooded countryside, is much sought after by London commuters. Its High Street is full of interesting and attractive old houses and shops, and the common, bright with gorse, looks out over the peaceful slopes of the Harpenden valley.

Continue on the Luton road and in 1¾ miles pass the Fox PH, then ¼ mile farther turn right, SP 'New Mill End'. In another 1½ miles turn left on to the B653 SP 'Luton'. Later, to the left, pass Luton Hoo.

LUTON HOO, Beds
The colourful Edwardian diamond magnate Sir Julius Wernher, decided to have Robert Adam's Classical 18th-century stone-built mansion remodelled in 1903 to suit his own extravagant tastes. His fabulous collection of art treasures includes Fabergé jewels and Imperial robes worn at the court of the Russian Tsars, paintings by Titian and Rembrandt, rare tapestries and old porcelain (OACT).

Continue into Luton.

LUTON, Beds
Luton is now Bedfordshire's largest town, a thriving centre of light industry and famous for its international airport. In the past, however, it was famed for the making of pillow-lace and the elegant straw-plaited hats worn by ladies to protect their complexions from the sun. Exhibits in the Wardown Museum illustrate the history of these crafts from a bygone era.

Leave on the A505, SP 'Hitchin', and after 3¾ miles pass the Silver Lion PH, then branch left, SP 'Lilley', and turn left into Lilley.

LILLEY, Beds
This quiet little village on the prehistoric track called the Icknield Way was the home of a 19th-century eccentric, John Kellerman. He claimed to be the last descendant of the medieval alchemists and to possess the secret of turning base metal into gold. The family crest of the Salusburys, local landowners, is carved on many of the cottages.

Continue on the unclassified road and in nearly 2 miles turn left, SP 'Streatley'. In another 2 miles cross the main road for Streatley. Here, turn right and continue to Sharpenhoe.

SHARPENHOE, Beds
A footpath winds from Sharpenhoe, a tiny village nestling at the foot of a steep hill, to a lovely area of high woodland known as the Clappers (NT). The views from the top explain why John Bunyan chose this for the 'Delectable Mountain' of *Pilgrim's Progress*.

Capability Brown landscaped the formal gardens of Luton Hoo which houses the splendid Wernher art collection

Turn left, SP 'Harlington', and in 1¾ miles turn on to the Westoning road and skirt the village of Harlington. After another 1¼ miles turn right on to the A5120, SP 'Ampthill', and continue through Westoning to Flitwick. Here, cross the railway bridge and turn left to reach Ampthill.

AMPTHILL, Beds
Sheltered by low hills, Ampthill presents a charming mixture of thatched cottages, Georgian houses, old coaching inns and a parish church set in a pretty square. Ampthill Park (house not open), is famous for the ancient oak trees in its grounds. Catherine of Aragon, first wife of Henry VIII, was dismissed to Ampthill when the king decided to divorce her.

A short detour can be made to visit the ruins of Houghton Park House, 1 mile north of the town.

HOUGHTON PARK HOUSE, Beds
The 17th-century mansion (AM) that was once the home of the Countess of Pembroke, sister of Sir Philip Sidney, fell into ruins nearly 200 years ago. This is thought to have been the 'House Beautiful' of *Pilgrim's Progress*, the book that John Bunyan wrote while a prisoner in Bedford gaol. The hill on which the gaol stands is thus his 'Hill of Difficulty'.

At Ampthill the main tour turns left on to the B530 SP 'Woburn'. In ¾ mile turn right on to the A507. Pass through Ridgmont and at Husborne Crawley join the A4012. In 1¾ miles turn left for Woburn

WOBURN, Beds
The village of Woburn has a number of attractive buildings dating from the post-coach era, and is filled with antique shops and boutiques catering for the thousands of visitors drawn to

Woburn Abbey (OACT), seat of the Dukes of Bedford. This most flamboyant of all Britain's stately homes is famous for its Wild Animal Kingdom. Herds of rare species of deer and numerous other exotic animals are housed in the beautiful 3,000-acre park and there are many other attractions, to suit the whole family. The abbey itself is a spacious 18th-century mansion designed by Henry Holland and contains a notable collection of paintings by Canaletto, Velasquez, Gainsborough and Van Dyck.

At Woburn turn right, SP 'Leighton Buzzard'. In 2 miles turn left and then right on to the A418 and continue through Heath and Reach to reach Leighton Buzzard.

LEIGHTON BUZZARD, Beds
A graceful 5-sided market cross with 2 tiers of arches holding carved figures, erected in 1400, stands at the centre of the market town. One of the attractive old buildings nearby, the Wilkes Almshouses, is the scene of a curious ceremony which takes place annually in May: while portions of the founder's will are read aloud, a choirboy stands on his head. As Leighton Buzzard has now been joined to Linslade on the opposite bank of the Ouzel, the town is sometimes called Leighton-Linslade. From Pages Park station, the Leighton Buzzard Light Railway, converted from industrial track, runs through nearly 4 miles of lovely wooded countryside.

Leave on the A4146, SP 'Hemel Hempstead'. Pass through Billington into Buckinghamshire, then continue to Edlesborough. In 1 mile turn left on to the B489, SP 'Dunstable'. Occasional views of the Whipsnade White Lion cut into the hillside can be seen on the right before reaching the outskirts of Dunstable. Here, at the mini-roundabout, turn right on to the B4541, SP 'Whipsnade', and climb on to the Dunstable Downs.

DUNSTABLE DOWNS, Beds
Rising dramatically from the surrounding farmland, Dunstable Downs, a steep scarp of the Chiltern Hills, is an ideal centre for gliding. Part of the downs, an area of woods and common land where many species of wildflowers grow, belongs to the National Trust. Two ancient highways cross the hills: the great Roman road of Watling Street, and the Icknield Way, a much older prehistoric track that may have been named after the tribe of the Iceni, whose queen, Boudicca, was eventually defeated by the Romans. Five Knolls, just outside Dunstable, is a group of round barrows where several Bronze-Age skeletons, knives and weapons have been excavated.

Near the top of the climb pass a picnic area and bear right. In 1¼ miles, at the crossroads, go forward SP 'Studham'. Alternatively, turn right on to the B4540 to visit Whipsnade Zoo.

WHIPSNADE ZOO, Beds
Over 2,000 wild animals roam the large paddocks of the 500-acre park set in the beautiful Chiltern countryside. Lions, tigers, bears and rhinos can be seen in almost natural conditions and there are many rare birds too. A passenger railway drawn by steam locomotives takes visitors through several of the paddocks, including the White Rhino enclosure. Special features include the dolphinarium and the children's zoo and farm.

The main tour continues to Studham. At the clock tower keep forward, SP 'Gaddesden Row', and in ½ mile go over the crossroads then bear left. Pass through Gaddesden Row and at the Plough PH bear left. In 2 miles turn left, SP 'Redbourn'. Later pass under the motorway bridge and turn left for Redbourn. Here turn right and at the roundabout take the 2nd exit on to the A5183, SP 'St Albans'. After 3 miles, near the Pré Hotel, a drive on the right leads to Gorhambury House.

GORHAMBURY HOUSE, Herts
Sir Francis Bacon, the Elizabethan writer and scholar who some believe to have been the real author of Shakespeare's plays, was born here. He rose to be Lord Chancellor of England under James I but was finally disgraced and impeached for embezzlement. His memorial stands in St Michael's Church, St Albans, a life-size marble figure showing the great philosopher asleep in a chair. The Tudor manor where Bacon lived is now partly ruined, but the present 18th-century house (OACT) contains relics of the Bacon family as well as a fine collection of Chippendale furniture.

Continue on the A5183 for the return to St Albans.

WINDSOR, Berks

The largest inhabited castle in the world rambles over 13 acres on a chalk bluff above the River Thames. Windsor Castle has been a royal residence since Henry 1's reign and every subsequent ruling English monarch has made additions to it. However, George IV contributed most and he was responsible for the distinctive multi-towered skyline of today. The parts of the castle open to the public are St George's Chapel, burial place of kings and queens; Queen Mary's Dolls' house, designed by Sir Edwin Lutyens and exquisitely perfect to the tiniest detail; the state apartments, full of outstanding paintings, carvings, furniture and porcelain; and the enormous Round Tower which surveys 12 counties. Most of the town's architecture is a mixture of Victorian and Georgian with the notable exception of the Guildhall (OACT). Sir Christopher Wren, whose father was Dean of Windsor, completed it in 1689 and it now displays various exhibits of local history, with portraits of kings and queens lining the walls.

WINDSOR GREAT PARK, Berks

Stretching south of the castle from the river to Virginia Water are some 4,800 acres of glorious open parkland, dense beech woods and beautiful formal gardens. Both Home Park, the private land around the castle, and the Great Park, are dissected by the Long Walk. This magnificent avenue of chestnut and plane trees leads from the castle to Snow Hill. Here, at the park's highest point, stands a towering equestrian statue of George III. Savill Gardens and the Valley Gardens within the park are both woodland areas of great beauty. Rhododendrons, azaleas, roses, camelias and magnolias are just some of the lovely flowers and shrubs that provide colour in them all year round.

Leave Windsor on the A308, SP 'Maidenhead'. In 4 miles pass under the motorway bridge and turn right on to the B3028 for Bray.

BRAY, Berks

The song called *The Vicar of Bray* has made the village name familiar. Just which vicar it refers to is uncertain, but Simon Aleyn of Tudor times seems to be the most popular candidate. The almshouses are a particularly attractive feature of this Thameside village. They were founded by William Goddard in 1627 and a figure of him stands over the gateway. A pretty lane leads from the main street to the churchyard, which is entered through a timber-framed gatehouse. This may have been the chantry house, for the chantry Chapel of St Mary stands inside the churchyard. It was used as a small school in the early 17th century.

REACHES OF THE THAMES AND ROYAL WINDSOR

The stern towers of Windsor's mighty castle look down in royal splendour on the ever-changing life of the Thames, where boats ply busily to and fro between leafy banks and beneath elegant bridges.

At the end of the village bear right, continue for 1 mile to the edge of Maidenhead then turn right on to the A4 (no SP) and shortly cross Maidenhead Bridge.

MAIDENHEAD, Berks

Maidenhead, so near to London and on one of the loveliest stretches of the Thames, has become a popular residential commuter town. The town first began to grow in the 13th century around the bridge which was replaced in 1772 by a fine stone one. During the Civil Wars and the 17th century Revolution Maidenhead was a strategic point. The Henry Reitlinger Bequest Museum in Oldfied House (OACT) by the bridge is filled with glass, pictures, ceramics and sculptures, as well as numerous other treasures. Just upstream is Boulters Lock Inn — a popular stopping place for river navigators since the 18th century.

After crossing the Thames continue for nearly ½ mile, then turn left on to an unclassified road, SP 'Wycombe'. After 2 miles, on the left, is the entrance to Cliveden.

In the 1820s Windsor Castle was transformed from a hotch-potch of apartments to a magnificent palace at a cost of about £1,000,000

CLIVEDEN, Berks

A house has stood at Cliveden (NT) since 1666, but it has not been the present one. Two fires burnt down the original and its successor, and this third house, built in the 19th century, is largely the work of Sir Charles Barry. Between the wars it was owned by the Astors and was a popular meeting place for influential politicians and social celebrities. The grounds are exceptionally beautiful, due to natural terrain as much as design. The site slopes down to a part of the Thames called Cliveden Reach and the views from the back of the house are superlative. Here, the huge terrace drops down to a great carpet of lawn patterned with low box hedges, and beyond lies the Italian Garden. Other features of the grounds include woodland walks, a monumental Victorian fountain, an elaborate water garden with a Japanese pagoda and glades of dark green ilex trees that provide an ideal setting for the stone statues scattered within them.

Continue on the unclassified road and in just over ¼ mile turn left, SP 'Bourne End'. In ¾ mile turn left still SP 'Bourne End'. Nearly ½ mile farther turn left on to the A4094, SP 'Cookham', and later cross the River Thames for Cookham.

Marlow's suspension bridge, built in 1831, and the 19th-century Church of All Saints — one of the town's 3 churches

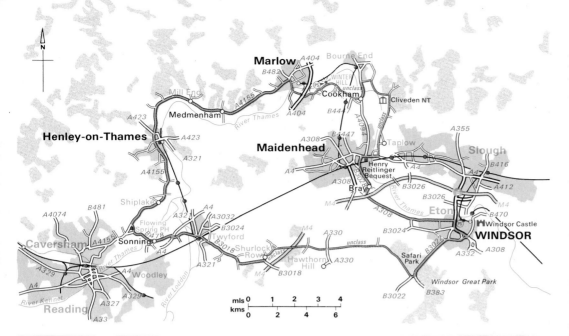

Looking upstream at Henley towards the 16th-century tower of St Mary's Church, distinguished by its flint and stone chequerwork and 4 octagonal turrets

COOKHAM, Berks

The modern painter, Stanley Spencer, was a native of Cookham. More people throng the streets and river since his days, but the redbrick cottages facing the green and the river scenes are easily identified in many of his paintings. Several of Spencer's works can be seen in the King's Hall Gallery in the unspoilt High Street. One of the boathouses along the river acts as the office of the Keeper of the Royal Swans. He is in charge of the annual ceremony of Swan Upping — the counting and marking of all cygnets on the Thames.

Turn right into the main street (B4447), SP 'Cookham Dean'. In almost ½ mile, before the White Hart Inn, turn right, SP 'Winter Hill Golf Club'. ¼ mile beyond the viewpoint of Winter Hill turn right, then right again, and descend through thick beech woods. At the next T-junction, turn right and cross the Thames for Marlow.

MARLOW, Bucks

The jewel of this busy town is its fine suspension bridge which was renovated to mint condition in 1966. It spans the river near a cascading weir and the beautiful beech trees of Quarry Wood form a backdrop for this, the lock and the lock house. By the bridge is the Compleat Angler Hotel, named after Izaak Walton's book about the delights of fishing as a pastime. Marlow's broad main

street and West Street are full of unspoilt buildings from the 16th to 18th centuries, among which was the home of Shelley and his wife.

At the end of Marlow High Street turn left on to the A4155, SP 'Henley' and continue to Medmenham.

MEDMENHAM, Bucks

A clique of roisterers in the 18th century came to be known as the Hellfire Club and their headquarters were at Medmenham. The leader, Sir Francis Dashwood, was a Chancellor of the Exchequer, and he rebuilt the Norman abbey here in which to hold his scandalous parties. Finally, public exposure and disgrace ended the club's activities for good. There is little sign of those revelries in the village

today, with its groups of cottages, 15th-century manor house and 16th-century inn with dormer windows.

Continue on the A4155 to Henley.

HENLEY-ON-THAMES, Oxon

Henley is the most famous of the Thames resorts due to the prestigious annual regatta held here in July. The first inter-varsity race took place here in 1829 and within 10 years it was a recognised national event enjoying royal patronage. The graceful bridge in Henley is 18th century, appropriately decorated with the faces of Father Thames and the goddess Isis. Apart from the boating available throughout the summer and the pleasant walks along the towpaths, there are lots of interesting shops, inns and teashops in Henley. Most of the inns are old coaching houses with squares that were once the scene of bull and bear fights. Kenton theatre, completed in 1804, is the 4th oldest theatre in England.

Leave Henley on the A4155, SP 'Reading'. In 2 miles pass the Shiplake war memorial, and after another 2½ miles, at the Flowing Spring PH, turn left (one-way), SP 'Sonning'. At the end turn left again on to the B478 (no SP) for Sonning.

SONNING, Berks

Eleven arches form the 18th-century bridge across the Thames at Sonning. The village is pretty and unspoilt, with little streets of cottages, grander Georgian houses and a lock gaily bedecked with flowers. The Bishops of Salisbury lived here centuries ago, but the only sign of their palace is a mound in the grounds of Holme Park.

Bear left through the village and at the roundabout take the 2nd exit on to the A3032, SP 'Twyford'. In Twyford turn right on to the A321, SP 'Bracknell'. After crossing the railway bridge keep forward on to the B3018 and remain on it to Shurlock Row. Turn left on to an unclassified road, SP 'Maidenhead', into the village, and at the far end turn right on to the Hawthorn Hill road. Later pass over the M4 and in 1¼ miles cross the A330, SP 'New Lodge'. In 4 miles turn left on to the B3022, SP 'Windsor', then turn left again and shortly pass Windsor Safari Park and Seaworld (left).

WINDSOR SAFARI PARK AND SEAWORLD, Berks

This was one of the first Safari parks to spring up in Britain. Apart from the fascinating drive-through reserves, aviaries and caged animals, there is a modern dolphinarium too. Here, bottle-nosed dolphins perform their incredible tricks, vying for popularity with the killer whale.

Continue on the B3022 for the return to Windsor.

BERKSHIRE'S WOODED VALLEYS AND ROLLING DOWNS

The rhythmic thud of horses hooves breaks the early-morning silence as racehorses at exercise gallop over the springy turf of the Lambourn and Berkshire Downs, high above the sheltered villages of the Kennet and Thames.

Boxford watermill on the River Lambourne

READING, Berks

The old town has all but disappeared under the impact of the 20th century, but it is still pleasant to stroll along the pretty riverside walk where the Thames runs between Reading and its quiet suburb of Caversham. In Whiteknights Park, the Museum of English Rural Life contains an interesting collection of agricultural implements and reminders of village life as it used to be. The town museum has remains from the nearby Roman fort of Silchester and the old Norman abbey, founded by Henry I who is buried in the Church of St Laurence. The Abbey Gate still stands in Forbury Street and here, from 1785-7, Jane Austen and her sister Cassandra attended a school that occupied 2 rooms above the gateway. Oscar Wilde wrote the moving *Ballard of Reading Gaol* about his imprisonment here from 1895-7.

Leave Reading on the A4, SP 'Newbury'. In 4¼ miles, at the motorway roundabout, take the 2nd exit, SP 'Theale'. At the next roundabout take the A340, SP 'Pangbourne', then turn left on to an unclassified road for Bradfield.

BRADFIELD, Berks

Set in the wooded valley of the River Pang, Bradfield, largely 18th-century, is best known for its public school, Bradfield College. It was founded in 1850 by Thomas Stevens, the local vicar, whose main concern was to train the pupils as choirboys for his church. The school has an open-air theatre, renowned for its good productions of Greek and other classical plays.

At Bradfield turn left, SP 'Bucklebury'. In 1 mile turn right through Southend Bradfield, then Chapel Row. Cross Bucklebury Common and continue to Upper Bucklebury. At the far end branch right, SP 'Cold Ash', and continue through well-wooded countryside. After 1½ miles pass the outskirts of Cold Ash, then in ¾ mile go over the crossroads and descend to Ashmore Green. Here, branch right into Stoney Lane (no SP) and continue to the suburbs of Newbury. At the T-junction turn right, then turn left on to the B4009 and continue to the edge of Newbury. For the town centre take the 3rd exit at the roundabout.

NEWBURY, Berks

This old market town is nowadays best known for its racecourse where major steeplechase and hurdling events are held in the winter season In the past, the town was noted for its weaving industry and its most famous resident was Jack of Newbury, John Smalwoode, who started life in the Tudor period as a penniless apprentice and became an immensely wealthy clothier. In 1513 he led 100 men to fight at the Battle of Flodden, and was important enough to act as host to Henry VIII. He paid for the building of the beautiful Tudor church of St Nicholas, where a brass (1519) commemorates him. The remains of his house can be seen in Northbrook Street, and the 17th-century timbered cloth hall now houses the town museum.

At Newbury the main tour joins the bypass, SP 'Hungerford A4'. At the next roundabout take the B4494, SP 'Wantage', and in nearly ¾ mile pass on the left the turning to Donnington Castle.

DONNINGTON CASTLE, Berks

The gatehouse and the massive round towers of the gateway of Donnington Castle (AM) stand as a reminder of the 2 Civil War battles of Newbury. The Royalist leader Sir John Boys beat off 2 attacks in 1643 after the first battle, even though his castle was pounded almost to rubble by cannon shot. Again in 1644, after the second battle, Donnington played its part by defending the king's retreat to Oxford, but the castle gradually fell into picturesque ruin.

Continue on the B4494 and in ¼ mile bear left (still SP 'Wantage'), then gradually climb over the well-wooded Snelsmore Common — now a country park. In 1 mile, before the motorway bridge, turn left on to an unclassified road for Winterbourne. At the far end of the village turn right, SP 'Boxford', and later descend into the Lambourn valley to Boxford.

BOXFORD, Berks

Old, weathered cottages and a lovely gabled watermill standing on a clear, bubbling stream make an idyllic rural picture in this charming Berkshire village set in the Lambourn valley.

Turn left and cross the river bridge, then keep left. At the main road turn right by the Bell Inn, SP 'Easton' and 'Welford', and continue to Great Shefford. Here, join the A338, then keep forward on to the unclassified Lambourn road and later skirt East Garston.

EAST GARSTON, Berks

Under the shelter of the Berkshire Downs nestle a medley of old brick and timber cottages, some thatched, some tiled. On the street that leads up to the church is an appealing group of black and white cottages, each with its own little bridge across the river.

Continue along the valley, through Eastbury for Lambourn.

LAMBOURN, Berks

Horses could be said to outnumber people in Lambourn, where almost every house has its own block of stables, and on the springy turf of Lambourn Down strings of highly bred racehorses can be seen at exercise against an exhilarating backdrop of open countryside. The village itself, in its downland setting, makes an attractive sight, especially around the medieval church where there are old almshouses and an ancient village cross.

At the crossroads turn right on to the B4001, SP 'Wantage', and cross the Lambourn Downs. After 6 miles, at the crossroads, turn right on to the B4507 for Wantage.

WANTAGE, Berks

The statue of King Alfred in the market place at Wantage commemorates the fact that this pleasant old town in the Vale of the White Horse was his birthplace in 849. No Saxon relics survive, but the town contains a number of attractive Georgian buildings.

Follow SP 'Newbury B4494' and climb on to the Berkshire Downs. After 4 miles turn left on to an unclassified road for Farnborough. Continue across the downs to West Ilsley and then East Ilsley.

Count Gleichen's statue of King Alfred, a tribute to a great warrior who united Saxon England, stands in Wantage market

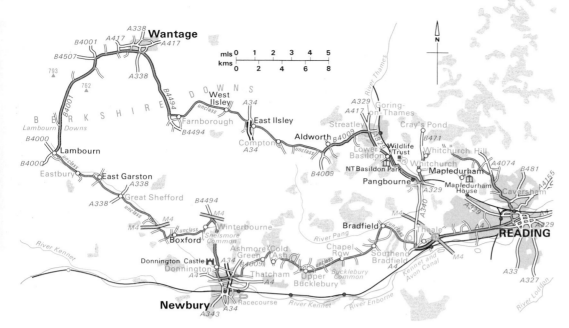

At the mini-roundabout in Pangbourne turn left, then left again on to the B471, SP 'Whitchurch'. Cross the Thames by a toll bridge and enter Whitchurch. After ¾ mile, at Whitchurch Hill, turn right, SP 'Goring Heath'. Nearly 1½ miles farther turn right again, SP 'Reading', then in 2½ miles pass on the right the turning for Mapledurham.

MAPLEDURHAM, Oxon

Wooded hills surround this peaceful little village where pretty cottages, 17th-century almshouses and an old watermill, the last one on the Thames to preserve its wooden machinery, are attractively grouped by the river. Mapledurham House (OACT) is a lovely brick manor house built in the reign of Elizabeth I by Sir Michael Blount, who entertained her here. Two of his descendants, the sisters Mary and Martha Blount, were friends of the 18th-century poet and satirist Alexander Pope, who wrote in a poem addressed to one of them: 'She went from Op'ra, park, assembly, play/To morning walks and pray'rs three hours a day;' John Galsworthy chose the village for the site of Soames Forsyte's country house in the Forsyte Saga.

Continue on the Reading road then in ¾ mile turn right on to the A4074 and later descend into Caversham. At the traffic signals turn right and recross the Thames for the return to Reading.

WEST AND EAST ILSLEY, Berks

At these twin villages the traveller stands in the heart of the Berkshire Downs, amid a seemingly endless panorama of superb country. East Ilsley seems to exist solely for the training of horses. There are stables everywhere and fenced-off rides cover the surrounding hills.

At East Ilsley bear left for Compton. Continue on the Pangbourne road then in 2¼ miles turn left on to the B4009, SP 'Streatley', and skirt the village of Aldworth.

ALDWORTH, Berks

The 9 'giants' of Aldworth were all members of the de la Beche family. Three of them are nicknamed John Long, John Strong and John Never-Afraid. A fourth one, John Ever-Afraid, has disappeared, but according to legend he was buried halfway up the church wall to fulfil an oath — he swore that the devil could have his soul if he was buried inside or outside the church. The village well, now disused, has the distinction of being one of the deepest (372ft) in the country.

The tour descends into the Thames valley to reach Streatley. At the traffic signals turn right on to A329, SP 'Reading'. Beyond Lower Basildon pass Basildon Park (right).

BASILDON PARK, Berks

This imposing 18th-century house, built by John Carr of York, was used by troops in both World War I and II but otherwise stood empty from 1910 until Lord and Lady Ilife bought it. After lovingly restoring the house, they gave it to the National Trust in 1977. The splendid plasterwork inside is attributed to William Roberts of Oxford.

½ mile further, on the left, is the Child Beale Wildlife Trust.

CHILD BEALE WILDLIFE TRUST, Berks

Colourful exotic birds, including ornamental pheasants, peacocks and flamingoes, strut around this unusual garden. A lake, a river and garden statuary provide an attractive setting for walking, and there is a special area for children.

Mapledurham, one of England's largest Elizabethan houses, was the home of the Blount family for 12 generations

Continue alongside the River Thames to Pangbourne.

PANGBOURNE, Berks

Kenneth Graham, author of The Wind in the Willows, lived and died at Pangbourne, and it is easy to imagine his characters Mole and Rat rowing up and down the river here, where the Thames meets the Pang. Above Pangbourne's pleasant houses is the Nautical College, founded in 1917 by Sir Thomas Devitt.

THE DOWNS AND TROUT STREAMS OF NORTH HAMPSHIRE

Peaceful lanes wind their way across the rolling North Hampshire Downs, then descend through strings of enchanting Saxon villages, where trout streams meander through the chalklands past green watercress beds and banks of wild flowers.

BASINGSTOKE, Hants
A town that is still expanding, Basingstoke was once a pleasant country town, but now it is surrounded by huge housing estates and the centre has been rendered unrecognisable by modern shopping precincts. The older buildings have to be sought out, but among them is the Willis Museum which is a gold mine for all those interested in Hampshire's history and archaeology. A local man, Mr Willis, founded the museum with his collection of clocks: they were his profession and his hobby.

From Basingstoke town centre, or the Ring Road, follow SP 'Aldermaston' to the Aldermaston Road Roundabout. Leave on the A340 and in 2½ miles turn right, SP 'The Vyne (NT)'. In 1½ miles, at the T-junction, turn left (no SP), or, alternatively turn right for a short detour to The Vyne.

THE VYNE, Hants
A lovely Hampshire lane leads down to The Vyne (NT) and a more charming or unpretentious country house would be hard to find. William Sandys, councillor to Henry VI, built it, and his family lived in it for the next century. Chaloner Chute was the subsequent owner and his descendants lived there until 1956. Among the best features of the house are the Gothic ante-chapel, the chapel itself with fine Flemish stained-glass and Italian glazed floor tiles, the sunny oak gallery and the neo-Classical hall and staircase decorated in pale blue and white. All the furniture and furnishings have been collected by the Chute family over several centuries. This redbrick house is set in simple but pleasant grounds; a grassy sward rolls down to the edge of a long narrow lake at the back and fields stretch away beyond. Looking somewhat out of place is the Classical portico overlooking the lake. Dating from 1650, it is the earliest example of a portico found on an English house.

The main tour continues to the edge of Bramley. Here, turn left, SP 'Silchester', and in ¾ mile turn right. In 1¼ miles, at the crossroads, turn left and in ¾ mile branch right, SP 'Silchester Ruins'. Shortly, to the right, is Silchester Calleva Museum.

SILCHESTER CALLEVA MUSEUM, Hants
This museum, housed in the grounds of Silchester rectory, was instituted in 1951 as a contribution to the Festival of Britain. It contains finds from excavations at nearby Silchester — the old Roman town called *Calleva Atrebatum*. Displays of drawings and models represent Silchester as it was in Roman times, namely a market town and a provincial administrative centre with a population of some 4,000.

Continue to the next road junction and keep left, SP 'Aldermaston'. At the end turn right, then immediately right again. In 1 mile cross the main road, then turn left and continue to Aldermaston.

ALDERMASTON, Berks
Despite the huge Atomic Research Station and accompanying housing estates on Aldermaston's doorstep, the village itself has not been marred by modern development. Its main street of colour-washed brick and timbered buildings runs uphill to Aldermaston Court which is barricaded by huge wrought iron gates known as the Eagle Gates. At the bottom of the street is the Hind's Head, an old coaching inn with a distinctive ornate black and gold clock and a gilt weather vane in the shape of a fox.

Turn right on to the A340, and at the Hind's Head PH turn left, SP 'Brimpton'. In 1¼ miles turn right, cross the River Enborne, then turn left. At Brimpton follow the Newbury road, then in 2¼ miles

Cloth used to be cleaned and thickened in the fulling mill at Alresford

turn left. In 1½ miles turn right on to the A339, then in another mile turn left, SP 'Burghclere'.

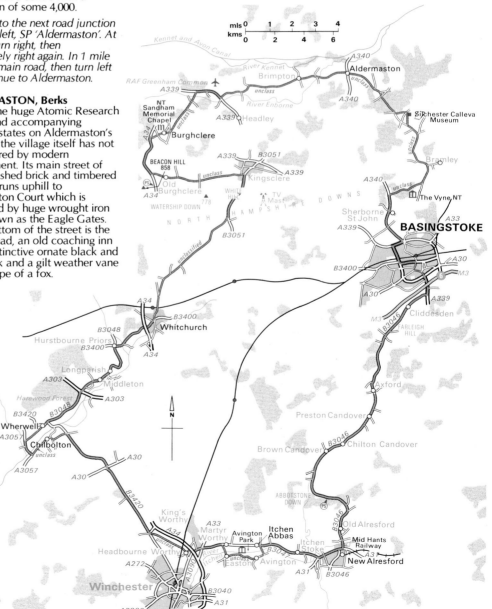

BURGHCLERE, Hants

In 1926 a chapel and 2 almshouses were built in the village of Burghclere to commemorate Henry Willoughby Sandham — a local World War I hero. The tiny Sandham Chapel (NT) is filled with visionary paintings by the English artist Stanley Spencer. Spencer served with the Royal Berkshire Regiment and the paintings here are his reflections of the war.

At the war memorial turn left and after ½ mile pass (right) the Sandham Memorial Chapel. At the A34, turn left, SP 'Winchester'. In 1¾ miles turn left, SP 'Kingsclere'. Ahead, on the A34, is Beacon Hill.

BEACON HILL, Hants

Beacon Hill rises to 858ft and is part of the chalk ridge running from Wiltshire through to Surrey and Kent. This windy, treeless viewpoint is a fine spot for picnicing and flying kites or model aeroplanes.

The main tour continues through the hamlet of Old Burghclere. In ½ mile bear right and follow a pleasant byroad along the foot of the North Hampshire Downs, with Watership Down prominent to the right, to Kingsclere. Here turn right, SP 'Whitchurch', then right again on to the B3051. Climb White Hill (to the left is a picnic area and Hannington TV mast) and continue for 5 miles, then turn left at the main road for Whitchurch.

WHITCHURCH, Hants

Anglers are familiar with the lovely trout-filled River Test and Whitchurch is one of the many villages lying along its valley. Of most interest here is the silk mill. The 18th-century brick building stands, crowned by a small bell tower, on an island in the river. Until the 1930s, when electricity deemed it redundant, water was the sole source of power. A shop (OACT) on the premises sells silk scarves, ties, shirts and so on, as well as an assortment of locally-made products.

At the mini-roundabout in Whitchurch turn right on to the B3400, SP 'Andover', and continue to Hurstbourne Priors. Here, turn left on to the B3048, SP 'Longparish', and follow a winding road along the Test valley to pass through Longparish (see tour 25). Beyond the village, at the A303, turn right then immediately left, SP 'Wherwell'. Remain on the B3420 into Wherwell.

WHERWELL, Hants

Elfrida, Saxon queen and mother of King Ethelred, founded a priory in this exceptionally picturesque thatched village. Unfortunately fires destroyed it and the few remains of the replacement nunnery are now part of priory house. The old pronunciation of the village name is 'Orrell'.

Continue through the village on to an unclassified road ahead, SP 'Fullerton'. In 1 mile turn left on to the A3057, then ½ mile further cross the River Test and turn left on to an unclassified road for Chilbolton.

CHILBOLTON, Hants

A huge, shiny, concave disc stands on the downs above Chilbolton on the site of an old airfield. This radio-wave reflector belongs to the Chilbolton Observatory, whose purpose is to discover more about the earth's atmosphere and interplanetary space.

At the end of Chilbolton turn right, SP 'Barton Stacey', then bear left. In ½ mile turn right on to the B3420, SP 'Winchester'. At the A30 turn right, then immediately left, to follow the line of an old Roman road. After 3½ miles, at the roundabout, follow SP 'The Worthy's', for Headbourne Worthy. Here, at the green, keep left then take the next turning right. In ¼ mile turn left on to the A3090 for King's Worthy. At the far end turn left and immediately right on to the B3047, SP 'Alresford'. After a mile, turn right and cross the River Itchen to Easton. At the Cricketers PH turn left and continue to Avington Park.

AVINGTON PARK, Hants

The River Itchen flows along the parkland boundary and its water meadows provide a tranquil setting for the 17th-century mansion (OACT), enhanced by cedar trees, tulip trees and a long avenue of limes. The front of the redbrick house is broken by a large, white, Doric portico on top of which sit 3 goddesses. For several years the house was lived in by the Shelley family. John, brother of the poet Percy, was the first. A previous owner, the Marquess of Caernarvon, built an

The silk mill at Whitchurch has always been a family business employing local women to work the looms

attractive Georgian church in the park and all the woodwork — gallery, reredos, pulpit and box-pews — is carved from rich dark mahogany.

After leaving the park turn left into Avington village. In ¼ mile keep left and recross the River Itchen to reach the edge of Itchen Abbas.

ITCHEN ABBAS, Hants

Itchen Abbas is another of the lovely villages along this valley. With the old mill and the lazy brown trout in the river, it is easy to see why Charles Kingsley was inspired to write *The Water Babies* here. He used to stay at the pub, now rebuilt and called The Plough.

Leave Itchen Abbas on the B3047, SP 'Alresford', and continue to Itchen Stoke, then in 1 mile turn left on to the A31 for New Alresford.

NEW ALRESFORD, Hants

This is one of Hampshire's loveliest small towns. Its main street, appropriately called Broad Street, is flanked with lime trees and colour-washed Georgian houses. The writer Mary Mitford was born in one of them in 1787. A tributary of the Itchen flows around the town and there is a pleasant walk along its banks past an old fulling mill — a reminder of Alresford's medieval days as a wool town. Another reminder of the past is a lake at the edge of the town. In the 12th century the Bishop of Winchester dammed the village pond to form a natural harbour and make the river navigable to the sea.

MID HANTS RAILWAY, Hants

The chalk streams of Hampshire feed beds of bright green cress and provide them with ideal growing conditions. Over half the country's supply of watercress comes from Hampshire and for a long time Alresford Station was an important despatch point. The railway transported the cress all over England and came to be known as the Watercress Line. Neglected and unused for several years, enthusiasts have now restored part of the line and in summer steam trains run between Alresford and Alton.

At Alresford turn left, SP 'Basingstoke B3046', into Broad Street. At the end bear right and cross a causeway over the River Alre to Old Alresford. Cross wooded Abbotstone Down and continue through the Candover valley and down Farleigh Hill, into Cliddesden. In 1¼ miles turn left on to the A339 for the return to Basingstoke.

The lake at The Vyne was landscaped in the 18th century to enhance the view

HIGH DOWNS AND HOCKTIDE REVELS

The bare uplands of the Marlborough and Berkshire Downs overlook open, windswept country, while the lush lowlands are dotted with small villages and noted beauty spots. At Hungerford, Hocktide is celebrated with an annual ceremony that has its origins in the pagan rites of ancient Britons.

Wansdyke, seen between Marlborough and Oare, was a 50-mile defensive earthwork thought to be built in the 1st century

MARLBOROUGH, Wilts
Marlborough's broad Georgian High Street was once a great livestock market where thousands of downland sheep were herded. Today it is a pleasant shopping centre, with a number of interesting old passages and side streets branching off on both sides. By St Peter's Church an arched gateway leads to the town's famous public school, founded in 1843 around the site of the old castle.

Leave Marlborough on the A4 Chippenham road, then turn left on to the A345, SP 'Salisbury', and continue to Oare.

OARE, Wilts
Oare sits beneath the Marlborough Downs at the head of the Vale of Pewsey, a fertile valley that separates the arid downland from the flat expanse of Salisbury Plain. The 18th-century mansion house was enlarged in the 1920s by Clough Williams-Ellis, creator of the 'Italian' seaside village of Portmeirion. He also designed other houses in the village: a T-shaped, thatched house with the unwelcoming name of Cold Blow, and a terrace of whitewashed cottages with a central archway.

Continue on the A345 to Pewsey.

A perfect combination of roses and thatch in Longparish

PEWSEY, Wilts
King Alfred's statue gazes out from the market place of Pewsey, a pleasant town sheltered by Pewsey Hill whose slopes are distinguished by a chalk white horse. The parish church rests on great sarsen stones, similar to those used at Stonehenge.

Continue on the Amesbury road, cross the River Avon and turn left, SP 'Everleigh', then immediately turn right. The outline of the Pewsey White Horse can be seen before ascending Pewsey Hill. Continue to the edge of Everleigh. Here, turn left on to the A342, SP 'Andover'. In 2 miles at the T-junction turn left then immediately right for Ludgershall.

LUDGERSHALL, Wilts
After the modern housing developments on the outskirts, the old village centre, with its almshouses, ruined castle and rambling church, comes as something of a surprise. The ruins were once a royal castle where Queen Matilda fled from King Stephen after one of their 12th-century battles.

At the T-junction turn left SP 'Andover' and continue into Hampshire. In 4¼ miles at the roundabout turn right, SP 'Thruxton'. In ¼ mile turn left, SP 'Amport'. Shortly turn right then immediately turn left across the main road for Hawk Conservancy.

THE HAWK CONSERVANCY WEYHILL WILDLIFE PARK, Hants
Opened in 1965, the park specialises in European birds, including hawks, falcons, eagles, owls and vultures; the hawks and falcons are flown whenever weather permits. Among the other wildlife represented are many native British mammals such as polecats, squirrels, foxes and wildcats.

Continue to Amport, turn left for Monxton, then go over the crossroads and continue to Abbots Ann.

ABBOTTS ANN, Hants
The 18th-century church at Abbotts Ann contains numerous white paper garlands; more, it is said than any other village in the country. This reflects well on the morals of the inhabitants because

these used to be carried at the funerals of men and women who had died chaste and celibate.

At Abbotts Ann turn right, then left at the Eagle PH and shortly keep left then bear right. At the A343 turn left then take the next turning right SP 'The Clatfords', into Anna valley. Continue through Upper Clatford and on to Goodworth Clatford. Here, turn left, SP 'Andover', and cross the river bridge. At the A3057 junction turn right SP 'Stockbridge', then in ¼ mile turn left on to the B3420 for Wherwell (see tour 24). Keep left through the village and at the far end go forward on to the B3048, SP 'Longparish'. At the A303 turn right, then immediately left for Longparish.

LONGPARISH, Hants
As the name suggests, this village consists of a long main street along which are spaced a number of pretty, thatched cottages. It stands in the valley of the River Test, noted for its excellent trout fishing.

Continue along a winding road to Hurstbourne Priors. Here turn right then immediately left, SP 'Hurstbourne Tarrant', and follow the Bourne rivulet to St Mary Bourne.

ST MARY BOURNE, Hants
The Bourne valley is watered by a pretty rivulet which in a dry summer sometimes disappears, as do many of the chalk streams in this area. There is enough moisture, however, to feed the many dark green watercress beds that surround this attractive village. Its church contains a massive, carved, black marbled font from Tournai, similar to the one in Winchester Cathedral. The yew tree in the churchyard is one of the oldest in Hampshire.

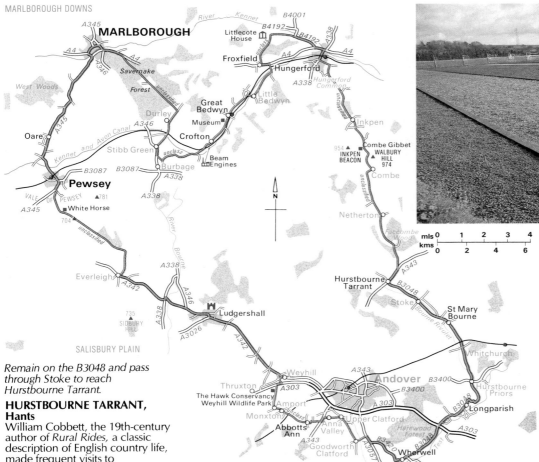

MARLBOROUGH DOWNS

Watercress, a member of the wallflower family, is cultivated as a food crop in beds such as these at St Mary Bourne

Remain on the B3048 and pass through Stoke to reach Hurstbourne Tarrant.

HURSTBOURNE TARRANT, Hants

William Cobbett, the 19th-century author of *Rural Rides*, a classic description of English country life, made frequent visits to Uphusband, as he called Hurstbourne Tarrant.

Turn right on to the A343, SP 'Newbury' then in ½ mile turn left, SP 'Netherton'. Follow this pleasant byroad for 3¼ miles, then keep forward, SP 'Combe' and Inkpen'. Later turn sharp right to reach the edge of Combe. Keep left and continue over the shoulder of Inkpen Hill and Walbury Hill.

INKPEN HILL & WALBURY HILL, Berks

Walbury Hill, at 974ft the highest point of the Berkshire Downs, is crowned by the forbidding banks of Walbury Camp, a massive Iron-Age hill fort. Almost opposite, Inkpen Beacon tops the barren, windswept upland of Inkpen Hill. Here Combe Gibbet stands as a sinister landmark. It was erected in 1676 for the hanging of 2 local villagers who had murdered 2 of their 3 young children. The gibbet was in use until the last century.

Descend and later go over the crossroads, SP 'Hungerford', to reach Inkpen. At the T-junction turn right, then take the first turning left. In 2½ miles bear right, then continue forward, SP 'Hungerford gated road', to cross Hungerford Common. At the next T-junction turn left for Hungerford.

HUNGERFORD, Berks

Hock Tuesday, the 2nd Tuesday after Easter, is the day to visit Hungerford, for the age-old Hocktide Ceremony, at which the town officials are elected for the coming year, takes place. Hungerford has no Mayor and Corporation, but instead, a governing body of Feoffees is elected from among the townspeople. While the elections take place, Tuttimen bearing long staves decorated with bunches (tutti) of flowers roam through the town demanding a kiss or a penny from any girl or woman they meet. In return, the Orange Scrambler, who goes with them, gives an orange. Hungerford is an attractive old town at any time of the year, and the many antique shops in its main street are fascinating.

At Hungerford turn right on to the A338. Cross the Kennet and Avon Canal, then turn left on to the A4. In ¼ mile turn right on to the B4192 SP 'Swindon'. In 1 mile keep forward, SP 'Littlecote'. After ¾ mile pass the entrance to Littlecote House.

LITTLECOTE HOUSE, Wilts

An early Tudor manor house (OACT) contains beautiful furniture, paintings and a rare example of an intact Cromwellian chapel. The magnificent Littlecote armour restored by the Royal Armouries at the Tower of London is on display in the Great Hall. Wax figures designed to appear in realistic settings to represent the domestic scene can be found in many rooms. A farm, self-sufficient in 17th-century manner, has had its original buildings restored and workers wear costumes of the period. Continuing the theme of original style and presentation, a company of six knights and their ladies are in residence and also wear costumes of the era. Excavations in the wooded grounds have revealed a large Roman mosaic, and a miniature railway system connects this to the house, gardens and play areas.

Continue to Froxfield.

FROXFIELD, Wilts

The centrepiece of this attractive village is the group of 50 redbrick almshouses, built around a peaceful courtyard in 1694 and later enlarged. They were originally endowed by the Duchess of Somerset as a refuge for poor widows.

Turn left on to the A4 and pass the Somerset almshouses on the left. In almost ½ mile turn right, SP 'Great Bedwyn'. Cross the bridges, then turn right again to follow the Kennet and Avon Canal. At Little Bedwyn continue on the Great Bedwyn road, recross the canal and railway bridge, then turn left.

GREAT BEDWYN, Wilts

Seven generations of stonemasons have lived and worked in Great Bedwyn. Their craftsmanship is commemorated in the Stone Museum, which contains monuments, gravestones, busts and sculpture going back to the 18th century.

At Great Bedwyn turn left, then right into Church Street, SP 'Crofton'. Shortly, on the right, is the Bedwyn Stone Museum. Continue to Crofton.

CROFTON, Wilts

Crofton stands at the highest point of the Kennet and Avon Canal, about 400ft above the River Kennet. Inside the early 19th-century pumping houses (OACT) in the village are 2 beam engines, designed by Boulton and Watt, which operate a massive cast-iron beam. They were used to pump water up to the canal and have now been restored; occasionally they are powered by steam and can be seen working.

Continue on the unclassified road then cross the canal and bear right, SP 'Burbage'. In 1¾ miles, at the T-junction, turn right, then at the A346 turn right again. In ½ mile, at Stibb Green, turn right by the Three Horseshoes PH, SP 'Savernake'. After 2 miles, opposite the gateway on the right, turn left (no SP) to enter Savernake Forest. (Forestry Commission road — rough surface in places).

SAVERNAKE FOREST, Wilts

This former royal hunting forest covers more than 2,000 acres. The walks and rides radiating from the superb Grand Avenue, a 3-mile drive lined by towering beech trees, are the handiwork of Capability Brown, who was commissioned by the Marquess of Ailesbury to landscape the natural woodland.

After 3 miles turn left on to the A4 for the return to Marlborough.

CHIPPENHAM, Wilts

Chippenham has been a market community since Saxon days when King Alfred stayed here and hunted in the neighbouring forests, and despite housing and industrial developments its character is essentially the same. The centre of this stone-built town is Market Place and the oldest building is the 15th century town hall.

Leave Chippenham on the A4, SP, 'Bath'. In 3½ miles turn left on to an unclassified road for Corsham.

CORSHAM, Wilts

The mellow, stone buildings of the old village centre are among the best in Wiltshire. Corsham was a weaving village in medieval times and the gabled weavers' cottages still stand in their cobbled street, as does the gabled block of the Hungerford Almshouses and School, dating from the same period. The school has kept its original seating arrangements and the master's old-fashioned pulpit desk. Near the church stands Corsham Court (OACT) — an Elizabethan stone manor house first built by 'Customer Smythe', a wealthy haberdasher from London. The present E-shaped design and pinnacled gables are a result of Paul Methuen's ownership from 1745.

Leave on the B3353, SP 'Melksham'. At Gastard, branch left by the Harp and Crown PH, SP 'Lacock', and continue to the A350 and turn right. Take the next turning left into Lacock.

LACOCK, Wilts

Lacock (NT) could stand as the pattern of the perfect English village with its twisting streets, packed with attractive buildings from the 15th to 18th centuries. Half-timbered, grey-stone, redbrick and whitewashed façades crowd together and above eye-level, uneven upper storeys, gabled ends and stone roofs blend with charming ease. Of all the outstanding buildings in the village, Lacock Abbey (NT) on the outskirts is the most beautiful. It began as an Augustinian nunnery in 1232, but after the Reformation Sir William Sharington used the remains to build a Tudor mansion, preserving the cloisters, sacristy and nuns' chapter house, and adding an octagonal tower, a large courtyard and twisted chimney stacks. It was here that W. H. Fox Talbot conducted his pioneer photographic experiments.

Turn right in Lacock, SP 'Bowden Hill', and shortly pass the entrance to Lacock Abbey. After crossing the River Avon ascend Bowden Hill, with fine views to the right. After 2 miles the tour reaches the A342. From here a detour can be made by turning left to Bowood.

BETWEEN THE COTSWOLD HILLS AND THE MARLBOROUGH DOWNS

Golden manor houses stud the countryside in the lee of the chalky heights of the Marlborough Downs and the gentler slopes of the Cotswold Hills. Between them glorious open vistas are broken only by wool towns and villages with their market crosses and stone church spires.

Silbury Hill, built c2500BC, would have taken 700 men 10 years to complete then

BOWOOD, Wilts

The magnificent Georgian house of Bowood is brilliantly complemented by its extensive gardens. The park was laid out by Capability Brown between 1762-1768 and is considered by many as the finest park in England, centring on a long narrow lake. The development of the formal gardens immediately surrounding the house and the establishment of the pleasure gardens, which cover almost a hundred acres, evolved between 1820-1850. The planting in the pleasure grounds, which began in 1820, now forms one of the great collections of trees and shrubs in England. It includes the tallest Cedar of Lebanon and poplar in the country. The whole area is mown. At the outfall from the lake are cascades and grottos, which give a sense of mystery and excitement. During May and June, a separate woodland garden is open which covers over 50 acres. The garden surrounds the family mausoleum, built in 1761 by Robert Adam. Interlinking paths wind beneath tall oaks, through banks of rhododendrons and azaleas. The house itself contains superb collections of paintings, sculpture, costumes and Victoriana. The fine library was designed by Robert Adam, and also on view is the laboratory where Dr Joseph Priestley discovered oxygen gas in 1774.

The main tour turns right, SP 'Devizes', into the village of Sandy Lane. Continue through Rowde to Devizes.

DEVIZES, Wilts

New shopping developments at Devizes have enhanced, rather than detracted from, its busy country town atmosphere. Market Square is the most attractive area and in the centre of this is the market cross, surrounded by 18th-century buildings, including the Black Swan and the Bear Hotel. Devizes, sited on the edge of Salisbury Plain, is a good centre for exploring this area rich in traces of prehistoric man.

Leave Devizes on the A361, SP 'Swindon'. In 2¼ miles turn right, SP 'Bishop's Cannings'. In ½ mile turn right SP 'Florton', into Bishop's Cannings.

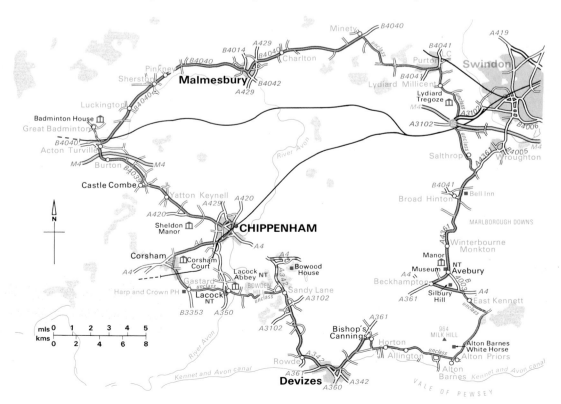

Lacock was built with the wealth brought by this wool trade and has remained intact since the 18th century

BISHOP'S CANNINGS, Wilts

Thatched cottages lie in the shadow of St Mary's Church which was built as a parish church on the Bishop of Salisbury's estate during the 13th century. There is a curious confessional chair inside, on which an enormous hand is painted together with a number of gloomy Latin inscriptions about death and sin, such as 'The hour of death is uncertain'.

In another ½ mile, at the T-junction, turn left, SP 'Alton Priors', then cross the Kennet and Avon Canal and continue to the outskirts of Allington. After 2 miles there are views to the left of the Alton Barnes White Horse.

ALTON BARNES WHITE HORSE, Wilts

Above the twin villages of Alton Barnes and Alton Priors is a white horse carved in chalk. An unlikely local story says a man called Jack the Painter was paid £20 to cut it, but he fled with the money instead. Rough justice was later done when Jack was caught and hanged, and someone else carved the horse in 1812.

At the T-junction turn left, SP 'Marlborough'. In 2 miles turn left, SP 'East and West Kennet'. Continue through East Kennet then at the A4 turn left, SP 'Chippenham'. Later pass the prehistoric mound of Silbury Hill to the right.

SILBURY HILL, Wilts

No-one knows why this huge, mysterious conical hill (AM) was created. One fanciful theory is that the devil made it and buried beneath is a mounted warrior in gold armour. At about 130ft high, it is the highest artificial mound in Europe and covers 5½ acres.

At the Beckhampton roundabout take the A4361, SP 'Swindon', and in 1 mile keep left for Avebury.

AVEBURY, Wilts

Avebury village stands inside the outer ditch of a huge prehistoric monument — Avebury stone circle (AM). Little is known about the purpose of these famous ancient standing stones, spread over about 28 acres, but the largest ring has 100 sarsen stones left now, and what are actually the remains of 2 inner circles are scattered, seemingly at random, about the village. Avebury Manor (NT) is an Elizabethan manor house standing on the site of a small Benedictine monastery. The gardens, bordered by stone walls, contain intricate topiary work and a large dovecot.

Continue on the Swindon road with views of the Marlborough Downs to the right. After 3½ miles pass the Bell Inn, then in another 1½ miles turn left, SP 'Wootton Bassett'. Follow this for 3¼ miles to the motorway roundabout and take the A3102, SP 'Swindon'. In ½ mile, at the next roundabout, turn left, SP 'Lydiard Millicent'. In 1 mile, to the left, lies the Lydiard Tregoze Estate.

LYDIARD TREGOZE, Wilts

Sir John St John was chiefly responsible for the spectacular monuments and decorations inside Lydiard Tregoze church which includes a splendid folding screen dedicated to his parents and an elaborate white marble monument for himself, his 2 wives and their 13 children.
The church stands in the park attached to the manor house of Lydiard Tregoze (OACT) in which the St John family lived for 4 centuries. It has been extensively restored and is mainly Georgian in appearance and interior furnishing.

Continue on the unclassified road and in ½ mile turn left, SP 'Purton', for Lydiard Millicent. At the far end of the village turn right and continue to Purton. Turn left in to the main street (B4041) and at the end of the village turn right on to an unclassified road (no SP). In 1¼ miles go over the crossroads, SP 'Minety', then ½ mile farther branch right. At the edge of Minety turn left on to the B4040, for Malmesbury.

MALMESBURY, Wilts

A tall, slender spire soars up above Malmesbury which, in turn, sits up on an isolated hill amid the surrounding water meadows. The spire belongs to the town's majestic abbey which has stood here since the 7th century. Look particularly at the splendid south porch covered in carvings and sculptures: it is one of England's best examples of Romanesque art.

Leave on the B4040, SP 'Bristol', and continue through Pinkney, Sherston and Luckington to Acton Turville. 1¼ miles to the north is Great Badminton and Badminton House.

BADMINTON HOUSE, Avon

The exciting 3-day event horse trials held annually at Badminton House have made the estate famous. Both the stables' and hunt kennels' magnificence reflect Badminton's long association with horses and hunting. At the heart of the great park is the Palladian mansion, remodelled by William Kent in about 1740. It has been the home of the Dukes of Beaufort since the 17th century. The entrance hall, hung with hunting scenes, was where the game of badminton evolved.

The main tour turns left, SP 'Chippenham'. At the Fox and Hounds PH turn left again on to the B4039. Cross the M4 and pass through Burton, then in 2½ miles turn right on to an unclassified road to Castle Combe.

CASTLE COMBE, Wilts

This village, portrayed on many a poster and picture-postcard as a haven of beauty and tranquility, well deserves its fame. A river, Bye Brook, flows through the streets under stone foot-bridges, and honey-coloured cottages — their roofs grown uneven with the passage of time — surround the market cross.

Return to the B4039, SP 'Chippenham', and turn right for Yatton Keynell. In 1¼ miles turn left on to the A420. In 1 mile, on the right, is the turning for Sheldon Manor.

SHELDON MANOR, Wilts

Terraced gardens, rose beds, water gardens and ancient yew trees encircle the Plantaganet manor house (OACT). The oldest part of the house is its 13th-century porch, still with its original stone water cistern which was fed from pipes in the roof. Within the grounds is a 15th-century detached chapel belonging to the house.

Continue on the A420 for the return to Chippenham.

COTSWOLD VALLEYS AT THE SOURCE OF THE THAMES

Stretching northwards from the infant Thames, the deep valley of the River Churn and the broader valleys of the Coln and the Leach bore into the wooded Cotswold Hills. The towns and villages of the Thames stand out amid the flat water meadows while the Cotswold valleys protect their own dreamy villages.

CIRENCESTER, Glos
This 'capital' of the Cotswolds is the epitome of an old market town, with its beautiful Tudor church dominating the busy market place. The church, built from the riches of the wool trade, has a magnificent 3-storeyed south porch with delicate fan vaulting and many interesting brasses. Around the attractive Georgian market place are a number of old streets where the stone-built houses of the wealthy Elizabethan wool merchants still stand. Cirencester stands at the meeting point of 3 Roman roads — the Fosse Way, Akeman Street, and one of the 2 Ermine Streets. Roman remains, including some fine mosaic pavements, are housed in the Corinium Museum. Cirencester Park (house not open) stands in lovely woodland and has a superb 5-mile-long avenue of chestnut trees. The 17th-century poet Alexander Pope was a frequent visitor to the house, and a rustic seat at the edge of the tree-lined avenues called the Seven Rides is named after him.

Leave on the A429, SP 'The South West' and 'Chippenham'. In 1½ miles go forward on to the A433, SP 'Bristol'. After another mile, in the meadow to the right, is the reputed source of the River Thames. Pass under a railway bridge and turn left on to an unclassified road for Kemble. Cross the main road into the village, then go over the staggered crossroads, SP 'Ewen', follow SP 'South Cerney'.

SOUTH CERNEY, Glos
Just outside South Cerney, old gravel pits have been transformed into lakes which form part of the Cotswold Water Park; the marina here is gay with sailing dinghies and motor boats on summer weekends. The village stands on the River Churn and has several attractive old streets, including one with the extraordinary name of Bow Wow.

Turn right at the war memorial into Broadway Lane. In ¾ mile pass the Costwold Water Park and in ½ mile turn right, SP 'Ashton Keynes'. In 1¼ miles turn left and shortly branch left to Ashton Keynes.

ASHTON KEYNES, Wilts
Small bridges spanning the little stream of the infant Thames lead up to the doors of several of the cottages at one end of Ashton Keynes, and at the other, a group of old stone houses form a picturesque scene with an old watermill. Just outside the village, the church and manor house look out over peaceful countryside.

At the end of the village turn left on to the Cricklade road then bear right. In 2 miles turn left on to the B4040, and in another 1½ miles turn left again to enter Cricklade. At the clock tower turn right and follow SP 'Swindon' then in ¾ mile join the A419. In 1 mile turn left on to an unclassified road for Castle Eaton. Continue on the Highworth road through Hannington and in 1¼ miles turn left on to the B4019 for Highworth. Turn left on to the A361 Stow road and after 4 miles pass a riverside park before reaching Lechlade.

LECHLADE, Glos
Just outside Lechlade, a pleasant riverside park extends along the banks of the Thames, locally referred to (as at Oxford) as the Isis. Halfpenny Bridge leads across the river and into the Georgian market place. A delightful characteristic of the village are the many gazebos in the trim gardens of the older houses. The poet Shelley, journeying upriver from Windsor, was inspired by the calm of the river and the churchyard to write the poem *Stanzas in a Summer Evening Churchyard* while staying at the local inn. By St John's Bridge 3 shires meet — Gloucestershire, Oxfordshire and Wiltshire — and the nearby lock is an ideal picnic spot.

Leave on the A417 Faringdon road and in ¾ mile cross St John's Bridge. In 2 miles pass the grounds of Buscot Park.

BUSCOT PARK, Oxon
The Classical mansion (NT), built the Edward Loveden Townsend in 1780, is the home of a notable collection of European paintings spanning several centuries, from the Italian Renaissance to the pre-Raphaelites and 20th-century works. 18th-century paintings include a Gainsborough landscape.

The collection was begun in the 19th century by Alexander Henderson, Lord Faringdon, and continued by his descendants. The most famous portrait is by Rembrandt of Clement de Jongh. The house also contains lovely furniture of rosewood and satinwood.

Continue to Faringdon.

FARINGDON, Oxon
A traditional market town famous for its dairy produce and fine bacon, Faringdon has many interesting old inns and an 18th-century Market Hall. Faringdon House (not open) was owned by Lord Barners and the folly in the grounds was built by him during the Depression of the 1930s to relieve local unemployment. The 14th-century Radcot Bridge between Faringdon and Clanfield is said to be the oldest of the Thames bridges.

From the market square branch left on to the A4095, and after passing the church turn left. In 2½ miles cross the historic Radcot Bridge. At Clanfield go forward on to the B4020 for Alvescot. In ¼ mile turn left on to an unclassified road to Kencot and 1¼ miles beyond the village turn right into Filkins.

FILKINS, Oxon
Wistaria and clematis, for which the Cotswold villages are so famous, clamber over the pale stone of houses, barns and garden walls. Chestnut trees, laden with flower in spring, spread over the quiet main street of Filkins.

In the village turn right and after 1 mile turn right on to the A361, SP 'Stow'. In 2 miles, at the crossroads, turn left, SP 'Wildlife Park', and pass the entrance to the Cotswold Wildlife Park.

COTSWOLD WILDLIFE PARK, Oxon
In 1969, 120 acres of wooded parkland were chosen to house the animal collection of the Cotswold Wildlife Park. They have taken as their emblem one of their most attractive creatures, the chestnut-coloured Red panda, a smaller relative of the Giant panda, whose natural habitat is the high forests of the Himalayas and western China. There are

Most Roman villas had mosaic flooring such as this which can be seen at the Corinium Museum, Cirencester

many African and South American mammals, an interesting Reptile House, with crocodiles, alligators and poisonous snakes, and numerous spacious aviaries of exotic birds, including a Tropical House where sunbirds, brilliant humming birds and bluebirds hover among the blossoms of hibiscus and bougainvillea.

Continue on the unclassified road, and in ½ mile go over the crossroads, SP 'Eastleach Martin', then ½ mile later branch left and follow a narrow byroad to the twin Eastleaches.

EASTLEACH, Glos
The village consists of 2 charming Cotswold hamlets, Eastleach Martin and Eastleach Turville, standing on opposite banks of the River Leach. An old stone clapper bridge leads from one to the other, named after John Keble (founder of Keble College, Oxford), whose family were lords of the manor of Turville. The 2 old village churches were built within sight of each other; that of Eastleach Martin has 5 old sundials; that of its neighbour, a fine Norman arched doorway with a carving of Christ in Glory.

At Eastleach Turville keep right through the village on the Hatherop road. At the T-junction turn left, then in ½ mile turn right, and 2 miles farther turn right again into Hatherop. Turn left for Coln St Aldwyn. Turn left, SP 'Fairford', then cross the River Coln and ascend to Quenington.

QUENINGTON, Glos
A number of lovingly-restored 17th-century stone houses grace the village street, but it is the 12th-century village church, with its 2 beautifully carved Norman doorways that attracts visitors from miles around. The north doorway depicts in vivid detail the Harrowing of Hell and the south doorway shows Christ placing a crown on the head of the Virgin Mary.

At the green, turn left then at the end of the village recross the Coln and continue to Fairford.

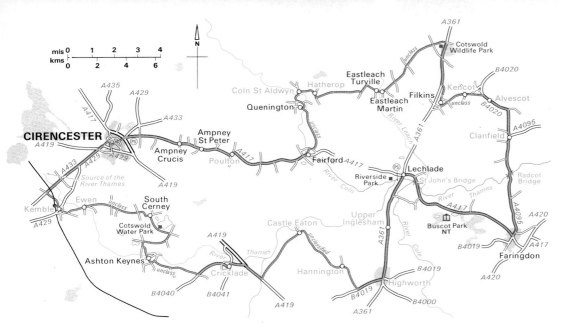

houses of all periods and, at the edge of the manor park, a picturesque stone watermill. The American air-base near Fairford was used for trials of *Concorde*.

Leave on the A417 and pass through Poulton to the villages of Ampney St Peter and Ampney Crucis.

THE AMPNEYS, Glos

Four villages all bearing the name Ampney. Ampney St Peter is generally thought to be the prettiest of them, with its village green bordered by old cottages. Ampney Crucis nearby, a pleasing blend of old and new, stands on the Ampney Brook. It takes the second part of its name from the ancient cross in the churchyard. At Down Ampney, some distance away, the composer Ralph Vaughan Williams was born.

Continue on the A417 for the return to Cirencester.

Fairford's 17th-century mill house stands beside the River Coln. St Mary's Church nearby marks the centre of the village

FAIRFORD, Glos

All the prosperity of the medieval wool trade is exemplified in the Church of St Mary at Fairford. The wool merchants, John Tame and his son Sir Edmund, paid for it to be built at the end of the 15th century and by a miracle the glorious stained-glass windows have been preserved almost intact. The church stands beside the river, overlooking the village square where houses of soft grey Cotswold stone have stood, their appearance virtually unaltered, for more than 200 years. A stroll around the streets leading off from the market place reveals old

OXFORD AND THE ISIS

Matthew Arnold's city of dreaming spires still enchants the visitor to Oxford, home of the oldest university in Britain. From Oxford, where the Thames is still called the Isis, the river winds its slow way through the broad green water meadows surrounding Abingdon and Dorchester.

OXFORD, Oxon

The splendour of the college architecture lends an unequalled dignity to Oxford's busy streets. Their enclosed courts and well-kept gardens (OACT) are a timeless haven from the pace of daily life outside. University, Merton and Balliol Colleges were all founded in the 13th-century and the oldest is probably Merton (1264). Edmund Hall is the only survivor of the medieval halls that pre-dated the colleges themselves. Most of the significant buildings in the city are connected with the university; The Bodleian Library's collection of rare manuscripts makes it second only in importance to the Vatican Library in Rome; the Ashmolean Museum, the oldest in the country, founded in 1683, contains opulent treasures from the Orient as well as from all the countries of Europe; the circular Sheldonian Theatre, opposite Blackwells, great rambling bookshop in the Broad, was designed in 1664 by Christopher Wren and from its cupola there are panoramic views of the city. The Broad, the Cornmarket and the High are the streets where life goes on. Here, and in the maze of side streets and winding narrow lanes that lead off, are most of the old colleges, the students' pubs, little restaurants, antique and curio shops. Eights Week, when college teams of rowing eights compete against each other in late spring, attracts hundreds of visitors to the lovely Meadows.

Leave on the A420, SP 'The West ' and 'Swindon'. In 1¼ miles turn right, then at the roundabout take the 2nd exit. In ¾ mile branch left, SP 'Eynsham', then turn right on to the B4044. After crossing the picturesque Swinford Bridge (toll) go forward to the outskirts of Eynsham and turn left on to the B4449. In 2 miles turn left to Stanton Harcourt.

STANTON HARCOURT, Oxon

The majestic tombs marking generations of the Harcourt family fill the Norman church which looks down upon medieval fishponds and the lovely 17th-century parsonage. Several thatched cottages grace the village, and there is a 15th-century tower in the grounds of the old manor house (not open). The poet Alexander Pope lived here while completing his translation of Homer's *Iliad* in 1718. Also in the manor grounds is an outstanding example of a medieval kitchen, with an octagonal pyramidal roof.

Morris Dancers celebrating May morning outside the Sheldonian Theatre, Oxford

Continue to the edge of Standlake and turn left, SP 'Kingston Bagpuize'. In ½ mile turn left on to the A415, SP 'Abingdon'. Recross the Thames at Newbridge and continue to Kingston Bagpuize. Here turn left then right. In 2½ miles cross the A338, and in another 2½ miles go forward at the roundabout for the outskirts of Abingdon. Keep forward at the mini-roundabout for a diversion to Abingdon.

ABINGDON, Oxon

A mixture of Georgian houses and buildings dating back to the 13th century characterise this old Thameside town, once the county town of Berkshire, but now within Oxfordshire's boundaries. The 17th-century County Hall, standing on graceful columns, houses the Town Museum specialising in local history, and the Guildhall has a fine 18th-century Council Chamber. Several portraits line its walls, including one by Gainsborough of George III and Queen Charlotte. Down by the river stands the abbey gatehouse and a reconstructed Elizabethan theatre where plays and operas are performed in summer. Of Abingdon's 2 churches, St Helen's is the more beautiful, its elegant spire dominating the town and surrounding water meadows.

The main tour turns right on to the B4017, SP 'Drayton'. At Drayton turn left on to the B4016 for Sutton Courtenay.

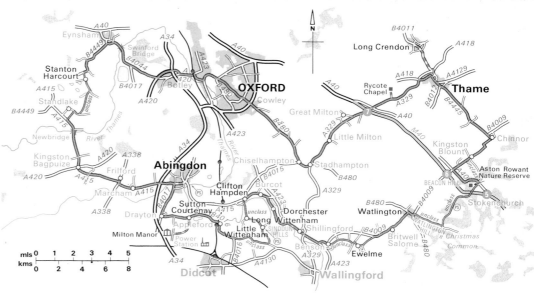

Rycote Chapel, with its fine wagon roof, has not altered since the 15th century

SUTTON COURTENAY, Oxon
One of the loveliest villages on the Thames, Sutton Courtenay's half-timbered houses and cottages are to be found along winding lanes and around a spacious green shaded by scented lime trees. In the churchyard rest the graves of Lord Asquith, who was Prime Minister at the outbreak of World War I, and Eric Blair, better known as George Orwell, author of *Animal Farm* and *1984*.

A diversion can be made to Milton Manor House by turning right in Sutton Courtenay on to an unclassified road.

MILTON MANOR, Berks
The 3-storey central portion of the Manor (OACT) was built during the 17th-century, but the 2 wings were added a century later by the Barret family. The house is remarkable for its elegant Gothic library, designed after the style of Horace Walpole's famous mansion at Strawberry Hill. The library contains a fine collection of English porcelain including Spode, Rockingham and Crown Derby.

Continue through Appleford, then go forward on to the Wallingford road. At the T-junction turn right and at the next T-junction, turn left. In ¾ mile turn left again, SP 'Little Wittenham'. Continue past the Sinodun Hills to Little Wittenham.

LITTLE WITTENHAM, Oxon
The hamlet lies in the shelter of the twin Sinodun Hills, which are crowned by a distinctive group of beech trees known as the Wittenham Clumps. A path through Wittenham Wood leads up to the ancient hill fort that commands the heights and provides superb views, westwards towards the Vale of the White Horse and eastwards to the Chiltern Hills.

In Little Wittenham turn left to reach the edge of Long Wittenham.

LONG WITTENHAM, Oxon
Half-timbered houses, an old inn and a medieval church form the long main street of this pleasant village. The Pendon Museum at the west end has fascinating detailed miniature scenes of rural life in the 1930s. Also part of the museum is the Madder Valley model railway. Built by one man, John Ahern, it pioneered the idea of setting model railways in a scenic landscape. Although Madder Valley is fictitious, many of the buildings along it are based on actual places around the country.

Continue on the Clifton Hampden road alongside the Thames. Cross the river and turn right into Clifton Hampden.

CLIFTON HAMPDEN, Oxon
By the old 6-acre bridge across the River Thames stands the Barley Mow Inn, immortalised by Jerome K. Jerome in *Three Men in a Boat*. On the other side of the river are the timbered, thatched cottages of Clifton Hampden.

In Clifton Hampden turn right on to the A415, SP 'Dorchester'. ½ mile beyond Burcot turn right on to an unclassified road for Dorchester.

DORCHESTER, Oxon
Dorchester's beautiful cobbled High Street contains a pleasing variety of interesting old buildings and the lanes leading off it are equally fascinating. In Samian Way, for example, is Molly Mop's thatched cottage; it was built in 1701 and the flint and brick walls are patterned in stripes and diamonds. The 200ft-long Abbey Church, standing on the site of a Saxon cathedral, is hidden among willow trees on a bend of the River Thame. It is famous for its magnificent sculpture and stained-glass window that traces the ancestry of the Virgin Mary.

In 1 mile turn right on to the A423 for Shillingford. In 1¼ mile turn left on to the B4009, SP 'Watlington', and enter Benson. Bear right through the village with the Ewelme road and in 1½ miles turn left, then right, into Ewelme.

EWELME, Oxon
Almost unchanged since the 15th-century when they were built, the almshouses, the old schoolhouse, and the church, form an exceptional medieval group among the brick and flint cottages of this charming village where watercress grows by the stream that runs parallel to the main street. Alice, Duchess of Suffolk, a granddaughter of the poet Geoffrey Chaucer, was responsible for them, and her imposing alabaster tomb is the most famous feature of the church. The grave of Jerome K. Jerome lies in the churchyard.

In Ewelme turn left on to the Watlington road and in 1 mile turn right on to the B4009. In 2½ miles join the B480 then turn left, SP 'Town Centre', into Watlington.

WATLINGTON, Oxon
Tucked away at the foot of the Chilterns, astride the prehistoric track known as the Icknield Way which stretches from Wiltshire up to The Wash, Watlington's Georgian architecture blends with the stone and half-timbered buildings of earlier centuries. At the centre stands the 17th-century brick market hall.

At the Market House in Watlington turn right (one-way) into Hill Road, and climb Watlington Hill, past the Watlington Mark — a chalk design cut into the hillside. At the top turn left, SP 'Kingston Blount'. After 1½ miles pass a picnic area on the right and in 1 mile cross the M40 and pass (left) the Aston Rowant Nature Reserve.

ASTON ROWANT NATURE RESERVE, Oxon
The whole of the Chiltern Hills, where the slopes and the high chalk ridges are clothed with beech woods, has been designated an Area of Outstanding Natural Beauty. Wildlife and plants are specially protected by a number of National Nature Reserves such as Aston Rowant (OACT), which lies on one of the highest ridges of the Chilterns.

Pass the Stokenchurch Wireless Mast before turning left on to the A40 and descending wooded Beacon Hill. At the foot, turn right on to the B4009, SP 'Princes Risborough'. Continue through Kingston Blount and in 1¼ miles turn left to reach the edge of Chinnor and go forward on the B4445 to Thame.

THAME, Oxon
The architectural styles of 5 centuries are well represented at Thame, where the picturesque gabled 15th-century Birdcage Inn could have served as the model for many Christmas card and fairy story illustrations. It stands on the immensely wide High Street, the scene in autumn of the annual fair. The Spread Eagle Inn was mentioned in John Fothergill's book of country inns, *An Innkeeper's Diary*. At the north end of the street stands an old stone house (1570) which used to be Thame Grammar School, its most famous pupil was the Civil War leader John Hampden.

A detour can be made by turning right in the High Street on to the Aylesbury road. After ½ mile, at the roundabout, take the B4011 to Long Crendon.

LONG CRENDON, Bucks
In the thatched cottages of Long Crendon needle-making flourished as a cottage industry until factories took the trade away in the 1830s. A long half-timbered building (NT), the Courthouse, dating from the late 14th-century, stands near the church. Its upper storey contains one long room with an open-beamed roof, which was used as a court house in the reign of Henry V and perhaps also as a wool staple hall during the 14th and 15th centuries.

The main tour turns left in Thame on to the Oxford road. In ¾ mile, at the roundabout, take the A329. In 2 miles an unclassified road on the right leads to Rycote Chapel.

RYCOTE CHAPEL, Oxon
This outstanding example of a medieval chapel was built by the Quartermaine family from Thame and consecrated in 1449. The interior is furnished with beautiful Jacobean pews and medieval benches; the gilded stars on the ceiling were originally cut from rare European playing cards. Elizabeth I and later Charles I both visited the chapel.

Continue on the A329 through Little Milton to Stadhampton and turn right on to the B480, SP 'Oxford'. After 4 miles enter the suburbs of Oxford before crossing the Ring Road for the return to the city centre.

BANBURY, Oxon

'Ride a cock-horse to Banbury Cross' begins the nursery rhyme, which, with the fame of Banbury's cakes, has made the name of this town a household word. The deliciously spicy cakes first appear in town records from the 16th century, and can still be bought freshly baked here. However, the original Banbury Cross was destroyed in a Puritanical frenzy of 1602; the cross now standing in the town centre was erected in 1859. A beautiful old church went the same way — rather than restore it, the inhabitants blew it up in 1792 and replaced it with the present rather stark neo-Classical building. Similarly the old castle disappeared stone by stone, dismantled by the townsfolk to repair damage suffered by the town in 2 Civil War seiges. Despite these depredations, Banbury is a town of great charm, and although a thriving industrial, marketing and shopping centre, the character of its ancestry can be found in the twisting little medieval streets, old houses and inns — especially the gabled, half-timbered Reindeer Inn with mullion windows, in Parsons Street.

Leave Banbury on the A361 and continue to Bloxham.

BLOXHAM, Oxon

From the bridge over the stream, on whose banks grow alder and willow, ironstone houses spread up the valley walls, on one side to the 14th-century church and on the other to a hill crowned by the Victorian buildings of a public school. The old streets and houses in the centre are so closely pressed together they discourage modern additions, and so Bloxham has remained unspoilt and interesting.

At the end of the village turn left on to the Adderbury road, then left again into Milton Road. Pass the edge of Milton, then in 1 mile turn left for Adderbury. Turn left again on to the A423, then right on to the A41, SP 'Aylesbury,' and continue to Aynho.

AYNHO, Northants

On either side of the street apricot trees shade the weathered walls of stone cottages set back in unfenced gardens. The golden fruit of these trees was required by the Lord of the Manor as a toll. The recipients of the apricots were, for nearly 350 years, the Cartwright family, who lived in Aynho Park (OACT), a 17th-century mansion. Monuments to the Cartwrights feature in the church, below whose splendid tower are the village square, shops and a row of thatched cottages, built, like most of Aynho, of local limestone.

¾ mile beyond Aynho, branch left on to the B4031, SP 'Buckingham', for Croughton.

'TO BANBURY CROSS'

Cut the corners of 3 shires, Oxfordshire, Northamptonshire and Warwickshire, gathering a taste of each while passing through truly English villages — satellites to Banbury, an old country town famous for its cakes and a children's nursery rhyme.

CROUGHTON, Northants

Croughton stands on the Oxfordshire border with an American Air Force base for company. Within the peaceful church are late 13th-century wall paintings, which were not discovered until 1930. Although unfortunately damaged by an unsuccessful attempt at protecting them with a layer of wax, these famous paintings are still reasonably clear, and include illustrations of the Flight into Egypt and the Epiphany.

Continue on the B4031 for 2 miles, then turn left on to the A43 for Brackley.

BRACKLEY, Northants

Although a busy place these days, Brackley, with a long tradition of fox-hunting, has retained its pleasant country town atmosphere. In the past, a number of important visitors have stayed here; in 1215 the Barons gathered in Brackley Castle (since demolished) to discuss the Magna Carta before meeting with King John, and Simon de Montfort tried to negotiate with Henry III's messengers here. The Earl of Leicester founded the Hospital of St John and St James in the 12th century, and his heart was buried in the chapel — only to be carelessly thrown away by a 19th-century workman who discovered a lead casket and threw away the 'bit of old leather' he found inside it. The Hospital, bought by Magdalen College, Oxford, in the 15th century, is now a well-known school and the chapel is one of the oldest school chapels in Britain.

Continue through Brackley and ¾ mile beyond the town turn left, SP 'Helmdon and 'Sulgrave', and continue to Helmdon. Here cross the bridge and turn left to Sulgrave. A detour (½ mile) can be made by turning right in Sulgrave for Sulgrave Manor.

Banbury Cross is adorned by statues of Queen Victoria, Edward VII and George V

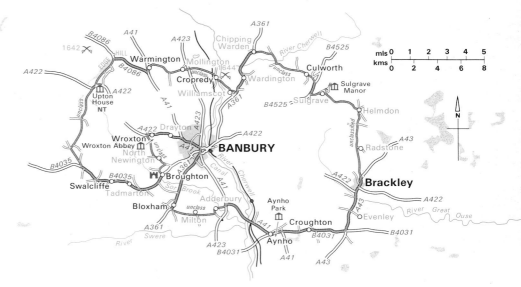

SULGRAVE MANOR, Northants

The forbears of American President George Washington lived in the Queen Anne north wing of Sulgrave Manor (OACT) between 1539 and 1610. The south wing was added in 1921, the same year the house opened its doors to the public. Carved above the porch entrance is the original American flag, 3 stars and 2 stripes, and in the hall hangs perhaps the most treasured possession of the house, an original oil painting of George Washington. Other relics include Washington's black velvet coat and a fragment of his wife's wedding dress. In the house there are great fireplaces, complete with their ancient implements; the original four-poster bed in the main bedroom; and a fascinating kitchen. The 14th-century church is closely linked to the manor and the Washington family, and includes the tomb of Laurence Washington, who built the house.

Continue on the Culworth road through Sulgrave, and in 1 mile turn right on to the B4525. In ½ mile turn left, SP 'Culworth', and at the T-junction turn left into Culworth.

CULWORTH, Northants

Culworth once had its own market and fair, but only a grocer's sign of a sugar-loaf and birch broom on a house by the green recalls these past days of importance. Charles I stayed in the village before the battle of Cropredy Bridge, and in the 18th-century the less respectable Culworth Gang, an infamous bunch of thieves, used it as their headquarters. The church has a tombstone of a negro slave who died in 1762 at the age of 16.

Continue for 1¾ miles, then turn right and later turn left for Chipping Warden. Join the A361 for Wardington, then in 1 mile turn right, SP 'Cropredy', and skirt the hamlet of Williamscot before reaching Cropredy.

CROPREDY, Oxon

Charles I won an early victory in Cropredy during his fight to keep the monarchy; a battle remembered by the 2 suits of armour hanging on the wall of an aisle in the spacious church. Chief among the church's treasures is the brass lectern, adorned by a glittering eagle. When the king came to fight his battle, the villagers hid the lectern in the River Cherwell for safety. Years later it was recovered, but one of the 3 brass lions which stand at the foot of the pedestal was missing. Another was made of bronze, which is why 2 lions shine brightly and the other is dull.

At the Brasenoes Arms PH in Cropredy, turn right, and in ¼ mile turn left, SP 'Mollington'. Later go over staggered crossroads into Mollington and continue to Warmington.

WARMINGTON, Warwicks

Warmington lies in rich farmland at the foot of Edgehill. Its cottages are gathered about a green, complete with a pond and sheep-dip, and nearby stands the Elizabethan gabled manor house of the village. Above the green the small brown-stone church is set on a steeply-sloping churchyard sheltered by shady pines. This was where soldiers killed in the Battle of Edgehill in 1642 were buried. The battle was the first in the Civil War between the Royalists and the Parliamentarians.

On entering Warmington bear left and cross the green and turn left on to the A41, then turn sharp right again on to the B4086, SP 'Kineton'. Continue for 2 miles with fine views from the Edge Hill plateau then turn left at a T-junction, SP 'Edge Hill'. Follow the hill for a further 1¾ miles before reaching the A422. From here a short detour can be made by turning left to Upton House.

A typical cottage in Culworth village

UPTON HOUSE, Warwicks

A wealthy London merchant of James I's reign built Upton House (NT), but it was not until Lord Bearsted bought the house in 1927 and filled it with an art collection of impeccable taste that Upton became exceptional. For here are kept outstanding paintings of the Flemish and early Netherlands school, the Florentine school, and a particularly fine collection of the English 18th-century school, including works by Stubbs and Hogarth. The exquisite collections of 18th-century porcelain include Sèvres and Chelsea pieces. Upton's delightful gardens include terraces, wooded combes, a lake and a water garden.

The main tour turns right on to the A422, SP 'Stratford', then take the next turning left, SP 'Compton Wynyates'. Continue for 3½ miles to a crossroads and turn left, SP 'Banbury'. In 1 mile turn left on to the B4035 for Swalcliffe.

SWALCLIFFE, Oxon

William of Wykeham, founder of New College, Oxford (1324-1404) and a builder of cathedrals, built the lofty and buttressed tithe barn in Swalcliffe. An impressive arch of cathedral proportions opens into the massive interior, where great roof beams can be seen in the half-light. A fine church and manor house overlook the tumble of thatched cottages clustered about a hollow.

Continue on the B4035 through Tadmarton to Broughton. Here turn left, SP 'North Newington', then bear right past the entrance to Broughton Castle.

The great hall at Sulgrave Manor was part of the original house

BROUGHTON CASTLE, Oxon

Broughton Castle (OACT) was last 'modernised' in about 1600, when the medieval fortified manor house of Sir John de Broughton was transformed into an Elizabethan manor by the Fiennes family. The improvements beloved by Victorians never took place because the 15th Baron was a notorious reveller and spendthrift, so no money was left for building. Indeed, the contents of the castle were auctioned to raise money in 1837, including the swans on the wide moat which surrounds the house. Across the bridge, through the battlemented gateway, great fireplaces, airy rooms, elaborate plaster ceilings and vaulted passages echo the past.

Shortly bear right again, then in ½ mile turn left for North Newington. Here turn right, SP 'Wroxton', then in 1¼ miles turn right on to the A422 and skirt the village of Wroxton.

WROXTON, Oxon

Mellowed, brown-stone cottages, many thatched, are overshadowed by Wroxton Abbey (OACT), a beautiful 17th-century house built on the foundations of a 13th-century Augustinian priory. The house possesses 3 paintings by Holbein and one by Zucchero, and of a more domestic nature, a quilt sewn by Mary, Queen of Scots.

Continue on the A422 through Drayton, then join the A41 for the return to Banbury.

REGENCY TOWNS AND COTSWOLD VILLAGES

Cheltenham has become a byword for refinement, elegance and gentility, qualities it has managed to preserve, with its tree-lined walks, exclusive shops and graceful architecture. More rural but scarcely less elegant is Pershore in the Vale of Evesham, while Tewkesbury is a rare survival of a medieval town.

CHELTENHAM, Glos

The architects of Regency Cheltenham created a supremely elegant town where houses are arranged in patterns of leafy squares, crescents and avenues. The material used was either cream-coloured ashlar from Leckhampton quarry, or brick faced with stucco of the same delicate shade. Balconies of finely wrought iron adorn many of the buildings, adding a Continental atmosphere to the streets and squares. Cheltenham became fashionable as a spa town in the 18th century after the discovery of what is now called the Royal Old Well, and, like Bath, the whole town was designed and rebuilt during the 18th and early-19th centuries. The atmosphere is best appreciated in Lansdown Place, the Promenade, Suffolk Square,

Montpellier Walk and Montpellier Parade. The Pittville Pump Room (OACT), with its colonnaded façade, portico and beautiful interior, is a masterpiece of the Greek Revival style. South of the High Street, is Cheltenham Ladies' College, one of the oldest and most famous girls' public schools in Britain.

Leave Cheltenham on the A46, SP 'Broadway', and continue to Prestbury.

PRESTBURY, Glos

Prestbury Park, the famous steeplechase course where the prestigious Gold Cup takes place every spring, is situated just outside the village, now a residential suburb of Cheltenham. Prestbury lies at the foot of Cleeve Hill, the highest (1,082ft) point of the Cotswold Hills; from the summit the views are superb.

At the end of Prestbury turn left and climb on to Cleeve Hill, then descend to Winchcombe.

WINCHCOMBE, Glos

Many pretty gardens in the main street slope down to the River Isbourne which flows by Winchcombe. Buildings of Cotswold stone, with uneven stone roofs, preserve the charm and character of the town, once the seat of a great Benedictine Abbey, which was so thoroughly destroyed by Lord Seymour of Sudeley Castle at the time of the Reformation, that no trace of it survives. The Railway Museum (OACT) has a fine collection of relics of the steam age. Overlooking the village is Sudeley Castle, (OACT) the home of Catherine Parr — one of Henry VIII's wives who married her lover, Seymour, after the king's death. She is buried in the chapel having died a year later during childbirth. Interesting art collections, costume and furniture exhibitions can be seen in the house, which was restored in the 19th century after suffering severe damage during the Civil War. The parkland surrounding the house has an ornamental lake with a colourful assortment of wildfowl.

Continue on the A46 and after 2 miles (right) a short detour leads to the remains of Hailes Abbey.

HAILES ABBEY, Glos

The romantic ruins of the great Cistercian abbey (AM, NT), founded in 1246, stir the imagination to reconstruct the austere monastic life of medieval times, when pilgrims came to revere the 'Blood of Hailes', a sacred phial said to contain the blood of Christ. The small museum on the site displays fragments of sculpture from the abbey.

The main tour continues on the A46. At the Toddington roundabout take the B4077, SP 'Stow-on-the-Wold'. ¾ mile farther, at a crossroads, turn left, SP 'Stanway'. Continue on this unclassified road, and in 1¼ miles keep right for Stanton.

STANTON, Glos

Beautiful villages abound in the Cotswolds, where the local golden stone blends so well with the wooded hills, but Stanton, thanks to the restoration of the 17th-century houses that line both sides of its main street, is exceptionally attractive. Village cross, church, manor house and cottages are all in harmony with the gentle countryside around.

Follow SP 'Broadway' and in ¾ mile turn right on to the A46. In 1 mile turn left for Aston Somerville, then at the T-junction turn right, SP 'Evesham'. In another mile, turn left on to the A435, SP 'Cheltenham', to reach the edge of Sedgeberrow. In 1¼ miles turn right for Ashton-under-Hill, then turn right and continue to Elmley Castle. Turn right through the village, then left, SP 'Pershore', for Little Comberton. At the crossroads turn right, SP 'Wick', and after 1½ miles turn right on to the A44, SP 'Evesham'. In 2 miles turn left on to an unclassified road for Cropthorne.

Bredon Hill — 961ft high

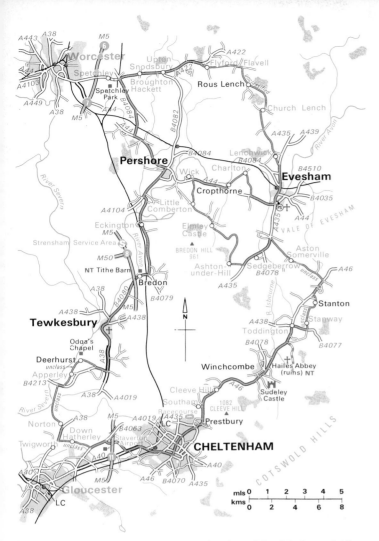

SPETCHLEY PARK, Herefs & Worcs
The house, home of the Berkeley family, is not open, but the beautiful wooded grounds (OACT) around the ornamental lake, and the garden centre, can be visited. Red and fallow deer roam the park which extends on both sides of the main road, and is linked by a graceful iron footbridge.

The main tour turns left on to the B4084, SP 'Pershore'. In 2 miles bear right, then in another 1½ miles turn left on to the A44 to reach the edge of Pershore.

PERSHORE, Herefs & Worcs
The River Avon flows past the end of the High Street of this enchanting market town in the Vale of Evesham. The land round about is celebrated for Pershore plums, which come in 2 varieties, purple and yellow. Pershore's architecture is classical Georgian, most of the elegant houses being faced in stone or stucco. The great abbey church was only partially destroyed at the Reformation, and what remains, the tower, crossing and transepts, is extremely fine.

At the edge of Pershore turn right on to the A4104, SP 'Upton', then in 2 miles turn left on to the B4080, SP 'Tewkesbury'. Cross the River Avon by a 16th-century bridge to reach Eckington. In 3 miles turn right into Bredon.

BREDON, Herefs & Worcs
Bredon, standing high above the River Avon, is a remarkably pretty village, with an impressive Norman church whose slender spire soars 160ft above the countryside around. A fine stone rectory and 2 large private residences, one Jacobean, the other Georgian, set off the church. Bredon tithe barn (NT) is a magnificent limestone structure with a steep-pitched, stone shingled roof, and dates from the 14th century.

3¼ miles beyond Bredon join the A38 to enter Tewkesbury.

TEWKESBURY, Glos
Almost all the buildings in Tewkesbury are old, timber-framed structures of considerable charm. Shortage of space in the multitude of narrow winding alleys leading off the main street has meant that the houses are tightly packed, producing a pleasing jumble of styles. It is a fascinating town to explore and Tewkesbury Abbey is one of the finest Norman buildings in the country. The interior is magnificent, particularly in the presbytery, where the roof is supported by superb vaulting. Several medieval stained-glass windows have survived, depicting the Last Judgment and the Coronation of the Virgin.

Leave Tewkesbury on the A38, SP 'Gloucester'. In 3 miles turn right on to the B4213, SP 'Ledbury', then in ½ mile bear right for Deerhurst.

DEERHURST, Glos
The village has the distinction of possessing 2 Saxon churches. St Mary's was built in the 9th and 10th centuries, while Odda's Chapel, an outstanding Saxon survival, was dedicated in 1056, as an inscribed stone, now in the Ashmolean Museum at Oxford, proves. The chapel was 'lost' for centuries, as it had been incorporated in a half-timbered farmhouse, until found in 1965.

Continue to Apperley and in 1 mile turn right on to the B4213 then take the next turning left, SP 'Norton'. Continue to Norton, and at the T-junction, turn right, then right again on to the A38, SP 'Gloucester'. In 1 mile turn left on to an unclassified road for Down Hatherley, then in another mile turn left on to the B4063, SP 'Cheltenham'. At the next roundabout join the A40 for the return to Cheltenham.

CROPTHORNE, Herefs & Worcs
Black and white cottages set in pretty gardens characterise this charming village overlooking the River Avon. In the church are monuments to the Dingley family, whose descendants became mayors of Evesham but lost respectability in the 18th century when Samuel Dingley murdered his brother in cold blood after years of quarrels and bitter rivalry.

Continue through Cropthorne to Charlton. Turn right, then in 1½ miles turn left to rejoin the A44. In 1¼ miles, turn left on to the A435 to enter Evesham.

EVESHAM, Herefs & Worcs
The town stands in a bend of the River Avon, the hub of a fertile region of orchards in the Vale of Evesham. In the centre of the market place is the charming half-timbered Round House (Booth Hall) with overhanging upper storeys and gabled attics. It was not a market hall originally, despite its position, but one of the many attractive old inns that Evesham has preserved in its pleasant streets. From the market place an old gateway leads to the abbey gardens where there is a splendid 16th-century bell tower, once a part of the ruined abbey. Flanking the bell tower are the 2

churches of St Nicholas and All Saints.

Leave Evesham on the A435, SP 'Birmingham', and in 1½ miles turn left for Lenchwick. At the T-junction, turn left, and continue to Church Lench. Here turn right then left for Rous Lench.

ROUS LENCH, Herefs & Worcs
There are 5 little villages, all within a stone's throw of each other, that bear the name Lench. Rous Lench is the largest and prettiest of the villages. It takes its name from the Rouses, a local family, one of whom, in the late 19th century, built most of the attractive houses that stand around the shady village green. The old manor house (not open) is famous for its topiary yew garden, which dates back 300 years, and can be glimpsed from the main road.

Continue through Rous Lench and in 1 mile, at a T-junction, turn left for Flyford Flavell. In ½ mile join the A422 and continue through Upton Snodsbury to Broughton Hackett. In 1¼ miles a detour can be taken by continuing on the A422 for ¾ mile to Spetchley Park.

The ornate Neptune Fountain in Cheltenham's Promenade is based on the famous Trevi Fountain in Rome

THE MALVERN HILLS AND THE VALE OF GLOUCESTER

The stark outlines of the Malvern Hills, an ancient natural rampart, are never far from view as the tour follows the pleasant valley of the River Leadon and skirts the fringe of the Royal Forest of Dean, before turning northwards to run through the Vale of Gloucester and the broad valley of the Severn.

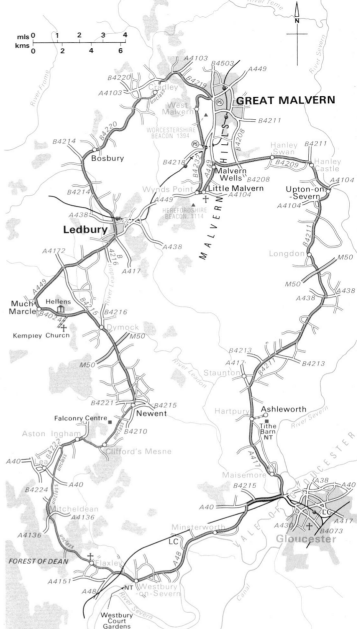

GT MALVERN, Herefs & Worcs

The distinctive character of this busy holiday centre was established in the Victorian and Edwardian periods when people came to take the waters and promenade in the Winter Gardens. Great rambling houses looking out across the town towards Worcester cling precariously to the steep slope of the dramatic Malvern Hills. The town itself clusters around the ancient priory church, a magnificent building which contains exquisite 15th- and 16th-century stained glass and beautiful tiles from the same period. Above the main street of the town by the Mount Pleasant Hotel, a steep flight of steps leads up to St Anne's Well, the source of the pure water for which visitors flocked to Malvern. Among many distinguished residents, the most famous was the composer Sir Edward Elgar, in whose memory an annual festival is held. George Bernard Shaw was a frequent visitor, and several of his plays received their world premiere at the festival.

Herefordshire Beacon, a summit of the Malvern range, is where Owain Glyndwr rallied his forces in 1405

THE MALVERN HILLS, Herefs & Worcs

The Malvern Hills rise abruptly from the broad, flat valley of the River Severn, an impressive 9-mile range of wild, upland country, from where 14 counties can be seen on a clear day. The Worcestershire Beacon at the northern end is the highest (1,395ft) point and the entire length of the ridge can be walked to the Herefordshire Beacon (1,114ft) at the south. The banks of a great Iron-Age fort, known as the British Camp, crown this hill, which Elgar used as the setting for *Caractacus*.

Leave Great Malvern on the B4219, SP 'Worcester' then 'Hereford'. In 2 miles turn left on to the A4103 and in 1 mile turn left on to an unclassified road for Cradley. Beyond the village turn right, SP 'Bromyard', and later turn left on to the B4220, SP 'Ledbury', and continue to Bosbury.

BOSBURY, Herefs & Worcs

Bosbury stands on the banks of the River Leadon, in the centre of a fertile hop and fruit growing region. The village has a charming street of black and white houses around an imposing Norman church with a detached tower. Inside the church, 2 remarkable 16th-century monuments to members of the Harcourt family face each other in baroque splendour.

¾ mile beyond Bosbury turn left on to the B4214, and continue past hop fields to Ledbury.

LEDBURY, Herefs & Worcs

An unspoilt town with a wealth of 16th- and 17th-century black and white buildings, Ledbury is set in a lovely corner of the English countryside where rich green meadows are watered by slow-moving streams. The main street, lined with old houses, leads to the market place where the 17th-century market house, timbered in a herringbone pattern, stands on pillars of oak. Here the Feathers Hotel rubs shoulders with the medieval chapel of St Katherine's Hospital, and a narrow cobbled lane where the houses project over the street takes the visitor straight back to Elizabethan England. At the end of the lane, St Michael's Church displays the grandeur of a small cathedral. Inside is a formidable collection of monuments of every period from the medieval to the 19th-century. Elizabeth Barrett Browning's stern father, Edward Moulton Barrett, lies in the north aisle.

At the crossroads in Ledbury turn right on to the A449, SP 'Ross', and continue to Much Marcle.

MUCH MARCLE, Herefs & Worcs

Cider-making has been a local industry around Much Marcle for nearly 400 years and in the 19th century a local firm was one of the first to build a cider factory. There are 2 manor houses in this attractive black and white village: Homme House (not open) and Hellens, a lovely old brick house (OACT) whose ancestry goes back to Norman times, although the present building is mostly 16th century. The church contains some exquisitely sculptured tombs, including a rare 14th-century oak figure of a man carved from a single block of wood.

Turn left on to the B4024, SP 'Newent'. After 1½ miles a detour can be taken to Kempley Church by turning right on to an unclassified road.

KEMPLEY CHURCH, Glos

The village, whose inhabitants once attended services in Kempley Church, has moved away to Kempley Green, leaving the old vicarage and 17th-century farmhouse isolated beside the Norman Church of St Mary. This small building is unique in England for the series of frescoes in the chancel painted between 1130 and 1140. The centre-piece shows Christ seated on a rainbow, surrounded by sun, moon, stars and the emblems of the Evangelists. Other figures include the Virgin Mary, St Peter and the Apostles.

The main tour continues on the B4024. In 1 mile, turn right on to the B4215 for Dymock, pleasantly situated in the Leadon valley. In 3½ miles turn right, then left, into Newent.

NEWENT, Glos

This small, essentially Georgian, town lies in the heart of an intensely rural part of Gloucestershire. The crooked main street has some well-kept 18th-century houses and a few older, timber-framed buildings, including a market house standing on posts, whose one large upper room is approached by outside stairs.

In the town turn right on to an unclassified road , SP 'Cliffords Mesne'. After 1¼ miles pass the Falconry Centre.

FALCONRY CENTRE, Glos

The ancient art of falconry can be studied at this fascinating centre (OACT) which specialises in birds of prey. There is an interesting museum with many photographs and displays about birds of prey; a wide variety of birds in aviaries; a falcon flying ground and a Hawk Walk where hawks are kept.

Continue through Cliffords Mesne SP 'Ashton Ingham', and in ¾ mile keep left to join the B4222, SP 'Ross', to Aston Ingham. In 1 mile keep forward, SP 'Mitcheldean'. In 1½ miles cross the main road, then in another 1½ miles join the B4224 into Mitcheldean which lies at the northern edge of the Forest of Dean.

THE FOREST OF DEAN, Glos

The Forest of Dean is one of the most ancient royal forests in Britain. For centuries this was an important industrial area, as a vast coalfield underlies the woodland, and iron ore has been worked here since Roman times. Weapons for the Crusades were forged here, and in Tudor times trees were felled to provide timber for warships. These days the Forest has been made more accessible by nature trails, picnic sites and way-marked routes.

At the far end of Mitcheldean go over the crossroads, SP 'Flaxley and Westbury', to follow a pleasant byroad, passing Flaxley. In 1½ miles turn left on to the A48, SP 'Gloucester', and at Westbury-on-Severn pass Westbury Court Gardens.

WESTBURY COURT GARDENS, Glos

Very few of the formal water gardens, modelled in the 17th-century after the Dutch style, survived the 'landscaping' craze of the 18th-century. However, Westbury Court Gardens (NT) lay forlorn and derelict for years, its hedges overgrown, its canals silted up, and its lawns covered with weeds and so remains as one of the best examples of its time. Ten years of devoted work and replanting have restored its elegant design, and the charming colonnaded pavilion has been rebuilt. Plants that are known from records to have flourished there originally have been replanted, including old roses, quince and morello cherry trees.

Continue on the A48, following the River Severn before reaching Minsterworth, a good viewpoint for the famous Severn Bore tidal wave. In 2 miles, at the roundabout, join the A40. There are distant views of Gloucester, with its cathedral, before the tour turns left on to the A417, SP 'Ledbury'. Follow the River Severn through Maisemore to Hartpury, where there is a fine, old tithe barn near the church. A detour can be taken by turning right to Ashleworth.

ASHLEWORTH, Glos

The pretty cottages in this charming little village, tucked away down a country lane, are grouped about a green. Another lane leads to Ashleworth Quay, down by the River Severn, where a church, a manor house (not open) and a great 16th-century tithe barn (NT) make up an outstanding group of medieval limestone buildings. The barn is 125ft long and has a magnificent roof.

The main tour continues on the A417. In 1¼ miles turn right on to the B4211, SP 'Upton-on-Severn'. In 5 miles, at the T-junction, turn right then left, continuing to Longdon with views of the distant Malvern Hills to the left. In 2¼ miles turn right on to the A4104 for Upton-on-Severn.

UPTON-ON-SEVERN, Herefs & Worcs

A delightful reminder of country towns as they used to be, with old-fashioned shops, old inns and streets where it is a joy to stand and look around. Looking out over the meadows of the River Severn, the old church tower, crowned with an 8-sided cupola, is the sole remnant of the original parish church. Locally known as the 'Pepperpot' it is now a Heritage Centre showing the development of the town and the Civil War battle of Upton Bridge.

In Upton-on-Severn turn left, then keep forward on the B4211, SP 'Malvern', to Hanley Castle. Turn left again on to the B4209, SP 'Malvern Wells', to pass through Hanley Swan, and continue to Malvern Wells.

MALVERN WELLS, Herefs & Worcs

Malvern Wells is a continuation of Great Malvern, liberally sprinkled with the gracious villas of a bygone age. In the churchyard of St Wulstan's Church at Little Malvern where primroses and violets flower among the graves in spring, is the simple tombstone to the composer Sir Edward Elgar and his wife.

At Malvern Wells turn left on to the A449, SP 'Ledbury', and 'Ross', and ascend to Wynds Point, a notable viewpoint beneath the Herefordshire Beacon. At the British Camp Hotel turn right on to the B4232, SP 'West Malvern', along Jubilee Drive. In 2¼ miles turn right, then left, and skirt the Worcestershire Beacon to West Malvern. Continue on the B4232 for the return to Great Malvern.

GLOUCESTER, Glos

The Romans, the first to build here, created a fortified port as a springboard for their invasion of Wales, and the town later became one of the 4 *coloniae* from which Rome ruled Britain. Today Gloucester is still an inland port; a canal, opened in 1837, connects the city's docks with the River Severn and can accommodate ships of up to 1,000 tons. After the Romans left the Saxons occupied the town, and made it a *burgh,* but it was not until the Normans arrived that tangible evidence of occupation was left, for they brought with them the will and knowledge to create Gloucester Cathedral. Their church remains at the heart of the cathedral, and, as later generations added without destroying what had gone before, Gloucester preserves an unparalleled display of ecclesiastical architecture through the ages. Within the church the tomb of murdered Edward II and the glorious east window, which commemorates the Battle of Crecy in 1346, are renowned for their quality and beauty. The city retains as its main streets the 4 Roman roads which meet at the cross in the town centre. Along these ancient routes survive some old houses from Gloucester's past. A little square of medieval England remains in Northgate Street as the outer galleried courtyard of the timbered New Inn. In 1555, Bishop John Hooper spent his last night before being burnt at the stake in the house which now bears his name in Westgate Street. This splendid 16th-century building houses a superb folk museum, where trades and crafts of the past are displayed, along with numerous items of historical interest connected with the city and the county.

Leave the city centre on the A430, SP 'Bristol (A38)'. In 2¼ miles, at the roundabout, take the B4008, SP 'Quedgeley'. In ½ mile, turn right, SP 'Elmore'. After ¾ mile, at the River Severn, the famous Severn Bore can be seen during the spring and autumn high tides, when the bore waves force their way up the narrow estuary. In 1¼ miles, at the T-junction, turn right for Elmore.

ELMORE, Glos

Tucked away in the Vale of Gloucester is Elmore village, a gathering of cruck-framed barns and timbered, thatched cottages clustered about a church and a churchyard renowned for its 18th-century table tombs. Acanthus and hart's tongue fern decorate the wrought iron gates of Elmore Court (not open), a mostly Elizabethan manor with a Georgian wing. Built on ground which the Guise family has owned since the 13th century, the house is delightfully situated in a loop of the Severn.

THE VALE OF BERKELEY AND THE SEVERN VALLEY

Along the Vale of Berkeley, beside the River Severn, are flat fertile lands where cattle grew fat and lords built great houses. Higher up, on the Cotswolds, the land changes and becomes a chequerboard of stone-walled fields beneath limitless skies.

A Whooper swan taking off — just one of the 2,500-odd birds kept at the Severn Wildfowl Trust

In 1¼ miles turn left and continue to Longney. Here turn right, SP 'Saul and Frampton', then in ¾ mile, at the T-junction, turn right again for Epney. At Saul join the B4071 and in ¾ mile turn left across the swing bridge, then in ½ mile, at the crossroads, turn right to Frampton-on-Severn.

FRAMPTON-ON-SEVERN, Glos

The road splits a 22-acre village green bordered by Georgian brick houses. On the left lies 18th-century Frampton Court (not open) home of the Clifford family. In the grounds, beyond the chestnut trees which partly screen the house from the road, a delightful Gothic orangery by William Halfpenny overlooks a rectangular canal sunk in landscaped surroundings. The green ends past the duck pond and thatched and gabled houses converge towards the heart of the village. Here is the spacious church, and closeby is the Berkeley-Gloucester canal, and a canal keeper's house with a pedimented portico.

VALE OF BERKELEY, Glos

Some 700ft below the Cotswold escarpment lies the Vale of Berkeley, a great expanse of flat land beneath huge skies bounded by distant horizons: a rich area of fat cattle, orchards and old timber-framed dairy-farms. The thick deposit of clay, in places over 700ft deep, is a prime raw material for the manufacture of bricks and tiles.

Return to the B4071 and turn right, then in 1½ miles, turn right on to the A38, SP 'Bristol', and continue to Cambridge. In ¾ mile, turn right for Slimbridge. 1 mile beyond the village, cross the canal bridge for the Severn Wildfowl Trust.

SEVERN WILDFOWL TRUST, Glos

An area of flat marshland between the Gloucester and Sharpness canal and the River Severn has been reserved solely for birds. Their host is a Wildfowl Trust, founded in 1964 by Sir Peter Scott to study and preserve wildfowl throughout the world. This is one of the finest collections in the world, where some 180 species are kept out of the known 247. The Trust caters admirably for the visitor, and its real work of preservation and research has an unparalleled record which is well documented in the main hall. One example of the value of the work is the story of the Hawaiian goose. Only 42 birds were known to be alive in 1952, but since then, from 3 birds procured by Sir Peter Scott, more than 800 have been bred and either distributed to zoos or returned to their natural habitat in the wild.

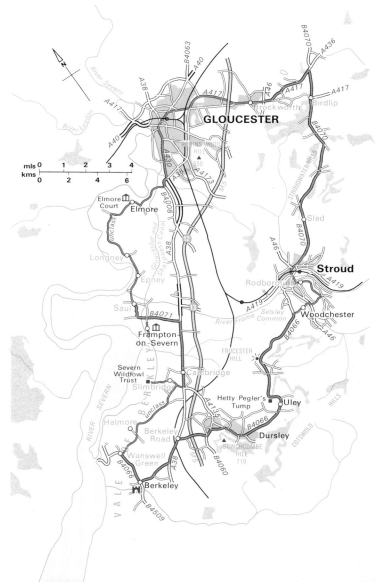

Return to Slimbridge and beyond the church turn right, SP 'Halmore', then in 1 mile, at the T-junction, turn right again. Follow a narrow byroad across flat countryside and after 2¼ miles turn left and immediately right for Wanswell Green. Here turn left on to the B4066 for Berkeley.

BERKELEY, Glos
A quiet Georgian town, Berkeley is dominated by 2 giants, Berkeley Castle from the past and an Atomic Power Station of the future. The castle (OACT) is a rugged sentinel of 900 years of English history, built in 1153 by permission of Henry I and home of the Berkeley family for centuries. It is still more a fortress than a stately home, and is best remembered for an act of violence. In 1327, Edward II was kept prisoner here and brutally murdered in the guardroom at the instigation of his wife and the Earl of Mortimer.

Follow SP 'Bristol' then keep forward, SP 'Gloucester', and in 1½ mile bear left to join the A38. At Berkeley Road turn right on to the B4066, SP 'Dursley'. In 2¼ miles turn right on to the A4135 for Dursley.

DURSLEY, Glos
Dursley's Market Hall of 1738, raised up on 12 arches of stone and graced by a statue of Queen Anne, keeps company with some elegant Georgian homes in a town which in recent years has experienced a flurry of new buildings and an influx of industry which has revitalised the community. The church has a 15th-century chapel, built of Tufa stone by a rich wool merchant, and a Gothic tower of the 1700s.

In Dursley turn left (one-way) and follow SP 'Stroud'. At the end of the town turn left on to the B4066 for Uley.

ULEY, Glos
Spilling down a hillside, distinguished houses of the 17th and 18th centuries are a legacy of Uley's success as a weaving community. Broadcloths, Spanish cloths and a blue dye of excellent quality were made here.

From Uley climb on to the Cotswolds. After 1½ miles, (left) is Hetty Pegler's Tump.

HETTY PEGLERS TUMP, Glos
Hetty Pegler's Tump (AM), is a Neolithic long barrow measuring 180ft by 90ft, where 28 people were buried in the stone-walled burial chamber. There are fine views over the Severn to the Welsh Mountains from the top.

Continue along a ridge, with good views, particularly at the Frocester Hill Viewpoint (NT). In 2¾ miles, turn right on to an unclassified road to Woodchester.

Above: a detail of the painting that decorates the inside of a wooden chest which belonged to Sir Francis Drake and is now kept at Berkeley Castle

Below: the cloisters of Gloucester Cathedral were built between 1351 and 1377

WOODCHESTER, Glos
One of the largest Roman villas found in England stood here, and in the churchyard a remarkable mosaic of Orpheus is occasionally on display, though it is mostly kept covered. The Industrial Revolution shaped the Woodchester of today and left it many fine clothiers houses, such as Southfield Mill House, and the Victorian mills which brought them prosperity.

Turn right on to the A46, then take the 1st turning left, SP 'Rodborough Common'. By the Bear Inn PH, turn left then left again, SP 'Rodborough', to cross the lofty Rodborough Common (NT). Descend through Rodborough before rejoining the A46 to enter Stroud.

STROUD, Glos
The River Frome and its tributaries powered 150 cloth mills here by 1824, and with the advent of steam, a canal was built to bring coal from the Midlands for the new machinery which brought Stroud into the forefront of England's broadcloth industry. The town still supplies most of the world's demand for greenbaize billiard table cloth. Stroud is also famous for its scarlet dyes, which were used to give the 'Redcoats' of the military their characteristic hue. Some of the old mills remain in this hilly town of narrow streets, though few of the wealthy clothiers houses have survived. The museum at Lansdown illustrates old methods of cloth weaving, many local crafts and past industries of the town. The Archaeological Room displays finds from barrows at nearby Rodborough and Nymphsfield.

Leave Stroud on the B4070, SP 'Birdlip', and gradually climb up to the Stroudwater Hills to Slad. Continue, to Birdlip. Turn right into the village then turn left on to the A417, SP 'Gloucester'. Magnificent views can be seen across the Severn Vale to the distant Malvern Hills. At the next roundabout take the 1st exit and return to Gloucester.

STRATFORD-UPON-AVON, Warwicks

Sir Hugh Clopton's 14-arched medieval stone bridge is still, as it has been since Shakespeare's day, the main gateway to Stratford. The house in Henley Street, where the poet was born on 23 April 1564, is a substantial timber-framed building preserved by the Shakespeare Birthplace Trust (OACT) as a museum, but the house he bought after becoming successful, New Place, was wantonly destroyed by an 18th-century owner. The foundations remain, however, and a delightful Elizabethan knot garden has been planted on the site. Hall's Croft, where the poet's daughter Susanna lived with her husband, Dr John Hall, contains a fascinating collection of Elizabethan medical implements. The most elaborate timbered house in Stratford is Harvard House, built in 1596 by the grandparents of John Harvard, who sailed to America, and on his death left £799 17s 2d with which to found Harvard University. The Royal Shakespeare Theatre, built in 1932, dominates the riverside, striking a startlingly modern note amid the old buildings of the town. It incorporates a museum and art gallery. Holy Trinity Church is Shakespeare's burial place: he died in 1616 and lies under the chancel with Susanna and John Hall. As a change from the Shakespearean connections of Stratford, the Motor Museum is a superb evocation of 1920s motoring history, specialising in sports and touring cars. There are several gardens laid out on the banks of the Avon which provide a welcome respite from the bustle of the town.

Leave Stratford on the A439, SP 'Evesham'. After ½ mile a short detour to the right may be taken along Shottery Road to the hamlet of Shottery.

The Tudor gatehouse of Coughton Court dominates the 18th-century west front that was built around it

SHOTTERY, Warwicks

Tourists flock to this pretty little hamlet across the fields from Stratford to see the idyllic thatched and timbered cottage (OACT) where Anne Hathaway lived and where Shakespeare came to woo her. Original Tudor furniture and fascinating domestic items are displayed in the old rooms. The Hathaway family lived in the house from 1470 until 1911, when it was acquired by the Shakespeare Birthplace Trust.

The main tour continues on the A439 along the shallow valley of the River Avon and later skirts Bidford-on-Avon.

A fascinating array of rural bygones can be seen in the barns belonging to Mary Arden's cottage in Wilmcote

78

SHAKESPEARE AND THE HEART OF ENGLAND

Among the winding lanes of Warwickshire and Worcestershire a wealth of timber, thatch and stone, seen in country cottage, village church and stately home, revives the atmosphere of Tudor England. From the interplay of forest and farmland, garden and park, Shakespeare drew the stirring imagery of his writing.

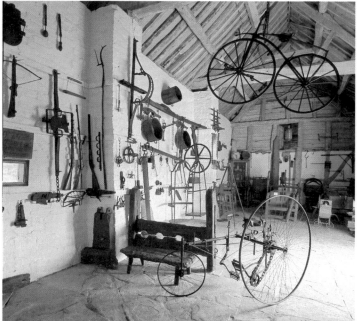

BIDFORD-ON-AVON, Warwicks

Shakespeare's connection with Bidford was the Falcon Inn, a handsome gabled building which still stands, though it is now a private house. The poet is known to have enjoyed many a drinking bout at the Falcon, and is popularly supposed to have composed the 4 lines of doggerel that end: 'Dodging Exhall, Papist Wixford, Beggarly Broom and drunken Bidford'.

Remain on the Evesham road and in 3 miles turn right on to an unclassified road to enter Harvington. Here turn right, SP 'The Lenches', then at the end of the village cross the main road and continue to Church Lench.

THE LENCHES, Herefs & Worcs

Five villages with the name Lench are dotted about the countryside north of Evesham, and 2 of them, Church and Rous Lench, lie on the route. Lench comes from an old English word meaning 'hill', and this part of the country, near the old Warwickshire border is an area of little hills. Each has a distinctive charm, but Rous Lench is perhaps the most interesting (see tour 30).

At Church Lench turn right to reach Rous Lench. Continue on the Inkberrow road and in 1 mile, at the T-junction, turn right, SP 'Alcester'. In another 1½ miles turn left for Abbots Morton.

ABBOTS MORTON, Herefs & Worcs

Often described as the most perfect village in the country, Abbots Morton is rich in black and white timbered cottages of all shapes and sizes. Its lovely 14th-century stone church stands surrounded by trees on a small mound overlooking the village, while on the green stands a thatched letterbox.

Bear right into the village and ¾ mile further, at the T-junction, turn left. In 1½ miles turn right on to the A441, then in another ½ mile, turn left on to the A435, SP 'Birmingham'. Later pass the entrance to Ragley Hall.

RAGLEY HALL, Warwicks

A stately Jacobean mansion of 15 bays, built between 1680 and 1690 by Robert Hooks for the 1st Earl of Conway, Ragley Hall (OACT) is one of the finest houses in England. Much of the sumptuous interior, however, was designed in the 18th century by James Gibbs for the 2nd Baron Conway, later created Earl, the Marquess of Hertford. Showpiece of the house is the great hall, 70ft long, 40ft wide and 40ft high, decorated with exquisite rococo plasterwork. Paintings by great European masters such as Reynolds and Hoppner, and collections of fine porcelain are on display.

Continue to Alcester.

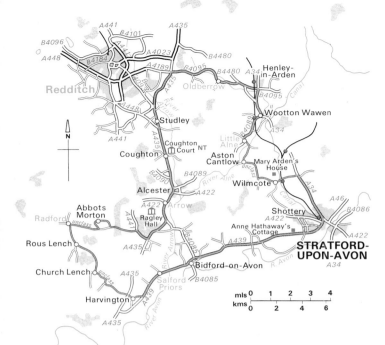

Malt Mill Lane in Alcester is lined by a
remarkable collection of ancient houses
which were renovated in 1975

ALCESTER, Warwicks
This attractive little market town
(pronounced Olster) lies at the
confluence of the Rivers Arrow
and Alne. Its oldest building is the
Old Malt House, a gabled, half
timbered structure dating from
1500, but the narrow streets
contain many charming Jacobean
and Georgian houses; Butter
Street in particular is a delight,
with its rows of picturesque old
cottages. Tudor cottages cluster
about the parish church with its
14th-century west tower, the nave
and aisles having been rebuilt in
the 18th-century. It contains the
fine alabaster tomb of Fulke
Greville, the grandfather of the
Elizabethan poet who was his
namesake. Alcester Mop is a
pleasure fair held in the town
each October.

*Leave on the A435 Birmingham
road and continue to Coughton.*

COUGHTON, Warwicks
The influence of the
Throckmortons predominates in
the 16th-century church, where
monuments and brasses
commemorate generations of this
staunchly Roman Catholic family.
Coughton Court (NT) was the
family home, its Tudor stone
gatehouse flanked by warm-toned
stucco giving entrance to a
courtyard with 2 timbered wings.
As befits a Roman Catholic house,
there is a hidden chapel, reached
by a rope ladder, in one of the
turrets, and many Jacobite relics.
The Throckmortons were
implicated in the 1605 Gunpowder
Plot, and it was at Coughton that
the family and friends of the
conspirators waited anxiously for
news. In the saloon is the famous
Throckmorton coat, made for a bet
in 1811 from wool sheared at
sunrise and woven into a coat by
sunset of the same day.

Continue through Studley.

STUDLEY, Warwicks
Pleasant countryside surrounds
this small town which is possibly
the largest centre of needle-
making in Europe. Since 1800,
when steam power was
introduced, the industry has been
mechanised, but the tradition goes
back for more than 300 years, and
there are many old houses dating
from the 17th century.

*At the end of the town go forward
at the roundabout, -SP
'Birmingham'. Nearly 2 miles
farther turn right on to the B4095
and continue to Henley-in-Arden.*

HENLEY-IN-ARDEN, Warwicks
Once, as the last part of the name
suggests, Henley lay in the great
Forest of Arden. Its ¾ mile-long
broad main street is bordered by
timbered houses and inns of all
periods and makes a charming
picture. Many of the inns date
from the great coaching age of the
18th-century when Henley was
served daily by a mail coach and 4
post coaches.

*Leave on the A34 Stratford Road to
reach Wootton Wawen.*

WOOTTON WAWEN, Warwicks
The fine village church exhibits
features of almost every style of
English architecture, from Anglo-
Danish to the late Middle Ages.
Parts of the crossing tower are the
most ancient, but there are
examples of Norman, early
English, Decorated and
Perpendicular styles as well as
features of the 17th, 18th and
19th centuries. The village is
attractive, with a graceful 17th-
century hall (not open) which was
the childhood home of Mrs
Fitzherbert whom the Prince
Regent, later George IV, loved and
with whom he illegally contracted
a secret marriage in 1785.

*Leave on the B4089 Alcester Road.
In 2 miles branch left, SP 'Aston
Cantlow'. Cross the river bridge and
turn right for Aston Cantlow.*

Ragley Hall commands sweeping views
over its parkland to the distant Cotswolds

ASTON CANTLOW, Warwicks
This church is very probably the
one in which John Shakespeare
and Mary Arden, Shakespeare's
parents, were married in 1557,
though the church records begin
only in 1560. The Victorian
architect William Butterfield
designed the pretty cottages,
vicarage, school and master's
house near the church, and the
rest of the village is a pleasing
mixture of black and white
timbered houses offset by terraces
of red brick. The name Cantlow
comes from the Cantelupe family,
and Thomas Cantelupe, rector of
the village church later became
Chancellor of England and Bishop
of Hereford. In 1282 he died while
on pilgrimage to Rome and was
subsequently (1320) canonized, the
only Warwickshire rector to be so
honoured and the last Englishman
to be canonized until after the
Reformation.

*Go forward through the village,
then turn left, SP 'Wilmcote'. In 1
mile turn left again for Wilmcote.*

WILMCOTE, Warwicks
The highlight of Wilmcote is the
lovely timbered farmhouse that
was the home of Mary Arden,
Shakespeare's mother. Simply
furnished, in period, the old
timbered house, surrounded by a
charming old-fashioned cottage
garden, retains a strong sense of
atmosphere, enhanced by the
collection of old Warwickshire
agricultural implements housed in
the stone barns belonging to the
house (OACT).

*Turn left, SP 'Stratford', then in 1
mile turn right on to the A34 for
the return to Stratford-upon-Avon.*

Wales and
the Marcher Lands

HAVERFORDWEST, Dyfed

Houses crowd the steep slopes of Haverfordwest under the stern gaze of the old castle which overlooks them all. Built in the 13th century by William de Valence, a Fleming, it has always been a centre of power. Haverfordwest, isolated from England by the southern valleys and constant battles, was ruled by Norman lords, who, unlike their fellow invaders elsewhere in the country, refused to inter-marry. Thus this part of Pembrokeshire became known as Little England beyond Wales. In 1405 Owain Glyndwr burnt the town during his bid to reassert Welsh independence, but the castle survived. Unscathed, it did surrender to Parliament in the Civil War, but when a fresh revolt against the Puritans broke out, Cromwell had the castle 'slighted'. The noble keep which remains is now the county museum and art gallery. Once the main sea-link with Ireland, before the growth of Milford Haven in the 19th century, Haverfordwest is now an important market and administrative centre. The old Butter Market survives, and of the 3 churches, St Mary's is the finest.

Leave Haverfordwest on the A4076, SP 'Milford Haven'. Pass through Johnston and Steynton to reach the coast at Milford Haven.

MILFORD HAVEN, Dyfed

Nelson called this drowned valley the best harbour in the world, and to it the town of Milford Haven owes its existence. In the late 18th century Milford was developed as a fishing port and naval dockyard by Charles Greville. Disaster struck in 1814 when the naval dockyard was moved to Pembroke Dock, but Milford retaliated by rapidly becoming a deep-sea fishing port with the fourth largest catch in Britain. The town's closely-ranked houses climb a smooth rounded hill, and from their perches witnessed the departure of 170,000 ships in convoys during World War II, and saw the growth of 4 great oil refineries and a massive power station along the Haven's shores. Yet despite this tremendous development, which obviously has had some effect on the natural surroundings, the greater proportion of the Haven has remained undisturbed and in fact the upper reaches have been designated a nature reserve. The town itself retains a neat harbour used by fishing trawlers, pleasant gardens and an excellent shopping centre.

Turn right along the promenade and at the war memorial turn left. At the end of the town turn left across the bridge then right, SP 'Hubberston' and 'Dale'. At the edge of Herbrandston turn right, SP 'Dale', and continue along a high-banked road. After 5 miles turn left on to the B4327 for Dale.

LITTLE ENGLAND BEYOND WALES

This is England's Wales, where the Normans settled and the Welsh never regained supremacy. Place-names in both languages appear in this corner of Wales that is mostly a National Park, catering for seaside tourists yet caring for the rare wildlife.

The Fishguard Bay Yacht Club has its headquarters at Fishguard's Lower Town, where the Gwaun joins the sea

DALE, Dyfed

Dale is a pleasant little village lying just within the mouth of Milford Haven. It has all the atmosphere, sights and sounds of a small yachting centre, and is conveniently placed near some fine sandy beaches; Musselwick Sands, Martin's Haven from where boats sail to Skomer Island, Marloes Sands and Westdale Bay. Henry VII landed from France at nearby Mill Bay in 1485, to begin a venture which brought him victory over Richard III at Bosworth and consequently the throne of England.

Return along the B4327 and in 1½ miles pass a turning to the left for Martin's Haven. In ¾ mile keep left, then bear right with the Haverfordwest road. Nearly 2 miles farther go forward SP 'Talbenny' and 'Little Haven'. Pass through Talbenny and later turn left for the descent to Little Haven. On the steep ascent turn sharp left, SP 'Broad Haven', then descend to Broad Haven.

BROAD HAVEN, Dyfed

A silver strand of sand a mile wide make Broad Haven and its neighbour, Little Haven, ideal stopping places for a day on the beach. Strangely-folded cliffs border the bay and this beautiful remote area is renowned for its rare wild flowers, sea-birds and magnificent coastal scenery. Broad Haven itself is a busy place and in the car park is the countryside unit of the Pembrokeshire Coast National Park, which provides information on talks, walks and excursions for those who would like to know more of this delightful countryside.

PEMBROKESHIRE COAST NATIONAL PARK, Dyfed

The upper reaches of Milford Haven, the Preseli Hills, the coast and its outlying islands are all included in a National Park covering about a third of Pembrokeshire. The wild coastline where seals breed and hundreds of seabirds feed is a naturalists' paradise — home of the peregrine falcon and the rare chough. The best way to explore the coastal areas is by way of the 167-mile coastal path which can be joined at almost any point along its length between Amroth and St Dogmaels. The path was officially opened in 1970.

At the end of Broad Haven keep forward (no SP) along highbanked roads. In 2¾ miles, at a crossroads, turn left, SP 'Nolton'. Pass through Nolton and bear right for Nolton Haven.

NOLTON HAVEN, Dyfed

In this narrow inlet of St Bride's Bay, high cliffs shelter a farm, a chapel, a few sleepy cottages and a sandy beach which is exposed only at low tide. A tradition associated with this coastline is the collection of seaweed for the making of laver bread, best eaten with bacon or, some say, with porridge.

Continue, passing the long, sandy beaches of Newgale Sands and at the main road turn left on to the A487 for Newgale.

NEWGALE, Dyfed

This modern holiday village faces 2½ miles of sandy beach backed by a pebble bank. At the north-east end of St Bride's Bay the winds whip up some fine surf, which has made Newgale a popular surfing resort. Very low tides reveal the stumps of a prehistoric forest.

Continue for 3 miles to Solva.

SOLVA, Dyfed

Solva appears at its best — a huddle of white, typically-Welsh cottages, hugging the hillside along the half mile of Solva Creek — from Gribin Head (NT). The village was favoured by smugglers, but this sheltered spot in an otherwise rocky and inhospitable coastline, was soon sought out by ships carrying lime and coal. Some disused lime kilns of the 19th century still stand near the road bridge. Today the amateur sailor reigns in the harbour, and the sailing club offers excellent facilities in St Bride's Bay. The Middle Mill at Solva, a watermill open to visitors, produces woollen weaves and hand-made furniture.

Continue on the A487 to St David's.

The Pembrokeshire Coast path near Solva

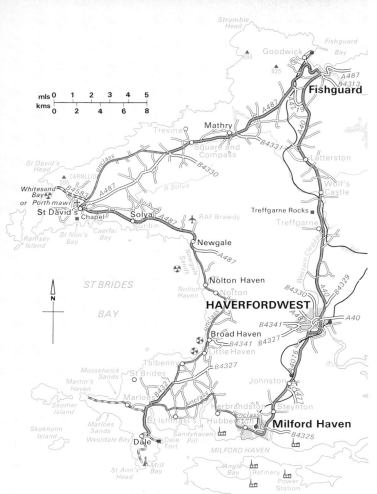

ST DAVID'S, Dyfed

Hardly more than a village, yet to every Welshman St David's is a hallowed place. St David, a descendant of the ancient Kings of Wales and patron saint of Wales, was born and lived here. Now his bones lie in the great cathedral, begun in 1180, which was some 500 years after his death. It was thought to be built in the shallow vale where it stands to hide it from the sea and possible invaders. The plain exterior belies the richly decorated interior. The floor slopes about 3ft from west to east, and the piers of the nave lean outward — an earthquake in 1248 was the cause of that. In front of the high altar lies the tomb of Edmund Tudor, father of Henry VII and between it and the Holy Trinity Chapel is an iron-bound chest containing the bones of St David and his teacher, St Justinian. Remnants of St David's original shrine are kept on the north side of the presbytery. It was badly damaged during the years in which the cathedral suffered neglect until Sir Gilbert Scott was commissioned in 1826 to renovate the building. The Bishop's Palace (AM) was built in 1340 to house pilgrims visiting the shrine, and there are extensive remains.

Leave on the A487 Fishguard road and in ½ mile turn left on to the B4583, SP 'Whitesands', then pass on the left the road which leads to Whitesand Bay.

WHITESAND BAY, Dyfed

Whitesand Bay, or Porth Mawr, is well-known for its excellent surfing and sweep of beautiful sands. In the early days of Christianity the bay saw many comings and goings to Ireland, and it is said St Patrick himself journeyed from here. The ancient chapel, excavated in 1924, is called St Patrick's Chapel in recognition of this.

The main tour continues forward along the unclassified road. In 4¼ miles bear right, SP 'Fishguard', then 1¼ miles further turn left on to the A487 for the outskirts of Mathry.

MATHRY, Dyfed

There is a legend here which tells of a father whose wife bore him 7 children at once; unable to support them and his already large family, he took them to a river to drown them, but they were saved by St Teilo, and thereafter the children were known as the Seven Saints of Mathry.

Continue on the A487, SP 'Fishguard'. At the edge of Goodwick turn right on to the A40 and ascend to Fishguard.

FISHGUARD, Dyfed

In the past herring fishing and pilchard curing were Fishguard's main industries: but in 1906 a new harbour was built, and in the following year so was a breakwater out to sea, both in the expectation that the new Atlantic liners would make Fishguard their first port of call. With the outbreak of World War I these hopes faded and the great liners never came. Fishguard is divided into 2; Upper Fishguard stands back from the sea and from it the road falls steeply to Lower Fishguard, which nestles beside the winding creek, indistinguishable from its counterparts in Cornwall or Brittany. Fishguard is noted in history as the scene of the last invasion of British soil. A French force landed here in 1797: the story goes that the French surrendered to a group of Welsh women in red cloaks and traditional tall hats; the French had thought they were Redcoats. There is a memorial in the churchyard to the heroine Jemima Nicholas, who rounded up a number of the French single-handed armed with only a pitch-fork. Fishguard is an ideal centre for touring, as the coastline here is truly magnificent, especially around Strumble Head and the beautiful Gwaum valley.

Leave on the A40 Haverfordwest road and continue through Wolf's Castle. The drive then enters a narrow Gorge and to the right are the prominent Treffgarne Rocks. From some angles these take on the fantastic shapes of a giant, a lion and a unicorn. Continue on the A40 for the return to Haverfordwest.

ALONG THE DYFED COAST

From the ancient borough of Pembroke with its magnificent castle, through picturesque inland villages, to the rugged red sandstone cliffs and mysterious caves of the coast that abound with mystery and superstition.

TENBY, Dyfed
One of the most popular resorts in South Wales, Tenby is a charming old port with many holiday facilities. See tour 36.

Leave Tenby on the A4139 Pembroke road, with glimpses of the coastline and Caldy Island, to reach Lydstep.

The neat and colourful resort of Tenby offers all the attractions of the seaside, including deep-sea fishing, boating, water-skiing and aqua-diving

LYDSTEP, Dyfed
Lying in the centre of the small village of Lydstep are the ruins of the Palace of Arms. This is said to have been a hunting lodge of Bishop Gower of St David's. The coastal views around Lydstep Point (NT) to the east are breathtaking, and Lydstep Caverns beneath are well worth exploring when accessible at low tide.

Continue on the A4139 and in ½ mile turn left on to the B4585, SP 'Manorbier', to reach Manorbier.

MANORBIER, Dyfed
An imposing stone castle (OACT) perches above the sandy beach of Manorbier Bay with its tidal pools and rocks of red sandstone. The de Barri family, Norman barons, built Manorbier Castle and it was always more a baronial residence than a fortress. Medieval castles were practically self-sufficient and had their own mills, orchards and fields: the stream below powered the castle's corn mills. Giraldus Cambrensis, 'Gerald the Welshman', was born here in 1146, and he claimed it was the 'pleasantest spot in Wales'. A wax model of him can be seen inside the castle.

Keep left (one-way) then turn right, SP 'Pembroke'. In ½ mile turn left on to the A4139 and pass through Jameston and Hodgeston to Lamphey.

LAMPHEY, Dyfed
Just north-east of Lamphey lie the remains of a 13th-century Bishop's Palace. The romantic ruins (AM) — originally set amid elegant gardens, orchards and fishponds — represent one of 7 medieval manors built as country retreats for the Bishops of St David's. Still visible are the arcaded parapets signifying the hand of Bishop Henry Gower, who also contributed to the design of Swansea Castle and the palace at St David's. The Earl of Essex, greatly favoured by Elizabeth I, lived here as a boy.

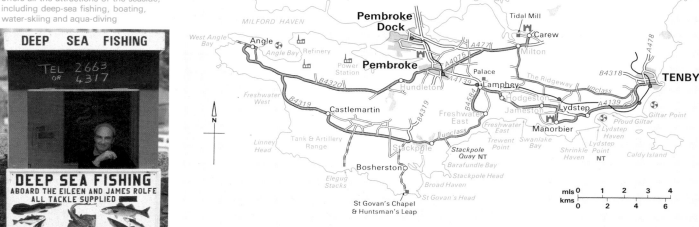

Turn sharp left on to the B4584 to Freshwater East, then turn right on to the unclassified Stackpole road. Descend (1 in 5) and follow a high banked road for 2¼ miles. A road to the left leads to Stackpole Quay.

STACKPOLE QUAY, Dyfed
Stackpole Quay (NT) is an extremely picturesque feature of this stretch of beautiful coastline. The stone jetty was used for the shipping of limestone when the nearby quarry was in use. The beach here is very rocky but a charming cliff path to the south leads to the peaceful sandy beach of Barafundle Bay, behind which lie the dunes of Stackpole Warren.

The main tour continues to Stackpole. Remain on the unclassified road, then turn left on to the B4319. In ½ mile turn right, SP 'Bosherton'. In ½ mile turn right, SP 'Castlemartin'. Alternatively, turn left on to an unclassified road for Bosherton.

BOSHERTON AND ST GOVAN'S CHAPEL, Dyfed
Bosherton is a peaceful village and its group of pools known as Bosherton Lakes make an enchanting picture when the hundreds of water lilies covering them burst into flower. The road through the village leads on to St Govan's Head and, by the steep steps leading down to the sea, lies St Govan's Chapel. The minute building, just 17ft by 12ft, wedged in to a crack in the cliffs, is shrouded with mystery and legend. Who Govan was is uncertain: suppositions vary between King Arthur's knight Sir Gawaine; Coren, wife of a 6th-century prince, or the Irish saint Gobham. Outside the chapel a boulder known as Bell Rock is said to contain a silver bell, which was in the bell tower, but was stolen by pirates; angels brought the bell back and hid it in the rock.

Another legend says the water from a well inside was able to cure skin and eye complaints and a second well below the chapel could cure cripples. Nearby there is a deep narrow ravine called Huntsman's Leap. The story behind the name is that a brave man jumped his horse over it and, having safely landed, died of fright when he realised the great risk he had taken.

The main tour continues to Castlemartin.

CASTLEMARTIN, Dyfed
The once flourishing village of Castlemartin is now a windswept place in the middle of a tank and artillery range. A breed of black cattle, called Castlemartin, was one of the 2 strains which were interbred to become the Welsh Black. The local Norman church contains an organ which belonged to the German composer Mendelssohn.

Turn left, SP 'Angle' and 'Freshwater West'. In 2 miles pass through the sand dunes of Freshwater West with views of St Ann's Head and Skokholm Island. In 1 mile turn left on to the B4320 with glimpses of Angle Bay and Milford Haven. In 1½ miles turn right on to an unclassified road, then descend and turn left into Angle.

ANGLE, Dyfed
A single main street of colour-washed cottages, dominated by the grand colonnaded front of the Globe Hotel, links Angle's 2 tiny harbours which face Milford Haven. Within the boundaries of the churchyard is a small Fisherman's Chapel — dating from 1447 — that has outside steps leading to its upper storey. North of the churchyard is an ancient dovecot: probably dating from

medieval days when doves were an important source of meat.

Pass the church and in ½ mile turn left (forward for West Angle Bay) to leave on the B4320 Pembroke road. In ½ mile turn sharp left and later pass through Hundleton and continue to Pembroke.

PEMBROKE, Dyfed
The ancient borough of Pembroke was built around the great 12th-century fortress of Pembroke Castle (OACT). Beside the sea on a rocky spur above the town, the castle, one of the finest in the country, was once the hub of a complex medieval defence system. Restoration work was started on the castle in 1880 and has been continued at intervals ever since. Beneath the castle lies a huge natural limestone cavern called the 'Wogan', which was linked to the main structure by a winding staircase and has an opening to the river. Pembroke's long main street, running east from the castle, is the scene in October of a centuries-old fair. In many places, notably the Park and the Mill Bridge, the old town walls are still visible. In Commons Road is the National Museum of Gypsy Caravans. It contains a fine collection of caravans, carts and other artefacts related to Romany life.

PEMBROKE DOCK, Dyfed
About 2 miles north of Pembroke town stands this stately dock, built on a grid-iron system with grey buildings lining its straight streets. Until the 1920s it was one of the chief Naval dockyards, but it is now used mainly by ship repairers and chandlers. An obelisk commemorating the launching of the Valorius and the Ariadne c1814, the first 2 ships made here, stands in Albion Square. It was here too that the first steam ship

There has been a mill at Carew on the tidal Cleddau River since 1560

man-of-war — The Tartar; the first Royal yacht — The Victoria and Albert; and the first iron-clad warship — The Warrior were made. The latter is moored at Portsmouth.

From Pembroke join the one-way system and pass Pembroke Castle. Keep forward along the main street, SP 'Tenby', and at the end of town turn left on to the A4075, SP 'Carmarthen'. In 2¼ miles, at the T-junction, turn right on to the A477 to reach edge of Milton. Keep forward, and in ½ mile turn left on to the A4075 for Carew.

CAREW, Dyfed
An ivy-clad ruin stands on the banks of the Cleddau River with only seagulls wheeling overhead for company. Just below the castle is a tidal corn mill and although a mill has stood here since the mid-16th century, the existing 'French' mill (OACT) — 3-storeyed and rectangular — dates from the late 18th century. It is open now as a working museum and utilises the tides by damming the water, then using it as required. A third feature of interest in the village is Carew Cross (AM). It was built during the 11th century and was a great technical achievement in those days. Standing 14ft high, its shaft is inscribed with several traditional Welsh patterns.

Return to the edge of Milton and turn left on to an unclassified road, SP 'Lamphey' and 'Manorbier'. Gradually ascend, and at the T-junction turn left. This road, known as 'The Ridgeway', has occasional all-round panoramic views. Continue following SP 'Tenby' and at the A4139, turn left for the return to Tenby.

THE HINTERLAND OF CARMARTHEN BAY

Ruined fortresses along the sandy coast of Carmarthen Bay stand guard over this peaceful corner of South Wales that inspired the poetry of Dylan Thomas. Carmarthen, at one end of the tour, reflects the antiquity of Wales, while Tenby at the other is a bustling tourist town.

CARMARTHEN, Dyfed

An important local centre with a busy food and cattle market, Carmarthen is believed to be the oldest town in Wales. Narrow, winding streets thread between old houses up to the ruins of the 14th-century castle, now almost completely masked by the imposing modern county hall. Down below, on the River Tywi, traditional Welsh coracles are still used for salmon fishing. The town has a long history going back to Celtic times and CAD75 the Romans built a major fort, *Moridunum*, here: the remains of an amphitheatre have been unearthed near Priory Street. Many fine Roman remains are now displayed in the Carmarthen Museum in the old Bishop's Palace (OACT) at Abergwili, to the north-east of the town. Of the many fine buildings in Carmarthen, the oldest is St Peter's Church, probably dating from the 12th century. The splendid houses beside the church and the elegant Guildhall of 1770 testify to the town's distinguished past. Carmarthen has always been associated with the Arthurian wizard Merlin. He was, reputedly, born near Carmarthen and hid in a crystal cave in Merlin's Hill. The decayed stump of Merlin's Oak is carefully preserved by the townspeople against the prophecy that 'When Merlin's oak shall tumble down then shall fall Carmarthen town'.

Leave Carmarthen on the A40, SP 'Haverfordwest' and 'St Clears'. In 1 mile turn left on to the B4312, SP 'Llanstephan', and at the T-junction turn right. Later run alongside the attractive estuary of the Afon Tywi to reach Llanstephan.

LLANSTEPHAN, Dyfed

The approach to Llanstephan is heralded by a glimpse of the ruined battlements of an impressive medieval castle. Its strategic position at the mouth of the River Tywi ensured a violent and cruel history for this most imposing fortress (OACT). The large, sandy beach below the castle runs up to the waterfront in the village marked by a pleasant, grassy area called The Green. In bygone days cockle-pickers and their donkeys tramped over the sands.

At the church keep forward along an unclassified road, then bear right, SP 'St Clears' and 'Llanybri'. At Llanybri keep forward, SP 'Bancyfelin'. Continue, then keep left and follow a sharply undulating byroad (narrow in places). Nearly 2 miles farther, at the Wern Inn, turn right, then at the war memorial keep left and pass through Llangynog. In 1¼ miles turn left, then ½ mile farther at the main road turn left on to the A40. In 2½ miles join the St Clears Bypass

ST CLEARS, Dyfed

This small agricultural town was famed as one of the centres of the Rebecca Riots in the 1840s (see Rhayader, tour 41). The riots obviously had some effect because in 1884 the toll system was reformed. St Clears' church is one of the oldest in the area and contains some fragments of Norman work, including a font and the carved chancel arch. It was originally the church of the Cluniac Priory, founded by the first Norman Lord of St Clears, of which nothing remains.

From the bypass branch left, SP 'Pendine', and at the T-junction turn right on to the A4066 for Laugharne.

Dylan Thomas's garden-shed workroom at his boathouse in Laugharne

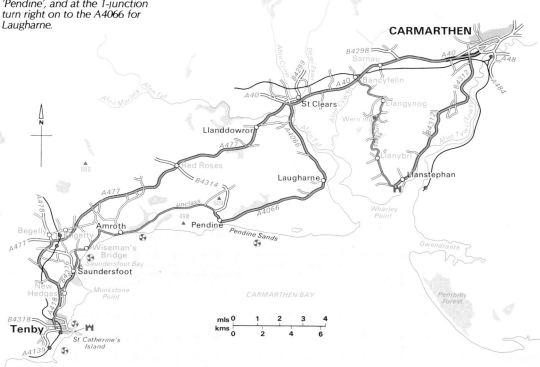

Above: the River Tywi snakes its way across its flood plain, passing Carmarthen to the right

Left: Saundersfoot — busy port turned holiday resort.

LAUGHARNE, Dyfed
Dylan Thomas said of Laugharne, 'this timeless, mild, beguiling island of a town . . .', and he will always be linked with this charming, modest place where he lived happily for 16 years in the Georgian boathouse romantically perched on Cliff Walk. Photographs, furniture and mementoes constitute a small museum here now. Many characters in his poem *Under Milk Wood* were probably based on local people and the play is still regularly performed in the town. The poet is buried in a simple grave in the churchyard The ruined castle on the water's edge was once an important strategic bastion, like that at Llanstephan, but was subsequently converted into a lavish Tudor residence by Sir John Perrot, illegitimate son of Henry VIII. In addition to the castle, the town has an attractive old harbour, a 13th-century church and a smart 18th-century town hall with a white tower and belfry. It is here that the Portreeve resides — an official post left over from Norman times. He wears a chain of golden cockleshells and has a retinue who attend him at town functions.

Continue on the A4066, passing on the right steep wooded slopes and on the left dunes and marshy land, to Pendine.

PENDINE, Dyfed
Five miles of firm, smooth sand form the extensive beach which made this resort a magnet in the 1920s for those seeking a seaside holiday. However, the hitherto peacefulness was shattered when motor speed trials were introduced to the area. Sir Malcolm Campbell broke the existing land speed record here in 1924, and a tragic accident in 1927 killed Parry Thomas when his car *Babs* crashed. The car was buried in the sand until 1969 when it was exhumed for restoration. Unfortunately peace has still not returned to Pendine Sands, for part of them are now used for missile testing.

Ascend steeply from the village on the B4314 and at the top turn left on to the unclassified road for Amroth.

AMROTH, Dyfed
Strangely-shaped petrified tree stumps can be seen here sticking out of the blue clay at exceptionally low tides. This forest was buried over 1,000 years ago, and the sea still eats away at the village. Several cottages and the old coast road have been washed away over the centuries. Amroth Castle (not open), an 18th-century house, was visited by Lord Nelson in 1802.

Continue for ½ mile then turn left, SP 'Tenby' and descend to Wiseman's Bridge. Continue through a wooded stretch and at the top of the ascent keep left, then descend to Saundersfoot.

SAUNDERSFOOT, Dyfed
During the 19th century Saundersfoot was a busy port shipping the local anthracite coal, but today it is an attractive and popular yachting and fishing village. The splendid sandy beaches either side of the harbour are ideal for safe bathing.

Go forward on to the B4316 and in 1 mile (at the roundabout) turn left on to the A478 for Tenby.

TENBY, Dyfed
Tenby's busy but sheltered harbour is the focal point of the town's narrow, winding streets bounded by remnants of the 13th-century town walls. Castle Hill is crowned by the remains of a Norman keep, and is also the home of the local museum, which houses a splendid collection of displays relating to the Tenby district. The Tudor gabled Merchant's House (NT) is a relic of the town's important seafaring history. It has been beautifully restored, revealing original beams and large areas of wall paintings and has a Tudor period museum. St Mary's Church in Quay Hill is a Norman building and is the largest parish church in Wales. Robert Recorde, the mathematician who devised the 'equals' sign, is buried inside it. The town was also the birthplace of the painter Augustus John in 1878. Just off the coast lies St Catherine's Island, which is accessible on foot at low tide. The fort on the island was originally built by Lord Palmerston as a defence against possible attack by Napoleon III. On Harbour beach is the tiny St Julian's Seamen's Chapel.

CALDY ISLAND, Dyfed
Motor launches run from Tenby harbour to Caldy Island, about 2½ miles offshore. The island is populated by Cistercian monks who farm the land and produce Caldy Island perfume, which they sell. The medieval church on the island contains a stone inscribed with Ogham lettering — and alphabet used by Irish Celts in the 6th century.

Return along the A478, SP 'Camarthen', to the Begelly roundabout and take the A477, SP 'St Clears'. Continue through a pretty wooded inlet and beyond Red Roses gradually descend through pleasant wooded country to Llanddowror.

LLANDDOWROR, Dyfed
The quiet atmosphere in this peaceful village of whitewashed houses gives no hint of the frenzy which was generated here in the 18th-century by the local vicar. Distressed by the ignorance and illiteracy of his parishioners, and of Welsh people in general, he started a system of travelling schools. Teachers travelled from parish to parish teaching children and adults of all ages to read the Bible and it was claimed that about 150,000 people learned to read through this scheme.

Continue on the A477 and in 1½ miles, at the roundabout, take the A40 for the return to Carmarthen.

TOUR 37   *73 MILES*

CORACLES ON THE TEIFI

Seaward lies the coast of Cardigan Bay, where Victorians transformed quiet Welsh villages into prosperous ports, now the playgrounds of yachtsmen and tourists. Inland the salmon waters of the Teifi cascade through a luscious valley to the town of Cardigan and flow on to swell the Irish Sea.

Ornamental ducks in Aberaeron's attractive harbour

CARDIGAN, Dyfed

On the banks of one of the loveliest rivers in Wales — the Teifi — stands Cardigan, once the headquarters of Welsh princes. In the past there has been many a bloody battle in the defence of the town's nationality, and it was here that Rhys ap Gruffydd won a rousing victory against a Norman-Flemish army in 1136. Perhaps the most outstanding architectural feature of Cardigan is the fine medieval 7-arched bridge over the Teifi. Old warehouses by the river are a reminder of Cardigan's former importance as a port, which flourished on the trade supplied by Cardiganshire's lead mines. Unfortunately, the Teifi silted up in the 19th century, and gradually trade died away. Today Cardigan is most concerned with its own affairs, generated through the rich farmland and forest which surrounds it, engendering in the town an air of independence. But this friendly town welcomes visitors, who come from the little seaside resorts up and down the coast to shop at the market which is still held beneath the arches of the Guildhall, and simply to enjoy the old-fashioned atmosphere and beautiful riverside setting. Two miles south off the A478 is the Cardigan Wildlife Park. This unusual mixture of Park and Sanctuary has a diverse range of mammals, birds and plants. Other features include fishing on the River Teifi, nature walks and disused slate quarries.

Leave Cardigan on the A487 Aberaeron and Aberystwyth road and gradually ascend to high ground beyond Penparc. In 2½ miles turn left on to the B4333 and continue, with views of the sea, to Aberporth.

CARDIGAN BAY, Dyfed

It is said that beneath the waters of Cardigan Bay lies a lost Atlantis. The seas were apparently kept from the Bay by a great embankment, which was put in the care of Siethenyn ap Siethenyn Sardi — one of Wales' greatest drunkards. He let the wall decay, and eventually it broke down altogether, destroying, so legend has it, 16 fortified towns. The plateau which meets the sea in a series of high cliffs is cut by narrow, wooded river valleys, such as the Teifi valley at Cenarth. The coastline itself is pierced at intervals by small, steep-sided river valleys which shelter fishing villages like Llangranog, where a small beach has formed at the river mouth. The people of Cardigan Bay are Welsh speaking, perpetuating a Welsh culture of fishermen and farmers.

ABERPORTH, Dyfed

Overlooking 2 sandy coves, this popular village is well sheltered from prevailing winds and so attracts flocks of visitors every year. Eastwards high cliffs stretch away to Tresaith, while westwards the coast climbs to the 400ft headland of Pencribach. The headland is inaccessible, and is used as a missile testing range.

Continue on the B4333 and after 2¼ miles turn left to rejoin the A487, SP 'Aberystwyth', for Tan-y-groes. For several miles there are views on both sides as the road keeps to high ground. At Brynhoffnant, the B4334 to the left leads to the attractive coastal village of Llangranog.

LLANGRANOG, Dyfed

A strange rock formation, likened to a lizard's head, overlooks the yellow sands of Llangranog where rocky outcrops are revealed at low tide. The slate-roofed houses of the village lie cramped by the walls of the narrow valley which shelters them. Up on the coastal hills cliff-top walks, preserved by the National Trust, give magnificent views along the coast.

The main tour continues on the A487 to Plwmp.

In 2½ miles, at Synod Inn, turn left on to the A486. Pass through Cross Inn before the descent (1 in 8), with coastal views ahead, into New Quay.

NEW QUAY, Dyfed

The New Quay Harbour Company, formed in 1833, developed a newly-established shipbuilding industry, which by 1860 employed some 600 shipwrights. However, road and rail gradually took away the coastal trade the port relied on, and although small fishing boats still land mackerel, herring and shellfish here, the amateur yachtsman has taken over the harbour. Yachting, and the sands revealed at low tide, have been the salvation of New Quay. During the summer months the neat, brightly painted Georgian and Victorian houses up on their terraced hillside look down upon a gay and lively scene and despite the tourist boom, New Quay remains one of the most charming little towns on the west coast.

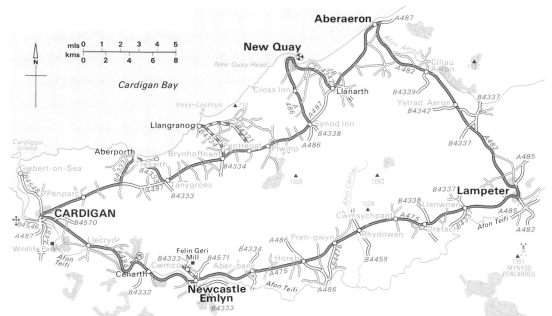

88

Continue on the B4342 Aberaeron road through a pretty wooded stretch. In 3 miles turn left on to the A487 to Llanarth.

LLANARTH, Dyfed

Llanarth lies partly alongside the road and partly up on the hillside above a steep ravine where the old village church stands. This holds objects of considerable antiquity within its walls: an 11th-century font; an ancient stone with an Ogham (ancient alphabet of the Celts) inscription superimposed with a carved Irish Celtic cross of the 9th century; and a collection of early English and Welsh bibles. Nearby, at Wern, is where Henry VII is said to have spent the night on his way to Bosworth Field, and to have had an affair with the daughter of the house from which the family, the Parry ap Harrys of Cardiganshire, claimed royal blood.

Continue on the A487 with excellent coastal views on the approach to Aberaeron.

ABERAERON, Dyfed

Aberaeron is a delightful town purposefully and attractively laid out by 19th-century planners who turned a small fishing hamlet into a flourishing trading port. Colour-washed Regency houses stand gathered about a square in orderly array and lined up on terraces overlooking the harbour. The earliest development provided the inner and outer harbours, the Harbour-Master's house, now a hotel, and the elegent brown-stone town hall. The town was renowned for its ship-builders, and schooners built here by master shipwright David Jones were highly prized. However the railways eventually took away the trade, and today the harbour is used primarily by yachtsmen and the quayside by holidaymakers.

At the far end of the town, turn right on to the A482, SP 'Lampeter', and follow the pleasantly wooded Aeron valley to Ystrad Aeron. Beyond the village a winding road leads through hill country before entering Lampeter.

LAMPETER, Dyfed

Lampeter is a busy trading centre at the confluence of several main roads, and market day, Tuesday, is a good time to experience the friendly atmosphere of this truly Welsh town. It is best known for St David's College, founded in 1822 by an Englishman, Bishop Burgess. The building, designed by C. R. Cockerell, was described by Sir Gilbert Scott as 'a most charming example of the early Gothic revival'. The original quadrangular building has not been marred by the modern additions and the remarkable library of some 80,000 books, medieval manuscripts and

This fine stained-glass portrait of St Christopher in Lampeter parish church is by R. J. Newberry, c1901

The Falls of Cenarth, a famous beauty spot on the River Teifi

first editions is housed here. A mound in the college grounds marks the site of a medieval castle, and on the opposite bank of the Teifi runs a stretch of Sarn Helen — a Roman road named after the Welsh wife of Magnus Maximus, who unsuccessfully attempted to become Emperor in AD 383.

In the town centre turn right into the High Street and leave on the A475 along the north side of the Teifi valley. Follow a 'switchback' road through several small villages. At Horeb, cross the A486 and later rejoin the Teifi valley before Newcastle Emlyn.

NEWCASTLE EMLYN, Dyfed

The castle, built in the 13th century, regularly changed hands between the Welsh and the English until 1403, when it finally fell to Owain Glyndwr's troops, but was almost destroyed in the process. Having fallen into disrepair, the castle was given to Sir Rhys ap Thomas by Henry VII, who rebuilt it for comfort rather than for security. It went the same way as its predecessor, however, when in 1645 Cromwell's troops found the castle in Royalist hands, won it, and then rendered it useless. So today little remains, except part of the walls and a ruined gatehouse standing on a grassy hillock. The town itself, although architecturally unassuming, is attractive. There is a town hall of 1892, and the Victorian church where slate from the Cilgerran quarries is used for the paving stones, the pillars, the chancel arch, the font, and even the sundial outside. A plaque on a house near the bridge over the Teifi commemorates Isaac Carter, who set up the first printing press here in Wales in 1718.

To the north-east near Cwmcoy is Felin Geri Mill.

FELIN GERI MILL, Dyfed

This watermill (OACT), built in the 16th century, was the last one in Wales to use the original production process for grinding wholemeal flour as a commercial concern. Visitors can see each stage of this ancient method and there is a museum, a water-powered saw mill, a shop and a bakery here as well.

The main tour turns left across the river bridge into the town centre, then right, SP 'Cardigan'. At the next T-junction turn right on to the A484 for Cenarth.

RIVER TEIFI, Dyfed

Flowing south and then west across the Cardigan plateau, the Teifi has beautiful carved valleys and steep gorges where waterfalls and rapids, such as those at Cenarth, challenge even the salmon's prowess. The Teifi and the Tywi are the only rivers where salmon are still fished from the coracle. These craft have been in use since prehistoric times. Built of interwoven ribs of ash, hazel or willow, and covered in a skin of tarred canvas, the coracles work in pairs with a net cast between them to trap the salmon. The Teifi also has the distinction of being the last refuge of the beaver, which probably became extinct in Britain during the 16th century.

CENARTH, Dyfed

The beauty of Cenarth Bridge and the Falls attract thousands of visitors every year. The Teifi cascades over a series of rocky ledges into swirling pools where sheep are washed prior to shearing during spring. Coracle men wait downstream to catch any luckless animals swept away by the current. Stone and colour-washed cottages around a simple church blend harmoniously with the delightful scenery surrounding the village.

Continue on the A484 along the Teifi valley through Llechryd to return to Cardigan.

THE BRECON BEACONS AND MYNYDD EPPYNT

Steep hills sweep down to verdant valleys where farmsteads are scattered over the wooded slopes and small towns occupy strategic crossing points on the swift-flowing rivers. North of the Brecon Beacons rises the harsh moorland plateau of the Mynydd Eppynt, an island of high ground bordered on all sides by rivers.

BRECON, Powys

Encircled by hills, the old county town of Brecknockshire lies at the meeting point of 2 rivers, the Usk and the Honddu. The narrow streets and elegant town houses are imbued with the atmosphere of the 18th and 19th centuries. At an inn in the High Street, Sarah Siddons (née Kemble) was born in 1755. Captain's Walk owes its name to the period of the Napoleonic Wars when it was a favourite place of exercise for captured French officers imprisoned here. The church of St John, raised to cathedral status in 1923, was originally the church of a Benedictine monastery founded in 1091. Most of the present building, however, belongs to the 13th and 14th centuries. The aisles were formerly filled with craft-guild chapels, of which only one, that of the corvizors (shoemakers)

remains. The Brecknock Museum contains an outstanding collection of local history and the barracks of the South Wales Borderers houses their Regimental Museum here.

From Brecon town centre follow SP, 'Upper Chapel B4520', and in ¼ mile turn left on to the B4520. Continue along the Honddu valley and later pass Lower Chapel at the southern edge of Mynydd Eppynt hills.

MYNYDD EPPYNT HILLS, Powys

Access to the high moorland summits of the Mynydd Eppynt hills is restricted because of an army firing range, but some roads and tracks do cross this exhilarating expanse of wild, bleak countryside. In the north the high sandstone scarps look down over Builth Wells; in the west, the dense woods of the Crychan Forest sweep down to the valley

of the River Bran, and in the south, the hillsides are studded with small farms interspersed with scattered trees.

½ mile beyond Upper Chapel keep forward on the steep (1 in 6) Builth Wells road. Later reach a summit of 1,370ft before a long descent into Builth Wells.

BUILTH WELLS, Powys

The mound of the 13th-century castle of Builth is all that is left, and from this period dates a shameful episode in the town's history, which earned the inhabitants the nick-name 'the traitors of Builth.' In 1282 a prince of Wales, Llewellyn the Last, hunted by the English, asked for shelter from the townspeople. They refused and he was later killed near Cilmeri. Builth today owes much of its character to the medicinal springs that made the town fashionable in the 18th century when it was a spa town. Its earliest buildings date from this period, as the town was totally destroyed by a fire in 1691 and money was sent from all parts of Britain to help the reconstruction. The River Wye, spanned by a graceful 6-arched bridge, and the River Irfon meet at Builth, and a little further up the Irfon valley is a delightful brook called the Nant-yr-arian, meaning the 'brook of silver'. In times of plague farmers brought produce to the brook and the townspeople threw coins into the water as payment.

Turn left on to the A483 and shortly cross the River Irfon by the Iron Bridge. Continue to Garth.

GARTH, Powys

Magnesium springs led to the establishment of a small pump room at Garth, but the village was never able to compete with its neighbours Builth, Llangammarch and Llanwrtyd Wells.

At the end of the village turn left for Llangammarch Wells.

LLANGAMMARCH WELLS, Powys

The smallest of the Welsh spas, Llangammarch was renowned for its success with heart complaints. Its springs were not sulphurous like those of many spas, but rich in barium chloride. For such a little village the unusually well-appointed hotel had its own lake, golf-course, tennis and shooting facilities. Just outside the village at Llwyn Einon, a charming triple-gabled house (not open), lived Theophilus Jones, whose classic history of Brecknockshire was published in the early part of the 19th century. He is buried in the churchyard.

By the church at the edge of the village turn right on to the Llanwrtyd Wells road and cross the Afon Cammarch. In 1 mile turn left.

The Brecon Beacons, seen from Llanhamdach
Inset: cattle market day at Llandovery

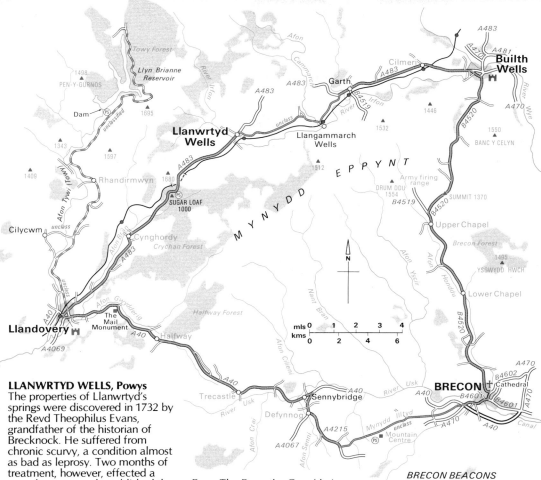

BRECON BEACONS

Follow SP 'Brecon A40' from Llandovery, shortly joining the deep, wooded valley of the Afon Gwydderig. There is a long, gradual climb passing, after 2½ miles, the Mail Monument set in a lay-by on the right.

THE MAIL MONUMENT, Dyfed
This simple stone obelisk is a reminder that drunkenness was sometimes a hazard of travelling even before the invention of the motor car, for here a coach and its passengers were driven off the road by an intoxicated driver and all were killed.

The tour continues up the Gwydderig valley past Halfway and the south-western corner of the Mynydd Eppynt to reach Trecastle on the upper reaches of the Usk valley. Continue to Sennybridge.

SENNYBRIDGE, Powys
Situated at the confluence of the Rivers Usk and Senni, Sennybridge was mainly developed in the 19th century when the large sheep and cattle market was transferred here from Defynnog after the turnpike road was opened. Sennybridge sheep sales became a major event in the area. They were started by Scottish farmers who bought large sections of sheep grazing in Fforest Fawr when it was sold in 1815, having been Crown property since the Middle Ages.

Beyond the village turn right on to the A4067 and shortly reach Defynnog. Here bear left on to the A4215, continuing along the Senni valley with views ahead of Fan Frynych (2,047ft). After 2¼ miles turn left, SP 'Mountain Centre', on to a narrow road which crosses the 1,100ft Mynydd Illtyd. To the right are excellent views of the Brecon Beacons, and to the right of the road is the Brecon Beacon Mountain Centre.

BRECON BEACONS, Powys
More than 500 square miles of wild mountainous country, stretching from the Black Mountains in the west to the Black Mountains in the east, were designated in 1957 as the Brecon Beacons National Park. From the highest of the red sandstone peaks, Pen-y-fan (2,906ft) and Corn-Du (2,863ft) there are wonderful views northwards over the bleak plateau of Mynydd Eppynt and westwards to the rugged grandeur of the Black Mountains. The Beacons are so called because in the days before telecommunications, they formed part of a chain of prominent hilltops on which beacon fires were lit to give warning of important events.

Gradually descend, with views of the Black Mountains ahead, and on reaching the roundabout take the B4601 for the return to Brecon town centre.

LLANWRTYD WELLS, Powys
The properties of Llanwrtyd's springs were discovered in 1732 by the Revd Theophilus Evans, grandfather of the historian of Brecknock. He suffered from chronic scurvy, a condition almost as bad as leprosy. Two months of treatment, however, effected a complete cure and established the village as a spa, with a pump room and large comfortable hotels making perfect centres for country holidays, with rambles along the banks of the lovely River Irfon or more energetic walks in the surrounding hills.

Turn left on to the A483. There is a gradual climb through the edge of the Crychan Forest to a 950ft summit below the easily-climbed Sugar Loaf (1,000ft) which stands at the head of the Bran valley and can be seen on the descent to Llandovery.

LLANDOVERY, Dyfed
Llanymddyfri, 'the church amid the waters', aptly describes the delightful little town with its picturesque ruined castle on a mound overlooking the River

The Tywi valley near Llandovery

Bran. The Bran, the Gwydderig and the Tywi (Towy) all meet at Llandovery, the market centre of the Upper Tywi valley. Pleasant Georgian and Victorian buildings are interspersed with a remarkable number of public houses, and historians will point out that in the days of Richard III the town charter gave Llandovery the sole right of keeping taverns in the area. The present bank stands on the site of the famous Bank of the Black Ox, founded in 1799 by cattle-drover David Jones when the town was the centre of the cattle trade and herds of black cattle passed through on their way to the English markets. Llandovery has 2 churches, both on the outskirts. The parish church is much restored but St Mary's-on-the-hill (Llanfair-ar-y-bryn) retains an atmosphere of great antiquity with its fine tie-beam roof and barrel-vaulted chancel.

In the town an unclassified road on the right, SP 'Rhandirmwyn', follows the Tywi valley for 11½ miles to the Llyn Brianne Reservoir and Dam. From the viewing point, a narrow road with passing places leads high above the shores for 7 miles into the Tywi Forest. On the way, another detour may be made to Cilycwm, SP to the left across the Tywi valley, 3 miles from Llandovery.

TYWI VALLEY, Dyfed
Hemmed in on either side by steep wooded hills, the River Tywi flows through one of the most beautiful of South Wales' valleys. Near Llandovery, the famous Dolauhirion bridge spans the river, a graceful single-arched stone structure built in 1773 by the self-taught builder William Edwards. Llyn Brianne reservoir was formed in 1972 by drowing part of the valley. Nearly 3 square miles of water are confined by a dam some 250ft high.

CILYCWM, Dyfed
On the west side of the Tywi valley nestles the village of Cilycwm, its little streets bright with white and colour-washed old cottages and its 15th-century church framed by ancient yew trees; inside the church are medieval frescoes and old box pews. The Methodist chapel is believed to be the first meeting house ever established in Wales.

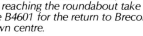

CHEPSTOW, Gwent

Chepstow, a border town, stands with its feet in the Wye on a stretch of the river that is distinguished by the high cliffs of its banks, and it was upon one of these natural fortresses that the castle (AM) was built — the first Norman stone castle in Wales. The cellar and the lower 2 storeys of the Great Tower survive from the original building erected by William Fitz Osbern. His castle was added to by later generations of the powerful de Clare family. After the Restoration, Henry Marten, one of those who signed the death warrant of Charles I, was subsequently kept a prisoner for 20 years, in the tower which now bears his name, until his death at the age of 78 in 1680. Another survivor from the Middle Ages is Westgate, part of the substantial town wall, where duty was collected on all goods which passed through it for the Lord of the Manor.

Follow SP 'Monmouth' and at the end of the town join the A466. Pass Chepstow Racecourse to reach St Arvans. Here, turn left, SP 'Trellech'. Later climb through wooded countryside to reach Devauden. Join the B4293 and continue through Llanishen to Trellech.

TRELLECH, Gwent

The village of Trellech takes its name from the 3 mysterious leaning standing stones by the village crossroads. Once part of a larger complex, their purpose is not really known, but perhaps, like Stonehenge, they were used for measuring time, or as the site of ancient religious rites. The stones appear again in carved relief on the remarkable sundial given to the church in 1689.

Continue on the B4293. In 4¼ miles bear right and later cross the A40. At the next T-junction turn left, then at the roundabout turn right and cross the Monnow Bridge to enter Monmouth.

MONMOUTH, Gwent

The Normans realised that to hold Monmouth, strategically placed on the Wye and Monnow, was virtually to control the whole of South Wales. The fortified bridge gateway (AM) which they built over the river in 1262, and guarded the town for centuries, is the only one now left in Britain. The castle has not lasted so well, being mostly destroyed in the Civil War of 1646. Harry of Monmouth, who became Henry V, was born within its walls. Such was his popularity that in 1673 the Duke of Beaufort built Great Castle House (exterior AM), in order that his first grandson could be born near the birthplace of his greatest hero, Henry V; he built the house from the stones of the castle and the interior has fine woodwork and

A WELSH BORDERLAND

From the cliff-edged River Wye on the long-contested Welsh border, travel along the outstandingly beautiful valley to White Castle and ancient Monmouth, historic bastion of Norman power. Continue on through the broad Usk valley to Caerleon, past powerhouse of Rome's legions in South Wales.

Monmouth's 13th-century gateway was originally used as a tollhouse, prison and watchtower

plasterwork. St Mary's Church stands on the site of Monmouth Priory, built by the same Fitz Osbern who founded the castle. A Monmouth Cap, the woollen headgear reputedly worn by the Monmouth archers at Agincourt on whom Henry V relied heavily for his victory, can be seen in the local museum. Today a statue of Henry V stands high up on the façade of the neo-Classical Shire Hall of 1724, overlooking Agincourt Square where there stands a statue of C. S. Rolls, co-founder of Rolls-Royce, pioneer aviator and the first man to fly the channel in both directions. A collection of Nelson's mementoes can also be seen in the town museum.

Return across the Monnow Bridge and at the roundabout turn right on to the B4233. At Rockfield bear left, SP 'Abergavenny', and later pass through Hendre. After 4¼ miles, at the edge of Llantilio Crossenny, a detour can be made by turning right on to an unclassified road to White Castle.

WHITE CASTLE, Gwent

Small, but powerful, White Castle (AM) is one of 3 fortresses which, in the 12th and 13th centuries, formed a strategic triangle of such importance that the Crown always kept direct control over them, lest they should be turned against the reigning monarch. The isolated castle gets its name from the white plaster which once adorned it, remains of which can still be found on the stone work. At the end of the 12th century the castle consisted merely of a stone tower surrounded by a curtain wall, but in the following century, in which the Welsh rose under the 2 Llewellyns, the castle was considerably refortified. Semi-circular towers were added, a gatehouse was built, and the outer ward enclosed by another curtain wall with attendant towers. Domestic buildings were built within, enabling many servants to be housed here in reasonable comfort. However, the castle was never tested in war, and after the Welsh retreat of 1277, it became a purely administrative centre, collecting tithes and levies from the residents of the surrounding countryside. With the decline of the feudal system, the castle finally fell into ruins through disuse.

Continue on the B4233 through Llanfapley to Abergavenny.

ABERGAVENNY, Gwent

Abergavenny stands upon the banks of the River Usk within a great green bowl, guarded by 4 hills. The Romans had a fort here, but the earliest evidence of Abergavenny's history is the Norman castle. It was founded before 1090 by Hamelin de Balun, but William de Breos is the name remembered by the Welsh. He came to the castle in 1176, and one of his first acts was to invite all the leading local chieftans to a Christmas banquet. While the chieftans ate, William ordered his soldiers to slay them all. The ruins consist of fragments of the curtain wall; the ruined gatehouse and a few other remnants and are now part of a pleasantly wooded park. The museum located within the castle grounds, houses many interesting exhibits associated with the history of Abergavenny. These include rural craft tools, Welsh kitchen, saddlers shop, costumes and Roman coins. St Mary's Church is built on the site of a Benedictine priory founded at the same time as the castle, and contains some outstanding relics of the past. Among these are the splendid tombs of the Herbert family, but outshining all their finery is a simple wooden effigy of a 13th-century knight. One mile west of Abergavenny off the A40 is the Sugar Loaf viewpoint offering wide views over the Usk valley and the Blorenge.

Leave the town centre on the A40, SP 'Raglan'. In 1¼ miles, at the roundabout, take the A4042, SP 'Newport'. Pass through Llanellen, Llanover and Penperlleni, then in 1¼ miles turn left on to the A472, SP 'Usk'. After another 4¼ miles, across the river bridge on the left, is the town of Usk.

USK, Gwent

Usk, meaning 'water', is, not surprisingly, named after the river on which it stands. It overlooks the broad meadows of the Usk valley, and is known for its excellent salmon fishing and inns; those around Twyn Square attest to Usk long being a market centre for the surrounding rural area. *Burrium*, the Roman station which stood here before the town, was an important fort from where the legions made unsuccessful sorties into the Welsh mountains. The Normans came and went, leaving behind them a castle and a church. The former stands ruined, just a gateway, a keep, round tower and remnants of the living quarters, yet still retains the grace and dignity of the finest Norman architecture. The castle suffered terribly during the 15th-century Glyndwr rebellion and was slighted in the Civil War.

The main tour continues forward on to the unclassified Llangybi/Caerleon road to Llangybi.

LLANGYBI, Gwent

An ancient mineralised spring here is dedicated to St Cybi, and was a place of pilgrimage to which people came seeking miraculous cures from its waters. The well chamber has a paved walk around it and niches in its walls for offerings. The beehive vault is thought to be unique in Wales. In this area there are a number of standing stones, cists and cromlechs, which mark the site of ancient burial sites.

Remain on the unclassified road to Caerleon.

CAERLEON, Gwent

This was *Isca*, home of the 2nd Augustinian Legion, one of 3 permanent legionary bases in Britain. It is estimated a population of some 6,000 lived here, and excavations have revealed a hospital, kitchens, baths, and outside the walls, a granary. Perhaps the most remarkable remain here is the amphitheatre (AM), the only one completely excavated in Britain. It is oval, and an earth bank, originally 8 yards high, held tiers of wooden seats that could seat several thousands. Ships from all over the world were said to dock at the Roman quays, bringing gold to decorate the palaces and churches, and finance the 200 schools which were said to thrive here. In the Middle Ages considerably more of the fort was visible, and these signs of a sophisticated civilisation gave rise to legends of King Arthur's Court.

Chepstow Castle, guarded on one side by the Wye and on the other by a ditch

From the one-way system follow SP 'Newport'. Cross the River Usk then turn left on to the B4236, SP 'Christchurch'. In ¾ mile turn right, then keep left. At the A48 turn left then ½ mile farther, at the roundabout, take the 3rd exit, SP 'Langstone'. In 1½ miles turn right on to the B4245 for Magor.

MAGOR, Gwent

Cadwaldwr, the last Welsh prince also to be king of England, founded Magor's spacious church in the 7th century. The Cathedral of the Moors, as the church is known, is mainly Norman, with a 13th-century tower which overlooks the Bristol Channel. In the churchyard lie the ivy-clad remains of a priory.

At the Wheatsheaf Inn turn left. In 2¼ miles skirt Rogiet, then 1¼ miles farther turn left on to an unclassified road to enter Caldicot.

CALDICOT, Gwent

New shops and industrial estates have turned Caldicot from a village into a sizeable town in little over a decade. The Romans had a pottery here when it stood on the busy *Via Julia*, and the Normans a castle. This was built in the late 12th century, but by the 17th century had fallen into decay. It was restored this century and medieval banquets and traditional musical entertainment take place within its walls.

At the roundabout take the 3rd exit, then in ½ mile turn left to rejoin the B4245. In 2 miles turn right on to the A48. After crossing the M4 a short diversion can be made by taking the 2nd turning right on to an unclassified road to Mathern.

MATHERN, Gwent

The old church at Mathern is dedicated to St Tewdric, a 6th-century king who ended his days as a hermit. Bishop Godwin buried his coffin in the chancel that was built in 1610. The nearby Bishops Palace (not open) was the residence of the Bishops of Llandaff from the time of the Glyndwr rebellion in the 1400s up until 1705. It has medieval and Tudor features and a glorious garden. Also near the village is Moynes Court (not open), a 17th-century building with a much older gatehouse, once the home of Bishop Godwin.

The main tour returns along the A48 by way of Pwllmeyric to Chepstow.

HEREFORD'S QUIET VALLEYS

Great Marcher fortresses like Ludlow Castle were built by the Normans to subdue the turbulent Welsh. Fierce battles have left no scars on these mild green hills and fertile valleys which epitomize the serenity and certainties of the rural way of life in one of the few remaining true pastoral regions of England.

LEOMINSTER, Herefs & Worcs

Hop gardens and orchards flourish around Leominster, one of the great wool towns of England from medieval times until the 18th century. Narrow medieval streets with their tightly-packed jumble of timber-framed houses contrast with the more spacious layouts of the Georgian era, best seen in Broad Street. A grey-stone priory church of 3 naves, stands amid green lawns shaded by trees. According to tradition it was founded in the 11th century by Earl Leofric, husband of Lady Godiva. A medieval ducking stool, last used to punish a nagging wife in the early 19th century, is on view in the church. Nearby, Grange Court, a delightful brick and timber house built in 1633 by John Abel, was moved to this site in 1855. It was originally the town hall and stood at the crossroads in the centre of Leominster. In Etnam Street is a folk museum devoted to the local history of the area.

Follow the A44, SP 'Rhayader', to Eardisland.

EARDISLAND, Herefs & Worcs

The village of Eardisland presents an exquisite picture in an idyllic setting among the green meadows bordering the River Arrow. Half-timbered black and white façades stand out among the old brick and colour-washed cottages that represent a medley of traditional styles of building. Near the old bridge over the river stands a 14th-century yeoman's hall, Staick House, and the old school house and village whipping post face the 17th-century manor house (not open) in whose garden stands a tall, 4-gabled dovecot of unusually charming design.

Continue on the A44 to Pembridge.

PEMBRIDGE, Herefs & Worcs

Pretty black and white timbered houses, their upper storeys drunkenly overhanging the pavements, are the keynote of this appealing village. Behind the New Inn, in the tiny market square, the old market house is raised on 8 oak columns. In the centre of the main street, weathered stone steps lead steeply uphill to a church with an unusual detached bell tower dating from the 14th century.

In 4½ miles pass the edge of Lyonshall and continue to Kington.

KINGTON, Herefs & Worcs

Sheltered by Hergest Ridge and Rushock Hill, Kington is an ancient town famous for its sheep markets. Offa's Dyke, the old Mercian defence against the Welsh, crosses Rushock Hill to the north. West of the town, the house called Hergest Court (not open) and for generations the home of the Vaughan family, was reputedly haunted by the ghost of 'Black Vaughan' until a 17th-century exorcism was said to have transformed his evil spirit into a bluebottle.

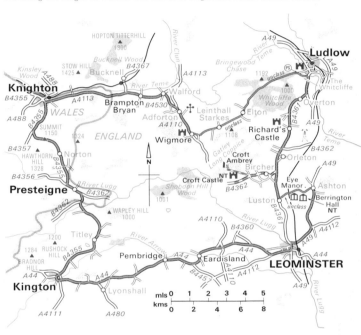

Crowning the height of Ludlow Hill is one of England's finest Norman castles

Turn right SP 'Presteigne' to join the B4355. After 6 miles cross the border into Wales and shortly enter Presteigne.

PRESTEIGNE, Powys

Presteigne stands on the bank of the River Lugg, at this point the boundary between England and Wales, in the rich green countryside of hill and vale so characteristic of the Welsh Marches. A priest hole, where a Roman Catholic priest remained hidden from persecution for 2 years, can be seen in the 17th-century Radnorshire Arms. In the churchyard is the grave of Mary Morgan, hanged in 1805 aged 17 for the murder of her illegitimate child. Her lover, who was a party to the crime and gave her the knife with which to do it, then sat as a member of the jury that condemned her. A royal pardon was granted but, sadly, arrived too late to save her.

Continue on the B4355 and at the end of the town turn right, SP 'Knighton'. Cross the River Lugg to reach Norton then ascend past Hawthorn Hill to 1,150ft before a long descent to the edge of Knighton.

KNIGHTON, Powys

In 1971 the Offa's Dyke Path was officially opened by Lord Hunt of Everest at a ceremony held in Knighton's riverside park. The earthworks of Offa's Dyke, the ancient frontier between England and Wales, built by King Offa of Mercia in the 8th century, are clearly visible on the west of the town, and Knighton stands at about the half-way point of the walk. The central Wales railway line, one of only 2 railways surviving in mid Wales, passes through Knighton at an enchanting neo-Gothic railway station. It owes its design to the owner of the land who, when he sold it to the railway, insisted in approving the plans of all the buildings.

Pembridge — typical Hereford architecture

At the near edge of Knighton turn right on to the A4113, SP 'Ludlow', to follow the Teme valley, later recrossing the border into England.

These splendid bow-windows, known as oriels, belong to the Angel Hotel — one of Ludlow's many memorable buildings

BRAMPTON BRYAN, Herefs & Worcs
The name of the village derives from Bryan de Brampton who built a massive fortress here in the 13th century. Two great round towers, the gatehouse and hall survive, standing in the grounds of the manor house (not open). De Brampton's daughter, Margaret, married Robert Harley, and one of their descendants became a Lord Mayor of London. Harley Street, fashionable West End home of many exclusive medical practices, is named after him.

In 1½ miles at Walford turn right on to the B4530, SP 'Hereford'. In 1 mile turn right on to the A4110, and continue through Adforton to Wigmore.

WIGMORE, Herefs & Worcs
Between the manor house (not open) and the church lie the delightful half-timbered cottages of Wigmore. Little remains of the moated 14th-century castle, owned by the Mortimer family, which was dismantled during the Civil War in 1643, but near Adforton are the picturesque ruins of an Augustinian abbey founded in 1179.

Turn left on to the Ludlow road, and pass through Leinthall Starkes and Elton. After the descent through Whitcliffe Wood there is a magnificent view of Ludlow before reaching Ludford Bridge. To reach Ludlow town centre turn left on to the B4361, cross the River Teme and ascend into the town.

Delightfully delicate 17th-century stucco work at Eye Manor

LUDLOW, Shrops
The tour climbs from the River Teme up the steep hillside whose summit is crowned by the mighty walls of Ludlow Castle (OACT), one of the great Marcher fortresses, constructed in 1085 by the Earl of Shrewsbury. It was to Ludlow Castle that Prince Arthur, elder son of Henry VII, brought his young Spanish bride Catharine of Aragon, and had gardens laid out for her in a series of pleasant walks. He died here and his younger brother not only ascended to the throne as Henry VIII, but also married his brother's widow. The town is a feast of old buildings, from the black and white Feathers Inn, its façade ornamented with rich carving, to the restrained elegance of Georgian town houses. Broad Street, leading up from the river to the castle, is said to contain no building later than the 15th century. Near the top, Broad Gate, the only one of the original town gates that remains, leads to the 18th-century stone Butter Cross where the town museum is housed. The great 15th-century church of St Lawrence bears a graceful spire 135ft high. The interior is famous for the exquisitely carved misericords of the choir stalls, and for its lovely east window which depicts the life and miracles of the saint in 27 separate scenes.

The main tour turns right on to the B4361, SP 'Leominster', and in 1½ miles turns right again, SP 'Presteigne', to reach Richard's Castle.

RICHARD'S CASTLE, Herefs & Worcs
A steep path leads north-west from the village through woodland to the earthworks of the ancient castle. It was built in the reign of Edward the Confessor and is one of only 2 in the county that pre-date the Norman Conquest.

Continue on the B4361, passing the edge of Orleton. The main tour continues south on the B4361, but from here a detour can be made to Croft Castle. Turn right on to the B4362, SP 'Presteigne', and in ½ mile bear right into Bircher. In 1 mile turn right for the entrance to Croft Castle and footpaths to Croft Ambrey.

CROFT CASTLE, Herefs & Worcs
Apart from a break of 173 years, from 1750 to 1923, this splendid Marcher castle (NT) has been the home of the Croft family ever since the medieval period. Walls and towers date from the 14th century, but the magnificent interior, with its superb collection of Gothic furniture, belongs to the 18th and early 19th centuries. The outstanding features of the extensive park, planted with many varieties of rare trees and shrubs, are the avenues of beech, oak and Spanish chestnut. The chestnut trees are particularly ancient — thought to be more than 350 years old. Close to the castle stands the church, with a monument to Sir Richard Croft. His finely carved armour represents the suit he wore at the Battle of Tewkesbury (1471).

Return to the B4361 and turn right to rejoin the main tour. At the edge of Luston turn left, SP 'Ashton', to reach Eye Manor.

CROFT AMBREY, Herefs & Worcs
This Iron Age fort is situated at 1,000ft on the edge of Leinthall Common. It covers an area of 24 acres and was occupied from 400 BC to 50 AD. The climb to the top is rewarded with wide views of several counties.

EYE MANOR, Herefs & Worcs
This Carolean manor house (not open) is renowned for its elaborate superbly moulded and painted plaster ceilings. The finest are those of the great parlour and the dining hall. Eye Manor originally belonged to a Barbados sugar planter and slave trader, Ferdinando Gorges.

Continue, passing in 1½ miles on the right, Berrington Hall.

BERRINGTON HALL, Herefs & Worcs
When the estate was bought by London banker and former Lord Mayor Thomas Harley, 3rd son of the 3rd Earl of Oxford, in 1775, he employed Capability Brown to create the park and choose the site for the house. Brown's son-in-law, Henry Holland, designed Berrington Hall (NT) as a neo-Classical building, completed in 1781. The style of the interior echoes the Classical theme: its outstanding features are the marble hall and the staircase hall.

At the A49 turn right, (care required), for the return alongside Berrington Park to Leominster.

LLANDRINDOD WELLS, Powys

Llandrindod stands just above the junction between the Rivers Ithon and Aran and the Church of the Trinity, built in the Middle Ages, marks the founding of the community. Llandrindod was no more than a scattered hamlet until 1749, when a hotel was built and the fashions of Bath were introduced — ballrooms, dining salons and gaming places. 1867 saw the arrival of the railway, and by the turn of the century Llandrindod had some 80,000 visitors a year and the town retains its spacious Edwardian streets and fine hotels from this heyday. In the War Memorial Gardens is the Llandrindod Wells Museum, which is chiefly devoted to finds from nearby Castell Collen, a Roman fort whose inhabitants may well have known of the curative properties of Llandrindod's waters. The Automobile Palace, in Temple Street, is a more contemporary museum. Here the Tom Norton Collection of bicycles and tricycles is kept. The waters which put Llandrindod on the map can still be taken at the pump room in Rock Park, now privately owned.

Leave on the A483 Newtown road. Pass through Crossgates and later reach Llanddewi.

LLANDDEWI, Powys

The village lies amid the beautiful scenery of the Ithon valley, and may be a site of ancient fortification as traces of tumuli and old defence systems have been found in the area. The church was rebuilt in 1890 on the site of a much earlier building, and preserves a walled-up Norman doorway and a 14th-century font. Perhaps the best building is Llanddewi Hall, now a farmhouse, opposite the church. This displays the simple, strong lines which gave it its authority in the days when it was the most important manor in the district.

Continue along the A483 to Llanbister.

LLANBISTER, Powys

Llanbister stands on a steep hill above the River Ithon and copes with the slope by a series of steps. It was the scene of bloody revenge in the 15th century; a quarrel among members of the Vaughan family resulted in a fight in which John Vaughan killed David Vaughan. David's sister took revenge by attending an archery competition, in Llanbister, dressed as a man. When her turn came to shoot, she turned from the target and shot John, and escaped during the ensuing confusion.

Continue along the valley to Llanbadarn Fynydd.

Penygarreg Dam holds back the waters of a 240-acre lake, which can be fished for trout by permit holders

96

AROUND THE WELSH LAKES

Victorian business acumen was responsible for the charming spa town of Llandrindod Wells; the 19th century created the lovely Elan Valley — the Welsh Lake District — and Newtown sprang up in the 20th century, but ancient Welsh culture marks the surrounding towns and hamlets with an indelible stamp of its own.

LLANBADARN FYNYDD, Powys

Close by the River Ithon stands the village church, rebuilt, but still with its original east window, remnants of its rood screen, and an altar rail of 1716. This lovely spot was once an isolated mountain village, and retains some of this character, but its position on the main Llandrindod Wells to Newtown road has inevitably resulted in development. The road was said to possess a bend for every day in the year — 365. An important cattle sale is held in the village street during late summer.

Pass the New Inn PH then turn right SP 'Dolfor'. Gradually ascend on to high moorland and later go forward on to the B4355, SP 'Newtown'. Descend to Dolfor and turn right on to the A483, then right again on to the narrow unclassified road past the church.

The red dragon of Wales has made the Dragon Pottery at Rhayader famous

DOLFOR, Powys

Dolfor stands at over 1,000ft above sea level, and from the hill above the village there are magnificent views, and from the summit of nearby Kerry Hill (1,565ft) the Brecon Beacons are visible to the south. The Rivers Teme, Ithon and Mule all have their sources in this area. The village inn is so unspoilt that from the outside it still looks like an ordinary house.

Garreg Ddu Reservoir, one of the Elan Valley reservoirs built between 1892 and 1907. Claerwen Reservoir was opened by Elizabeth II in 1952

Keep forward on this road, climbing to 1,200ft with magnificent views over the Severn valley and distant mountains. After a long descent turn left at the crossroads on to the A489 and descend into the Severn valley to Newtown.

NEWTOWN, Powys

Although originally established in 1279, the 20th century has virtually seen another Newtown arise. Extensive building, including a theatre and civic offices, have appeared in a variety of styles, ranging from Tudor to contemporary; such diversity imparts its own charm. In Llanllwchaiarn, a district of Newtown where some of the old town still exists, the Newtown Textile Museum has established itself in one of the blocks where weavers used to work. The museum includes exhibits of the wool trade, old tools and machinery and other general items of local history, giving a picture of Newtown life in the past. In 1885, the little stone and half-timbered building in which Owain Glyndwr held one of his parliaments during the first decade of the 15th

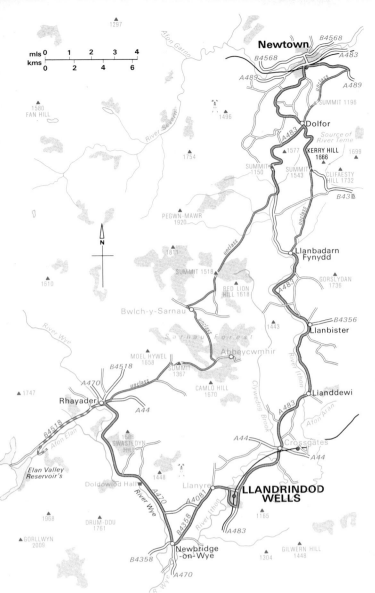

century, was brought from Dolgellau and re-erected on its present site in Newtown. The most honoured native of Newtown is Robert Owen, the great social reformer who is known as the father of trade unionism. He is buried in the churchyard of the old parish church. Also buried here are a boy and girl, lovers who were denied marriage by their families and consequently made a suicide pact and took poison. Thousands attended the funeral: in death the couple were allowed to be together and were buried in the same grave.

At the crossroads in the town centre turn left on to the A483. A long, winding ascent leads past Dolfor to a 1,200ft summit. In 1 mile, on the descent, go forward on to the Bwlch-y-sarnau road (main road bears sharply left, care required), and cross the River Ithon. In 5¼ miles bear right to reach Bwlch-y-sarnau. Here go forward at the crossroads and at the T-junction turn right, SP 'Rhayader'. At the next T-junction turn left and in 1 mile turn right and continue to Rhayader, joining the A44 on entering the town.

RHAYADER, Powys

A busy, bustling little town which has kept a 19th-century atmosphere even though many of its shop fronts have been modernised. Far below, the River Wye bounces over boulders and rocky platforms towards pretty falls below the bridge. Although some light industy has grown up, Rhayader is essentially a market town noted for its sheep fairs, nestling as it does above the River Wye on the edge of vast moorlands, often referred to as the Welsh desert. The most notable

historical event at Rhayader was the Rebecca Riots during the 19th century. Men, dressed as women and calling themselves Rebecca's Daughters, tore down the turnpike gates in protest against high toll charges. They took their name from the biblical quotation Genesis 24:60 'And they blessed Rebekah, and said unto her, Thou art our sister, be thou the mother of thousands of millions, and let thy seed possess the gate of those which hate them'.

From Rhayader, a detour can be made to the Elan Valley Reservoirs. At the crossroads go forward on to the B4518, SP 'Elan Valley', cross the Wye and in ¼ mile bear left. Later pass the Elan Valley Hotel and in ½ mile go forward for Caban Coch, Garreg Ddu and the other reservoirs.

ELAN VALLEY, Powys

During the 19th century a new reservoir complex constructed by the Corporation of Birmingham created a beautiful series of lakes and wooded slopes known as the Welsh Lake District. Before the Elan Valley was flooded, it was famous for its wild, haunting beauty. Beneath the waters of Caban Coch lies a house in which the poet Shelley lived for a while with his young wife Harriet.

The main tour turns left at the crossroads on to the A470 following the Wye valley.

WYE VALLEY, Powys

Running along the southern boundary of old Radnorshire, the Wye is a delightful river to either fish in or walk beside. It is a true mountain stream, its bed strewn with great boulders interspersed with deep, swirling pools, rapids and falls and it is a paradise for trout fishermen, as well as being famous for salmon. In 1308 Edward II took with him 3,000 dried salmon for his Scottish Campaign and many of them came from the Wye.

5 miles from Rhayader, pass Doldowlod Hall (not open), where the famous engineer James Watt spent his retirement, and continue to Newbridge-on-Wye.

NEWBRIDGE-ON-WYE, Powys

This pretty village beside the sparkling waters of the River Wye is a very popular base for fishermen as both the Wye and nearby Ithon offer excellent sport. In the village itself is the Mid Wales House Gallery — an art gallery and craft shop.

Turn left on to the B4358, SP 'Llandrindod', then in 2½ miles go forward on to the A4081. Shortly beyond Llanyre cross the River Ithon then bear right to re-enter Llandrindod Wells.

Rhayader's 2 main streets meet at the town's clock-tower war memorial

CADER IDRIS

Between the wide watery expanses of the Dyfi and
Mawdacch estuaries lies the unyielding massif of Cader
Idris. The tour winds in a figure of eight round both these
startlingly contrasting landscapes, introducing each with
stretches of seaside motoring.

MACHYNLLETH, Powys
Magnificent scenery surrounds the
historic market town of
Machynlleth. Its attractive tree-
lined main street, Maen Gwyn,
takes its name from a direction
stone of extremely ancient date,
no doubt used by the earliest
inhabitants, who made a
prehistoric trackway along the
Dyfi valley. The stone, now in 2
fragments, is set against the wall
of a house in the street. The
pinnacled Victorian clock tower in
the centre of the street was
erected by the Marquess of
Londonderry in the 1870s. He had
aquired the local Plas (manor),
now used as council offices, and
where sheepdog trials are held
annually in the grounds.

*Leave Machynlleth on the A487,
SP 'Dolgellau'. In ¾ mile cross the
River Dyfi and turn left on to the
A493 and in 3 miles enter Pennal.*

PENNAL, Powys
Low, slate-roofed cottages cluster
about a church rebuilt, in early
Classical style, during the 19th
century, with a hipped roof and
gilded weathercock. It stands
within a circular enclosure which
in turn acts as Pennal's central
roundabout. The salmon of the
Dyfi and trout from neighbouring
streams are a great attraction for
anglers, and the peaks of Tarren
Hendre, Tarren y gesail and Tarren
Cadian, which soar above the
village, invite walkers and climbers
to explore their crags and valleys.

*Continue on the A493, later joining
the shores of the Dyfi estuary to
reach Aberdyfi.*

ABERDYFI, Gwynedd
Seafaring and shipbuilding was the
business of quiet and genteel
Aberdyfi — formerly one of the
most important ports along the
Welsh coast; in the 16th century it
accommodated both coastal and
Continental shipping. The last boat
was built here in 1880, so the
scene today is a far cry from the
days when at one time 180 ships
loaded with coal, malt, flour and
salt, which was traded for woollen
cloth and slate from the Welsh
hillsides, were recorded waiting for
a berth outside the harbour. The
seafaring tradition is continued by
the Outward Bound Sea School,
and by the town's sailing club,
which first adopted the GP14
sailing dinghy as a club boat.

*Follow the A493 behind sand-
dunes then continue inland to
Tywyn.*

TYWYN, Gwynedd
Surrounded by the foothills of the
Cader Idris range, the town lies in
the plain of the Dysynni River. The
older part of the town is about 1
mile from the sea, but over the
years it has grown towards a sandy
beach where safe bathing and a
fine esplanade attract tourists. The
church is 12th century, although it
was extensively restored in the
1880s. Within is the 7th-century St
Cadfan's Stone, 7ft high and
inscribed with the earliest known
Welsh writing. Three miles of sand
and shingle beach stretch to
Aberdyfi, and the river and sea
afford excellent fishing, while
Cader Idris offers beautiful
scenery; but perhaps the greatest
attraction to visitors is the Talyllyn
Narrow Gauge Railway.

**TALYLLYN NARROW GAUGE
RAILWAY, Gwynedd**
The Talyllyn Railway celebrated a
centenary of unbroken passenger
service in 1966. It was opened in
1866 to service the slate quarry
above Abergynolwyn, but when
the quarries declined in 1947 the
2ft 3in-gauge railway found itself
having to rely solely on passenger
service. It was taken over by the
Talyllyn Railway Preservation
Society in 1950, and through their
efforts the run-down line has been
refurbished and developed into
the remarkable tourist attraction
and museum it is today. The 7¼
mile-long track begins at Tywyn
Wharf station and ends at Nant
Gwenol.

*Follow SP 'Dolgellau' and in 2¼
miles turn right on to the B4405.
This road follows the attractive
steep-sided Fathew valley, past
Dolgoch and its well-known Falls,
to Abergynolwyn station. In ½
mile reach Abergynolwyn village.
Continue on the B4405 into the
Dysynni valley and follow the river
below high mountain ridges to its
source at Tal-y-llyn Lake.*

TAL-Y-LLYN LAKE, Gwynedd
Tal-y-llyn Lake lies at the foot of
Cader Idris, which towers above to
a height of 2,927ft — the second
highest mountain outside the
Snowdon range. These glittering
waters, over 1 mile long, were
formed during the last Ice Age.

*A mile beyond the lake turn left on
to the A487, gradually climbing to
a 938ft summit, below the
overhanging cliffs of Craig-y-Llam.
Descend to the Cross Foxes Hotel
and turn left on to the A470. A
long, winding descent leads to
Dolgellau. Turn left at the start of
the bypass for Dolgellau town
centre.*

DOLGELLAU, Gwynedd
Dolgellau's ancient stone houses,
narrow streets and austere beauty
lies under the shadow of massive
Cader Idris. Now a delightful
touring centre, in the distant past
the town was a more important
place nationally, for here Owain
Glyndwr held his last Parliament,
and in 1199 Cymer Abbey was
founded nearby; of which only the
church and a few fragments
survive. In Dolgellau itself perhaps

*Looking towards the bulk of Cader Idris
from the twin lakes of Llynnau Cregennen*

the most outstanding feature is the
7-arched 17th-century bridge over
the Afon Wnion which divides the
town.

*Leave Dolgellau on the A493 to
follow the south shore of the
Mawddach estuary. For a detour to
the magnificently scenic Llynnau
Cregennen (NT) below Cader Idris,
turn left on to an unclassified road,
SP 'Cader Idris', on leaving the
town. This road climbs to Llyn
Gwernan, with excellent views to
the left. Continue, below Craig-Las
(2,167ft), and later turn right, SP
'Llynnau Cregennen, Arthog', to
reach the Llynnau Cregennen.*

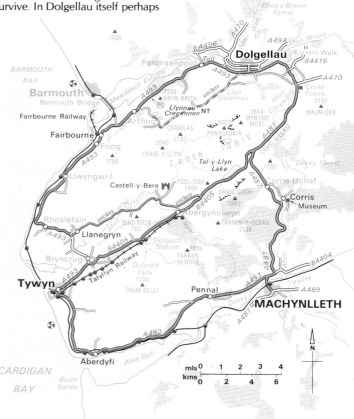

LLYNNAU CREGENNEN, Gwynedd

Situated at over 800ft, the Llynnau Cregennen are 2 small lakes at the foot of the main Cader Idris range, surrounded by 700 acres of National Trust property. Nearby, a marked footpath leads to the summit of the conical Bryn Brith (1,256ft). From here, and from near the car park, there are magnificent views of the Mawddach estuary.

Return to Dolgellau and turn left on to the A493 then follow the main road through Penmaenpool and Arthog to Fairbourne, with views on the right of the railway bridge.

FAIRBOURNE, Gwynedd

Here is one of the finest beaches in Wales and miles of golden sand and safe bathing make it a popular spot. Anti-tank blocks, a legacy of World War II, are scattered along the shoreline. This is the home of the Fairbourne Railway, first laid as a tramway to transport stone and materials for the construction of Barmouth Railway Bridge, before the road was built. However, it was soon realised that the locality and splendid sands were a potential tourist attraction, so the village of Fairbourne was created and developed on reclaimed land along the Mawddach estuary. Until 1916 the tramway was horse-drawn, but later became the Fairbourne Miniature Railway, devoted to passenger service, until its closure in 1940. Six years later it was bought by enthusiasts who were also business men, and has since been rebuilt and renovated.

Beyond Fairbourne the main road climbs high above the shore, with extensive views across Barmouth and Tremadoc Bays. Pass through Llwyngwril and later turn sharply inland. 1 ½ miles beyond Rhoslefain turn left, SP 'Llanegryn' for Llanegryn.

An engine in the dark Brunswick green of the Talyllyn Railway — one of the Great Little Trains of Wales — which operates in the Fathew valley

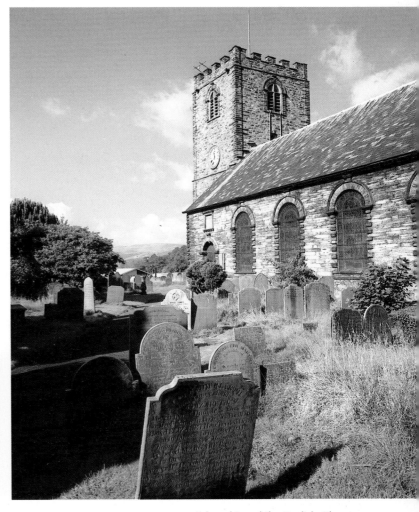

St Mary's Church, Dolgellau

LLANEGRYN, Gwynedd

Llanegryn stands at the mouth of the Dysynni valley, which, broad, flat and unspoilt, stretches away to the summits of the Cader Idris range. Three miles away, but clearly visible, is the extraordinary Bird Rock. This rises to 760ft above the valley floor and is the only inland nesting site of cormorants in Britain. The village itself lies in a hollow, gathered about a short main street which crosses a stream, near which stand 2 chapels joined by their vestries.

Keep forward across the river bridge and follow the Dysynni valley. Later, at the foot of the Bird Rock, turn left, SP 'Abergynolwyn'. In 2 miles turn right to follow the river though a narrow gap. For Castell-y-bere (AM) 1 mile away, turn left at this point.

CASTELL-Y-BERE, Gwynedd

Hidden by trees lies Castell-y-bere (OACT), ruined fortress of the Dysynni valley and once the most important castle in Wales. Great expense was lavished on this castle by the independent Welsh, and here Dafydd, Llewelyn the Last's brother, held out against Edward 1 and the English. The castle, however, eventually surrendered, and Dafydd fled. Victorious Edward took over the castle and gave it borough status, but a town never developed here, as around other castles, and the scant ruins remain lonely, and beautifully unspoilt.

The main tour continues alongside the river through a narrow gap in the hills, then turns left, SP 'Tal-y-llyn'. Shortly rejoin the B4405, again passing Tal-y-llyn Lake. In 1 mile turn right on to the A487. Shortly enter Corris Uchaf (Upper Corris) before descending past Corris village (left) in the valley.

CORRIS, Gwynedd

The village is surrounded by fir-clad slopes, almost the southern boundary of Snowdonia National Park, and consists of a tortuous main street, old solid stone houses and an old stone bridge over the River Dulas. In the village is a small museum of the Corris Railway (closed in 1948) which ran alongside the main road to Machynlleth.

Continue down the winding and thickly wooded Dulas valley to rejoin the Dyfi valley. Turn left and shortly re-enter Machynlleth.

FROM MAWDDACH TO SNOWDONIA

The wooded mountains of Merioneth hide sparkling waterfalls, deserted gold mines and Iron-Age forts, but the highlight of this tour is undoubtedly the ancient castle at Harlech behind which rise the massive Rhinogs.

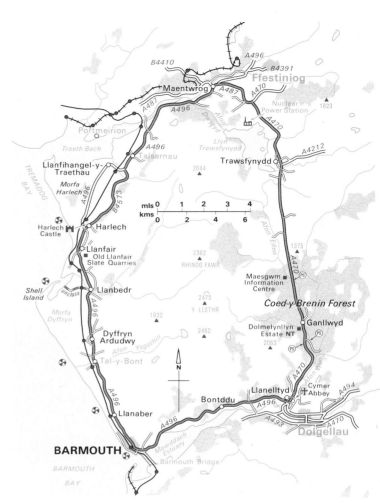

BARMOUTH, Gwynedd

Traditional seaside attractions characterise the popular resort of Barmouth with its long, wide promenade that sweeps up to the busy harbour at the estuary mouth and large, sandy beach. From the quayside a ferry plies to Penrhyn Point, linking with the Fairbourne Railway, a narrow-gauge steam line that runs down from the point for 2 miles along the beach to Fairbourne. Splendid views along the way make this a most rewarding outing. One of the most historic buildings in the quaint Victorian town is Ty Gwyn yn y bermo, on the quayside. This 15th-century house is supposed to have been built for Henry Tudor, Earl of Richmond, before he became Henry VII. However, probably the most dominating feature of the town is the wooden railway bridge spanning the estuary. This also carries a footpath, enabling visitors to enjoy the wonderful scenery along the estuary and to enjoy good views of tiny Friar's Island, just off the coast.

Leave Barmouth on the A496 Harlech road and continue for 1 ¾ miles to Llanaber.

LLANABER, Gwynedd

Perched on the clifftop, just north of Barmouth, is Llanaber's old church which was used rather irreverantly by smugglers in days gone by. Legends say they hid their booty inside the table tombs in the churchyard. The church itself is full of interesting features, such as some 10th-century inscribed stones in the north-west corner, and its doorway is one of the best examples of early English work to be seen anywhere in Britain.

Remain on the coast road and pass through Tal-y-bont to Dyffryn Ardudwy.

DYFFRYN ARDUDWY, Gwynedd

The hills and mountains around this scattered village are full of the remains of Bronze- and Iron-Age settlements. One of the best is Arthur's Quoit, a huge cromlech (prehistoric burial chamber) which can be seen in a field to the west of the village. The capstone is said to have been thrown by King Arthur from the summit of Moelfre (1,932ft), which lies 2 miles away.

Continue to Llanbedr.

LLANBEDR, Gwynedd

Fascinating shells of all kinds are found in abundance on Mochras, or Shell Island, near Llanbedr, and well over 100 different varieties have been found. The 'island' is actually a peninsula which is cut off from the mainland at high tide — a paradise for children and equally popular with holidaymakers and yachtsmen. The village makes an excellent centre for walking in the area, particularly along the valleys of the Cwm Bychan and Nantcol which lead to the enchanting lakes of Cwm Bychan, Gloyw, Du and Bodlyn. Many of the paths follow the tracks made by miners who worked the local manganese deposits. The Cefn Isaf farm trail, starting near Salem Chapel, winds for 2 miles round a typical Welsh hill farm, the workings of which are fully explained along the way.

Follow the A496, and pass (right) the Old Llanfair Quarry Slate Caverns.

The seaside resort of Barmouth stands at the mouth of the tidal Mawddach estuary, which at low tide reveals acres of golden sands that provide a common feeding ground for many species of birds

Harlech Castle cost nearly £9,000 to build in 1290, an astronomical sum in its time. The builder was Master James of St George, Edward 1's chief architect

OLD LLANFAIR QUARRY SLATE CAVERNS, Gwynedd

Slate mining was an important industry in several areas of North Wales a century ago, and it is possible to recapture something of the grim conditions which prevailed then by visiting the Old Quarry Slate Caverns (OACT). The tunnels and caves which were created by the blasting of the hillsides are now specially illuminated and make a fascinating tour.

In 1¼ miles branch right on to the B4573 for Harlech.

HARLECH, Gwynedd

The name Harlech means 'high rock', an apt description of this small town clinging to the cliffside and overlooked by the majestic 13th-century castle (AM). Edward I built the fortress in 1283 with the purpose of controlling the newly-subjugated Welsh people. Its lofty position, which at that time was right by the sea, guaranteed the castle's impregnability and it successfully resisted rebel attacks for 120 years. The military life of the castle ended during the Civil War when the Royalists who lived there finally surrendered to the Roundhead forces in 1647. The best way to see the layout of the castle is to walk along the walls. Its plan consists of 2 rings of walls and bastions, with the inner wall considerably higher than the outer, a pattern derived from one of the strongest Crusader castles. The nature reserve of Morfa Harlech lies to the north of the town, covering a large plain which was reclaimed from the sea in 1908.

Continue along the B4573 and in 3¼ miles rejoin the A496, SP 'Maentwrog'. (The A496 to the left leads to Llanfihangel-y-traethau).

LLANFIHANGEL-Y-TRAETHAU, Gwynedd

Before the land around it was reclaimed, the old church here was isolated on an island. An inscribed stone pillar stands in the churchyard and inside there is a 17th-century stone inscribed in both Latin and Welsh. On the far side of the Traeth Bach Estuary can be seen the fairytale village of Portmeirion, created by Clough Williams-Ellis in 1926, in the style of the Italian resort, Sorrento.

The main tour passes through Talsarnau then follows the south bank of the Afon Dwyryd to enter the Vale of Ffestiniog at Maentwrog.

MAENTWROG, Gwynedd

This village is reputed to be one of the prettiest in Wales. Most of it was built in the heyday of the local slate industry at Blaenau Ffestiniog, and small quays by the river downstream from here were loading points for the slates. The church of St Twrog was largely rebuilt in 1896, but it is said to date from c 610, possibly because Twrog, a 7th-century giant, is said to have hurled a stone from the hillside into the churchyard, where it still lies buried beneath the turf.

Beyond the village turn right on to the A487. Ascend and continue to Trawsfynydd.

TRAWSFYNYDD, Gwynedd

The huge bulk of Britain's first inland nuclear power station dominates the countryside around Trawsfynydd. Llyn Trawsfynydd is a man-made reservoir and provides all the cooling-water needed by the power station, which can sometimes be visited by arrangement; the parkland around incorporates some nature trails and excellent fishing is available in the lake. The village of Trawsfynydd lies just off the main road where there is the house of a remarkable poet, Hedd Wyn. He was a local shepherd boy who

won the poetry competition in the National Eisteddfod in 1917, but was killed in action on the Somme, in France, before he could collect the award. A bronze statue of him, dressed in gaiters and shirtsleeves, stands in the village main street where it was unveiled in 1923.

Continue southwards on the A470 across a stretch of bleak moorland, then after 4 miles enter the Coed-y-brenin Forest.

COED-Y-BRENIN FOREST, Gwynedd

To either side of the road south of Trawstynydd lies the huge forest of Coed-y-brenin. Its name means King's Forest and it is the fourth largest in Wales, covering an area of more than 16,000 acres. In 1922 the first Douglas fir was planted and this is still the predominant species in the forest, although there are also quantities of larch, spruce and pine. The scenery within the forest is superb, surrounded by a ring of mountains taking in the Rhinogs in the west and Rhobell Fawr in the east. The sparkling river Mawddach and its tributaries flow through the area, breaking out into a series of tumbling waterfalls. An excellent information centre is sited at Maesgwrn and this shows what part the forest plays within the local community, what products come from it, the wildlife which inhabits the area and has descriptions of the various facilities available. Planned forest trials start from the picnic sites at Dolgyfeiliau and Tyn-y-groes. This part of Wales used to support a large number of gold mines, and an exhibition of mining machinery can be seen at this information centre.

Near the south end of the forest is the hamlet of Ganllwyd.

GANLLWYD, Gwynedd

The centre of gold mining in the old county of Merioneth used to

be at Ganllwyd and the most prosperous mine, at Gwynfynydd, was the scene of a mini-gold rush in the 1880s, when 250 men worked here. It finally closed in 1917 after producing 40,000 ounces of gold. The Dolmelynllyn Estate (NT) at Gallwyd embraces the superb falls, Rhaiadr-Du, or Black Waterfall. Many rare species of ferns and moss grow in the moist soil around the waterfalls in this nature reserve.

Continue to the outskirts of Llanelltyd.

LLANELLTYD, Gwynedd

Cottages surround the ancient church dedicated to Illtud, a famous Welsh saint of the 6th century. A medieval stone in the church is inscribed in Latin which says that Kenyric's footprint was impressed on it before he set out for foreign parts. Ruins of Cymer Abbey (AM) stand beside the river nearby in a beautiful stretch of the Mawddach valley. The abbey was established by Cistercian monks in the 12th century but was abandoned in about 1350. As well as parts of the south wall of the church there are also the ruins of the refectory and the chapter house.

From Llanelltyd follow the A496 along the Mawddach estuary to Bontddu.

BONTDDU, Gwynedd

Nowadays it is a pleasant holiday village, but about 100 years ago Bontddu was one of the thriving centres of the Welsh gold-mining industry. There were 24 mines in the Merioneth Hills behind the village, and the Clogau mine provided gold for the use of the Royal Family. Nothing now remains of the mine workings, although occasionally fragments of gold may still be found in this area.

The A496 continues beside the estuary for the return to Barmouth.

BANGOR, Gwynedd

Bangor's cathedral is the oldest bishopric in Britain, founded in AD550 by St Deiniol. Bangor means a circular enclosure, or wattle fence, and probably referred to the fence around Deiniol's first church. The present cathedral was rebuilt between 1496 and 1532, after destruction in 1407 by Owain Glyndwr's troops, and its present appearance is due to total restoration by Gilbert Scott in 1866-7. Bangor was not much more than a village until the 19th century, when, during a space of 50 years, Penrhyn's quarries were opened, the docks were built, Telford's road and his suspension bridge were completed, and the railway was laid. The maze of streets and unremarkable architecture of Bangor is dignified by the presence of the University College of North Wales, designed in 1906 by Henry T. Hare. It is a fine English Rennaissance building, unspoilt by the modern extensions added since 1950. Lower Bangor dips down to the shores of the Menai Straits, where a Victorian pier stretches a third of the way to Anglesey. In the town centre, the museum of Welsh Antiquities, housed in the Old Canonry, has exhibits of prehistoric and Bronze-Age implements, Roman and early Christian finds, Welsh furniture and costumes.

Leave Bangor on the A5122, SP 'Conway (A55)', and in 2½ miles pass Penrhyn Castle.

PENRHYN CASTLE, Gwynedd

Penrhyn Castle (NT) is a Victorian extravaganza, financed in 1827 by G. H. Dawkins, the extremely wealthy owner of the Penrhyn slate quarries. The exterior is styled after Norman military architecture — a mass of great walls and crenellated towers built on a fanciful scale. The interior is spacious, lavishly decorated with a richness and complexity that is bewildering and overpowering. Penrhyn Castle was bought by the National Trust in 1951, who have since established a worldwide collection of some 800 dolls, a natural history room, and in the stable block an industrial locomotive museum.

At the roundabout turn left on to the A55 and continue to Aber.

ABER, Gwynedd

Lying just ½ mile from the sea, Aber was a starting point for the journey over the water to Anglesey before the Menai Bridge was built. This involved crossing the vast expanse of Lavan Sands at low tide, beneath which a drowned palace 1,000 years old is alleged to lie, and undergoing a dangerous ferry trip from Beaumaris. Nearby is Coedydd Nature Reserve, set in a beautiful glen, and the spectacular Aber Falls, a 170ft waterfall.

AROUND CARNEDDAU

Encircling the impenetrable bulk of wild Carneddau, the road travels to the mighty fortress at Conwy, meanders along the lush Conwy valley, then twists through the wooded ways of Betws-y-coed: a journey though wild passes, green valleys and coastal plains that sees Wales at her most varied.

Remain on the A55 to Llanfairfechan.

LLANFAIRFECHAN, Gwynedd

The little stream of Afon Llanfairfechan drops 2,000ft over a distance of 3 miles, passing through the old village in the lower and flatter part of its valley. The newer village lies a little to the north where there is a pleasant beach and promenade; good sailing can be had off this coast, and there are fine walks along it.

The tour follows the coast road alongside Conwy Bay to Penmaenmawr.

PENMAENMAWR, Gwynedd

Penmaenmawr has changed very little since it became popular with holidaymakers in the last century, encouraged by William Gladstone, Prime Minister, who made this his summer retreat. The resort offers safe bathing from a good beach backed by a promenade and the pleasant streets and Victorian terraces of the town itself. The headland of Penmaenmawr grows smaller every year, for its stone is continually used in roadbuilding, and quarrying has scarred and disfigured it. An important Iron-Age fort was destroyed in the process, but one of Wales' best-known Bronze-Age stone circles still survives. An urn was

Enchanting Betws-y-coed has attracted tourists since Victorian times when it was a haven for artists and honeymooners

discovered here containing the cremated remains of a child and a bronze dagger, suggesting a ritual sacrifice was performed to consecrate the site.

CONWY, Gwynedd

Three bridges cross the wide estuary of the Conwy on which the town stands; Telford's suspension bridge of 1826; Stephenson's tubular railway bridge; and a modern road bridge. Conwy is the most perfectly preserved of Edward I's walled towns and its castle (AM) is one of the great fortresses of Europe; begun in 1248, it was a key element in Edward I's control of Wales. The town itself began with the building of the castle, and is still largely contained by the medieval walls — 30 ft high with 21 towers built along its length. There are 3 other important survivals from Conwy's past. Plas Mawr (OACT) is a fascinating Elizabethan mansion, built between 1577 and 1580, with courtyards, stepped gables and an octagonal watch-tower, and is now the home of the Royal Cambrian Academy of Art. The Church of St Mary in the town centre incorporates parts of a Cistercian abbey and a worn gravestone to Nicholas Heotes, who died in 1637, 41st child of his father and father of 27 himself. On the corner of High Street and Castle Street is a building, c1500, which is claimed to be the oldest house in Wales, while on the quayside is a tiny house squeezed between 2 terraces, claimed to be the smallest house in Britain (OACT).

From the castle leave on the B5106, SP 'Betws-y-coed'. Continue along the west side of Conwy valley and pass through Tyn-y-groes, Tal-y-bont and Dolgarrog before reaching Trefriw.

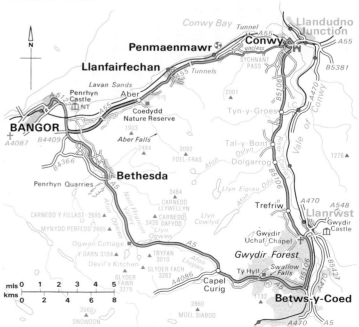

TREFRIW, Gwynedd

Trefriw was briefly a spa town as the local wells lying a mile north of the village are rich in iron and sulphur. The pump rooms and baths were built in 1835 and by 1867 100 people were visiting the spa each day. Within the village itself is the largest woollen mill in Wales, where visitors can observe all the processes required to turn fleece into woollen products. Llanrhychryn Church, a refreshingly primitive building of ancient timbers, slate floors and whitewashed walls, lies hidden by trees from the village and can be reached by a short climb through woods.

In 1¾ miles turn right with the B5106, still SP 'Betws-y-coed', and pass Gwydir Castle.

GWYDIR CASTLE, Gwynedd

More a Tudor mansion than a castle, Gwydir (OACT) became the seat of the Wynn family around 1500. They altered and added to the original hall over the following 100 years, which resulted in the existing layout. In 1944 the house was bought by Arthur Clegg, who renovated the house which had been greatly damaged by a fire between the 2 world wars. Among the furniture with which Clegg refurnished the house is a magnificient bed, *c*1570, which bears carvings illustrating scenes from the Bible. Peacocks arrogantly strut around the grounds and there is an arch built to mark the end of the Wars of the Roses, and a 700-year-old yew tree. Nearby are the Gwydir Uchaf Chapel (AM) and house. The house is now used as a Forestry Commission office and exhibition, but the 17th-century chapel retains many of its contemporary features, and possesses a remarkable painted ceiling.

Continue along the valley to Betws-y-coed.

BETWS-Y-COED, Gwynedd

Three rivers meet in the wooded valley that holds Betws-y-coed and the village has 3 attractive bridges. Telford's graceful, iron Waterloo Bridge of 1815 spans the Conwy, and the beautifully-proportioned Ponty-y-Pair dating from about 1470 spans the Llugwy. Downstream, beside the church, is an iron suspension footbridge smartly painted white. Not surprisingly, the area is renowned for its beautiful waterfalls, the most famous being the Swallow Falls, the Conwy Falls and the Fairy Glen Ravine.

At Betws-y-coed join the A5, and follow the wooded valley of the Afon Llugwy. In 2 miles pass (right) the entrance to the Swallow Falls, then in ¼ mile pass (left) a picnic site and arboretum. After another ½ mile is Ty Hyll.

TY HYLL, Gwynedd

In the wooded Afon Llugwy valley, near the Swallow Falls, is the Ty Hyll — the Ugly House — built of massive irregular rocks, thrown together without any cement. This is supposedly an example of hurried construction in order to obtain freehold right on common land. It was used as an overnight stop by Irish drovers taking cattle from Holyhead to the rich markets of England.

Continue to Capel Curig.

CAPEL CURIG, Gwynedd

Capel Curig is a popular resort with climbers, hill walkers and anglers, and there are numerous hotels to accommodate them in this small but somewhat scattered village. Ringed by mountains, it is the natural home for the National Centre for Mountaineering Activities, housed in Plas Y Brenin, formerly the Royal Hotel built by Lord Penrhyn when Capel Curig was developed as a resort.

Remain on the A5 Bangor road, following the Afon Llugwy. Continue through the Nant Ffrancon Pass (NT) before reaching Bethesda.

BETHESDA, Gwynedd

Bethesda takes its name from the Noncomformist chapel which was established here. However, the village is primarily a quarryman's community, for nearby, gouged out of the steep slopes of Bron Llywyd, is the world's largest opencast slate quarry. It is 1 mile long by 1,200ft deep, covering a total of 560 acres. Richard Pennant was the entrepreneur who created the quarry in 1765, building Port Penryn in 1790 specifically to serve the quarry. By 1875 the quarry employed 2,300 men, but competition from abroad and the increase in production of roofing tiles at the turn of the century caused a decline of the industry.

Continue on the A5 for the return to Bangor.

Above: Conwy Castle, seen between Telford's bridge and Stephenson's bridge

Below: this 4-poster bed in Penrhyn Castle is made of slate and weighs 4 tons

THE DEE VALLEY AND THE VALE OF CLWYD

From the small town of Llangollen, where streets are filled with the sound of music from the International Eisteddfod every July, the drive crosses by the lofty Horseshoe Pass into the rich farmland of the Vale of Clwyd and carries on through Clocaenog Forest to the pretty lakeside town of Bala and the picturesque Dee valley.

LLANGOLLEN, Clwyd
In July every year this small Welsh town on the River Dee plays host to thousands of visitors and competitors who flock to the International Musical Eisteddfod, which was instituted in 1947. Llangollen's old stone bridge dates from 1345-6 and is doubly acclaimed: firstly as one of the Thri Thlws Cymru, the 3 beauties of Wales; secondly in a traditional rhyme as one of the Seven Wonders of Wales. 'Pystyll Rhaeadr and Wrixham Steeple/ Snowdon's Mountain without its people;/Overton Yewtrees, Saint Winifred Wells,/Llangollen Bridge and Gresford Bells.' A source of wonder in their own lifetimes were the Ladies of Llangollen, Miss Sarah Ponsonby and Lady Eleanor Butler. These eccentric ladies left their native Ireland and defied convention by setting up house together in 1778 at Plas Newydd, a handsome black and white timbered house (OACT), inaccurately described by the poet Wordsworth as a 'low-browed cott'. The ladies always wore severely masculine dress and were often mistaken for men. It became fashionable to visit them and among their distinguished guests were Sir Walter Scott and the Duke of Wellington. To the west of the town are the Horseshoe Falls, not a tumbling cascade, but an elegant semi-circular weir designed by Thomas Telford to take water from the Dee to his canal. There is a small canal museum on the town wharf.

Leave Llangollen on the A542 Ruthin road, and follow the Eglwyseg valley to pass ruined Valle Crucis Abbey.

VALLE CRUCIS ABBEY, Clwyd
Set amid hill and valley, the original majestic ruins (AM) evoke the splendour of the abbey. It was built by Madog ap Gruffydd Maelor, Prince of Powys, and destroyed by order of Henry VIII 3 centuries later. Of the abbey church only the west front, with its beautifully carved doorway, survives. The Cistercian monks ate fish not meat, and had fishing rights in the River Dee.

Continue on the A542 and shortly pass (right) the Pillar of Eliseg.

PILLAR OF ELISEG, Clwyd
Prince Eliseg fought a great battle against the Saxons in 603 to reclaim his inheritance of Powys. Concenn, his great grandson, had the 12ft-high pillar cross erected on the hillside in Valle Crucis 2 centuries later to commemorate the victory, and its history was inscribed in Latin on the stone. This is one of the oldest surviving records of pre-Norman Britain. During the Civil War, Cromwell's soldiers threw the cross down and broke it. The remaining portion was re-erected in the 18th century.

Continue up to the Horseshoe Pass.

HORSESHOE PASS, Clwyd
The spectacular Horseshoe Pass (1,367ft) leads over the eastern edge of Llantysilio Mountain into the undulating pastures of the Vale of Clwyd. From the summit there are superb views of the rocky ridge of Eglwyseg Mountain and the wooded Dee valley.

2½ miles beyond the summit go forward at the roundabout, then in ½ mile turn left on to the A525. Descend the wooded Nant-y-garth Pass into the Vale of Clwyd and continue to Ruthin.

RUTHIN, Clwyd
'Rhyl, St Asaph, Denbigh and Ruthin lie along the Vale of Clwyd like beads threaded on a string and the fairest of these is Ruthin', wrote the novelist Stanley Weyman in 1928. Ruthin, encircled by wooded hills, is an old market town where Edward I built a stronghold in the 13th century to keep the troublesome Welsh in check. In September 1400 however, the Welsh prince Owain Glyndwr rebelled against the English and sacked Ruthin in September 1400. After the Civil War the medieval castle fell in ruins and the present structure, now a hotel, dates from the 19th century. A number of attractive 16th- and 17th-century timbered houses stand in the old streets which meander up to the little square. Here the Maen Huail stone is kept, where, according to legend, King Arthur slew Huail, his rival in love. The old court house and prison is now a bank; projecting from the eaves is the stump of a gibbet last used in the reign of Elizabeth I.

At the roundabout in the town centre go forward, SP 'Cerrig-y drudion', then keep forward on to the B5105. Cross rolling countryside and pass through Clawdd-newydd, before entering Clocaenog Forest.

CLOCAENOG FOREST, Clwyd
The vast green expanse of Clocaenog Forest clothes the slopes of the Denbigh moors. Like many of the woodlands in North Wales, this is the creation of the Forestry Commission, who started planting in the 1930s: the trees are mostly conifers — larch and sitka spruce. There are picnic areas and way-marked forest trails.

Descend to Llanfihangel Glyn Myfyr and cross the Afon Alwen then continue to Cerrigydrudion.

The 4-arched medieval bridge over the River Dee at Llangollen

CERRIGYDRUDION, Clwyd
English author George Borrow describes Cerrigydrudion in his book *Wild Wales* as a 'small village near a rocky elevation from which no doubt the place takes its name . . . the rock of heroes.' The rocky elevation is the nearby hill of Pen y gaer, crowned by an Iron-Age hill fort where it is said that King Caractacus was betrayed to the Romans by Cartimandua and taken in chains to Rome. His bearing so impressed his captors that they set him free.

Pont Cysyllte aquaduct is still used, 176 years after its completion, by pleasure craft on the Llangollen Canal

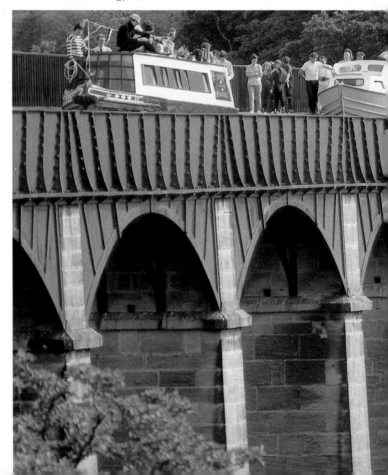

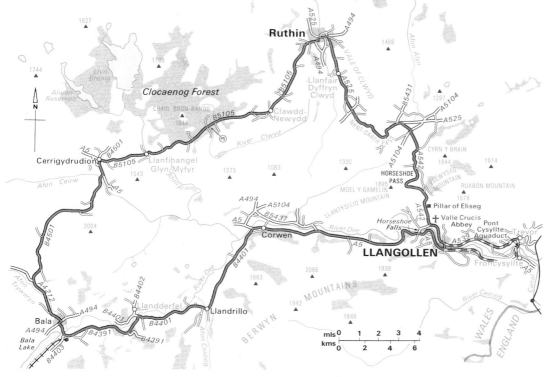

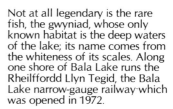

Not at all legendary is the rare fish, the gwyniad, whose only known habitat is the deep waters of the lake; its name comes from the whiteness of its scales. Along one shore of Bala Lake runs the Rheilffordd Llyn Tegid, the Bala Lake narrow-gauge railway which was opened in 1972.

Cross the River Dee and follow the valley, then in 3¼ miles turn left on to the B4402, SP 'Corwen'. In 1 mile turn right on to the B4401 for Llandrillo.

LLANDRILLO, Clwyd
This small village on the Afon Ceidiog, which flows down a narrow valley into the River Dee, is an excellent starting point for walks in the Berwyn Mountains, one of the 3 great mountain ranges of North Wales. The lowest pass over these hills is higher than 900ft, and many of the summits top 2,000ft.

Continue through pleasant countryside and after 7¾ miles turn right on to the A5, SP 'Llangollen', to reach Corwen.

CORWEN, Clwyd
Corwen lies amid the beautiful scenery of the wooded Dee valley, overlooked by the Berwyn Mountains. The Welsh hero Owain Glyndwr, who raised a revolt against Henry IV, had estates near Corwen from which he took his name. A groove in the lintel of the church doorway was reputedly made by Glyndwr hurling his dagger at it in a fit of rage. Some of the gravestones in the churchyard are hollowed out to allow mourners to kneel and pray over the dead.

Remain on the A5 through the beautiful wooded Dee valley for the return to Llangollen.

A 9 mile extension to the drive can be made as follows: from Llangollen follow the A5 to Froncysyllte. Here, turn sharp left on to the B5434, SP 'Trevor', and descend into the valley. On the right is Pont Cysyllte.

PONT CYSYLLTE, Clwyd
The wonder of Pont Cysyllte is the spectacular aqueduct, built by Thomas Telford in 1805 to carry the Llangollen branch of the Shropshire Union canal over the Dee valley. The 1,007ft-long aqueduct is the longest in the country, supporting a cast-iron trough on 18 tapering stone piers 127ft above the river. At the time, people scoffed at Telford, but boats still cross the aqueduct and after all this time there is scarcely any leakage of water from the dovetailed joints of the iron trough.

Cross the River Dee, then bear right. At the T-junction turn left on to the A539 (no SP) and return along the north side of the valley to Llangollen.

Ringed by hills, 140ft-deep Bala Lake is said to conceal a drowned city

In Cerrigydrudion turn left on to the Llangollen road, then left again on to the A5. In ½ mile turn right on the B4501, SP 'Bala'. After 7 miles turn left on to the A4212 and continue to Bala.

BALA, Gwynedd
Knitting warm woollen stockings was Bala's main industry in the 18th century: they were so famous that George III insisted on having a pair to ease his rheumatism. Bala is a pretty town on the northern shore of Bala Lake, and was made an important centre of Welsh Nonconformism by its minister, Thomas Charles, born in 1755. His aim was to provide Bibles for his people, and hearing of this, a village girl, Mary Jones, made an epic journey in 1800 on foot, 25 miles across the mountains, to obtain a Bible from him. Her determination inspired him to become one of the founders of the British and Foreign Bible Society, an organisation dedicated to the dissemination of Bibles throughout the world.

Leave on the B4391, SP 'Llangynog', and pass the northernmost end of Bala Lake.

BALA LAKE, Gwynedd
This 4 mile-long lake is the largest natural expanse of water in Wales. Its Welsh name is Llyn Tegid, and it is also known as Pimble Mere — the lake of 5 parishes. Legends include the story that the Dee flows through the lake without its waters mingling with those of the lake. Tradition gives the source of the Dee as 2 fountains, Dwy Fawr and Dwy Fach, named after 2 people who escaped the Great Flood, represented by Bala Lake.

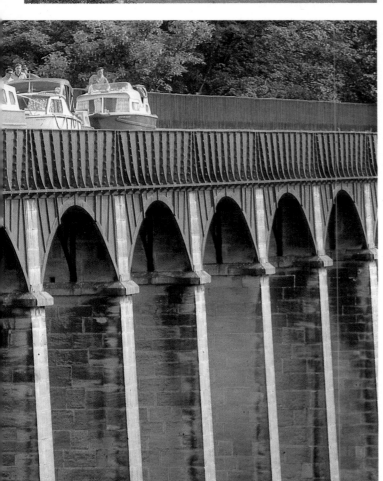

OSWESTRY, Shrops

Sometimes in England, sometimes in Wales, Oswestry was for centuries a battleground between the 2 countries, until the Act of Union in 1535 permanently established the border to the west of the town. Three times ravaged by fire, and by plague in 1559, when nearly a third of the inhabitants perished, few of Oswestry's medieval buildings have survived. Among those which have, Llwyd Mansion, a black and white timbered building in the centre of the town, bears the double-headed eagle of the Holy Roman Empire on one wall. The crest was granted to the Lloyd family in recognition of its services during the Crusades. Other noteworthy ancient buildings include the row of cottages near the church which originally housed Oswestry Grammar School. This was founded in 1407 and is thought to be the oldest secular foundation in the country. In Morda Road, the Croeswylan Stone, or Cross of Weeping, marks the place to which the market was shifted during the plague. Oswestry supported the Royalist cause in the Civil War, but Cromwell's forces took the town and destroyed the castle, of which only a grassy mound and a few fragments of masonry survive. King Oswald's Well sprang up, according to legend, on the spot where an eagle dropped one of the limbs of King Oswald of Northumbria, slain at the Battle of Maserfield by King Penda of Mercia in 642. The parish church is dedicated to Oswald, and Oswestry is a corruption of his name.

Leave Oswestry on the A483 Wrexham road, and in 1 mile pass (left) Old Oswestry.

THE WELSH MARCHES AND THE BERWYN MOUNTAINS

The turbulent history of the borderlands between England and Wales resulted in a series of magnificent Norman castles. The tour leads from the Border town of Oswestry, to Chirk, through the delightful woodlands of the Ceiriog valley, across the foothills of the wild Berwyn Mountains and along the Cain and Vynrwy valleys.

The coat of arms decorating the wrought iron gates of Chirk Castle belongs to the Myddleton family, who have lived in the castle since 1595

OLD OSWESTRY, Shrops

On a ridge a little to the north of Oswestry lie the remains of a massive Iron-Age hill fort, known in English as Old Oswestry and in Welsh as Yr Hen Dinas, 'the old fort'. It dates from about 250BC, when the first lines of defence, 2 great banks and ditches, were constructed. At a later date a third bank was added and the whole site was enclosed by a formidable double rampart. The fort was inhabited for more than 300 years, until the Romans destroyed it in AD75.

Continue on the A483 and at Gobowen turn left at the roundabout on to the A5, SP 'Llangollen'. In 2 miles descend into the Ceiriog valley where the Chirk Aqueduct can be seen ahead. Cross the river into Wales and ascend to the edge of Chirk.

CHIRK, Clwyd

Chirk is an attractive small town with streets of pleasant houses shaded by trees. A short footpath leads west from Chirk to the stone arched aqueduct built by Thomas Telford between 1796 and 1801. Its 10 great arches carry the Shropshire Union Canal high over the Cairiog valley. Alongside runs the railway viaduct, built in 1848.

A detour can be taken by keeping forward with the A5, then take the next turning left on to an unclassified road to Chirk Castle.

CHIRK CASTLE, Clwyd

The Welsh name of the castle, Castell y waun, meaning 'meadow castle' aptly describes its beautiful setting. Built by Edward I in 1310, Chirk (NT) is a fine example of a border stronghold — a rectangular stone fortress with massive, round drum towers at the 4 corners. In 1595 it became the home of Sir Thomas Myddelton, later Lord Mayor of London. His son held the castle for Parliament during the Civil War, and relics of that period can be seen in the courtyard. Later, the family supported Charles II, and the magnificent long gallery contains portraits and furniture dating from the Restoration. There is a beautifully decorated and furnished suite of 18th-century rooms, whose elegance is echoed by the graceful wrought iron gates at the entrance to the park. These, with their delicate tracery of foliage, were the work of Robert and John Davies, 2 brothers who lived near Wrexham. Through the park runs a part of Offa's Dyke, which for many centuries after King Offa's death in AD796, marked the boundary between England and Wales. There is a walk to Llangollen from here.

The main tour turns left at the edge of Chirk on to the B4500, SP 'Glyn Ceiriog'. Follow the Ceiriog valley, through Pontfadog, to Glyn Ceiriog.

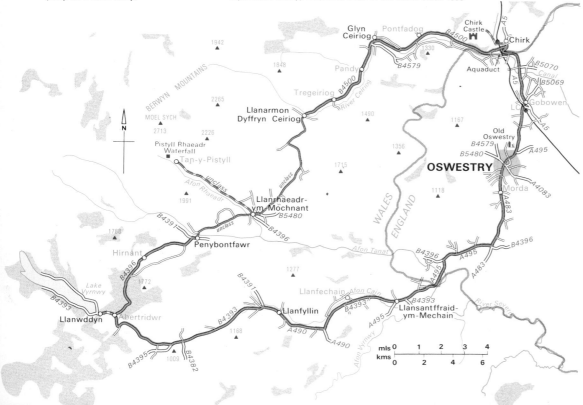

The dramatic waterfall of Pistyll Rhaeadr is the highest in Wales

GLYN CEIRIOG, Clwyd

Llansantffraid Glyn Ceiriog, to give the village its full name, stands on the swift-flowing River Ceiriog and is the main centre for exploring the lovely Ceiriog valley. Quarrying was once a major industry and in the Village Institute there are relics of the narrow-gauge tramway that ran from the quarries to the canal at Chirk.

Continue on the Llanarmon road for the gradual climb through the narrowing valley, passing the villages of Pandy and Tregeiriog and approaching the foothills of the Berwyn Mountains, to Llanarmon Dyffryn Ceiriog.

LLANARMON DYFFRYN CEIRIOG, Clwyd

Situated at the head of the Ceiriog valley, Llanarmon, a secluded village hidden in the foothills of the Berwyn Mountains, makes an excellent centre for walkers and for riding holidays. Penybryn, just above the village, was the birthplace of the great lyric poet John Ceiriog Hughes (1832-87). A farm labourer, who later became stationmaster at Glyn Ceiriog, Hughes wrote in Welsh but is, paradoxically, best remembered among the English for the translation of one of his less accomplished poems, *God Bless the Prince of Wales.*

Go forward over the crossroads, SP 'Llanrhaeadr', and climb out of the valley. In 1¾ miles, at the top, turn left and descend following a hilly, narrow byroad to Llanrhaeadr-ym-mochnant.

LLANRHAEADR-YM-MOCHNANT, Clwyd

This large market village has grown up around a tiny square where the 17th-century inn and the solid, square tower of the parish church make a pleasant group. The village was the birthplace in 1540 of William Morgan, later Bishop of St Asaph, who made the first translation of the Bible into Welsh, thus helping to preserve the language from extinction. It was published in 1588 by permission of Elizabeth I, who revoked a decree of Henry VIII which had officially banned Welsh.

A detour can be taken by turning right in the village to Tany-y-pistyll and the remarkable Pistyll Rhaeadr waterfall.

PISTYLL RHAEADR, Clwyd

The falls of Pistyll Rhaeadr, rightly considered to be one of the Seven Wonders of Wales (see Llangollen, tour 45), cascade down a tree-covered gorge high up in the Rhaeadr valley. The water falls for 200ft, then pours through a natural rock arch to tumble down a further 100ft in a series of leaps and rocky pools.

The main tour continues through the village. Cross the river bridge and by the Three Tuns PH, go forward for Penybontfawr.

PENYBONTFAWR, Powys

Its picturesque setting amid the Berwyn Mountains is the charm of this small village on the Afon Tanat. As with many hill villages, church, vicarage, school and terraced houses were all built in the 19th century and only the outlying farms date from an earlier period. To the north-east of the village rises the bleak summit of the 3,713ft-high Moel Sych.

At the T-junction turn right then left on to the B4396, SP 'Lake Vyrnwy', and follow a winding narrow road to Llanwddyn.

LLANWDDYN, Powys

This is a new, model village, built in the 1880s when the Afon Vyrnwy valley was drowned to form Lake Vyrnwy. The old village, which lies at the bottom of the lake, originally grew up around the church of a 6th-century Celtic saint, Wddyn. Later it became part of the principality of Powys and in the 13th century was acquired by the Jerusalem Knights of St John.

Leave Llanwddyn on the B4393 Llanfyllin road, passing through rolling hill scenery. In 7¾ miles turn right on to the A490 to enter Llanfyllin.

LLANFYLLIN, Powys

This little market town on the River Cain centres on a pleasant square where the town hall used to stand. In olden days, Llanfyllin had a dubious reputation for strong ale — Old ale fills Llanfyllin with young widows — ran the saying. During the Napoleonic Wars French prisoners were quartered here and a room in the chemist's shop still displays frescoes painted by them during their captivity.

Follow the Welshpool road and in 2 miles turn left on to the B4393, SP 'Llansantffraid' and 'Oswestry'. Continue along the Cairn valley then in 3¾ miles turn left on to the A495 to enter Llansantffraid-ym-mechain.

LLANSANTFFRAID-YM-MECHAIN, Powys

The village strays along the main road in 3 stages. First comes the church, with vicarage, school hotel and timbered brick cottages gathered close around it. Next, a group of new houses spread out around the flour mill, and finally set around the 18th-century arched bridge stands a collection of tidy Victorian houses.

Follow the Vyrnwy valley before crossing the border into Shropshire. Later, at the T-junction turn right, then in 2¼ miles turn left on to the A483 for the return to Oswestry.

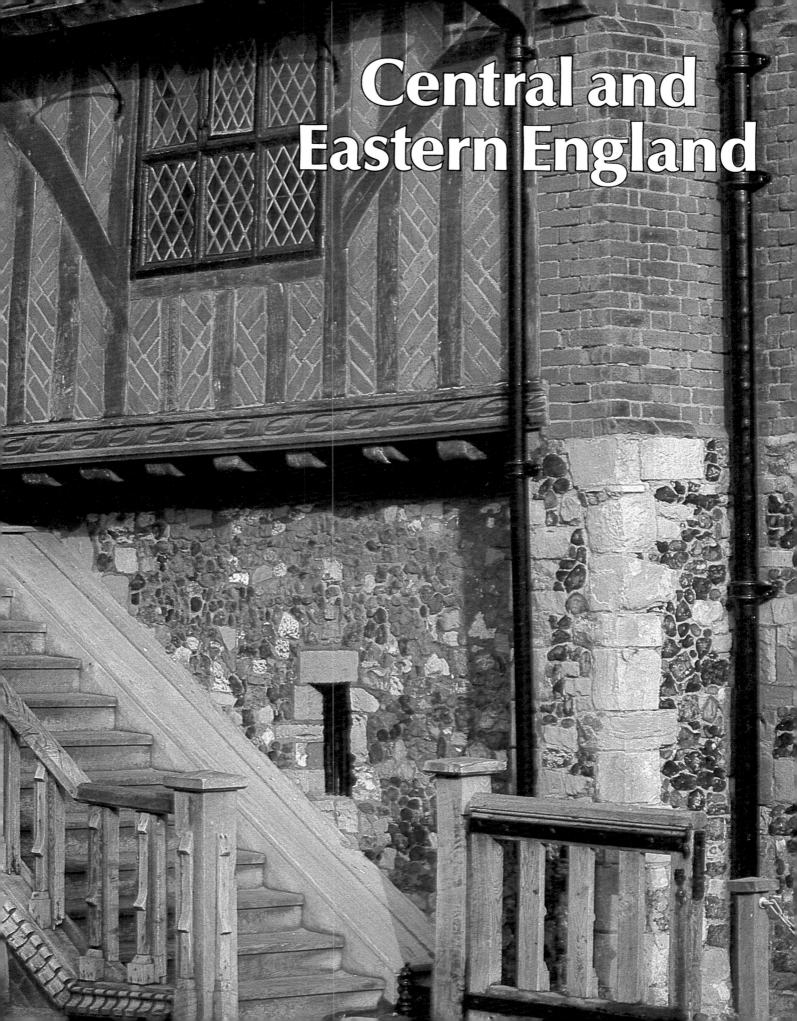

Central and Eastern England

STAFFORD, Staffs

New buildings encircle the county town, but despite this the old centre retains its dignified character. In Greengate Street stands the aptly named High House, 4 storeys high, and a beautiful example of timberframe construction. St Chad's is a fine Norman church with carvings said to have been the work of Saracens brought back to England after the Crusades by Lord Biddulph. The parish church, St Mary's, contains a monument to Izaak Walton, the noted angler, who was born at Stafford in 1593. Noel's Almshouses in Mill Street, a group of stone houses round a spacious courtyard, date from 1660. The William Salt Library in Eastgate Street is a remarkable collection of old deeds, drawings and books on Staffordshire history amassed by William Salt.

Leave on the A518, SP 'Telford' and 'Newport', and pass through Haughton for Gnosall.

GNOSALL, Staffs

Gnosall's church has a superb Norman interior, featuring massive pillars and decorated arches. An interesting item near the altar, in the pavement of the south aisle, is the rough carving of a pair of sheep-shearer's shears, no doubt a tribute to the importance of the wool trade. High on the tower outside can be seen a mason's mark of shield and hammer.

WHERE A HUNTED KING FOUND REFUGE

The capital of the Black Country is, unexpectedly, the gateway to the leafy woodlands and deer-haunted glades of Cannock Chase — noble remnant of a royal forest — and to the quiet pleasures of Staffordshire's unassuming countryside, where a succession of stately homes once gave shelter to the exiled Charles II.

Continue to Newport.

NEWPORT, Shrops

A town of great charm, Newport's broad main street passes on either side of its imposing church, whose 14th-century tower looks out on a vista of handsome 18th-century houses. There is a famous grammar school near the church, founded by William Adam in the Commonwealth period, that still has its original 17th-century clock. One of its most famous pupils was Sir Oliver Lodge, who was one of the pioneer experimenters in wireless telegrams.

Turn left then right, still SP 'Telford', to remain on the A518. In 2 miles turn left on to an unclassified road and enter Lilleshall. In 1¼ miles turn left, SP 'Lilleshall Abbey', and pass the remains in 1 mile (left).

LILLESHALL ABBEY, Shrops

Lilleshall Abbey (AM) now consists of graceful ruined arches and walls but some idea of its former magnificence can be gained by looking through the west front down the length of the ruins to the east window. It was founded in 1148 and after the Dissolution Henry VIII gave the abbey to the Leveson family, who were local landowners at that time. It stands in the grounds of the Hall that has now been turned into the National Sports Centre, which is where the English team trained before winning the World Cup in 1966.

In 2 miles turn left on to the B4379, then turn right, SP 'London'. Later cross the A41 to join the B5314. In another 2 miles turn left on to the A5, then take the next turning right on to an unclassified road and pass the entrance to Weston Park.

WESTON PARK, Staffs

This Classical 17th-century house (OACT) has been the family home of the Earls of Bradford for 300 years. The rooms are mainly of 18th and 19th-century inspiration, and the tapestry room, lined with rose-pink Gobelin tapestries, is particularly notable. However, the real treasure of Weston is the magnificent collection of paintings, which includes portraits of the Bradfords and works by leading Dutch, Italian and French masters.

Continue along the unclassified road to Tong.

TONG, Shrops

Thatched cottages, a distant mock-castle, wooded slopes and an ancient church give Tong its charm and character. When Charles Dickens wrote *The Old Curiosity Shop* he had this village in mind as the final haven of Little Nell and her grandfather. The red sandstone church, with unusual battlements, has one of the most splendid arrays of monuments in the Midlands. Many are of Lady Elizabeth Pembruge — who founded the church in the early 15th century — and her husband. Others include effigies of the Vernon family, including Sir Richard, Speaker of the House of Commons in 1428.

The Shropshire Union Canal at Gnosall, which links the Mersey to the Severn

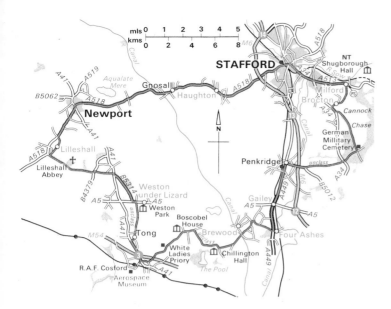

At the church turn left, then shortly turn left again on to the A41. In almost 1 mile, at the start of the dual-carriageway, turn left on to an unclassified road (no SP). Alternatively, turn right to visit the Aerospace Museum.

AEROSPACE MUSEUM, Shrops
Two hangars within the grounds of Cosford RAF station house the museum. One hangar concentrates on rockets, ranging from the earliest German model to more modern ones. The other hangar has over 50 aircraft, including a World War II Lincoln Bomber which is being meticulously restored by teams of volunteers. Here too is a prototype of the TSR2 — a new fighter-plane which Harold Wilson cancelled because it was costing too much money. Each exhibit has a placard describing its history, and outside there are picnic sites and a souvenir shop.

The main tour later joins a narrow byroad, SP 'Shackley', and continues to Boscobel House.

BOSCOBEL HOUSE, Shrops
Built in 1600 for the Roman Catholic Gifford family, Boscobel House (AM) was amply provided with secret hiding places to shelter priests, and it was here that Charles II, defeated and weary, found refuge in 1651 after the Battle of Worcester. Hunted high and low by soldiers, he spent the day in an oak tree near the house hidden by the loyal Penderel family, who were Boscobel's tenants. The present oak tree, although ancient, is not the original, but grew from one of its acorns. Whiteladies nearby, is a ruined 12th-century nunnery where the king also sheltered from pursuit.

At the T-junction turn right, then branch left on to another byroad (no SP). In ¾ mile turn right and 1¼ miles farther pass (right) Chillington Hall.

CHILLINGTON HALL, Staffs
For 800 years, Chillington Hall (OACT) has belonged to the Gifford family through direct male descent, but it was not until 1724 that Peter Gifford began to build the existing redbrick mansion. He demolished part of the Tudor house and bought in Francis Smith of Warwick as the architect. Later, in about 1750, Sir John Soane built the east front and one of the most interesting rooms is Soane's saloon, which replaced the Tudor great hall. It has an oval ceiling which leads up to an oval lantern and over the chimneypiece is the Gifford family arms. Capability Brown landscaped the grounds in the 18th century and formed the beautiful ornamental lake that occupies 75 acres.

After passing the main gateway turn left then in 1 mile turn left again. In ¾ mile go over the crossroads, SP 'Four Ashes', then in another ¾ mile, at the T-junction, turn left. At the next T-junction turn right and cross the river bridge then turn right again, still SP 'Four Ashes'. In 1¼ miles turn left on to the A449, SP 'Stafford', then at the Gailey roundabout take the 2nd exit and continue to Penkridge.

PENKRIDGE, Staffs
Of the several pleasing old buildings in this quiet little town near the River Penk, the old stone and timber deanery, dating from the 16th century is the most outstanding. The large parish church is packed with interesting monuments and was once the collegiate church of the area which maintained a dean and 4 canons. North of the church is the timber-framed Old Deanery.

At Penkridge turn right on to the unclassified road, SP 'Cannock', then turn right again. Cross the M6 then in ½ mile turn left, SP 'Rugeley'. In 2 miles cross the A34 and enter Cannock Chase.

CANNOCK CHASE, Staffs
Conifers, silver birches, heathland and little valleys cover a wide area of countryside that was for centuries the royal hunting forest of Cannock Chase. Fallow deer, descendants of the vast herds that roamed the Chase in medieval and Tudor times, graze among the surviving areas of oakwood, and in marshy areas the rare sundew flourishes. Soaring up above the treeline, the Post Office tower looks down on the German Military cemetery where the dead of 2 wars lie buried, including the crew of the first Zeppelin shot down in World War I.

At the next crossroads turn left, SP 'Brocton' and 'Stafford', and pass the German Military cemetery. Descend to the A34 and turn right. In ¼ mile, at the crossroads, turn right into Brocton, then continue to Milford. From here a short diversion to the right along the A513 leads to Shugborough Hall.

SHUGBOROUGH HALL, Staffs
The white, colonnaded mansion (NT) set in beautiful grounds has been the home of the Anson family, Earls of Lichfield, since the 17th century. The fortune of

The dining room fireplace and a portrait of Admiral Lord Anson at Shugborough

George Anson, the celebrated admiral and circumnavigator of the world, paid for much of the splendour of house and park. Mementoes of the admiral's voyages and victories are an outstanding feature of the house, which also contains fine paintings and 18th-century furniture. In the park, the flamboyant Triumphal Arch, modelled on that of the Emperor Hadrian at Athens, commemorates Admiral Anson's victory over the French in 1747. Other particularly charming features are the elegant little Tower of the Winds and, on an island in the lake, the Cat's Monument in memory of a favourite pet of the Admiral that sailed round the world with him. The Staffordshire County Museum and Farm Park are also contained in the grounds of Shugborough Hall. Museum exhibits include social history, crafts and agricultural subjects, and the park has rare farm livestock.

The main tour leaves Milford on the A513 and later joins the A34 for the return to Stafford.

STAFFORDSHIRE'S VALLEYS

Three valleys, Dovedale, the Manifold and the Churnet,
offer some of the loveliest scenery to be found anywhere
England. Often, and unfairly, dismissed for the industrial
sprawl of the Potteries, the countryside of north
Staffordshire changes from a patchwork of small, hedged
fields to the bleak grandeur of the open moors.

A piece of 'jasperware' pottery made by
Wedgwood in Stoke-on-Trent

STOKE-ON-TRENT, Staffs

In 1910, the towns known as the
Potteries — Hanley, Burslem,
Tunstall, Fenton, and Longton —
were amalgamated and named
Stoke-on-Trent. Pots dating from
before the Roman era have been
discovered in the area, but the
great English porcelain companies,
Wedgwood, Minton, Spode and
Doulton, were all established in
the late-18th and early-19th
centuries. Most of the factories
organise conducted tours and the
Gladstone Pottery Museum in
Longton, with its carefully restored
and preserved traditional bottle-
shaped kilns has practical
demonstrations of the craft as well
as exhibitions. Hanley's City
Museum contains one of the finest
collections of pottery and
porcelain in the world. Novelist
Arnold Bennet, who wrote books
about the Potteries, or 5 Towns
was born in Hanley in 1867.
Drawings, manuscripts, letters and
other relics of the writer can be
seen in the City Museum. Another
native of the Potteries represented
in the museum is the aeronautical
engineer R J Mitchell who
designed the first 'Spitfire'
aeroplane in 1936 which became
famous as a World War II fighter.
Also near Cobridge is Ford Green
Hall (OACT), a 16th-century
timber-framed mansion built for
the Fords, a family of yeoman
farmers, which contains
English furniture and domestic
items of the 16th to 18th
centuries. Some idea of the
development of mining
technology can be gained from

the Chatterley Whitfield Mining
Museum near Tunstall. Guided
tours take you 700ft below the
ground around the workings and
there is a colliery lamphouse
exhibition and museum

*From the city centre at Hanley
follow SP 'Burslem A50', and in ¾
mile turn right on to the A53. Pass
through Baddeley Green and
Endon then in 1¼ miles turn left,
SP 'Rudyard', into Dunwood Lane,
and continue for 2½ miles to
Rudyard.*

RUDYARD, Staffs

This charming little village was
made famous by the parents of
the novelist and poet Rudyard
Kipling, whom they named after
the place where they had spent
many holidays, and where it is said
Lockwood Kipling proposed to
Alice Macdonald. The lake lies in
a deep wooded valley surrounded
by high moors, and along the
shores of the nearby reservoir are
pleasant walks, with picnic sites.

*Turn right on to the B5331. In 1
mile, at the T-junction, turn right on
to the A523 then take the next
turning left, SP 'Meerbrook'. In ½
mile turn left again and later skirt
Tittesworth Reservoir before
reaching Meerbrook.*

MEERBROOK, Staffs

A lonely village surrounded by
bleak moorland, Meerbrook lies in
the shadow of Hen Cloud (1,250ft).
Nearby are the Staffordshire
Roaches, a forbidding outcrop of
dark millstone grit rocks rising to
1,658ft which have been
weathered over the ages into
fantastic shapes.

*Turn right at the church, SP
'Blackshaw Moor' and 'Leek' and in
1¼ miles turn left on to the A531.
In 2 miles go forward over a
crossroads then turn right, SP
'Longnor'. A long descent leads to
the Manifold valley and Longnor.*

LONGNOR, Staffs

Longnor is the market centre of
the far north of Staffordshire, a
charming stone-built place
surrounded by superb hill scenery,
whose narrow streets and alleys
end abruptly in magnificent views
of the Peak District.

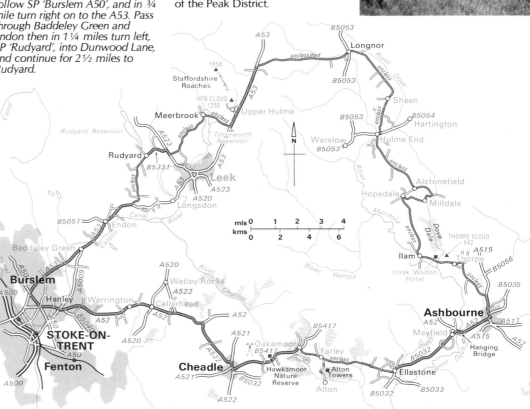

Dovedale's alpine scenery has earned it the title Little Switzerland

Follow SP 'Bakewell' and in ½ mile branch right, SP 'Hulme End'. Continue, through Sheen, then in 1½ miles turn right on to the B5054 into Hulme End, and at the Light Railway Hotel turn left on to the unclassified road for Alstonefield. Here keep left, SP 'Ashbourne', and in 1¼ miles turn sharp right (care needed) SP 'Milldale'. At Milldale, turn right and ascend a narrow gorge to Hopedale. At the Watts Russell Arms turn left, SP 'Ilam', and in 100 yds turn left again. After 2 miles descend into Ilam.

ILAM, Staffs

Ilam owes its delightful and unique appearance to the 19th-century manufacturer Jesse Watts Russell, who bought the village and estate. The cottages he built are completely different in design from the traditional Staffordshire style, with steep-pitched, gabled roofs covered with dark red, shaped tiles. Ilam Hall is now a youth hostel, but the spacious park in the lower reaches of the Manifold valley belongs to the National Trust.

At the war memorial turn left, SP 'Dovedale, Thorpe'. In ¾ mile, by the entrance to the Izaak Walton Hotel, a short detour can be made by turning left to reach a car park at the entrance to Dovedale (reached on foot).

DOVEDALE, Staffs

Dovedale, at the southern edge of the Peak District National Park, is one of the most beautiful valleys in England. The River Dove, the boundary between Staffordshire and Derbyshire, runs through a deep, wooded limestone gorge, where high white cliffs,

Below: 150 years ago Alton Towers was no more than a bare and rocky wasteland

honeycombed with caves, have been weathered into distinctive shapes — the 12 Apostles, Dovedale Castle, Lion's Head, and so on. At the southern end of the valley, annual sheepdog trials draw crowds at the end of August from all over the region.

Cross the River Dove into Derbyshire then skirt the village of Thorpe and in ½ mile, at the Dog and Partridge Hotel, turn right, SP 'Ashbourne'. In 2 miles turn right on to the A515 to enter Ashbourne.

ASHBOURNE, Derbys

Ashbourne has some fine architecture, particularly in Church Street, where 2 sets of almshouses, an Elizabethan grammar school, a mansion house and an old inn make a pleasing group. The parish church, St Oswald's, is considered one of the best examples of Early English style in the North Midlands. Ashbourne holds a traditional football game on Shrove Tuesday, when the inhabitants of the 2 banks of Henmore Brook compete in a riotous game with few rules and unlimited numbers. The locally famous Ashbourne gingerbread is still made to a secret recipe, taught to the town's bakers by French soldiers held prisoner during the Napoleonic Wars.

Leave on the A52, SP 'Uttoxeter (B5032)', and in 1½ miles cross the Hanging Bridge.

HANGING BRIDGE, Staffs

The Hanging Bridge leads the way from Derbyshire across the River Dove to the small stone-built village of Mayfield, clinging to the Staffordshire bank. The name is said to commemorate the hanging of Jacobite supporters of Bonnie Prince Charlie in 1745 — his army had reached Derby on the march south, but then retreated back to Scotland. Records show, however, that the name is much older than the 18th century.

Beyond the bridge turn immediately left on to the B5032. Continue through Mayfield following the Dove valley, to reach Ellastone.

ELLASTONE, Staffs

Robert Evans, father of the novelist George Eliot (Mary Ann Evans), worked as a carpenter here for a time, and the village features in her novel *Adam Bede* under the name Hayslope. Not far from the village, Wootton Lodge (not open) looks out over the Churnet valley. A tall, graceful building, it is one of the finest examples of Jacobean architecture in the county.

Turn left in the village then in ¼ mile turn right on to an unclassified road. In ½ mile go forward over crossroads and in another ½ mile turn left. In 1½ miles, at the edge of Farley, a detour can be made by turning left, 'SP 'Alton', for Alton Towers.

ALTON TOWERS, Staffs

The 15th Earl of Shrewsbury, whose family had acquired vast estates in Staffordshire, came to Alton in the early 19th century and fell in love with the rugged scenery of the Churnet valley. The 600-acre gardens of Alton Towers (OACT) are the result of his work. Thousands of trees and flowering shrubs — rhododendrons, azaleas, Japanese maple, cedars, dwarf and giant conifers, tulip trees — cover the hillsides and set off a series of gardens, ornamental ponds and fountains, connected by winding paths designed to offer an ever-changing succession of views. Soaring above the gardens, the towers and pinnacles of Alton Towers seem like something from a fairy tale. Most of the house, built by the 16th Earl, is just a shell, but the chapel, with its splendid roof designed by the Victorian architect, Pugin, is intact and now houses a superb model railway. Other modern innovations include a miniature scenic railway, an aerial cable car and numerous amusements for children.

The main tour continues into Farley. At the end of the village turn left, SP 'Oakmoor', and in 1 mile turn left again on to the B5417. Cross the River Churnet into Oakmoor and later pass (right) the Hawksmoor Nature Reserve.

HAWKSMOOR NATURE RESERVE, Staffs

This part of the Churnet valley, between Oakmoor and Cheadle, was presented to the National Trust in 1926 by J. R. B. Masefield, a well-known Staffordshire naturalist and cousin of the poet John Masefield. Several rare varieties of tree, such as the lodge pole pine and the red oak flourish alongside the native plants, and many birds — curlews, pheasants, redstarts, nightjars and warblers — have found refuge in the woodland. Nature trails are well marked.

Continue on the B5417 to Cheadle.

CHEADLE, Staffs

High moorland surrounds this small market with a high street of pleasant 18th-century and Victorian buildings, but dominating it all is the massive Roman Catholic church whose lofty spire (200ft) is a landmark for miles around. The church was built in 1846 by Pugin and is regarded as one of his masterpieces. The interior is a magnificent tableau of rich colour, creating an atmosphere of 19th-century opulence.

At the town centre turn right on to the A522, SP 'Leek', and in 2¼ miles turn left on to the A52 for Cellarhead, Werrington and Bucknall. At the traffic signals beyond Bucknall turn right, then at the next traffic signals go forward on the A5008 for the return to Hanley (Stoke-on-Trent).

113

SHEFFIELD, S Yorks

Chaucer's *Canterbury Tales* refer to Sheffield cutlery as early as the 14th century, and when Flemish craftsmen settled here in the 16th century Sheffield began to specialise in cutlery in earnest. In about 1740 Benjamin Huntsman discovered how to produce steel, and Thomas Boulsover discovered how to roll silver plate; the 2 products for which Sheffield is world famous. Bomb damage in World War II necessitated the rebuilding of the city centre and there is little pre-Victorian building. The town hall, with a statue of Vulcan on the very top, was opened in 1897, and nearby the Cutlers Hall of 1832 contains a fine collection of silver from 1773 to the present. The City Museum in Weston Park, however, has the best collection, and the world's largest collection of Sheffield plate. There are 2 art galleries in Sheffield; the Graves, above the Central Library, which has an excellent collection of Chinese ivories and Mappin Art Gallery in Weston Park, specialising in English art.

Leave Sheffield on the A625, SP 'Chapel-en-le-Frith', and climb out of the suburbs on to Totley Moor (1,254 ft). To the left there are fine

THE PEAK DISTRICT

Great dams and small stone villages, bleak moorlands and narrow wooded valleys, fast-flowing rivers and placid lake waters; here is a mountain country in miniature, where ruined mills and tumbled stone walls testify to nature's supremacy. However, man has long inhabited the Peaks, and remnants of prehistoric cultures litter the hillsides.

views of the Derwent valley before entering Derbyshire and the well-known 'Surprise View', from where the entire Hope valley can be seen. Descend to Hathersage.

HATHERSAGE, Derbys

This small town in the Hope valley was well-known by the Brontë family, and nearby North Lees Hall and Moorseats Hall were depicted in Charlotte Brontë's novel *Jane Eyre*. Charlotte stayed with her friend Ellen Nussey in the vicarage, and her pearl inlaid writing desk is kept here. Over the church porch are the arms of the Eyre family, and within are fine brass portraits representing generations of Eyres. A grave in the churchyard is said to be that of Little John, Robin Hood's comrade.

Continue along the Hope valley and in 1 ¾ miles pass the junction with A6013, SP 'Glossop', which provides a short detour through Bamford to the Howden, Ladybower and Derwent reservoirs.

LADYBOWER, HOWDEN & DERWENT RESERVOIRS, Derbys

Howden, Derwent and Ladybower reservoirs lie in the valley of the Upper Derwent, forming a lovely landscape of tree-clad slopes and glittering lakes. Howden and Derwent, built in 1912 and 1916 with great castellated dams, were used for target practice during World War II by the famous Dambusters squadron. Ladybower was opened later, in 1945, at the cost of 10 farmhouses and 2 villages which lay in its path.

An unclassified road to the right immediately beyond the 2nd viaduct (A57) leads past an arm of the Ladybower reservoir up to the Derwent reservoir. The main tour continues for 2 ½ miles to Hope.

HOPE, Derbys

The village stands in the middle of a valley named after it, and was an important trading centre in medieval times. Today it is noted for the fishing and rough shooting to be had hereabouts. A weekly stock market is still held here and during late summer the Hope valley agricultural show with its popular sheepdog trials is a local highlight. Before this on Midsummer Day (25 June), a well-dressing ceremony takes place in which the village well is decked in flowers. The ceremony is pagan in origin and the flowers were offerings to the gods who supplied the spring water.

Continue on the A625 to Castleton.

The Mam Tor/Losehill ridge is a 3-mile barrier which separates Edale from the Hope valley

Inset: many Peak District villages ceremonially decorate their wells with clay panels inlaid with flower petals, such as this one at Hope

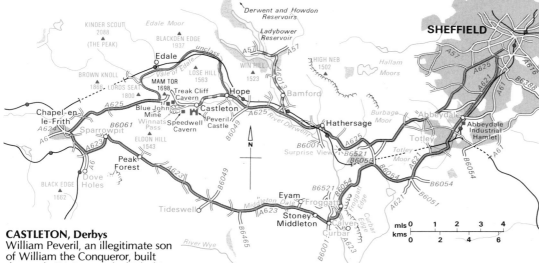

SHEFFIELD

CASTLETON, Derbys
William Peveril, an illegitimate son of William the Conqueror, built the castle (AM) around which this popular Peak District village grew. The keep which remains today was erected by Henry II in 1176, and is the most impressive medieval landmark in the Peak National Park. However, the feature which attracts the visitor most to this pleasant village is its group of limestone caverns (OACT): Peak, Speedwell, Treak Cliff and Blue John, the last named after the rare, blue semi-precious stone found in these hills. Speedwell Cavern is the most spectacular as it consists of one huge chamber and has to be toured in a boat. The nearest cavern to the village is Peak Cavern which is the largest and stretches 2,000ft into the hillsides. Castleton Garlanding, held on 29 May, is a strange custom, believed to be a fertility rite praising some long-forgotten god. A bell-like garland covers the wearer who is usually led through the village on horseback.

To visit Speedwell Cavern and the Winnats Pass, continue on the A625 (now closed at Mam Tor) and at the end of the village branch left on to the unclassified road. The Blue John Cavern can be reached by turning right beyond the end of the gorge, and Treak Cliff is reached by staying on the old A625 at the end of Castleton village. The main tour returns along the A625 to Hope and at the church turns left on to the Edale road.

EDALE, Derbys
In the shadow of the Kinder massif — the highest point in the peak District — is broad, green Edale valley. Along its length are hamlets known as booths (Upper Booth, Barber Booth, Grindsbrook Booth and so on), the name refers to the shelters used by cattle herdsmen in Elizabethan times when the valleys were divided into great ranches. Today sheep rather than cattle roam the valley pastures. On the other side of the valley from Kinder is a massive 3-mile-long ridge, with Mam Tor

(1,696ft) as the highest point. This is crowned by a great Iron-Age fort, which was once a sizeable town. Part of the earthworks have fallen away on the east side, giving rise to landslides which have given Mam Tor the nickname 'shivering mountain'. These slides have recently destroyed the main road running along its lower slopes. Mam Tor is a very old name, the 'Mam' referring to a pagan belief in a mother goddess.

Follow this unclassified road through the valley passing Edale village, and near the end bear left and later ascend to a 1,550ft pass, behind Mam Tor. Descend to the A625 and turn right and in 4¼ miles enter Chapel-en-le-Frith.

CHAPEL-EN-LE-FRITH, Derbys
The first church here was a chapel built in the 13th century by local foresters, and the site would then have been at the edge of the forest — hence, en-le-Frith. The present church dates from the early 14th century. The position of this small market town is high up in the Peak District and it is the gateway to the famous walking and climbing country for which the Peaks are renowned.

Follow SP 'Buxton' to join A6 and in 1½ miles turn left again on to the A623, SP 'Chesterfield'. At Sparrowpit turn sharp right, and in 2 miles pass through Peak Forest.

PEAK FOREST, Derbys
In high, exhilarating countryside this straggling village was once the 'Gretna Green' of the Peak District. The original church, dedicated to King Charles the Martyr in 1657, was extra-parochial, and therefore independent of episcopal jurisdiction, and so up until the early 19th century was able to hold marriage services outside usual church law.

In 2½ miles pass an unclassified road on the right for Tideswell. In 4 miles start the descent into Middleton Dale and in 1½ miles the B6521 to the left leads to Eyam.

EYAM, Derbys
One day in 1665 a clothes chest was delivered to a cottage in Eyam from plague-ridden London. The chest carried plague germs, and between 1665-1666 two-thirds of the population was wiped out. The villagers, led by their rector William Mompesson and his

predecessor Thomas Stanley, resolved to isolate themselves to prevent the plague spreading. Whether this heroic act saved or lost life is disputed by modern-day theorists, but either way it has earned Eyam an honoured place in history. The cottage which took delivery of the clothes chest still stands, and Cucklett Church, a nearby crag, where Mompesson held open-air services during the plague, is the scene of an annual commemorative service.

Shortly pass through Stoney Middleton.

STONEY MIDDLETON, Derbys
Stoney Middleton is as beautiful as Castleton, except for the white dust from the nearby limestone quarries, which covers trees for miles around and produces a most eerie landscape on a moonlit night. In the village is one of the few truly octagonal churches in the country. Two wells stand before the church, and are decorated every August with pictures from the Bible made from thousands of flower petals and bits of bark and moss which are pressed into soft clay.

Continue to Calver and turn left at the traffic signals on to the B6001, SP 'Grindleford', and in ¼ mile branch right on to the B6054, SP 'Sheffield'. Shortly turn left across the River Derwent and climb to Totley Moor. At the summit keep right. To the left is a ventilation shaft of the 3½ mile-long Totley railway tunnel which lies 650ft below the top of the moor. Further on join the A621 before reaching the Abbeydale Industrial Hamlet.

ABBEYDALE INDUSTRIAL HAMLET, S Yorks
Ranged round a large courtyard on a half-acre site on the banks of the River Sheaf, is a remarkable piece of industrial archaeology. This is the Abbeydale Industrial Hamlet, dating mainly from the 18th century, and consisting of workshops and workers' cottages. The main industry here was scything and there is a grinding shop, a tilt-hammer house, a steel melting shop and 6 hand forges. The hamlet has been restored to working order and opened to the public.

Continue on the A621 for the return to Sheffield.

THE PEAK NATIONAL PARK, Derbys
The National Park was the first to be designated as such in Britain, the green 'lung' of industrial England. Peak incidentally comes from Old English 'peac' for knoll or hill. The area comprises the White Peak central and southern limestone area, a gentle, rolling countryside of wooded slopes and rounded hills, and Dark Peak the northern gritstone region, hard, bleak and wild.

115

THROUGH THE DUKERIES

The open countryside of the Trent valley gives way to the ancient woodlands of Sherwood Forest, the traditional hunting ground of Robin Hood and his merry men. Here, a series of palatial estates known as the Dukeries were created in the 18th and 19th centuries by 4 dukes.

NEWARK-ON-TRENT, Notts

At the centre of the old market town whose ruined castle walls are reflected in the river, is the old cobbled market place surrounded by attractive buildings. Most famous is the 14th-century timbered White Hart Inn, its façade adorned by figures of angels. Nearby stands the Clinton Arms, where William Gladstone, who became Prime Minister in the late 19th century, gave his first public political speech. In the streets around the market place fine Georgian buildings lend character to the town, and opposite the castle is a remarkable Victorian extravaganza, the Ossington Coffee Palace, built by Lady Ossington to promote the cause of temperance. The castle (AM), of which only the west wall, towers and north gateway remain, was where King John died of a surfeit of food and drink at the end of the disastrous journey during which he lost the crown jewels in the Wash. The castle, held for the king during the Civil War, proved impregnable to siege, but its commander surrendered after King Charles had given himself up to the Scots, and Cromwell's troops destroyed it. The church of St Mary Magdalen is remarkably beautiful and has a soaring 240ft slender spire.

Leave Newark on the A46, SP 'Lincoln'. In 2½ miles, at the roundabout, turn left on to the A1133, SP 'Gainsborough', and continue to Collingham.

COLLINGHAM, Notts

A plaque on the village cross records that in 1795 the River Trent burst its banks and swept through the village causing a flood 5ft deep. In the following century there was another flood almost as bad, but the Trent has since been diverted and its old course through Collingham is followed now by the River Fleet, which is no threat to this pleasant village strung out along the eastern river bank.

At the end of the village turn right on to the South Scarle road, then in ¼ mile turn left. Later, at the T-junction, turn right into South Scarle. Follow the Swinderby road, then shortly turn left, SP 'Eagle'. In ½ mile bear right and later, at the T-junction, turn right. In another ½ mile turn left, SP 'Lincoln', and ¾ mile further turn left again. Pass through Eagle and after 1½ miles turn left, SP 'Doddington', then in ¾ mile turn left again to reach Doddington.

Mighty Newark Castle was 'slighted' by Cromwell's soldiers in the Civil War

DODDINGTON, Lincs

The focal point of the village of Doddington is its lovely Elizabethan mansion (OACT), owned by the Jarvis family. Portraits by Reynolds, Lawrence and Lely decorate the walls, and the rooms contain fine period furniture, porcelain and ceramics. Among the curiosities on show is a medieval scold's bridle — a fearsome contraption put on a nagging wife to stop her talking.

Go forward on to the B1190. In 3¼ miles turn left on to the A57, and in just over ¼ mile turn left on to the Worksop road. Continue past Newton On Trent and Dunham, then in 1¾ miles turn right, SP 'East Drayton'. In 1 mile at the T-junction, turn left for East Drayton. At the church turn right and continue to Stokeham. Here, turn right then left on to the Leverton road. After 1¼ miles turn left into Treswell, then turn right for South Leverton and North Leverton.

NORTH & SOUTH LEVERTON, Notts

Dutch-gabled houses dating from the 17th and 18th centuries give these 2 villages a distinct resemblance to Holland. At North Leverton, a trim tower windmill, 3 storeys high and still in working condition, also echoes the atmosphere of the Netherlands. The mill, erected in 1813, is known as a subscription mill because all the neighbouring farmers banded together to finance it.

Continue on the unclassified road to Sturton-le-Steeple. From here a detour can be made by turning right to visit Littleborough.

LITTLEBOROUGH, Notts

As its name suggests, this is a tiny village with an even tinier Norman church. It was here that King Harold and the Saxon army crossed the Trent in 1066 on their desperate march south to Hastings to stop the Norman invasion. A drought in 1933 lowered the river level to reveal a paved ford, which has been in existence since the village was built.

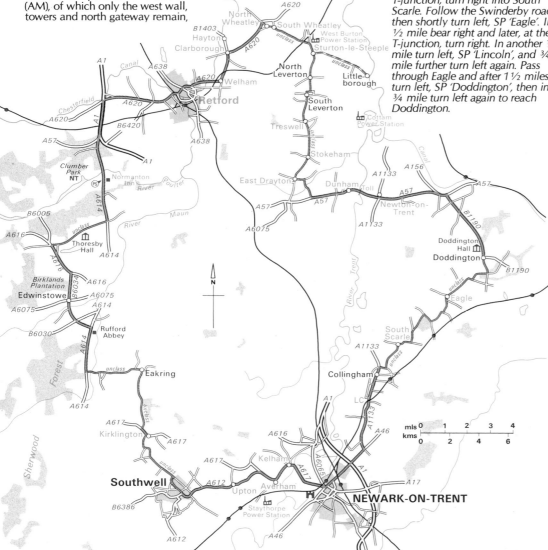

Southwell minster; unique in having pyramidal roofs to its towers

The entrance to Thoresby Hall

At Sturton-le-Steeple, follow SP 'Gainsborough', then 'Wheatley', to pass near West Burton Power Station. Beyond South Wheatley turn left into North Wheatley and at the end of the village turn left again on to the A620 and continue through Retford, SP 'Worksop'. In 3¾ miles turn left, SP 'Newark', to join the A1. Later, at the roundabout, take the A614 to enter Sherwood Forest and the area known as the Dukeries.

THE DUKERIES, Notts
The name Dukeries was given to the northern part of Sherwood Forest because, in the 18th and 19th centuries, no less than 4 dukes and several earls and marquises bought estates in the area. Most of the forest had been completely denuded of trees in the aftermath of the Civil War, and the land was desolate. It was not until the Dukes of Norfolk, Kingston, Newcastle and Portland began to establish plantations of woodland that the forest regained something of its traditional appearance. Three of the ducal estates remain: Clumber Park, Thoresby Hall and Welbeck Abbey; Rufford Abbey, an estate of the Earls of Shrewsbury is just outside the boundary of the Dukeries proper.

After 1¼ miles cross the River Poulter, with Clumber Park to the right.

CLUMBER PARK, Notts
The Duke of Newcastle created this 3,400-acre park (NT), one of the original Dukeries, in the 18th century. It was planted with noble trees, the showpiece of which is the 3-mile avenue of lime trees called the Duke's Drive. Near the ornamental lake stands an elegant 19th-century church in red and white sandstone, built by the 7th Duke as a private chapel. The imposing ducal mansion was, however, demolished in the 1930s when the estate was sold.

Continue past the Normanton Inn and in 1½ miles, at the crossroads, turn right on to the unclassified Thoresby Hall road.

THORESBY HALL, Notts
This gigantic Victorian mansion (OACT), home of the Countess Manvers, is the third stately home to stand on the 12,000-acre Dukeries park. It was designed by Anthony Salvin, who restored Windsor Castle, and is probably the largest Victorian house in England, with 29 main apartments and 78 bedrooms. The interior is lavishly decorated, and there are statues of Robin Hood and Little John in the library, carved by a Mansfield woodcarver. The estate was originally enclosed in the 17th century by the 1st Earl of Kingston. The park was laid out around beautiful ornamental lakes surrounded by avenues of chestnut trees. On the edge of the lake stands a 'model' village, built in 1807, and on the hillside above it is a folly called Budby Castle.

After 2½ miles turn left and join the A616, then in 1½ miles turn right on to the B6034 and continue to Edwinstowe.

EDWINSTOWE, Notts
This substantial colliery village is the biggest of the villages in the Dukeries area. The Birklands plantation, the oldest part of Sherwood Forest, comes right up to the edge of the village. Birklands means birch, and silver birch and oak trees are the main species in the estate. Part of Birklands is now the Sherwood Country Park and here the Major Oak stands. Named after a local historian, Major Rooke, the oak is the oldest tree in the forest, with a girth of 30ft around its hollow trunk. Although damaged by a storm in recent years, its massive branches spread a circumference of 270ft. This is said to have been Robin Hood's hideout for his outlaw band, and there is a local tale that Robin Hood and Maid Marion were married in Edwinstowe Church.

Continue on the B6034, and in 1 mile, at the traffic signals, go forward, then in ½ mile turn right on to the A614 to pass the entrance to Rufford Abbey.

RUFFORD ABBEY, Notts
A Cistercian abbey stood here from medieval times until the Dissolution of monasteries in Henry VIII's reign, when the estate was given to the Earl of Shrewsbury. It later passed into the hands of his daughter-in-law, Bess of Hardwick, who built a great mansion on the site which over the centuries has fallen in ruins. Her descendant, Sir George Savile, planted most of the oak and ash woodlands in the 18th century, and the estate is now a country park (OACT) with a lake and formal gardens.

Continue along the A614 for 1¾ miles, then turn left on to an unclassified road to Eakring.

EAKRING, Notts
Oil was first struck near this surprisingly rural village in 1939, which today stands at the centre of the Nottinghamshire oilfield. The village church contains a brass to the Revd William Mompesson who came here as vicar in 1670 from plague-ridden Eyam (see tour 49) in Derbyshire. When he arrived in Eakring, however, his parishioners still feared the plague and at first refused to let him enter the village; a stone cross on the outskirts marks the place where he preached his sermons. Eventually all was well, and he remained in Eakring till his death in 1708.

Leave Eakring on the Kirklington road then ascend. On the descent there are good views before turning left on to the A617 for Kirklington. By the nearside of the village turn right on to the Southwell road. After 2½ miles turn right for Southwell town centre.

SOUTHWELL, Notts
The glory of Southwell is its great minster, a 12th- and 13th-century building with a Romanesque nave and transept. In the octagonal chapter house are exquisite carvings of foliage — oak, hawthorn and vine leaves. Vicar's Court, in the precinct, is a delightful group of 17th-century houses with hipped roofs. King Charles I spent his last night as a free man at the Saracen's Head, an old coaching inn in the town.

Leave Southwell on the A612 Newark road, and continue through Upton to Kelham then cross the Trent and return to Newark.

THE FEN COUNTRY

For centuries farmers have been draining the fens and creating new fields, but Oliver Cromwell, the farmer's son who became Lord Protector of England, would still recognise the broad horizons of the Cambridgeshire-Northamptonshire border, his old school in Huntingdon, and his family home — Hinchingbrooke House.

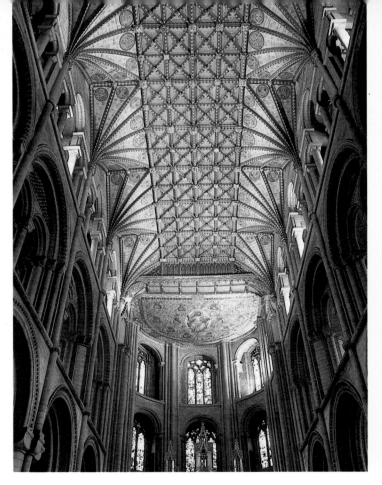

The 15th-century roof of the presbytery and chancel in Peterborough Cathedral

PETERBOROUGH, Cambs
Factories, office blocks and extensive housing estates have turned the ancient settlement of Peterborough into a 'New Town', unfortunately with little charm. Until the 19th century and the development of the railway, it was a peaceful river port on the Nene with an outstanding cathedral. The latter, built of local Barnack stone, is still magnificent and the triple-arched front is its chief glory. Catherine of Aragon and Mary, Queen of Scots were buried here, although Mary's body was subsequently reburied in Westminster Abbey by James I. Another fine building still standing is the old Guildhall in Market Place. It was built to commemorate the Restoration of Charles II and at one time was used as a Butter Market. A few old stone houses have also survived such as those in Preistgate and among them is the Museum and Art Gallery. Here there are bone carvings made by French prisoners during the Napoleonic Wars.

From Peterborough city centre follow SP 'Leicester (A47)' and cross the railway bridge. In 1¾ miles, at the roundabout, take the unclassified road for Longthorpe.

LONGTHORPE, Cambs
Longthorpe Tower (AM) was added to the village manor house in the 14th century as fortification. On one floor of the square tower there are some rare wall-paintings dating from about 1330, but they were not discovered until after World War II. The paintings represent religious and allegorical tales such as the Three Living and the Three Dead, and the Wheel of the Five Senses, figured as animals.

Beyond the village, at the T-junction, turn right. At the roundabout take the A47, SP 'Leicester', and continue to Castor.

CASTOR, Cambs
When the Romans occupied Britain they built *Durobrivae* by the Nene and took over the potteries at Castor, and Castor ware was subsequently sent to all corners of their Empire. The Normans built the village church, using Roman remains, and it is the only one in England dedicated to St Kyneburgha, the sister of King Peada who founded Peterborough Abbey.

After 3 miles cross the A1 then turn left on to the A6118 for Wansford.

WANSFORD, Cambs
Crossing the River Nene at Wansford is a medieval 10-arched bridge which links the village on either side of it. Wansford is sometimes known as Wansford in England, and this dates from the 17th century when a traveller called Drunken Barnabee arrived at the village inn (now called Haycock Inn) and, finding a plague sign on the door, slept on a haycock. During the night the Nene swept him downstream and when he awoke people said to him: 'Whereaway, from Greenland?' to which he replied: 'No; from Wansford Brigs in England.'

Continue on the B671, then in 3½ miles turn right on to the A605, SP 'Oundle', and enter Elton.

ELTON, Cambs
Along the village's 2 main streets — Over End and Middle Street — are ranked stone-built cottages and houses, many with mullioned windows. All Saints Church has 2 Saxon crosses in its churchyard which indicates there may have been a church on this site since the 10th century. Elton Hall (OACT) in Elton Park, dates from the 15th century but has had 18th- and 19th-century alterations

Continue on the A605 to Oundle.

OUNDLE, Northants
This lovely old county town has been unspoilt by time; alleyways thread their way past ancient inns, tall stone houses with steep roofs and tiny cottages with the smallest of windows. Oundle's famous public school was founded in 1556 by William Laxton, a grocer of the town who became Lord Mayor of London; the school is still owned by the Grocers' Company. The Nene flows round the town, making it a very popular sailing centre with beautiful views of the surrounding countryside.

Leave by the Kettering road. Cross the river and pass Barnwell Country Park. Join the A605 then in 1¾ miles (on right) is the turning for Lilford Park.

Wansford Bridge has been added to over the years which accounts for its irregular arches

LILFORD PARK, Northants
The 4th Baron Lilford, a keen ornithologist and naturalist, focused attention on Lilford Park at the end of the last century through the aviaries and gardens he built here. These have been restored or rebuilt, and the gardens are stocked with hundreds of birds, including the Lilford crane, named after the baron, and the Little owl, which Lilford introduced to Britain from Europe by releasing breeding pairs from aviaries in this park. The grounds, covering about 240 acres, offer a range of attractions for the whole family, including a children's farm, a craft and museum centre and an antique centre. The 17th-century house, Lilford Hall, is only open for special events such as motor shows and craft markets.

Continue on the A605 and in 1 mile pass the edge of Thorpe Waterville, then in another mile turn left on to an unclassified road for Titchmarsh.

TITCHMARSH, Northants
There is a splendid Perpendicular tower on the village church, which has a ha-ha (sunken ditch which cannot be seen from a distance) as a boundary. Two painted monuments inside the church are by Mrs Elizabeth Creed, cousin of John Dryden, the poet. The delightful thatched almshouses which stand to the south of the church and green, were provided by the Pickering family in 1756.

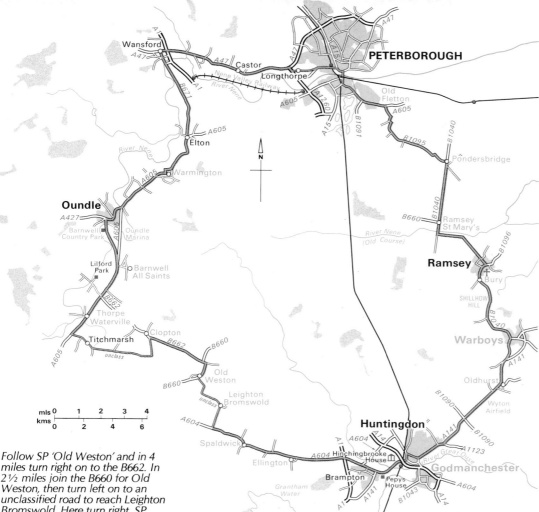

From the Ring Road (one way) follow the A141, SP 'March'. Pass RAF Wyton before reaching the edge of Oldhurst. In ½ mile turn left on to the B1040, SP 'Ramsey'. Pass through Warboys and Bury before entering Ramsey.

RAMSEY, Cambs

Ramsey Abbey, built in 969 on a tiny island in the marshland of the Fen country, prospered to become one of the 13th century's most important abbeys. As a result of this prosperity a town grew up around it. The Dissolution, however, brought an end to both: the abbey was destroyed and the lands sold off. Thereafter a series of misfortunes befell the town: the Parliamentarians destroyed many buildings during the Civil War; the Great Plague struck in 1666, and a series of devastating fires ravaged the town in the 17th and 18th centuries. All that remains of the abbey now is the gatehouse (NT) which looks across the smooth lawns of Abbey Green. A few 18th-century houses surround the green, but the rest of Ramsey is mostly 19th century. Great Whyte is the town's wide, main street, built in 1852 over Bury Brook which flowed through the town.

Turn left to continue on the B1040, SP 'Pondersbridge'. In 2¾ miles turn right and cross the river bridge then at Pondersbridge turn left on to the B1095, SP 'Peterborough'. In 4 miles turn left on to the A605 and pass through Old Fletton before the return to Peterborough.

Follow SP 'Old Weston' and in 4 miles turn right on to the B662. In 2½ miles join the B660 for Old Weston, then turn left on to an unclassified road to reach Leighton Bromswold. Here turn right, SP 'Huntingdon', and descend, then in 1 mile turn left on to the A604. Nearly 6 miles farther, at the roundabout, take the 2nd exit, then join the A141 before reaching the edge of Brampton.

BRAMPTON, Cambs

Among the reddish-yellow cottages in Brampton is the gabled house once owned and lived in by diarist Samuel Pepys's family (open by appointment). It is said that Pepys buried his money here when an invasion from Holland was feared.

At the roundabout go forward and in 1 mile pass (left) Hinchingbrooke House.

HINCHINBROOKE HOUSE, Cambs

A medieval nunnery was the foundation of Hinchinbrooke House (OACT), the remains of which were given to Oliver Cromwell's grandfather in 1538, but it was Oliver's father who began to adapt the ruins and build a country home. The house was damaged by fire in 1830 but afterwards restored by Edward Bore. One of the best features of the interior is the 17th-century carved staircase, which was installed during the 1950s from a house in Essex (now demolished). Hinchinbrooke has been used as a school since 1962.

Continue into Huntingdon.

HUNTINGDON, Cambs

Once a county town, Huntingdon has ancient origins, its history stretching back to Roman times — coins and pottery of that era have been found here. By the end of the 10th century a market and a mint were established, and the town grew in prosperity. However, the Black Death of 1348 drastically reduced the population, and the town sank into obscurity. Always a centre for local agriculture, Huntingdon survived the setback, and was again a substantial little market town by the 18th century, when the impressive town hall was built. In 1599 Oliver Cromwell was born here, and both he and Samuel Pepys attended the grammar school (OACT), now a museum of relics associated with Cromwell. The famous poet William Cowper lived in Cowper House in 1765. Most of the town is Georgian, but the George and Falcon inns are fine examples of 17th-century building and the finest medieval bridge in the county links the town with Godmanchester.

The George Inn in Huntingdon retains its courtyard, galley and external staircase of the 17th century.

BURY ST EDMUNDS, Suffolk

'Shrine of a King, cradle of the Law' runs the city motto, which refers to the 2 great events of the city's history. St Edmund was buried here 33 years after his death in 869 at the hands of the Danes. The monastery where he lay was given abbey status in 1032 by King Crut, eager to please his new subjects. The 'Law' in the motto refers to an event in 1214 when King John's barons swore on the high altar of the abbey church to force the king to accept the Magna Carta. The best preserved remains of the abbey are 2 gatehouses, one 12th-century, the other 14th-century. Two churches stand at the edge of the abbey precincts, St Mary's, a 15th-century church with a fine hammerbeam roof, and St James', built a little later. The rest of the town follows the rectangular plan set out by Bishop Baldwin in the 11th century, but the houses are essentially Georgian, or appear so; Bury kept up with fashion, often not by rebuilding, but by adding new façades in the latest style to the fronts of existing buildings. Angel Hill is a fine example, it is a square surrounded by some of Bury's best houses — including Angel Corner (OACT), a Queen Anne Mansion which houses one of the largest collections of clocks and watches in Britain. The oldest Norman house in East Anglia is claimed to be Moyse's Hall (OACT), c1180, in the Butter Market. It is now a museum displaying Bronze-Age weapons, medieval relics and other items of Suffolk archaeology and natural history.

Leave on the A143, SP 'Sudbury', then 'Haverhill'. At Horringer is the entrance to Ickworth.

ICKWORTH, Suffolk

The centre of this most unusual house (NT) is a great rotunda with 2 arms curving away which end in square blocks, each the size of a substantial country house. The interior of the rotunda is lit by a glass dome 100ft above the floor, and the odd-shaped rooms, hung with paintings by Titian, Velasquez, Hogarth, Reynolds and Gainsborough, are furnished with fine 18th-century English and French furniture. Earl-Bishop Frederick Hervey designed the house to hold a collection of choice artefacts (now at Ickworth), collected on his European tours but sadly he died abroad before the house was finished. Capability Brown landscaped the surrounding parkland which features majestic oak and cedar trees.

Continue on the A143 and pass the edge of Chedburgh. In 3 miles, at the Plumbers Arms PH, turn right, SP 'Lidgate'. In ¾ mile bear left then turn right on to the B1063 Newmarket Road, and continue to Lidgate.

HORSES AND KINGS

From Bury St Edmunds, shrine of a martyred king, to Newmarket, the headquarters of horse racing in Britain since the 17th century — but the glamour of the sport of kings soon gives way to the continuity of tradition — lands and buildings owned by the same families for centuries.

LIDGATE, Suffolk

Suffolk House (not open), brick-gabled and timber-fronted, was the birth-place of the poet John Lydgate, who was born c1370 and lived as a Benedictine monk at Bury. He imitated Chaucer in his work and although he became a court poet, he died in poverty. In the mainly 14th-century church there is a brass of a cleric, said to be Lydgate.

In 1¼ miles keep forward on to the B1085 Kentford road to Dalham.

DALHAM, Suffolk

Thatched cottages set back from the road in their own gardens line both banks of the River Kennet, and woods climb an escarpment to the church at the north end of the village. Paintings inside depict the building of the steeple in 1625. There is a monument of Sir Marten Stukeville and his 2 wives: Stukeville was probably with Sir Francis Drake on his last fateful voyage.

Turn left across the bridge, SP 'Moulton', and ascend past a windmill. At Moulton turn left, beyond the post office, on to the Newmarket road. Gradually ascend Warren Hill, passing several racing stables on either side of the road. There are good views of Newmarket and the surrounding country on the descent into the town. At the bottom turn right, then at the clock tower turn left to enter Newmarket.

NEWMARKET, Suffolk

Newmarket, the home of English horse racing. James I often came here, hunting and tilting, and organised the first recorded horse race in 1619. The High Street, which follows the ancient road, has Jubilee Clock tower at one end, and at the other the Cooper Memorial Fountain. In between are many fine houses and hotels, including the headquarters of the Jockey Club formed in 1750. Next door is the National Horseracing Museum telling the story of horseracing development in this country. The racecourse itself has been painted by many great artists — the wide downland, high elevation and magnificent views creating a memorable setting, enhanced by the massive Anglo-Saxon earthwork known as Devil's Dyke.

Leave Newmarket on the A1304, and in ¾ mile turn left on to the B1061, SP 'Haverhill'. Shortly bear right, then go over a level crossing into Cambridgeshire. In 1 mile cross the Devil's Dyke, marked by a line of trees. Continue to Dullingham then in 1 mile turn left and pass through Burrough Green. Continue to Great Bradley.

Ickworth's central feature, the great rotunda, was built in the 1790s

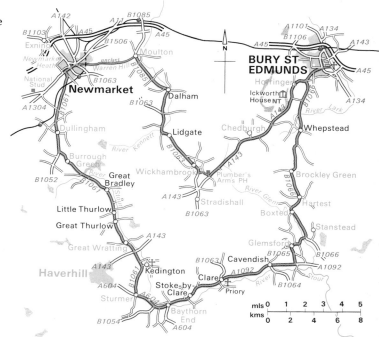

120

Continue to Great Wratting, then at the main road turn right, then left, on to the B1061 and shortly skirt Kedington.

KEDINGTON, Suffolk

Kedington possesses one of the foremost churches in Suffolk. Stepping on to the uneven brick floor, seeing the ancient pews and monuments that have not changed in centuries, is like stepping back in time. There are separate little pews for boys and girls, and another angled so that the overseers could keep an eye on their charges, a triple-decker pulpit, and the Barnardister pew. The Barnardister family was one of Suffolk's most important and oldest families, stretching back for 27 generations in an unbroken line.

Continue on the B1061 and at Sturmer turn left on to the A604. Follow the River Stour round to Baythorn End, then turn left on to the A1092 Clare road and recross the river into Suffolk to reach Stoke-by-Clare.

STOKE-BY-CLARE, Suffolk

Strung out along the road in the Stour valley, is Stoke-By-Clare, with houses of the 15th-19th centuries, some of which are timber-framed or plastered and decorated with chevrons or fish-scale patterns. Near the church stands a tall Tudor dovecot, resembling a gatehouse, which belonged to a college of priests who were transferred from a priory in Clare in 1124. A Queen Anne house, now a private school, has the remains of the old priory built into it. In 1948 wall-paintings were revealed in the church; they are thought to be some of the last executed before the Reformation.

Continue to Clare.

CLARE, Suffolk

Clare is an ancient little market town on the River Stour with a history centred upon its Norman castle of which only the 53ft-high motte and some masonry remains. Lady Elizabeth Clare, who founded Clare College, Cambridge, in the 14th century, lived here occasionally, and in those days the castle was large enough to house her 250-strong retinue and several hundred horses. The Augustinians founded their first priory in England here in 1248, and there are extensive remains still visible near the river. The Prior's house was turned into a dwelling house after the Dissolution and is complete. Among the many old houses in the town is the Ancient House, c1473. This timber-framed building is renowned for the fine plaster-work, or pargetting, on its exterior walls. Also of interest is the Swan Inn, which has a remarkable carved bracket of a swan with a crown round its neck.

Leave on the A1092, SP 'Sudbury' and continue to Cavendish.

CAVENDISH, Suffolk

Cavendish is one of Suffolk's show-pieces. A noble church rises above half-timbered thatched cottages around a village green. By the pond is the Old Rectory, a 16th-century building which was used by Sue Ryder as a home for concentration-camp victims. St Mary's Church dates from the 13th and 14th centuries and has within it 2 lecterns; one is a brass 16th-century eagle, the other is a wooden lectern with 2 17th-century books chained to it.

In 1 mile turn left on to the B1065 for Glemsford. Follow SP 'Bury St Edmunds' through the village and ¾ mile beyond the church turn left on to the B1066, following the attractive Glem valley to Boxted. Beyond the village the road becomes more winding and hilly and passes through Hartest and Brockley to Whepstead.

WHEPSTEAD, Suffolk

Set in splendid rolling country, Whepstead possesses the only church dedicated to St Petronilla, and its fair share of Suffolk manor houses (not open); Plumpton Hall, where 2 of Cromwell's brothers-in-law lived; Doveden (pronounced Duffin) Hall, moated with Tudor chimneys, and Manston Hall, red-brick, half-timbered and now a farmhouse.

3½ miles beyond Whepstead turn right on to the A143 for the return to Bury St Edmunds.

GT BRADLEY, Suffolk

The church at Great Bradley — a village set in meadowland beside the River Stour — is reputed to have the best brick porch in Suffolk: its bricks made by the 'King's own brickmaker' in early Tudor times. The tower, built in the early 14th century, retains one of its original bells and also has a fire-place, which may have been used in the preparation of the holy wafers used in communion.

Continue on the B1061 to Little and Great Thurlow.

The best of Britain's horses compete on the famous Newmarket turf, the centre of the English horse racing world

Cavendish, once the ancestral village of the Dukes of Devonshire

LITTLE & GT THURLOW, Suffolk

The 2 villages are so close together as to be almost one. Great Thurlow has a fine Georgian Hall and a Perpendicular church, originally Norman, in which there is a sanctuary chair where criminals could claim safe refuge. Little Thurlow has a past dominated by the Soames family, who built the almshouses and grammar school in the 1600s.

ALDEBURGH, Suffolk

There is more to this small, salt-laden town with its long, straight, somewhat desolate shingle beach than at first meets the eye. The musicians Benjamin Britten and Peter Pears made their homes here and an annual music festival, founded by Benjamin Britten, takes place every June and focuses on the Maltings at Snape, just west of the town along the broad Alde estuary. One of Britten's most popular works is *Peter Grimes,* which is set against the background of Aldeburgh's Moot Hall. This is the town's most striking building, with its 2 tall Jacobean chimneys, dating back to the time of Henry VIII, and now standing defiantly facing the advancing sea. The council chamber (open to the public in summer) is on the upper floor, where visitors can see old maps, prints and objects of local interest. *Peter Grimes* was inspired by the work of the poet George Crabbe. He lived in the town during the 17th century when its fortunes had considerably declined since its earlier heyday as a port and ship-building centre: the Dutch Wars, the transition of shipbuilding to the Blackwall yard, and sea damage had taken their toll. At least half this Tudor town has now been destroyed by the encroachment of the sea.

Leave Aldeburgh on an unclassified road for Thorpeness.

THORPENESS, Suffolk

The building of Thorpeness began just 70 years ago and was deliberately planned as a resort of quiet and refinement. A large boating lake, called the Meare, was created and a number of pleasant houses were built

VILLAGES OF EASTERN SUFFOLK

The coastline from Aldeburgh to the vanished city of Dunwich is an area of haunting bleakness that is the prelude to an extremely varied tour through Suffolk's most delightful villages, past several bird sanctuaries, some splendid churches and a historic castle.

The curious House in the Clouds and the post mill at Thorpeness

between this and the sea. One of the town's most distinctive buildings is the extraordinary House in the Clouds. It looks like a mock-Tudor building, but beneath the facade is a water tower on stilts. The post windmill standing beside it was brought from Aldringham so the tower could use it as a pump.

At Thorpeness turn inland and follow the B1353 to Aldringham. Here turn right on to the B1122 for Leiston.

LEISTON, Suffolk

Leiston is distinguished by having one of the most advanced schools in the country — Summerhill. It was founded by educationalist A. S. Neill as an experiment in self-education and has proved very successful. The surrounding marshes were first drained between 1846 and 1850 by the Garretts of Leiston Iron Works. Richard Garrett created a portable steam engine and threshing machine and a bust of him can be seen in the town's Victorian church.

Leave on the B1122, SP 'Yoxford', and in 1 mile pass the remains of Leiston Abbey.

LEISTON ABBEY, Suffolk

Leiston Abbey (AM) was first founded on the Minsmere Marshes in 1182, and was moved to its present site in 1363 and then rebuilt by Robert de Ufford, Earl of Suffolk. The ruins incorporate an octagonal brick gate-turret which was added when it was converted into a diocesan retreat during Tudor times.

Continue to Theberton and ½ mile beyond the village turn right on to the B1125 for Westleton.

WESTLETON, Suffolk

Farmland and heathland surround the village of Westleton which consists of a variety of attractive buildings — redbrick and colour-washed. A shaded duck pond lies at one end of the village green where every summer a week-long fair is held featuring races and general festivities. Westleton used to have 2 windmills, but one, the smock mill, has been converted into a house and the other, a tower mill, is derelict.

At the end of the village turn right on to the unclassified Dunwich road and shortly pass the Minsmere Bird Sanctuary on Westleton Heath.

THE MINSMERE BIRD SANCTUARY, Suffolk

This is one of the Suffolk reserves where avocets — a rare black and white wading bird — breed, and the public are allowed access to some parts of the reserve as well as to several hides. The sanctuary covers 1,500 acres and the varied habitats it provides include reed beds, woodland and heathland.

Continue to Dunwich.

DUNWICH, Suffolk

Dunwich was a city about the size of Ipswich in the 12th century, but everything from those days has all gradually been washed away by savage sea storms. It was still an important port in Roman times, but the sea started its onslaught in 1326 and by the 16th century most of the city lay on the sea bed. It is said that church bells can be heard ringing out across the lonely beach. All that remains now beneath the crumbling cliffs is a scattering of cottages, an inn and a general store. However, a dramatic idea of the city's former glory and importance can be gained by studying the relics and pictures in the museum in St James' Street. North-east of this lonely and evocative place is the extensive Dunwich Forest where there is an excellent picnic site.

Leave on the Blythburgh road and pass through Dunwich Forest. In 1½ miles, at the crossroads, turn right on to the B1125. In 1 mile a detour may be taken by turning right on to the B1387 to Walberswick.

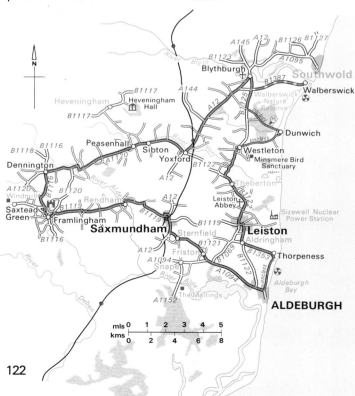

Blythburgh's church tower was crowned by a spire until 1577 when it fell through the roof, killing a man and a boy

WALBERSWICK, Suffolk

Walberswick's ruined church tower stands proudly as a landmark to those at sea. The pleasant houses around the village green have attracted artists over many years and it was a favourite spot of the artist Wilson Steer earlier this century. Just across the estuary (crossed by ferry) is the smart little town of Southwold (see tour 54) with brick and colour-washed Georgian houses. A national nature reserve, overlooking the Blythe estuary, is home to an interesting variety of waders and rare birds.

The main tour keeps forward on the B1125 into Blythburgh.

Aldeburgh is famous for its 'long-shore' herring and the best sprats in England are caught here in November and December

BLYTHBURGH, Suffolk

The collapse of the fishing trade along the east coast contributed to Blythburgh's decline from a prosperous town to the village it is today. The huge and magnificent church rising up above the marshes is the only reminder of the town's importance in the 15th century when there was a mint here, a gaol, crowded quays and 2 annual fairs. It is a light and spacious building with a great wooden roof decorated with carved angels and painted flowers. Another notable feature of the church is the bench-ends depicting the 7 deadly sins, and a wooden clock with a quarter jack.

At Blythburgh turn left on to the A12 Ipswich road for Yoxford.

YOXFORD, Suffolk

Locally known as 'The garden of Suffolk', because it is surrounded by the parkland of 3 country houses (not open), Yoxford is packed with attractive timbered houses featuring balconies and bow-windows. Cockfield Hall was originally a magnificent Tudor house built during Henry VIII's reign; it was altered in the 19th century, but is still most impressive and has a thatched Victorian lodge in the village.

Turn right on to the A1120, SP 'Stowmarket', for Sibton.

SIBTON, Suffolk

Sibton stands at the junction of 2 Roman roads in the Minsmere valley. It is a pretty place, with a group of cottages and small 18th-century bridges cross the Drain, a ditch that drains the farmland along its length. Romantic, overgrown ruins of Sibton Abbey, the only Cistercian house in Suffolk, lie in the woods near the village. It was founded in 1150 but was never prosperous and fell into neglect after the Dissolution.

Continue to Peasenhall.

PEASENHALL, Suffolk

Trickling through the village is a little stream that brings an air of serene tranquillity to the cluster of houses on its banks: the stream is actually part of the Drain. Peasenhall's claim to fame is that the Suffolk seed drill was originally manufactured here. The Wool Hall has been discovered and restored only recently. About 4 miles to the north of the village stands Heveningham Hall (see tour 54), a lovely Palladian house set in magnificent grounds landscaped by Capability Brown.

Remain on the A1120 for Dennington.

DENNINGTON, Suffolk

Treasures which fill the 14th-century church at Dennington include an extremely rare altar canopy, some beautiful screens and, on a bench-end on the south side, a curious carving of a giant with a webbed foot.

At the church branch left on to the B1116 for Framlingham.

FRAMLINGHAM, Suffolk

The Earls of Norfolk used to own the impressive castle in this lively market town. The castle (AM) was destroyed in 1639, but before that it was the home of Mary Tudor during her attempts to gain the throne. The ruins of the original castle are extensive and are an unusual example of the 12th-century style, using square towers rather than round ones. Next door to the castle is the church with its memorials to the Norfolk family and one of the most splendid wooden church roofs in Suffolk. The rest of the old town consists of many attractive cottages, and historic buildings, centred on the market square. Saxted Green lies 2 miles to the east of Framlingham and is the site of a famous windmill (AM). It is a very good example of an 18th-century post mill — the oldest type of windmill — where the body carrying the sails and machinery rotates on an upright post.

Leave Framlingham on the B1119, SP 'Saxmundham'. In 4 miles pass through Rendham, then in another 2¾ miles reach the outskirts of Saxmundham. Here, turn left then right, and at the T-junction turn right on to the A12 for the town centre.

SAXMUNDHAM, Suffolk

One of the more modern towns in this part of Suffolk, its origins actually go back to the 13th century when there was a market here occupying 7 acres. However, most of the existing buildings in the main street are 19th century.

Continue on the Ipswich road for 1 mile and turn left on to the B1121, SP 'Aldeburgh'. Pass through Sternfield and Friston, then later join the A1094 for the return to Aldeburgh.

GREAT YARMOUTH AND HER HINTERLAND

Something for everyone; traditional seaside entertainment is to be had at lively Yarmouth, with its pier, arcades and illuminations. Southwold offers the homely attractions of a small fishing town (as well as fresh seafood), and for those who prefer to get away from it all, and admire unspoilt coastal scenery, there is Covehithe.

GT YARMOUTH, Norfolk

Three rivers, the Yare, the Bure and the Waverley, flow into the sea at Great Yarmouth which stands on the long spit of land separating the fresh and salt waters. For over 1,000 years Yarmouth has been a great herring fishing port, but its fleet has dwindled during this century and the tourism which began in the 18th century has overtaken it. A promenade runs along the seaward side of the town and behind there are entertainments of every kind: bowling greens, tennis courts, boating lakes, theatres, amusement arcades and piers which are brilliantly illuminated during the summer season. Although air raids in World War II devastated much of the old town, there are still remains of its medieval town walls and a part of the Rows, a complex grid-iron pattern of narrow streets which grew up within the walls. The Old Merchants House (AM) in Row 117 is a 17th-century house typical of those owned by merchants not quite rich enough to live in the great houses on the quayside. A museum of local history is sited in the Tolhouse (OACT) in Tolhouse Street, a 13th-century building said to be the oldest civic building in Britain. On South Quay the rich merchants had their houses, such as the Customs House of 1720 where John Andrews lived, the most famous of herring merchants, and the Elizabethan House (OACT), a 16th-century house which had a new façade added in the 19th-century. In one corner of the market place is the attractive Fishermen's Hospital, founded in 1702, and next to it is Sewell House (OACT) (1646), where Anna Sewell, authoress of *Black Beauty*, was born in 1820.

Leave Yarmouth on the A12. At the roundabout at the edge of Gorleston-on-Sea, take the 3rd exit, SP 'Burgh Castle'. In 2 miles turn right for the village of Burgh Castle.

BURGH CASTLE, Norfolk

The village is named after the Roman fort (AM) here, which was one of a chain the invaders built along the east coast. After the Romans left, St Fursey, an Irishman, built a monastery within the fort walls, but the site was later used again as a castle by the

Normans. In later centuries stone from the castle was used for building in the village. The substantial walls and bastions, still held together by Roman mortar, give an idea of the scale of the fort, built in about AD 300.

From Burgh Castle follow the Belton road and in 1½ miles, at the T-junction, turn left, SP 'Yarmouth'. In 1 mile turn left on to the A143, then immediately right, SP 'Blendeston'. In 1½ miles turn right, SP 'Somerleyton', then after another mile turn left. Later pass (left) Somerleyton Hall.

SOMERLEYTON HALL, Suffolk

The Victorian railway entrepreneur Sir Morton Peto had this Anglo-Italian mansion (OACT) built around an old Elizabethan hall in 1844. He also had the church, school and cottages of the village built to complement it. The house stands among magnificent trees and shrubs, and of particular interest is the clipped yew maze. The oak parlour in the house has beautiful carved panelling by Grinling Gibbons, and the dining room is hung with paintings by old masters. The game trophies proudly displayed throughout the house are the victims of the sporting Crossley family, who bought the house in 1866.

At the next T-junction turn right on to the B1076 and continue to St Olaves. From here a short detour can be made by turning right on to the A143 to visit Fritton.

FRITTON, Suffolk

The church here has a Saxon tower and a chancel showing the work of Norman stone masons. There are several notable wall-paintings, and a trap door under the thatched roof of the chancel is said to have been used by smugglers when prudence required them to lie low. Near the partly-ruined St Olave's Priory (AM), is the Fritton Decoy, a long, wooded lake used to trap wildfowl.

At St Olaves the main tour turns left on to the A143. Cross the River Waveney and continue through Haddiscoe to Tofts Monks. In 2¼ miles, at the roundabout, take the A146. After 1 mile turn right on to the A145 into Beccles.

The superbly restored post mill at Holton: the mill is pivoted on a central post and turns with the wind

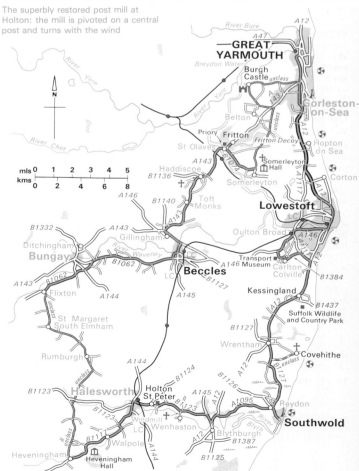

The River Blythe at Southwold

Southwold — a pleasant seaside resort with the character of a fishing port

BECCLES, Suffolk
Beccles quay on the River Waveney is an ideal centre for exploring the network of local waterways, and the boats provide a colourful scene in the summer months. The 14th-century chapel is unusual in having a separate 92ft-high bell tower, holding a peal of 10 bells.

Leave Beccles on the B1062, and follow the Waveney valley to the outskirts of Bungay (see tour 55). Here, turn left on to the B1062, SP 'Diss'. In ½ mile go over the staggered crossroads and continue to Flixton. Pass the Buck Inn and at the next road junction turn left, SP 'St Margarets', and in 1¾ miles turn left into St Margaret South Elmham. Continue to Rumburgh and in 1 mile turn right, SP ''Cookley', then in 1 mile bear right, SP 'Heveningham'. In another mile go over the staggered crossroads and continue to Heveningham. Turn left into the village and join the B1117, SP 'Halesworth', and in 1 mile pass the entrance to Heveningham Hall.

HEVENINGHAM HALL, Suffolk
In 1777 Sir Gerald Vanneck MP commissioned Sir Robert Taylor to enlarge the family's Queen Anne house, Heveningham Hall. Taylor built an impressive

Palladian mansion; he screened the north front with Corinthian columns and added a wing to either side. Then James Wyatt took over, his task being to oversee the interior decoration. Biagio Rebecca, an Italian artist, was employed to do the house painting. The result is a magnificent Georgian house typical of all that is fine of the period. The grounds were landscaped by Capability Brown, and include one of Suffolk's finest 'crinkle-crankle' walls (curves in and out to give plants' protection) and a beautifully-proportioned orangery by Wyatt.

Continue through Walpole and in 2 miles join the A144 for Halesworth. At the end of the main street turn right on to the B1132, SP 'Southwold', and continue to Holton-St-Peter.

HOLTON ST PETER, Suffolk
An attractive village which takes the latter half of its name from the Church of St Peter. This has a round Norman tower, a Norman doorway, a 15th-century octagonal font and a 16th-century linenfold pulpit. Overlooking the village from a hillside is a post mill situated among pine woods.

At the edge of the village bear right, then in 3½ miles turn right on to the A145. At the next T-junction turn left on to the A12, then skirt an inland lake formed by the River Blyth before turning right on to the A1095. Continue through Reydon to Southwold.

SOUTHWOLD, Suffolk
Southwold, perched on cliffs overlooking the North Sea, has flint, brick and colour-washed cottages, a church and a market place. There are 7 spacious greens which resulted from a disastrous fire in 1659, because as the herring trade declined, there was less money for rebuilding, and the damaged areas were left as open spaces. There is, however, evidence of Dutch influence in the buildings that did arise, as can be seen in the gabled cottages in Church Street, and the museum in Bartholomew Green (OACT). The museum displays relics of the Southwold Railway (1879-1929), and illustrates local history, including an archaeological collection.

The tour returns to Reydon and turns right on to the B1127, SP 'Wrentham'. After 3 miles a byroad (right) may be taken to visit Covehithe.

COVEHITHE, Suffolk
This delightful, unspoilt village has a stretch of sandy beach that is often empty. The beach is backed by cliffs and the village dominated by the ruins of a huge 14th-15th century church. Judging by the size of the church, Covehithe must once have been a prosperous place; the church fell into disrepair in the 17th century.

Chinese ring-necked pheasants in John Gould's *Book of Birds*, which can be seen in the library of Somerleyton Hall

The main tour continues to Wrentham. Here turn right on to the A12 and continue to Kessingland.

KESSINGLAND, Suffolk
The village is mainly in 2 parts; near the coast road, from where the church's 13th-century tower has served for centuries as a landmark for sailors; and the popular beach and caravan site by the sea. Nearby is the Suffolk Wildlife and Country Park, (OACT) a small, attractive zoo with a mixed collection of animals, including lions, tigers, a walk-through aviary, monkeys, badgers and a lake full of waterfowl.

Remain on the A12 for another 2 miles, than at the roundabout take the A1117, SP 'Great Yarmouth'. At the next roundabout take the B1384. In ¾ mile turn right, SP 'Beccles', then at the T-junction turn left and shortly pass the East Anglia Transport Museum at Carlton Colville.

EAST ANGLIA TRANSPORT MUSEUM, Suffolk
The museum covers 3 acres which can be seen from a tramway and narrow-gauge railway, and exhibits include historic cars, commercial vehicles, trams, buses and trolleybuses as well as collections of curios connected with the historical development of transport.

Continue to the A146 and turn right to reach Oulton Broad. At the traffic signals turn right with the A146 and continue into Lowestoft.

LOWESTOFT, Suffolk
During the 14th century Lowestoft was an important fishing port, valuable to the nation, and although the fleets are now a shadow of their former glory, the town is a lively place, and the trawlers docking and unloading their catch to be cleaned and gutted on the quayside ready for the busy fish market, is an exciting spectacle. South Town is the tourist section, with many seaside lodgings giving it a traditional seaside atmosphere, and a long esplanade runs alongside the beach to Claremont Pier. At one end is a children's corner, a boating lake and a miniature steam railway. The northern limit of the old town is marked by the Upper Lighthouse, open at weekdays. A feature of this part of the town are the 'Scores', narrow alleys which cut steeply down from the High Street to the shore, where the fish-houses for curing herring used to stand, few of which still survive.

Leave on the A12. In 5 miles re-enter Norfolk and later skirt Gorleston-on-Sea before the return to Great Yarmouth.

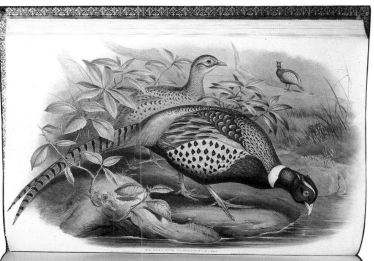

NORWICH AND THE WAVENEY VALLEY

South of the fine old cathedral city of Norwich lies an area of lovely wooded countryside that stretches down to the Suffolk border, where the River Waveney meanders through a tranquil valley of great beauty.

NORWICH, Norfolk

East Anglia's capital city is full of curious old streets and alleys, antique and curio shops, with interesting buildings at almost every turn. Elm Hill, a narrow cobbled lane, pretty, and crowded with ancient shops and courtyards, is the best known of all the old streets, but there are many more around the market place. Every day, except Sunday, there is a large bustling market beside the old Guildhall, built in the 15th century of local knapped flints. Not far away on St Andrew's Street, Strangers' Hall museum is a fascinatingly-preserved medieval merchant's house, its rooms furnished in the style of different periods. Nearby, in a little alley off Bedford Street stands the Bridewell Museum of local crafts, and near to it is a Dickensian-looking mustard shop and small museum run by Colmans, who still manufacture mustard in Norwich. The castle, a square Norman keep raised high on a mound overlooking the centre, is now the city museum and art gallery, with a fine collection of pictures by John Crome and John Sell Cotman, leaders of the Norwich School of painters who flourished in the last century. Undoubtedly the finest sight in Norwich, however, is the beautiful Norman cathedral, whose slender spire rises above the water meadows of the River Wensum. Work on the cathedral began in 1069 and continued for over 50 years. There are 2 medieval gates to the precincts, the Ethelbert and the Erpingham; just inside the latter stands Norwich School, founded in 1316, at which Horatio Nelson was a pupil for a short time. The lovely walled cathedral Close, bordered by elegant 18th-century houses, stretches down to the river where a charming 16th-century house known as Pull's Ferry (not open) is portrayed in many local paintings and postcards. Apart from the great Norman cathedral, Norwich has a Roman Catholic cathedral and 32 medieval churches; once there were even more and it was said that the city had a church for every week of the year, but a pub for every day.

Leave Norwich on the A11, SP 'Thetford'. In 9 miles turn right, SP 'Town Centre', into Wymondham.

Colman's Mustard Shop in Bridewell Alley, Norwich, has a small museum

WYMONDHAM, Norfolk

This small country town, pronounced Windham, is a delightful jumble of old cottages, traditional shops, timbered inns and 18th-century houses. At the centre of the old streets is an ornate half-timbered Butter Cross, raised on wooden pillars. The spectacular abbey church, with 2 great towers at each end, was once shared by the monks of the priory (now ruined) and the townspeople. As a result of a quarrel with the town, the monks built a wall to isolate their part of the church and so the townsfolk built the great square west tower for themselves. The monks' part of the church was later destroyed, leaving only the tower.

Leave Wymondham on the B1135, and continue to Kimberley, then turn left on to the B1108 for Hingham.

HINGHAM, Norfolk

The large number of elegant redbrick Georgian houses in this attractive village show that it was once a thriving market town. Hingham was the birthplace of one Samuel Lincoln, who emigrated to America in 1637 and there raised a family whose most famous descendant, 2 centuries later, was Abraham Lincoln, who became president of the United States. The bust of Lincoln in the imposing village church was presented by the people of Hingham, Massachusetts, the New World town in which Samuel Lincoln had settled.

Continue on the B1108 and later pass Scoulton Mere (right) before reaching Scoulton. 1½ miles beyond the village turn left on to the B1077, SP 'Attleborough'. In 2 miles, at the T-junction, turn left. The B1077 leads through Great Ellingham to Attleborough.

ATTLEBOROUGH, Norfolk

Although not a particularly attractive town, there is a fine church with a famous and beautiful 15th-century rood screen. The countryside round here is celebrated for the rearing of fine turkeys and ducks and until recently there was a vast annual turkey fair at Attleborough.

Leave Attleborough on the B1077 Diss road and continue to Old Buckenham.

OLD BUCKENHAM, Norfolk

The village green is so enormous that the groups of cottages round the edges have remained as separate little hamlets, each with its own delightful name — Hog's Snout, Puddledock and Loss Wroo are just a few examples.

1½ miles beyond the village turn left on to the B1113 to visit New Buckenham.

NEW BUCKENHAM, Norfolk

'New' is a relative term, for this charming village is at least 8 centuries old and preserves a street plan laid out in medieval times. Its pretty cottages lead up to a village green, near which stands a 17th-century market house supported on wooden posts. The one at the centre served in bygone days as a whipping post. A little way outside the village is the castle mound with the ruins of the castle built in 1145.

Return along the B1113 and follow the Stowmarket road to Banham.

BANHAM, Norfolk

The village of Banham is exceptionally pretty with elm trees round its green. Nearby, Banham Zoo and Monkey Sanctuary is famous for its colony of woolly monkeys, one of only 6 in the whole of Europe. Woolly monkeys came originally from the rain forests of the Amazon Basin in South America, and are a delicate breed, difficult to rear in our climate. Many other species of monkeys from Africa and Asia can be seen here too, as well as other types of animals and birds of prey. Also within the zoo grounds is Lord Cranworth's motor museum. Racing cars, motorcycles and children's pedal cars dating from the 1920s to the 1960s are all displayed in an imaginative setting.

Continue on the B1113 to Kenninghall, and at the end of the village turn left for North Lopham. In 1 mile, at South Lopham, turn left on to the A1066. Later (right) are Bressingham Gardens.

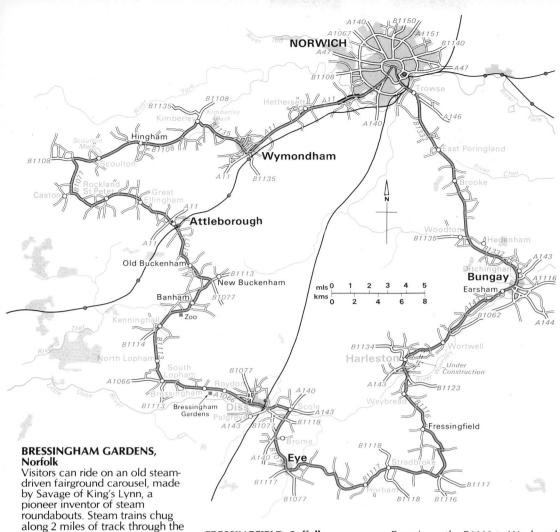

EARSHAM, Norfolk

In 1965 naturalist Philip Wayre set up an Otter Trust (OACT) on the banks of the Waveney at Earsham, and now it has the largest collection of otters in the world. As well as British otters, European, North American and Asian otters are bred here in semi-natural conditions. There are also large lakes with a variety of waterfowl and a pleasant walk can be taken alongside the river.

Continue on the A143 to Bungay.

BUNGAY, Suffolk

Bungay is a fascinating place, with a history that goes back long before the Norman Conquest. There was a massive castle here in Norman times, and in a part of the ruins, traces of an old mining gallery can be seen. This is thought to date from the days of Henry II, when the lord of the castle, Hugh Bigod, defied the king, and an attempt was made to undermine the castle walls by tunnelling. The castle in fact survived many years after this, only to be demolished by local entrepreneurs looking for good building stone. Bungay has many fine buildings, including an outstanding 17th-century Butter Cross, built to keep the butter cool on market days, surmounted by the figure of Justice. Printing and leather-working have been the town's major industries since the 18th century.

Follow SP 'Norwich' to join the B1332. Continue through Brooke and Poringland and in 3 miles, at the traffic signals, turn left on to the A146 for the return to Norwich.

The delightful village green at Banham, overlooked by church and Guildhall

BRESSINGHAM GARDENS, Norfolk

Visitors can ride on an old steam-driven fairground carousel, made by Savage of King's Lynn, a pioneer inventor of steam roundabouts. Steam trains chug along 2 miles of track through the beautiful countryside of the Waveney valley, and the 6 acres of gardens specialising in alpine plants and hardy perennials, are a delightful spectacle at all seasons of the year.

Remain on the A1066 and beyond Roydon bear right to reach Diss. Leave on the A1066 and at the end of the town join the A143 for Scole. Here, turn right on to the A140, SP 'Ipswich'. Cross the River Waveney into Suffolk then in 1½ miles turn left on to the B1077 for Eye.

EYE, Suffolk

The church at Eye, with its wonderful tower of superb Suffolk flushwork, rising over 100ft, is the pride of this enchanting little place, but its appealing streets are packed with interesting old buildings of all periods. The timber-framed Guildhall dates from the 16th century and there are a number of fine houses in the streets leading up to the ruins of the Norman castle.

At Eye branch left, then left again on to the B1117. Follow a winding road to Horham, where the road bears left and continues to Stradbrooke. In 2¾ miles turn left on to the B1116, SP 'Harleston', and later pass through Fressingfield.

FRESSINGFIELD, Suffolk

This attractive village, deep in the Suffolk countryside, is a mecca for gourmets who come from all over the country to dine at the Fox and Goose Inn, a charming timber-framed building, once the Guildhall of the village.

Remain on the B1116 to Weybread and later cross the River Waveney back into Norfolk. On reaching the main road turn right and enter Harleston. Continue on the A143 Yarmouth road, which follows the Waveney valley through Wortwell to Earsham.

GREAT HOUSES OF NORFOLK

From Norwich, the beating heart of Norfolk, the tour
meanders to the peaceful seaside resorts of Cromer and
Sheringham, through a landscape of broad fields and
slumbering villages overlorded by churches of medieval
splendour and great manor houses.

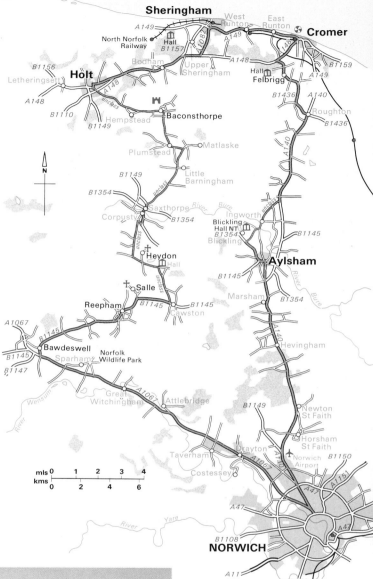

NORWICH, Norfolk
Onetime centre of the worsted
trade, Norwich is now a county
borough, port, industrial centre
and cathedral city. The charm of
Norwich lies in its combination of
antiquity and modernity and the
history that has made it one of
Britain's most flourishing cities.
See tour 55.

*Leave Norwich on the A140, SP
'Cromer', and beyond the Airport
continue to the edge of Marsham.
In 1 mile, at the roundabout, go
forward on to the B1145 into
Aylsham.*

AYLSHAM, Norfolk
This is a charming little market
town with many old buildings,
brick-built and Dutch-gabled.
Wherries — light flat-bottomed
rowing boats — sailing up the
Bure, now no longer so navigable,
brought wealth in the Middle Ages
to this town noted for its worsted
cloth and linen. John of Gaunt is
said to have held the manor at
Blickling, and to have founded the
church in 1380. The church has
altered little since his day, and
contains a fine font and, of
particular interest, a copy of the
Breeches Bible of 1611; so called
for the passage in Genesis which
reads 'they sewed fig leaves
together and made themselves
breeches'. The famous landscape
gardener Humphry Repton
(1752-1818) is buried in the
churchyard.

*In Aylsham turn left, SP
'Saxthorpe', on to the B1354. In
1½ miles (right) is Blickling Hall.*

BLICKLING HALL, Norfolk
Yew hedges (15ft across) planted
in the late 17th century line velvet
lawns either side of the driveway
which sweeps up to the pleasingly
symmetrical Jacobean front of
Blickling Hall (NT). Between 2 tall
turrets a Dutch-gabled roofline
culminates in a central domed
turret, beneath which mullioned
windows complete the picture of a
perfect English country house. The
house was begun in 1616 within a
dry moat on the side of an old hall
in which Anne Boleyn was born.
The Jacobean exterior hides a
Georgian interior; much was
remodelled by the 2nd Earl of
Buckinghamshire during the 18th
century, although the long gallery
still keeps its splendid plaster
moulded ceiling of the 1620s.

*Return along the B1354 for ½
miles then turn left, SP 'Cromer'. In
1 mile turn left and cross the River
Bure into Ingworth and in 1½
miles turn left on to the A140.
At Roughton turn left on to the
B1436 which leads to Felbrigg.*

FELBRIGG, Norfolk
The Felbrigg estate lies on top of a
ridge, now divorced from the
village of Felbrigg which may have
been moved as a result of the
plague and re-established in its
present position to avoid further

infection. The Jacobean entrance
front of Felbrigg Hall (NT) was
built in the 1620s, and in 1665 a
new brick wing was added to the
south. Then in the 18th century
William Windham II had the
house refurbished in
contemporary style, after the
completion of his Grand Tour of
Europe, creating a new dining
room, staircase and a Gothic
library. The glorious plaster ceiling
in the dining room was left
untouched and dates from 1687.

*½ mile beyond the entrance to
Felbrigg Hall turn right on to the
A148 for Cromer.*

The garden at Blickling Hall has a long
history, but the main flower beds and
lawns seen here date from the 1930s

CROMER, Norfolk

The splendid Perpendicular church tower, 160ft high, of this ancient fishing village served as a lighthouse before the construction of a purpose-built one. The old village survives in the midst of a Victorian seaside resort born of the railway age. The impressive seafront is backed by high cliffs topped by hotels which are reached by steep stone steps. The crabs along this coast are the best in England and Cromer crab is renowned. It is the chief catch here, and the boats used are a special small double-ended broad-beamed variety — a version of the Shetland boats which came down this coast after herring. There is no harbour here, and the boats are launched and landed from the beach.

Traditional gardens in Heydon

Leave on the A149, SP 'Sheringham', and pass through East and West Runton to Sheringham.

SHERINGHAM, Norfolk

Sheringham, like Cromer, was also established as a resort during the railway age, and the old flint village is still discernible within the Victorian brick town. Crab is also the main catch here, but when the weather is bad the fishermen collect the pebbles from the beach which are then ground down to make glazes for the local pottery. Sheringham Hall (open by appointment) is a Regency building in a beautiful park (OACT), both the work of Humphry Repton. The highlight of the estate is perhaps the mile-long rhododendron drive which was planted in the 19th century. Sheringham Station is the headquarters of the North Norfolk Railway and steam-hauled trains operate. There is also rolling stock and a museum.

Leave on the A1082, SP 'Holt'. Climb through wooded country then turn right on to the A148, SP 'King's Lynn', and continue to Holt.

HOLT, Norfolk

The town of Holt has a well-kept appearance and there is nothing to offend the eye. Here and there among the smartly painted walls the flintwork shows itself to advantage, indicating that this stone is the main building material of the area. Most famous of its buildings is Gresham's School, founded by Sir John Gresham who was born here in 1519. Gresham became Lord Mayor of London and also founded the Royal Exchange there.

From the town centre follow the unclassified Baconsthorpe road and continue to Baconsthorpe.

BACONSTHORPE, Norfolk

Baconsthorpe Castle (AM) stands sadly forgotten among muddy Norfolk farmland which now has greater importance than the castle itself. It was a fortified manor house built by Sir Henry Heydon in 1486. The gatehouse stands well preserved, as do the curtain walls, the remains of a 17th-century dwelling hall and an 18th-century Gothic mansion, built in front of the castle largely from stone taken from the original building.

Follow SP 'North Walsham' to Plumstead. ½ mile beyond the village, at the crossroads, turn right on to the Saxthorpe road. In 3¼ miles keep forward on to the B1149 into Saxthorpe. Cross the River Bure and turn right, SP 'Heydon', then immediately turn left at the Dukes Head Inn. In 2 miles, at the T-junction, turn left. In ½ mile, at the crossroads, turn left again into Heydon.

HEYDON, Norfolk

This is an extremely pretty village of pleasant houses centred around a charming village green. Heydon Hall (open by appointment) begun in 1581 but much enlarged since, is the home of the Bulwer family, of whom Lord Lytton, author of *The Last Days of Pompeii* was a member. The house has an E-shaped 3-storey front and the grounds include an ice-house and a lookout tower.

Return to the crossroads and turn left, SP 'Cawston'. In 1 mile turn right and continue to the edge of Cawston. Turn right on to the B1145 Bawdeswell road, and in 1½ miles pass the turning on the right leading to Salle.

SALLE, Norfolk

The tiny village of Salle is the unlikely site of a cathedral-like church full of rich treasures, totally out of proportion to the almost non-existent parish which it serves. It was built by 3 immensely wealthy local families; the Briggs, the Fountaynes, and the Boleyns. Anne Boleyn (wife of Henry VIII) is said to be buried here, but it is more likely her remains lie in the Tower of London where she was beheaded. Over the west door are 2 lovely feathered angels carrying censers. Within is an unusual font on which the symbols of the 7 sacraments are carved.

Continue along the B1145 into Reepham.

REEPHAM, Norfolk

This little 18th-century town has outdone other similar East Anglia towns with 2 parish churches sharing the same churchyard, because Reepham has 3. Hackford parish church burnt down in 1543, and only a ruined wall remains, but the other 2 are still standing. St Mary's is the parish church of Reepham and contains an especially delicate altar-tomb to Sir Roger de Kerdiston, who died in 1337. Nearby St Michael's has an excellent Jacobean pulpit.

Cromer's Victorian seafront. The tower of the old village church soaring above the 19th-century town was used as a lighthouse in days gone by

At the crossroads turn right with the B1145 for Bawdeswell.

BAWDESWELL, Norfolk

This village lies on an ancient route once used by pilgrims on their way from Norwich to the shrine of Our Lady of Walsingham. A timber-framed house in the village street, called Chaucer House, recalls that the reeve in Chaucer's *Canterbury Tales* came 'from Norfolk, near a place called Bawdeswell.'

At the end of the village turn left on to the A1067, SP 'Norwich'. In 2¼ miles pass, (left), the Norfolk Wildlife Park.

NORFOLK WILDLIFE PARK, Norfolk

The well-known naturalist Philip Wayre opened the Norfolk Wildlife Park and Pheasant Trust in 1961, which was originally his private collection. It boasts the largest collection of European animals in the world, but the zoo breeds more animals than it takes from the wild, and where possible returns animals bred in captivity to their natural habitat to boost the native population. The zoo has a remarkable breeding record, and is dedicated to the conservation of endangered species. Animals which are kept here range from the European beaver to the European bison, stone curlews to European eagle owls. This 50-acre site is also the home of the Pheasant Trust. This was started in 1959 to begin the captive breeding of endangered species of wild pheasants in order that natural populations could be restocked, a policy carried out with outstanding success.

Follow the A1067 through the Wensum valley and pass through Great Witchingham (Lenwade) before the return to Norwich.

The North Country

MORECAMBE BAY AND THE LANCASHIRE MOORS

Between Morecambe Bay and the western edge of the Yorkshire Dales stretch the wild, remote moors of the Forest of Bowland, the haunt of grouse and hardy moorland sheep. North and west the steep fells drop down to one of the loveliest valleys in Lancashire, that of the River Lune, painted by Turner and extolled by Ruskin.

This lonely pass across the Forest of Bowland is called the Trough of Bowland

MORECAMBE, Lancs
Second in popularity only to Blackpool as a holiday resort for the north-west, Morecambe has excellent sands and a wealth of seaside entertainments, culminating in the famous 'illuminations' which take place every autumn. Its Marineland complex, billed as the first oceanarium ever built in Europe, boasts a vast swimming pool as well as a dolphinarium and fascinating aquaria displaying all types of marine life. The name Morecambe, as it applies to the town, is of very recent date. Until the railway era in the last century there was only a fishing village, Poulton-le-Sands, here. When the railway line was built, the new resort sprang up, engulfing not only Poulton but also the neighbouring villages of Bare and Torrisholme, and came to be known as Morecambe, which had formerly been simply the name of the bay.

Leave Morecambe on the A5105, SP 'The North and Hest Bank', and follow the seafront to Hest Bank.

HEST BANK, Lancs
From Hest Bank, there is a magnificent view of the bay to the hills of the Lake District. Morecambe Bay was, until the last century, the regular route to and from the Lake District. It was always a perilous journey, as there are shifting sands and 3 treacherous river estuaries to negotiate. Many people lost their lives, and the guides were even known to abandon travellers to their fate if they had not sufficient money to pay the charges. The 3-hour walk at low tide along the beach to Grange-over-Sands is still popular, but it must not be undertaken without an official guide, as the estuaries and shifting sands are a definite hazard.

Continue on the A5105 and in 1 mile turn left on to the A6, SP 'Kendal'. Pass through Bolton-le-Sands to reach Carnforth.

CARNFORTH, Lancs
To railway enthusiasts a visit to Steamtown, the railway museum that now occupies Carnforth's old locomotive sheds and marshalling yards, is a must. The *Flying Scotsman* is the most famous of the 30 steam engines from Great Britain, France and Germany that are maintained here. In the summer season, engines are in steam on Sundays (daily in July and August) and rides in vintage coaches are an added attraction.

On entering the town turn left (one-way), SP 'Warton', and shortly turn left again. Pass the railway museum (left) and continue to Warton.

WARTON, Lancs
The arms of the Washington family, ancestors of George Washington, once decorated the church tower and are now preserved inside the 15th-century church of this pleasant village. Although age has made it difficult to distinguish the symbols, it is said that this coat of arms was the inspiration of the stars and stripes motif of the United States flag. The last member of the English Washington family, Thomas, was the vicar of Warton until 1823.

Remain on the unclassified road for Yealand Conyers.

YEALAND CONYERS, Lancs
Tucked away in the far north of the county, Yealand Conyers is an outstandingly attractive village whose stone-built houses are fine examples of traditional architecture. An early Friends' Meeting House reminds the visitor that this is what the Quakers call '1652 country' because in that year the founder of the movement, George Fox (1624-91), first came into North Lancashire to preach.

From here a turning on the left leads to Leighton Hall.

LEIGHTON HALL, Lancs
Sheltering under Warton Crag, Leighton Hall (OACT) stands in extensive grounds. The Hall, built on the site of an earlier medieval one, dates from 1760-63, a Classical stone mansion with a charming Gothic façade that was added in the early 19th century. The home of the Gillow family for generations, their descendants still live here. In 1826 the estate was bought by Richard Gillow, a distinguished Lancaster furniture maker, and the house is a showplace for his artistry. There is a large collection of Birds of Prey with regular flying displays.

The main tour continues to Yealand Redmayne. Near the end of the village turn right, SP 'Kendal' on to a narrow byroad. In ¾ mile cross the M6 (no SP), then pass over the railway line, canal and M6 to reach the edge of Burton. Here turn left, then take the next turning right on to the Kirkby Lonsdale road. In 4¼ miles bear right and descend into Whittington. In the village turn left on to the B6254 and continue to Kirkby Lonsdale.

KIRKBY LONSDALE, Cumbria
Devil's Bridge (AM), 3-arched and possibly as old as the 13th century, spans the River Lune outside Kirkby. One of the finest ancient bridges in the country, it is now closed to traffic. Kirkby is a delightful small market town and it is an excellent centre for exploring the Lune valley. John Ruskin, the 19th-century writer and painter, was captivated by this, describing his favourite view as 'one of the loveliest scenes in England and therefore in the world'. Ruskin walks are signposted north of the churchyard.

Leave on the A65, SP 'Skipton', and re-enter Lancashire before reaching Cowan Bridge.

COWAN BRIDGE, Lancs
A few cottages mark the site of the Clergy Daughters' School to which Charlotte and Emily Brontë were sent as boarders from 1824-5. Later Charlotte was to describe the harsh treatment they suffered in her novel *Jane Eyre*, where the school appears under the name of Lowood.

In 1¾ miles enter North Yorkshire. In 2 miles a turning to the left may be taken to visit Ingleton.

INGLETON, N Yorks
Ingleton thrives as a centre for climbers, potholers and visitors to the Yorkshire Dales. The limestone hills of this region are honeycombed with caves, most of which are accessible only to experienced potholers, but the White Scar caves, with their stalactites, stalagmites, underground river and lake, are a noted tourist attraction. Above Ingleton loom the heights of Whernside (2,419ft) and Ingleborough (2,373ft). With Penyghent, these peaks are the most formidable in the Dales, and a walk taking in all 3 is a favourite feat of endurance for fell walkers. Even more gruelling are the 3-peaks races, one for runners and one for cyclists.

Continue on the A65 and after 4 miles pass the turning for Clapham.

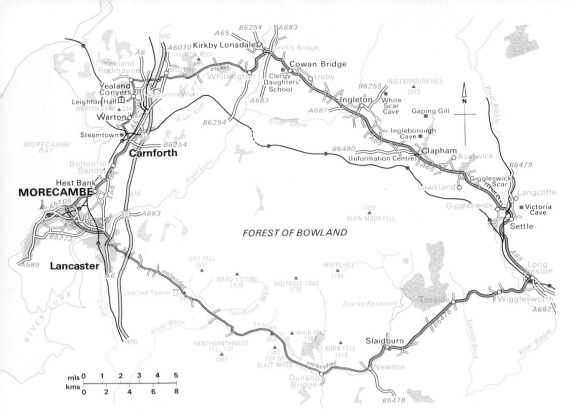

SCALE

| mls | 0 | 1 | 2 | 3 | 4 | 5 |
| kms | 0 | 2 | 4 | 6 | 8 |

FOREST OF BOWLAND, Lancs

This wild region of grouse moor and high fells, dissected by deep, narrow valleys, was one of the ancient royal forests of Saxon England. There are no towns and few villages in the Forest, and no roads cross it, except for the lonely moorland road from Newton through the pass known as the Trough of Bowland to Lancaster. Parts of the Forest have now been designated an Area of Outstanding Natural Beauty and are therefore accessible, but much of the area remains a wilderness.

Continue on the unclassified road towards Lancaster. On entering the suburbs follow SP for city centre.

LANCASTER, Lancs

Lancaster, county town of the shire, was throughout the 18th century England's chief port for trade with America. St George's Quay, the elegant Customs House designed by Robert Gillow, whose family were famous furniture makers, and the many Georgian houses around the centre, are eloquent reminders of this prosperous era. The massive keep of the castle, 78ft high with walls 10ft thick, dates from the Norman era, when virtually the whole of Lancashire was given to Roger de Poitou by William the Conqueror. The castle was enlarged by King John and its magnificent gateway was built by John of Gaunt, 1st Duke of Lancaster, in the 14th century. The castle also served, and still does, as the county gaol. Among many distinguished prisoners was the Quaker leader George Fox, who was incarcerated in appalling conditions in the 17th century. Earlier in the same century, in 1612, the famous trial of the Lancashire Witches was held in Lancaster, and the iron rings by which they were chained can still be seen in the Well Tower. The City Museum in the Market Square is also the Museum of the Royal Lancashire Regiment.

Leave on the A589 for the return to Morecambe.

CLAPHAM, N Yorks

Stone-built cottages in trim little gardens straggling along the banks of a stream characterise this delightful Yorkshire village where a National Information Centre for the Yorkshire Dales is situated, and where the monthly *Dalesman* magazine is published. Like Ingleton, this is a noted potholing centre. To the north of the village is Ingleborough Cave (access by foot only). The famous Gaping Gill pothole, 378ft deep with a central chamber vast enough to hold a small cathedral, lies not far away.

Remain on the A65 for Settle.

SETTLE, N Yorks

Just outside Settle rises one of the most impressive natural features of the region, the massive rock wall of Giggleswick Scar. Settle itself is one of the most delightful towns in Ribblesdale, with picturesque narrow streets and Georgian houses, sometimes

Leighton Hall's façade, built of a white local limestone, was added in 1810

grouped around small courtyards. Castleberg Crag, 300ft high, dominates the town centre, and from the summit the visitor can enjoy panoramic views of the town and the surrounding dales. In 1838 a chance discovery of the feature now known as Victoria Cave led to the retrieval of many fascinating prehistoric remains, including the bones of animals long extinct in the British Isles.

Leave on the A65 Skipton road and follow Ribblesdale to Long Preston. Here turn right on to the B6478, SP 'Slaidburn'. Beyond Wigglesworth gradually climb through moorland countryside to Tosside. Re-enter Lancashire and later descend to reach Slaidburn.

Displays of heraldic shields and coats of arms of all sovereigns since Richard 1 adorn the Shire Hall in Lancaster Castle

SLAIDBURN, Lancs

Although only a village, Slaidburn was for centuries the administrative 'capital' of the Forest of Bowland, and boasted the only grammar school for miles around. The Forest 'court' next to the inn was in use until the outbreak of World War I. The inn itself bears the unique name of Hark to Bounty. The story goes that Bounty was a foxhound belonging to a local vicar and that whenever his master and other hunting friends were in the inn, Bounty's barking was easily distinguishable above the hullabaloo of the whole pack.

At the war memorial keep left, then turn left, SP 'Trough of Bowland'. At Newton continue forward to reach Dunsop Bridge. After crossing the river bridge turn right and later ascend the Trough of Bowland.

YORK, N Yorks

The many strands of York's proud history can be traced in its fascinating streets, its ancient buildings, superb museums and, above all, in the fabulous minster, the largest Gothic church in England. The Romans built *Eboracum* at this point on the River Ouse; the Anglo-Saxons made the city capital of their kingdom of Deira and, when the Vikings came, they named it Jorvic, from which we get the name of York. Sacked by the Normans, York rose again as a great medieval city, surrounded by massive walls within which a maze of narrow streets grew up around the towering minster. The medieval atmosphere is felt most vividly in the Shambles, the street of the butchers, where in places the overhanging storeys of the ancient houses almost touch across the narrow way. Old street scenes and exhibits of life in bygone times can be seen in the fascinating Castle Museum, and the power of the medieval guilds is displayed in the Merchant Adventurers' House, a restored 14th-century guild house in Fossgate. The minster reigns majestically over the city as it has done for more than 700 years, its beautiful interior lit by glowing stained-glass windows, created by medieval craftsmen at the height of their powers. The graceful design of the west window has earned it the title of the Heart of Yorkshire. The minster undercroft houses the cathedral treasury. In Jacobean and Georgian times York had 2 famous citizens, both of

TOUR 58   *75 MILES*

THE VALE OF YORK

Yorkshire's mighty capital city looks out over the ancient kingdom of Elmet and the lowlands of the Vale of York where 3 great rivers, the Ouse, the Derwent and the Wharfe, meander through rich farmland sheltered by the rolling hills of the Yorkshire Wolds.

whom met a tragic fate: the first was Guy Fawkes, born at a house in Petergate and executed for treason in 1605; the second was Dick Turpin, a legendary hero of the ride from London, hanged as a highwayman in 1739 on the Knavemire, now York racecourse. At the Jorvik Viking Centre is one of Britain's newest and most exciting museums. Here visitors are transported — in 'time cars' — back to the sights, smells and sounds of 10th-century York. Providing a contrast is the National Railway Museum, which pays tribute to York's importance as a railway centre from the early days of steam. Here can be seen locomotives, rolling stock, models, films, and posters.

Leave York on the A1036, SP 'Leeds (A64)'. In 3¼ miles join the A64 and after 6 miles branch left on to the A659 for Tadcaster.

TADCASTER, N Yorks

Tadcaster is the home of traditional Yorkshire ales and the scent of the breweries pervades the old streets which are famous for the large number of public houses. A restored 15th-century house called the Ark (OACT) has been converted into a museum of pubs and brewing, with a unique collection of fascinating relics of British drinking habits. The dignified stone church has an interesting past; it was completely dismantled in the last century and reconstructed on a site higher above the River Wharfe to save it from flooding. The limestone for the church was quarried locally, and much of this stone was used to build York minster.

In Tadcaster turn left on to the A162, SP 'Sherburn-in-Elmet', and continue to Towton.

TOWTON, N Yorks

One of the most savage battles in English history took place near this peaceful little village in wooded Wharfdale. A stone cross just outside Towton marks the place where more than 30,000 men were slaughtered on Palm Sunday, 1461, during the Wars of the Roses. The bodies were interred in a mass grave in a field nearby, and for centuries after ploughmen would often turn up bones.

At the end of the village turn right on to the B1217, SP 'Garforth'. After ½ mile pass (right) the War of the Roses memorial cross and continue for 2½ miles to reach the entrance to Lotherton Hall.

LOTHERTON HALL, N Yorks

Lotherton Hall (OACT), with its outstanding collection of European works of art, furniture and porcelain, was given to the city of Leeds by the Gascoigne family and is now a country house museum. In addition to the Gascoigne collection, there are superb Chinese ceramics, 20th-century pottery and a fascinating display of historical costumes, including examples of the best of the fashion designs of our own time.

Return along the B1217 for 200 yards and turn right on to an unclassified road, SP 'Sherburn-in-Elmet'. In 3¼ miles turn left on to the B1222 for Sherburn-in-Elmet.

SHERBURN-IN-ELMET, N Yorks

A white church stands like a beacon on the hill above Sherburn, once the eastern capital of the ancient Brigantine kingdom of Elmete. The church, built of local limestone, was the secret meeting place for loyal Catholics during the Reformation, when they are said to have made their way by night through underground passages, to worship according to their faith. The medieval Janus cross in the church, so called after the double-headed Roman deity because the carved figures face opposite directions, was buried for safety during the 16th-century Reformation; when it was later exhumed, a quarrel over its ownership caused it to be sawn in half vertically, but the 2 sections have finally been brought together. The old gabled grammar school dates from the 17th century.

At the crossroads turn right on to the A162, SP 'Ferrybridge', and proceed to South Milford. From here an unclassified road on the right may be taken to Steeton Hall Gatehouse.

STEETON HALL GATEHOUSE, N Yorks

Across the woods and meadows from the village of South Milford, stands the 14th-century gatehouse (AM) of a medieval castle, once owned by the Fairfax family. A forbear of the famous Cromwellian general is said to have ridden out from here to escape with his sweetheart, a wealthy heiress, who was incarcerated in Nun Appleton Priory.

York minster, one of England's best examples of Gothic architecture, has the largest lantern tower in Britain and contains more stained glass than any other cathedral in the country

Water lilies are the speciality of Burnby Hall's lovely gardens

Continue on the A162 and in 1¼ miles, at the roundabout, turn left on to the A63, SP 'Selby', for Monk Fryston.

MONK FRYSTON, N Yorks
This delightful little village with a Tudor Hall (not open) and old cottages around a small square was given to the monks of Selby Abbey in Norman times, hence the first part of its name. The village church predates the Norman Conquest and has preserved intact its Anglo-Saxon tower.

Remain on the A63 to Selby.

SELBY, N Yorks
Famous for its beautiful abbey church, Selby is an ancient town and port on the River Ouse, where small ships still put in and out of the small dock. When boats were built here they had to be launched sideways because the river was too narrow for the usual method. The abbey was founded in 1069 by a monk of Auxerre in France who, following a vision, came to England and sailed up the River Ouse, stopping at a place where 3 swans settled on the water. Here he built a hermitage and received permission from the king to found an abbey. Unfortunately he fell out with the authorities before work could begin, and the present church was started by Hugh de Lacy in 1100. Building went slowly and was not finally completed until the 14th century. The abbey stands, surrounded by lawns, in the attractive little market-place at the heart of the town.

Leave on the A19, SP 'York', and cross the River Ouse by a wooden toll bridge. Pass through Barlby and at the end turn right on to the A163, SP 'Market Weighton', then right again across the railway. Later cross the River Derwent for Bubwith and continue to Holme-upon-Spalding-Moor.

HOLME-UPON-SPALDING-MOOR, Humberside
Lonely Beacon Hill, crowned by Holme Church, looks out over the surrounding flat plain, once a marshland where travellers were guided by the welcome sight of the church tower. Monks kept a nightly vigil, tolling the church bell as a signal to anyone who might be lost. The church is a charming medieval structure, its walls whitewashed inside to show off the beautiful wood furnishings.

At the end of the village turn left, SP 'Bridlington'. In 1¾ miles, at the roundabout, turn left, and 2½ miles farther, at the next roundabout, turn left again on to the A1079, SP 'York'. Pass through Shiptonthorpe to Hayton, then in 1 mile turn right on to the B1247 for Pocklington.

POCKLINGTON, Humberside
This red-roofed little market town sits snugly in the shadow of the Yorkshire Wolds, with many attractive houses along the cheerful streets leading up to the medieval church, sometimes called the Cathedral of the Wolds. A memorial on the church wall commemorates an 18th-century flying man, Tom Pelling, who performed acrobatic tricks on a tightrope slung from the church tower to a nearby inn.

BURNBY HALL GARDENS, Humberside
These beautiful water gardens (OACT) on the outskirts of Pocklington were created by Major Stewart, a world-traveller in the old tradition, who gathered rare plants on his travels and brought home one of the finest collections of water lilies in Europe. Specimens of more than 50 varieties of lily bloom here all summer long. Nearby, in the Stewart Museum, is his collection of hunting trophies.

At the roundabout in Pocklington keep forward, SP 'Malton', then go over the crossroads. Nearly ½ mile farther turn right into Garth Ends, SP 'Millington'. At the next roundabout turn left, then in 1¾ miles keep forward, SP 'Givendale'. This byroad climbs on to the Wolds and passes the hamlet of Great Givendale. Continue for 1¾ miles and turn left on to the A166, SP 'York', to reach Stamford Bridge.

STAMFORD BRIDGE, Humberside
The first of the 2 decisive battles of English history was fought at this quiet village on the River Derwent in 1066. King Harold was threatened by 2 invading forces: across the North Sea were the combined fleets of Tostig of Northumbria and Harold Hardrada of Norway; on the French side of the channel lay the ships of William of Normandy. Both fleets were waiting for a favourable wind to bring them to England, and the Norsemen arrived first, obliging Harold to march his army north to Yorkshire, where he inflicted a crushing defeat on the invaders. In the meantime, however, William had landed in Kent and the Saxon army, exhausted from their long march south, were defeated at the Battle of Hastings and Harold was killed.

Beyond the town cross the River Derwent, then in 5 miles, at the roundabout, take the A1079 for the return to York.

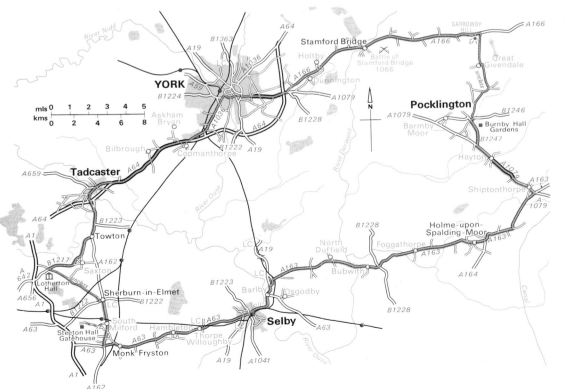

THE NORTH WOLDS

In this area of North Yorkshire and Humberside, lush green meadows, rich in wildlife and scattered with tiny villages, slope gently seawards beyond the resorts of Filey and Bridlington to the chalky cliffs of Flamborough Head

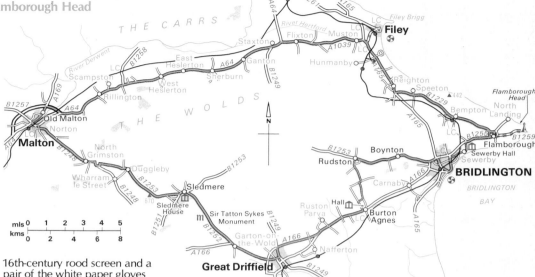

BRIDLINGTON, Humberside

Bridlington has less of the 'genteel' Yorkshire resort atmosphere of days gone by, but it is still a very popular seaside town boasting an attractive and historically interesting centre. The main point of interest in old Bridlington is the Priory Church of St Mary, which is particularly noted for its nave — the remains of an Augustinian priory founded here in the 12th century. The richly-decorated north porch, the 14th-century south aisle and the beautiful west doorway are also of note. Across the green is the priory's Bayle Gate which was built in 1388 and has, at various times since, served as the prior's courtroom, a sailors' prison, a barracks and a school, before being used in its present role of museum. Stones from the old priory were used in the building of 2 piers in the harbour which still services a small fishing fleet. The long stretches of fine sandy beach to the north and south of the harbour, on Bridlington Bay, enjoys a sheltered location protected by the great headland of Flamborough.

Leave by the Promenade for Flamborough Road. In 1¼ miles, at the roundabout, take the 3rd exit into Sewerby Road. Go over the level-crossing into Sewerby for Sewerby Hall.

SEWERBY HALL, Humberside

Sewerby Hall (OACT) was built between 1714 and 1720 and is surrounded by a fine park of 50 acres, which sweeps down to striking cliffs overlooking Bridlington Bay. The mansion has been turned into a museum, and included in this is the Amy Johnson Room, where many of the pilot's momentoes are kept. The grounds are also open to the public, and a miniature golf course, croquet lawns, a putting green and a children's corner provide entertainment.

At the entrance to the Hall keep left. In ½ mile turn right on to the B1255 (no SP) then bear right for Flamborough.

FLAMBOROUGH, Humberside

About 1,000 years ago the area around Flamborough was taken by the Vikings, and is still sometimes called 'Little Denmark'. The sprawling village stands 2 miles inland from Flamborough Head and the lighthouse, and boasts a much restored but delightful church, in which there is a fine

16th-century rood screen and a pair of the white paper gloves which were traditionally worn at the funeral of a maiden. There is also a monument of a man with his heart bared; he is Sir Marmaduke Constable who died in 1520, because, it is said, a toad which he swallowed ate his heart. Flamborough Head is where the Yorkshire Wolds meet the sea in glistening white 400ft cliffs. From here onlookers watched John Paul Jones, the Scottish-born American sailor who performed a number of daring naval exploits during his career, win a sea battle with 2 British men-of-war. The cliffs between Flamborough and Bempton are famous as a valuable breeding ground for seabirds, and here the only mainland gannetry in Britain is to be found.

Continue on the B1229, SP 'Filey', and at the end of the village turn right. Pass through Bempton, then in 4¼ miles turn right on to the A165, SP 'Scarborough', and enter Reighton. In 3 miles a detour along the A1039 (right) leads into Filey.

FILEY, N Yorks

Filey is now a popular holiday town, standing mostly on the cliff tops overlooking the bay. The old village has quaint streets and several houses dating from the 17th century, and the modern town boasts a fine promenade, a sandy beach and well-kept gardens. A lovely wooded road called the Ravine leads down to the beach, and at the top of it stands St Oswald's Church. The oldest parts are 12th century, and the great square medieval tower bears not a weathercock, but a 'weatherfish'. One of the windows commemorates all the Filey men

lost at sea. A great attraction nearby is Filey Brigg, a mile-long reef jutting out from the Carr Naze headland with caves, coves, cliffs and rock pools which are a delight to explore.

The main tour continues on the A165 for ¼ mile and turns left on to the A1039, SP 'Malton'. Pass through Flixton, then in 1 mile at the roundabout join the A64, SP 'York'. After 14 miles join the Malton Bypass and in 1¼ miles branch left, SP 'Malton B1257'. At the roundabout turn left for Old Malton and Malton.

MALTON, N Yorks

Malton is actually divided in half by the site of a Roman station which lies in between. New Malton is the busy market town serving a large farming community and its large market square is

Cobles — open-decked fishing boats — run holiday fishing trips from Bridlington's harbour which is also still a working port

always a hive of activity. The 18th-century town hall around the corner from the market square bears a plaque recording the fact that Edmund Burke was Malton's MP from 1780 to 1794. Other buildings of interest include the Cross Keys Inn in Wheelgate, which has a medieval crypt, and the former Hospital of St Mary Magdalene. The quaint old-fashioned cottages and inns of Old Malton lie a mile north-east of the town. Here, the Church of St Mary was built on the remains of a Gilbertine priory founded in the 12th century. South-east of Malton, at Langton Wold, is a famous training ground for race horses.

Above: the cliffs of Flamborough Head

Left: the elegant furnishings of King James's bedroom at Burton Agnes Hall are shown off by the Jacobean panelling

GT DRIFFIELD, Humberside
Driffield is a busy agricultural town on the edge of the Yorkshire Wolds, boasting an annual show and a regular Thursday cattle market. Anglers come to Driffield to fish for trout in the numerous streams which flow down from the Wolds.

Leave by the Bridlington road A166 to reach Burton Agnes.

BURTON AGNES, Humberside
The magnificent Elizabethan mansion, Burton Agnes Hall (OACT), is the main attraction in this sleepy village. The mellow redbrick exterior with stone trim is an impressive sight, distinguished by semi-octagonal bays on the south front. Octagonal towers are a feature of the gatehouse which was built a little later than the house. It provides an elegant entrance-way to the house via velvet lawns complemented by almost 100 clipped yew trees. The Hall is still owned by the Griffith family, whose ancestor, Sir Henry Griffith, built it more than 350 years ago. The splendid interior is just as impressive as the outside and visitors may require more than one trip to absorb all details of the richly-furnished rooms. Of special note are the stone and alabaster chimneypiece and oak and plaster screen of the great hall, the massive staircase and the beautifully-restored long gallery. The house also contains a fine collection of paintings.

The main tour turns left on to an unclassified road for Rudston.

RUDSTON, Humberside
In 1933 a ploughman uncovered a Roman villa at Rudston, and 3 fine mosaic pavements from the site are now on view in the Hull Transport Museum. The largest pavement measures 13ft by 10ft 6in and depicts a voluptuous Venus with flying hair, holding an apple and a mirror and surrounded by leopards, birds and hunters. An enormous monolith, a relic of earlier times, stands in the churchyard at Rudston.

At the far end of the village turn right on to the B1253, SP 'Bridlington'. In 2½ miles skirt the village of Boynton.

BOYNTON, Humberside
This small, picturesque village of whitewashed houses is set amidst woods on the slopes of the Gypsey Race valley. The Stricklands of Boynton Hall (not open) are thought to have introduced the turkey to England from America and there are monuments to the family in the church, rebuilt during the 18th century. Their family crest includes a turkey and a portrait.

Remain on the B1253 for 2 miles, then turn left on to the A165 for the return to Bridlington.

Leave Malton on the B1248, SP 'Beverley'. Cross the River Derwent then the level-crossing and keep left. In almost ½ mile turn right, still SP 'Beverley', then at the T-junction turn left. Beyond North Grimston ascend, then branch left on to the B1253, SP 'Driffield'. At Duggleby, bear right, then cross the Wolds to enter Humberside. In 2 miles turn left into Sledmere.

SLEDMERE, Humberside
This neat little village forms part of the Sledmere estate of which Sledmere House (OACT) is the centre. The estate is the property of the Sykes family who were largely responsible for the development of the Wolds from bare open wasteland into the richly-wooded agricultural land that exists here today. Beside the main road in the village stand 2 remarkable war memorials. One, known as the Waggoners' Memorial, is a tribute to the 1,200 men from the Wolds who died in World War I, and the other is a replica of the nationally famous Eleanor Crosses. The elegant 18th-century mansion, Sledmere House, was burnt down in 1911 but was rebuilt later in the same style. A great attraction at Sledmere is the beautifully-landscaped park designed by Capability Brown. A church within the park is reputedly one of the loveliest parish churches in England. Arguably the most famous member of the Sykes family was Sir Tatton. Born in 1823 and a legend in his own time, he excelled in the skills of farming, hunting, racing, boxing, building schools and breeding sheep. He also established the Sledmere stud before he died at the age of 91. Just outside the village, on Garton Hill, is a great spire dedicated to the celebrated Sir Tatton, which has a carving on the front depicting the great man on horseback. Garton Hill is a good vantage point from which to view the magnificence of the Wolds.

Continue on the B1252 Driffield road, and in 2¼ miles pass Sir Tatton Sykes's monument. After another 2 miles turn left on to the A166 for Great Driffield.

NB: The early part of this tour uses a Forestry Commission Forest Drive (toll). During periods of extremely dry weather the road may be closed owing to the high fire risk. If wishing to avoid this portion, leave Pickering on the A169, SP 'Whitby', and pick up the tour at the Saltersgate Inn (11 miles shorter).

PICKERING, N Yorks

This ancient market town, situated amidst beautiful countryside, is known as the Gateway to the Moors. The market place façades are mainly Georgian or Victorian, but older structures are often concealed behind them. The 12th century is evoked in the robust towers and ruined remains of Pickering Castle (AM), where Richard II was confined after his abdication. The Church of St Peter and St Paul, which stands above the main street, has retained fragments of a similar date. Its main attraction is the fine 15th-century wall paintings, depicting Bible stories with the figures in daily costumes of over 500 years ago. The Beck Isle Museum of Rural Life is housed in a fine Georgian house, formerly the home of William Marshall, a noted agriculturalist, and displays folk exhibits of local interest. Pickering is also the terminus of the North Yorkshire Moors Railway.

NORTH YORKSHIRE MOORS RAILWAY, N Yorks

The North Yorkshire Moors Railway operates over 18 miles of track between Pickering and Grosmont, taking in some superb panoramic views along the way. The private company which runs the railway was founded in 1967, and became a trust in 1972. Steam and diesel locomotives pull the trains, and at Grosmont there is a loco shed, viewing gallery, gift shop and catering facilities. At Pickering station there is an excellent bookshop and also a National Park information and audio-visual centre.

From the North Yorkshire Moors railway station at Pickering follow the Newton-on-Rawcliffe road to Newton-on-Rawcliffe.

NEWTON-ON-RAWCLIFFE, N Yorks

Newton-on-Rawcliffe stands close to the woodlands of Newton Dale on high ground overlooking a stupendous panorama of the Newton Dale canyon — a beautiful moorland glen bordered in places by crags and steep cliffs. The White Swan Inn in the village stands on one of the oldest hostelry sites in the district.

Continue to Stape.

STAPE, N Yorks

The hamlet of Stape was at one time the centre of besom-making; a besom being a kind of broom

made of a bundle of supple twigs tied to a handle. This little community is also the home of the Stape Silver Band — many of these northern villages boast their own bands, which are the objects of much fierce competition and pride. Closeby a footpath, near Mauley Cross, leads to Needle Point, where well-dressing ceremonies — the garlanding of wells with flowers once connected with pagan worship — and rural fairs used to be held.

Continue on the Stape road and in 1 mile descend (1 in 6). In 1¾ miles keep left then in ½ mile bear right to enter Cropton Forest and join the Newton Dale Forest Drive (toll). In 3 miles pass a picnic area and turn right. After another 2¼ miles leave the Forest Drive and continue to Levisham.

LEVISHAM, N Yorks

Levisham, high on open moorland, has a green and a Hall and a church with a Saxon chancel arch. This church, St Mary's, stands forlorn at the bottom of a glen beside Levisham Beck, with an old watermill for company. Because the descent from the village to the church is so steep, a new church, St John the Baptist, was built in the village in 1884. Levisham has a typical North Riding main street, with a wide lawn to the left and right, although the view at one end is obscured by a cottage. At the head of Levisham Beck is a great natural amphitheatre called the Hole of Horcum.

Continue to Lockton.

NORTH YORKSHIRE'S MOORS AND DALES

Savage, desolate moorland, lush farmland and deep peaceful dales blend into an area of unique contrasts and beauty where picturesque grey-stone villages are centres for magnificent walks by streams and waterfalls.

Part of the 15th-century wall paintings in Pickering's church

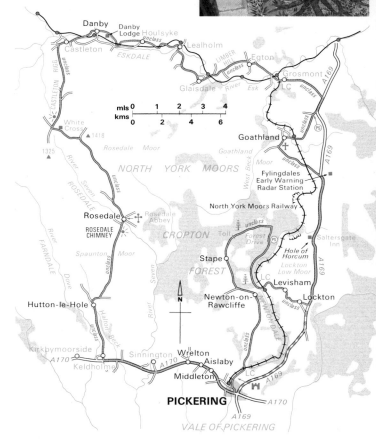

The Hole of Horcum, a great natural hollow, is the curious product of erosion during the Ice Age

LOCKTON, N Yorks

Lockton, across the dale from Levisham, is another moorland village with a spectacular view. The 13th-century Church of St Andrew and St Giles has been greatly modified over the years and has a Jacobean pulpit, reading desk and communion table. There is no village public house, but over Lockton Low Moor to the north, past the gorge known as the Hole of Horcum, is the picturesque Saltersgate Inn. Smugglers, running silk and gin inland from Robin Hood's Bay, are said to have used the inn as a refuge.

At Lockton keep left, SP 'Whitby', then in ½ mile turn left on to the A169. Climb on to Lockton Low Moor and later pass the Hole of Horcum before descending to the Saltersgate Inn. After 2¾ miles (right) there are views of the Fylingdales Radar Station.

FYLINGDALES EARLY WARNING RADAR STATION, N Yorks
A futuristic sight on the desolate Fylingdale Moor is the white domes of the Radar Station. This defence installation is a gaunt reminder of the consequences of technological development in an area which was previously uninhabited. The gruelling Lyke Wake Walk across the North Yorks Moors passes through Fylingdales Moor.

Turn left, SP 'Goathland', and cross Goathland Moor before descending to Goathland. Bear right to enter the village.

GOATHLAND, N Yorks
The grey-stone buildings of this delightful moorland village are set around a large village green where a group of sword dancers, the Plough Stotts, regularly perform traditional dances. Sheep graze between the houses scattered on the perimeter of the village. This is a marvellous centre for walking, and the local streams tumble over rocks forming spectacular waterfalls, some of which are named; for example: Mallyan Spout, Thomason Foss, Nelly Ayre Foss and Water Ark.

Follow SP 'Whitby' and cross the railway, then ascend. In 2 miles turn left on to the A169, then ¼ mile farther turn left again, SP 'Grosmont'. Cross Sleights Moor and later descend into Grosmont.

Hutton Beck tumbles down from the Yorkshire Moors through the enchanting village of Hutton-le-Hole to Westfield Wood which lies behind it

Continue over the level-crossing and the River Esk, then ascend to Egton. In the village bear right and at Wheatsheaf Inn turn left, SP 'Glaisdale'. In 1¾ miles descend (1 in 3), then cross the Esk and ascend through Glaisdale. Follow the Castleton road and in 1 mile bear right. In another ¾ mile turn right for Lealholm. Recross the Esk, then turn left, SP 'Danby'. Continue through Esk Dale and pass Danby Lodge before reaching Danby.

DANBY, N Yorks
Close to this village in the Esk valley is Danby Lodge, a former shooting lodge and now a visitor centre for the North Yorks Moors National Park. The village is also called Dale End, as it lies at the head of Danby Dale, which runs south into the moors. One mile south-east of the village is ruined 14th-century Danby Castle. The ruins have had a farmhouse added to them and are used as farm buildings. This was the home of the Latimers, and of their successors the Nevilles. Close to the castle is Duck Bridge, a packhorse bridge over the River Esk which dates from about 1386. All around are obscure circles and stones which are remnants of the Bronze and Iron Ages.

At Danby go over the staggered crossroads and continue to Castleton. Follow SP 'Rosedale' and in ½ mile bear left to climb along the 1,000ft-high Castleton Rigg. After 4 miles turn left (still SP 'Rosedale'). Cross the plateau of Rosedale Moor and after another 4 miles descend into Rosedale.

ROSEDALE, N Yorks
In the churchyard, near the attractive green of this main village in the dale of the same name, are a few stones which represent the remains of a 12th-century Cistercian abbey. South of the village, as the dale narrows, is the Rosedale Chimney, which is the remnant of an iron-ore working. What used to be the mineral railway at the head of the dale is now a walking trail with superb views of the countryside.

At the end of the village turn right and ascend Rosedale Chimney Bank (1 in 3). Beyond the summit cross Spaunton Moor and after 3 miles, at the T-junction, turn right for Hutton-le-Hole.

HUTTON-LE-HOLE, N Yorks
This attractive village was built randomly around wide greens dissected by 2 becks and various picturesque bridges, at the foot of a limestone escarpment. Grey-stone houses with red pantiled roofs complete the showplace-effect. Ryedale Folk Museum is housed here in an ancient cruck-type (timbered) building, once the home of prosperous Quakers. Craftsmen's tools, farm implements, an ancient dairy, Roman pottery and a reconstructed Elizabethan glass furnace are among the exhibits. The oldest building in the village, dating from 1695, belonged to John Richardson, who was a friend of William Penn the English Quaker who founded Pennsylvania. It is called, appropriately, Quaker Cottage.

Leave on the Kirkbymoorside road. In 2¾ miles, at the T-junction, turn left on to the A170, SP 'Scarborough', and continue to Wrelton.

WRELTON, N Yorks
The junction of the westward road from Pickering and the Roman Road is marked by the old village of Wrelton. The crossing is distinguished by a tiny green, set amidst sturdy Georgian farms and houses, and a substantial restored cruck building of 1665. An ancient alehouse, the Buck Inn, contains curios such as an old witness dock from Pickering magistrates' court. Back in 1779, the inn had its own brewhouse and served 'Old Tom' ale to passing stagecoach travellers.

Continue on the A170 to Aislaby.

AISLABY, N Yorks
One of the smallest villages on the main road, Aislaby was built by the Vikings. Among its most attractive buildings is the Georgian Hall (not open), with its lead statuettes and regal summer house which presides over a group of solid farmhouses.

Continue to Middleton.

MIDDLETON, N Yorks
A string of pleasant buildings lining the road make up the village of Middleton, with the early Georgian Middleton Hall (not open) just visible through the trees. Opposite the New Inn is the Church of St Andrew. The north aisle contains fragments of 3 fine Anglo-Danish crosses dating from the 10th century and the sculpted decorations include a dragon and an armed warrior.

Remain on the A170 for the return to Pickering.

Fylingdales Early Warning Radar Station was set up jointly by the British and United States governments in 1961

HELMSLEY, N Yorks

Helmsley is an old stone market town with venerable houses gathered about the borders of its spacious market square, which has an old market cross as its focal point. Among the buildings is the modest town hall and several old inns; the Black Swan has 2 Georgian houses and a 16th-century timber-framed house incorporated in it. All Saints Church, just off the square, was rebuilt in the 1860s, but retained some Norman characteristics. Walter L'espec, founder of Rievaulx Abbey, built Helmsley Castle (AM) in the 12th century. Although the stronghold rarely saw action, perhaps because of the strength still evident in the ruins of the great keep, tower and curtain walls, it did suffer a 3-month siege during the Civil War before being taken by Parliamentary forces. In 1689 Sir Charles Duncombe, a banker, bought the town of Helmsley and built Duncombe Park (now a school) and the picturesque ruins of the old castle lie in the grounds of the park.

Leave Helmsley on the B1257, SP 'Stokesley'. In 1½ miles turn left, SP 'Sawton'. Later descend through woodland before turning right for Rievaulx Abbey.

RIEVAULX ABBEY, N Yorks

Rievaulx Abbey (AM), magnificent even in ruin, lies in the richly-wooded valley of the River Rye and is a favourite subject of artists. Walter L'espec gave the site to the Cistercians in 1131, and this was the first church they built in the north of England. The ruins consist of the choir and transepts of the church, the lower walls of the nave and its attendant chapels, and the chapter house. Other remains include the shrine of the first abbot and the refectory. One of the best views of the abbey can be obtained from Rievaulx Terrace (AM), high up to the south, where 18th-century garden temples were built to take advantage of the delightful landscape. It belonged to Duncombe Park and the gentry used to drive out and enjoy the magnificent views.

Continue on the unclassified road and ascend to the junction with the B1257. To the right is the entrance to Rievaulx Terrace. Here, turn left, SP 'Stokesley', and climb to over 800ft before the descent into Blisdale.

BLISDALE, N Yorks

It was said that a Blisdale man left his dale so rarely that when he did he was regarded as a foreigner in his own county. It is only in comparatively recent times that a proper road was laid along the valley floor, giving the outside world access to one of the wildest and most picturesque dales in this part of Yorkshire. Between

THE LESSER-KNOWN DALES

Solid little market towns of grey stone dot the dales, above which rise the heather-clad slopes of the Cleveland Hills. Medieval monks found the peace and solitude they sought in the secluded river valleys of the North Riding, and here still stand the ruins of their beautiful abbeys.

Helmsley and Chop Gate the bubbling River Selph flows through a dale luxuriously wooded with birch and aromatic pine, but northwards, through Great Broughton to Stokesley, a moorland landscape emerges. Up on the high moors above the road are old coal-workings and lime pits — all that remains of the iron-smelting activities of the monks from Rievaulx Abbey.

Continue on the B1257 and beyond the hamlet of Chop Gate reach the summit of Clay Bank — a fine viewpoint. Descend from the Cleveland Hills to Great Broughton. In 2 miles, at the roundabout, take the 2nd exit to enter Stokesley.

STOKESLEY, N Yorks

This old market town of narrow, cobbled streets lies at the foot of the Cleveland Hills. At each end of the long market place is a green, and standing on an island in the middle is the 19th-century town hall. The River Leven runs along one side of the town and is spanned at frequent intervals by footbridges. Stokesley's many trees were planted in memory of Miss Jane Page, who, in 1836, emigrated to become the first white woman to settle in Victoria, Australia. Every September this normally quiet town explodes into activity when its fair and major agricultural show takes place.

Follow SP 'Thirsk (A172)'. In ¾ mile turn right on to the A172 and continue along the foot of the Cleveland Hills.

CLEVELAND HILLS, N Yorks/Cleveland

This great mass of sandstone hills runs in high ridges separated by secluded valleys and patches of open moorland; one of these is Urra Moor, at 1,500ft the highest point in the hills. The moorlands are famous for the bilberries which grow here, possibly an important part of the diet of the lost civilisation which left their burial chambers, tumuli, scattered all over the region. In winter snow covers the hills in a blanket, in summer they are carpeted in the glowing colours of flowering heather.

Remain on the A172 for 8 miles then branch left to join the A19. In ½ mile a track (left) may be taken to visit Mount Grace Priory.

MOUNT GRACE PRIORY, N Yorks

The old Carthusian monastery (AM, NT) was built towards the end of the 14th century by an order which vowed to austerity, isolation and silence. Within the inner cloister the remains of 15 cells survive, one of which has been restored. Hermit-monks lived in these self-contained apartments, working each day in their own private gardens and only meeting for services in the church and for a Saturday meal. On other days of the week their food was passed to them through a right-angled hatch so that the monks could not see or touch the server. It is a peaceful place, and pleasant to wander in, but the architecture, though softened by time, still reflects the grim austerity of its former inhabitants.

In another ½ mile branch left on to the A684 for Northallerton.

Top: the Fauconberg Arms in Coxwold dates from the 17th century. It still has the right to graze 4 cows on village land

Above: the striking ruins of Byland Abbey still show something of the great rose window that was 26ft in diameter

NORTHALLERTON, N Yorks

This old posting station retains many of its old inns in which travellers stayed while waiting for the stage coaches, which were given romantic names like the *High Flyer* and the *Wellington*. The town is built along a curving street, which broadens in the middle to form a market square, and narrows again at its north end near the church. There is a lot of Georgian housing, and a town hall, built in 1873, stands in the square.

Leave on the A168, SP 'Thirsk'. In 7 miles turn right on to the B1448 to enter Thirsk.

Sutton Bank, a dramatic escarpment of the Hambleton Hills, is a famous viewpoint. The white horse was cut in 1857

THIRSK, N Yorks

As an important coaching station, Thirsk once boasted 35 pubs and 4 breweries; determined, it would seem, to send travellers merrily on their way. Many of these establishments still ply their trade, perhaps foremost among them is the Georgian Golden Fleece Inn, formerly the most important coaching inn, and now the hub of the town on market days and race days. The vast square is still cobbled as it was when bull-baiting was held here in the 18th century. The church is probably the finest Perpendicular church in the county. Begun in 1430, it was founded on a chantry built by Robert Thirsk, who died in 1419. He was a member of the ancient family which gave the town its name.

From the one-way system leave on the A170, SP 'Scarborough'. Beyond Sutton-under-Whitestonecliffe climb on to the Hambleton Hills by means of Sutton Bank (1 in 4). Continue for 3¾ miles before turning right, then immediately right again, SP 'Wass' and 'Coxwold'. To the south-west of Wass short detours can be made to visit Byland Abbey, Coxwold and Newburgh Priory.

BYLAND ABBEY, N Yorks

Here stood the largest Cistercian church in the county. The great west front, incorporating the broken circle of what must have been a magnificent rose window, stands starkly with a single turret as a reminder of its past glory. The monks of Furness who founded it searched for 43 years for a suitable site, and after several false starts settled in the village of Old Byland, only to discover this was too close to the existing abbey at Rievaulx for comfort, so they moved to this pleasant broad valley, drained the marshes, and began to build. Until the Dissolution they led an uneventful life, apart from a visit by Edward II. He stayed briefly while fleeing the Scots whose country he had tried to conquer. Unfortunately, after he left the Scots followed, sacked the abbey and ousted the indignant monks as further punishment.

COXWOLD, N Yorks

Coxwold, with a wide sloping street lined with cottages of golden stone set back beyond broad green verges and spreading trees could be called the 'perfect' village. At one end the 15th-century church, with an unusual octagonal tower, serenely stands as guardian. Its fame as a beauty spot has brought many tourists, but the inhabitants have resolutely kept the village community, which has evolved over the centuries, intact. Fame also came to Coxwold in the form of Thomas Sterne, author of *The Life and Opinions of Tristram Shandy*. Sterne was a rector here for 7 years, and although he died and was buried in London, the Sterne Trust brought his remains back to the village churchyard. The Trust also owns the house in which he lived, Shandy Hall (OACT). It is an old brick farmhouse with medieval timber-framing and a warren of rooms.

NEWBURGH PRIORY, N Yorks

This is essentially an 18th-century hall (OACT) built on a site where Augustinian canons settled in 1150. It is set amid pleasant gardens featuring a pond and striking ornamental hedges. At the Dissolution Henry VIII gave the property to Anthony Belayse, who rebuilt the house. In time it passed to Lord Fauconberg, who, it is said, married a daughter of Oliver Cromwell's who brought her father's heart to Newburgh and had it bricked-up in an attic room of the house to save it from desecration. The vault has never been opened so the story has never been proved.

At Wass the main tour turns left, SP 'Ampleforth', and follows the foot of the Hambleton Hills to Ampleforth.

AMPLEFORTH, N Yorks

Perched upon a shelf of the Hambleton Hills, this village was chosen in 1802 as the site of a Roman Catholic school by English Benedictine monks who had fled from France to escape the French Revolution. The college and abbey of St Lawrence stands at the eastern end of the street along which most of the stone-built houses of the village are ranked, overlooking magnificent views towards Gilling Castle 2 miles to the south. Within the college library are some of Robert Thompson's earliest pieces of furniture. His much sought-after work is easily recognisable by the handcarved mouse he always hid somewhere on his furniture as his signature.

At the end of the village bear right, SP 'Oswaldkirk', and pass Ampleforth College. At Oswaldkirk keep forward and join the B1363, SP 'Helmsley', then in ¼ mile turn left on to the B1257. Continue to Sproxton and turn right on to the A170, SP 'Scarborough', for the return to Helmsley.

LAKES AND FELLS

Magnificent lakes, fells and mountains border the winding roads in this area beloved by poets, writers and painters, and immortalised by William Wordsworth. Some of the most dramatic scenery in England is here, including Kirkstone Pass — the highest pass open to motorists in Cumbria.

WINDERMERE, Cumbria

The quaint, crowded town of Windermere lies on the eastern shore of Lake Windermere which has been a well-known centre for sailing and boating since the 19th century, and a number of clubs are based on its shores. Lake Windermere, at 10½ miles, is the longest lake in England. It has 14 islands, including the delightful privately-owned 38-acre Belle Island which can be visited by steamer and has a historic round house (OACT) full of curios. The Steamboat Museum has a collection of Victorian and Edwardian boats that were used on the lake in the days of steam. They are kept in working order in a covered dock and an exhibition recalls the development of navigation at Windermere. Casual visitors can travel up and down the lake by steamer and it is an ideal way to enjoy the scenery.

Leave Windermere on the A591, SP 'Kendal', and proceed to Staveley.

STAVELEY, Cumbria

This small village is set beside the second fastest-flowing river in England — the Kent. The Kentmere valley to the north of Staveley was once a lake, but it was drained a century ago for the mineral deposits on the bed. At the head of the valley, at Kentmere, is the 16th-century ruin of Kentmere Hall, birthplace in 1517 of the evangelist Bernard Gilpin. High fells dominate this lovely, lonely valley, with Ill Bell, to the north, the loftiest peak at 2,476ft.

In 3 miles, at the roundabout, take the A5284 for Kendal.

KENDAL, Cumbria

The largest of the south Lakeland towns, Kendal, known as the Auld Grey Town, is a blend of both ancient and modern architecture. Limestone buildings, their walls a dozen subtle shades of grey, dominate its narrow old streets and picturesque yards. The River Kent meanders through the town, its banks lined by well-tended gardens and high on the hill in the centre of the town are the imposing ruins of Kendal Castle. Built during the 14th century, the castle was the birthplace of Catherine Parr, last of Henry VIII's 6 wives. A famous son of the town is George Romney, the portrait painter, born in 1734, and a collection of his works hangs in the Mayor's Parlour. Other collections can be viewed at Abbot Hall Art Gallery, close to the 12th-century parish church, and in the Borough Museum, which specialises in natural history. The Castle Dairy in William Street is a well-preserved example of vernacular Tudor architecture. Kendal has long been a centre of commerce and in 1331 a woollen industry was established and became famous for 'Kendal Green', mentioned by Shakespeare.

Leave on the A6, SP 'The North' then 'Penrith'. Later climb across Shap Fell and continue to Shap.

Ullswater, second largest lake in the Lake District, is a popular centre for boating and water sports

LOWTHER PARK, Cumbria

This 3,000-acre park is sculpted out of beautiful countryside that surrounds the ruins of Lowther Castle (not open). This was once a grand house, home of the Earls of Lonsdale and visited by Mary, Queen of Scots. Also in the park is the 12th-century church of St Michael. This was considerably rebuilt during 1686 and outside it stands the mausoleum of the Earls of Lonsdale.

After 1 mile, at the crossroads, turn left, SP 'Lowther Wildlife Park', and in ½ mile reach the A6. At Hackthorpe (right) is the entrance to the Wildlife Adventure Park.

WILDLIFE ADVENTURE PARK, Cumbria

About 100 acres of parkland provide a natural setting for deer, rare breeds of sheep and cattle, and cranes. There are also special enclosures for many European mammals, including otters, badgers and wild pigs.

The main tour turns left on to the A6, SP 'Penrith', and continues through Clifton to Eamont Bridge.

EAMONT BRIDGE, Cumbria

The village of Eamont Bridge is distinguished by a triple-arched medieval bridge which carries traffic over the River Eamont. Nearby is a prehistoric earthwork, 300ft in diameter, called King Arthur's Round Table. It is nearly circular and originally had 2 entrances, one of which survives, and is surrounded by a ditch and a 5ft-high bank. Mayburgh, ¼ mile to the west, is another prehistoric site. This originally occupied 1½ acres and still has 15ft ramparts.

Continue from Eamont Bridge on the A6 and at the roundabout take the 2nd exit to enter Penrith.

PENRITH, Cumbria

Capital town of the old Cumbria in the 9th century, Penrith was probably occupied by the Celts c 500BC. Penrith Castle (AM), built in the 14th century as a defence against the Scots, is now just a ruin. The castle was enlarged by the Duke of Gloucester, later Richard III, who is said to have resided in The Gloucester Arms; dating from 1477, it is one of the oldest inns in England. Penrith town hall, built in 1791, is constructed from 2 houses designed by Richard Adam. In the graveyard of the partly-Norman church are 2 strange stone monuments named 'Giant's Grave' and 'Giant's Thumb'. They are believed to commemorate Owen, King of Cumbria c 920.

Return along the A6, SP 'Shap', and at the roundabout take the 3rd exit to re-enter Eamont Bridge. Here, turn right on to the B5320, SP 'Ullswater', for Yanwath. Continue on the B5320 and pass through Tirril to reach Pooley Bridge.

POOLEY BRIDGE & ULLSWATER, Cumbria

Pooley Bridge, a small village beside the River Eamont, is an ideal centre from which to explore the majestic, spectacular Ullswater lake and its surrounding fells and mountains. Boats may be hired from Pooley Bridge and passenger vessels sail regularly in summer. A small, unclassified road to the south of the lake ends at Martindale where there is a forest with red deer and 2 lonely old churches. The lake is 7 miles long, and about 5 miles from the east end is Gowbarrow Park, seen in spring as a sea of golden daffodils and immortalised by Wordsworth in his famous poem. Close by is Aira Force, a splendid waterfall. High mountains dominating the south-western end of the lake include some of the High Street peaks to the east and the Helvellyn range to the west. Glenridding is a hamlet towards the south-westerly tip of the lake, dominated by a large hotel; boats from Pooley Bridge put in here.

At Pooley Bridge cross the river bridge and in nearly ½ mile turn left on to the A592, SP 'Windermere'. Continue along the shore of Ullswater to Patterdale.

PATTERDALE, Cumbria

This attractive village at the head of Ullswater is encircled by mountains — Place Fell to the east is over 2,000ft and Helvellyn and Lower Man to the south and west are over 3,000ft. The summit of Helvellyn, the third highest peak in the Lake District, is a 3-mile walk along the mile-long Striding Edge, approached by the Grisedale valley. On a clear day, almost every peak in the Lakes is visible from the summit, with the mountains of Scotland rising to the north and the Pennines to the east.

The tour continues southwards and later ascends the dramatic Kirkstone Pass. Beyond the summit (1,489ft) there is an easier descent for 3 miles before turning right, SP 'Ambleside', to enter Troutbeck.

TROUTBECK, Cumbria

Spread along the side of a wild and beautiful valley of the same name, Troutbeck is dominated by lofty pikes of the Kirkstone Pass to the north. At the south end of the village is Townend — a typical yeoman's house (NT) of the early 17th century, with whitewashed walls and mullioned windows: it still retains much of the original oak furniture. At the north end farms and houses cluster around a 17th-century inn called The Mortal Man. The east window in the church was designed by the artist, Edward Burne-Jones.

Follow the Windermere road and in 1¼ miles turn right on to the A591 for the return to Windermere.

A British Rail steamer on Lake Windermere

At the end of the village turn left, SP 'Bampton'. In ½ mile bear right (passing the track to Shap Abbey) and continue to Bampton Grange. Cross the river bridge and turn right for Bampton.

BAMPTON & HAWESWATER RESERVOIR, Cumbria.

The small village of Bampton lies about 2 miles north-east of the spectacular Haweswater Reservoir which can be reached via an unclassified road from Bampton. The reservoir was created to supply Manchester with water and although the road to the north of the lake was submerged in the waterworks scheme, a footpath along the valley remains.

At Bampton turn right, SP 'Penrith', and later skirt Helton to reach Askham. At the crossroads turn right, SP 'Lowther'. Cross the river then pass through Lowther Park.

SHAP, Cumbria

Shap village, nearly 1,000ft above sea level, lies north of the wild, desolate Shap Summit which reaches to 1,300ft. The A6 crosses the summit and is frequently blocked by snowdrifts in winter. Hidden in the valley west of Shap village are the ruins of Shap Abbey (AM). Founded around 1191 by Premonstratensian canons (a French order) most of the ruins date from the early 13th century. There are dramatic views of the High Street group of peaks here.

WAST WATER AND THE WESTERN DALES

The high fells sweep down almost to the sea and above Wast Water, deepest and wildest of the Cumbrian lakes, tower the formidable peaks of Scafell and Scafell Pike. In the shelter of the mountains lie 2 of the loveliest and quietest of the valleys, Eskdale and Dunnerdale, whose scenery inspired many of Wordsworth's poems.

SEASCALE, Cumbria
Good sandy beaches and long rolling breakers, ideal for surfing, make Seascale a popular seaside resort. The village lies on a narrow coastal strip of flattish land, with the magnificent scenery of the distant fells of the Lake District as a backdrop. To the north loom the giant towers of Windscale and Calder Hall Nuclear Power Stations; the latter was the first atomic reactor in the world to generate electricity on a commercial scale. Recently, both plants were re-designated and are now known collectively as Sellafield. There is an information centre here open to the public.

Leave Seascale on the B5344 Gosforth road. In 2½ miles cross the main road on to an unclassified road and enter Gosforth.

GOSFORTH, Cumbria
In this remote Cumbrian village churchyard stands one of a very few survivals of the earliest Christian times in these islands, Gosforth Cross. This 1,000-year-old sacred monument is intricately carved with figures of men and beasts which may represent the pagan gods of Norse mythology, as well as orthodox Christian symbols, a sign that the 'new' religion had not yet completely supplanted the old beliefs of the Viking settlers.

Turn right, SP 'Wasdale Head', then in ¼ mile turn left. In ¾ mile bear right and continue to the shores of Wast Water.

WAST WATER, Cumbria
Bleak fells and cliffs of wild, grey scree sweep down to the shores of Wast Water. In places the water is more than 260ft deep, making this the deepest of the English lakes. To the east, dominating the surrounding hills, rise the towering jagged crags of Scafell and Scafell Pike, at 3,162ft and 3,206ft, the highest peaks in England. The mountain scenery of this remote stretch of water is incomparable.

From here a short detour to the left leads to Wasdale Head.

WASDALE HEAD, Cumbria
The only road through Wasdale ends abruptly at this small village, overshadowed by the massive bulk of Great Gable. From here the only way into the neighbouring valleys is on foot: over Black Sail Pass into Ennerdale, or by Sty Head into Borrowdale. The village is a famous centre for rock climbers: tracks lead up from Wasdale to climbs on Scafell, Napes ridges on Great Gable, and Pillar Rock. The first recorded ascent of Pillar was in 1826; Scafell Pinnacle and Lord's Rake were not climbed until the 1890s, and the Central Buttress not until 1914, but now climbers come from all over the country to tackle these ascents. In the graveyard of the tiny church at Wasdale Head several of the unsuccessful lie buried.

The main tour turns southwards alongside Wast Water, SP 'Santon Bridge'. In 1¾ miles turn left then left again and continue to Santon Bridge. Here turn left, SP 'Eskdale', and ascend through the Miterdale Forest, then continue to Eskdale Green.

Above: Eskdale, ideal for walking, is one of the few Lakeland valleys with no lake

Right: Scafell towers above the River Irt which flows through Wast Water

ESKDALE GREEN, Cumbria
The easiest way to enjoy the scenery of this beautiful lakeland dale is to take the miniature railway, either at Irton Road, nestling in the shelter of Miterdale Forest, or at Eskdale Green station in the nearby village. The line runs from Ravenglass on the coast high up the valley to Dalegarth station at the foot of Hard Knott Pass, one of the highest and steepest motor roads in the Lake District. It was laid in 1875 to transport slate and minerals from the hills to the coast, but the steam locomotives, named after Lake District rivers, are not antique; they have been specially made by the railway company to carry passengers. The local name for the railway, 'Laal (little) Ratty', still sometimes used, comes from the name of the original contractor, Ratcliffe. From the top of the road leading from Eskdale Green into Ulpha can be seen one of the finest Lake District views, a panorama of the high fells, encompassing Harter Fell, Crinkle Crags, Bow Fell, Esk Pike, Scafell, Great Gable, Kirk Fell and Pillar.

Continue on the unclassified road and in ½ mile branch right, SP 'Ulpha'. Follow a narrow moorland road across Birker Fell then later descend and, at the T-junction, turn right into Ulpha.

Above: during medieval times the present entrance hall of Muncaster Castle was used as the great hall. It contains some intricate panelling and several family portraits of the Penningtons

ULPHA, Cumbria
Ulpha lies at the foot of the steep fell road out of Eskdale, looking across the River Duddon to the slopes of the Dunnerdale Fells. The poet Wordsworth wrote about the Chapel of St John, calling it the Kirk of Ulpha, in one of his sonnets. The chapel contains wall paintings dating from the 17th and 18th centuries.

In ¼ mile bear left across the river bridge, SP 'Broughton', and follow a winding road through Dunnerdale.

DUNNERDALE, Cumbria
Dunnerdale is the name given to the lower reaches of the lovely Duddon valley whose beautiful scenery inspired no less than 34 of Wordsworth's best-known sonnets. The poet had come to know the valley as a boy when staying with relations at Broughton. The River Duddon, which rises in the bleak moorland near Wrynose Pass, was until 1974 the old county boundary between Cumberland and Lancashire. It flows out to the sea beneath Duddon Bridge, into the deep estuary of Duddon Sands which washes the western shore of the Barrow-in-Furness peninsula.

After 3¼ miles turn right on to the A595, SP 'Workington,' cross Duddon Bridge, then continue to Whicham.

WHICHAM, Cumbria
A footpath from the village winds up the steep hillside to the summits of Black Crags and Black Combe with superb views on all sides. Black Combe, in the days before the postal service had established a reliable nationwide system of communications, was one of a chain of beacon hills stretching across the country, on which signal fires were lit to warn the people of danger or inform them of important events.

At the T-junction turn right and follow the foot of the fells to Bootle. Remain on the A595 and pass the edge of Waberthwaite, then in 1 mile descend into the River Esk valley. Cross the Esk and later pass the entrance to Muncaster Castle.

MUNCASTER CASTLE, Cumbria
The castle (OACT) stands on a superb site near Ravenglass, looking out westwards to the sea and eastwards to the high hills of Cumbria. The old medieval castle and pele tower still form part of the building which was enlarged and remodelled by Anthony Salvin in the 19th century. The Penningtons have lived here since the 13th century and there is a curious tradition associated with the family that dates back to 1461, when they gave shelter to King Henry VI after his defeat at the Battle of Towton. In gratitude, he gave them a bowl of greenish glass, enamelled and gilded, which has been known ever since as the 'Luck of Muncaster' because it is believed that while the bowl remains unbroken the Pennington succession at Muncaster will be assured. Among the other treasures of the castle is a fascinating collection of 17th-century miniature furniture. Muncaster is also famous for its bird gardens; small, brightly-coloured exotic species flit about the old courtyard and stately flamingoes, ibises and storks adorn the lakes.

½ mile beyond the castle keep forward on to an unclassified road for Ravenglass.

RAVENGLASS, Cumbria
Three rivers, the Irt, the Mite and the Esk, flow into the sea at Ravenglass, forming a sheltered, triple-pronged estuary, at the head of which lies the small resort. The town was granted a market charter in 1209, and flourished through the Middle Ages. In 1825 the beacon on the hill above the port was built as a lighthouse for the coastal traffic Ravenglass relied on, until alternative inland routes and the railway took this trade away. Today the sandy beaches, seafront and good bathing attract another trade — tourism. The village, as it now is, is the starting point of the Ravenglass and Eskdale Railway. On the north shore of the estuary, at Drigg Point, the Ravenglass Gullery and Nature Reserve (permit only) has the largest colony of black-headed gulls in Europe. Straight through the entrance of the harbour the Isle of Man can be seen 40 miles out to sea.

To the south of the village is Glannaventa.

GLANNAVENTA, Cumbria
Ruined walls, in places 13ft high, mark the site of a Roman fort, sometimes known as Walls Castle. The course of the old Roman road can still be traced along Eskdale to the site of another fort that once commanded the strategic heights of Hard Knott Pass, and thence by way of Wrynose Pass down to Ambleside.

Return to the A595 and turn left. At Holmrook turn left on to the B5344 for the return to Seascale.

145

COCKERMOUTH, Cumbria

This attractive small town, situated at the point where the Rivers Cocker and Derwent meet, is rich in history and has the distinction of being one of 51 towns in Britain recommended by the British Council for preservation. The ruined Norman castle (OACT), which overlooks the River Derwent, was built of stone taken from a Roman fort at Papcastle. During the 16th century Cockermouth was a busy market town, and became the country's commercial centre in the 17th century. Today it is a rural town with a broad main street and a number of Georgian houses and squares and is a popular base for touring the Lake District. The most famous people in Cockermouth's history are, of course, the Wordsworths, and Wordsworth House (OACT) is internationally known as one of the 2 principal residences in the Lake District of Dorothy and her famous poet brother, William. The other is Dove Cottage at Grasmere. Their home in Cockermouth is a handsome house (NT) on Main Street which was built in 1745 and became the home of Wordsworth's father in 1766 when he was made steward to Sir James Lowther. William was born here in 1770 and his sister in 1771. Much of the house remains unchanged since Wordsworth's day, and he made reference to the garden in *The Prelude*. A stained-glass memorial window to him can be seen in the 19th-century Church of All Saints situated south of the market place.

From Cockermouth follow SP 'Workington', then in 1¼ miles turn right on to the A66 and follow the valley of the River Derwent to Workington.

NORTHERN LAKES AND THE SOLWAY FIRTH

This is Wordsworth's country, where the romance of majestic mountain scenery, flawless lakes and lush green valleys give way gently to flat pastoral farmland sprinkled with handsome Georgian farmhouses and tiny hamlets: a delicately-proportioned tapestry fringed with glittering stretches of golden sands and unspoilt resorts.

Above: the Norman doorway of the church at St Bees

WHITEHAVEN, Cumbria

Sir John Lowther was responsible for bringing industry to Whitehaven in 1690, transforming it from a cosy hamlet into the bustling seaport and coal-mining town it is today. During the 18th century, his son, Sir James Lowther, built Whitehaven Castle (now a hospital), and St James's Church was also built at this time. In 1701 George Washington's grandmother was buried in St Nicholas's Church, where she is commemorated by an inscribed tablet. The Washingtons were a Lancastrian family who later emigrated to America. The colourful American sailor John Paul Jones fired on Whitehaven in 1788.

Leave the one-way system on the B5345 for St Bees.

ST BEES, Cumbria

St Bees is a small coastal resort with fine cliffs and bathing sands. The 12th-century Benedictine priory church of SS Mary and Bega is reputed to be one of the most outstanding in Cumbria. It is thought that a princess, St Bega, came from Ireland in about AD650 to found a nunnery that preceded the priory. St Bees' church has an impressive Norman doorway, and a fine carved stone in the churchyard wall depicts St Michael fighting a dragon. A local man, who became Archbishop of Canterbury in 1576, founded St Bees Grammer School, which is now a public school.

Go over the level-crossing and at the end of the town keep left, SP 'Egremont'. After 2¾ miles go forward on to an unclassified road and continue to Egremont.

WORKINGTON, Cumbria

A onetime Roman fort and town called *Gabrosentum*, Workington has an interesting history. It was from this port, where the River Derwent enters the Solway Firth, that the Lindisfarne monks fled from the Danes in the 9th century. In 1568 Mary, Queen of Scots, was received at the fine old mansion of Workington Hall (not open). An important industrial town in the area, Workington's main industries are iron and steel. An interesting museum known as the Helena Thompson Museum was bequethed to the town by the late Miss Thompson MBE, a native of Workington. Opened in 1948, it contains a fascinating collection of costumes, glass, ceramics and local history exhibits.

Leave on the A596, SP 'Barrow'. In 2¾ miles, at the T-junction, turn right on to the A595. Pass the edge of Distington, then in 3½ miles branch right on to the A5094 for Whitehaven town centre.

Left: Whitehaven's harbour and lighthouse date from the 18th century

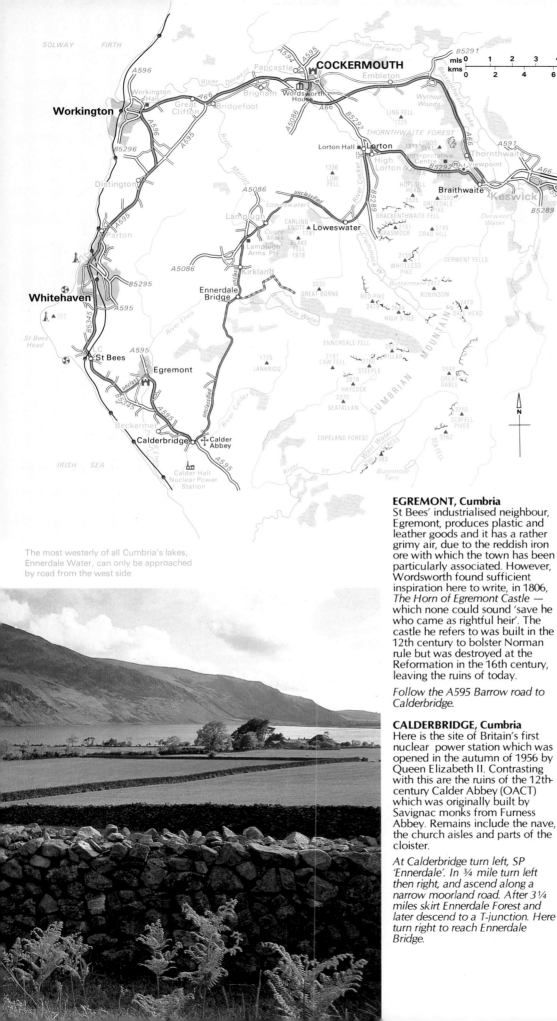

The most westerly of all Cumbria's lakes, Ennerdale Water, can only be approached by road from the west side

EGREMONT, Cumbria

St Bees' industrialised neighbour, Egremont, produces plastic and leather goods and it has a rather grimy air, due to the reddish iron ore with which the town has been particularly associated. However, Wordsworth found sufficient inspiration here to write, in 1806, *The Horn of Egremont Castle* — which none could sound 'save he who came as rightful heir'. The castle he refers to was built in the 12th century to bolster Norman rule but was destroyed at the Reformation in the 16th century, leaving the ruins of today.

Follow the A595 Barrow road to Calderbridge.

CALDERBRIDGE, Cumbria

Here is the site of Britain's first nuclear power station which was opened in the autumn of 1956 by Queen Elizabeth II. Contrasting with this are the ruins of the 12th-century Calder Abbey (OACT) which was originally built by Savignac monks from Furness Abbey. Remains include the nave, the church aisles and parts of the cloister.

At Calderbridge turn left, SP 'Ennerdale'. In ¾ mile turn left then right, and ascend along a narrow moorland road. After 3¼ miles skirt Ennerdale Forest and later descend to a T-junction. Here turn right to reach Ennerdale Bridge.

ENNERDALE BRIDGE, Cumbria

This tiny hamlet on the banks of the River Ehen is situated just a mile or so west of Ennerdale Water, amid breathtaking scenery. Its churchyard was the setting for Wordsworth's poem *The Brothers*.

The main tour turns left, SP 'Cockermouth', and proceeds to Kirkland. In 1 mile turn right on to the A5086, then in ½ mile right again, SP 'Loweswater'. Pass through the hamlet of Lamplugh and turn right. Follow this narrow road for 1¾ miles, then turn right and descend to pass Loweswater, and continue to the outskirts of Loweswater village.

LOWESWATER, Cumbria

A narrow road leads to this attractively-positioned village which lies halfway across the plains towards Crummock Water. Carling Knott rises to 1,781ft behind Loweswater lake and the great peak of Grasmoor (2,791ft) lies to the east. Opposite Grasmoor, the impressive screes of Mellbreak rise on the west side of Crummock Water.

Continue on the unclassified road then in ½ mile cross the River Cocker. Later join the B5289, SP 'Cockermouth', and continue to the edge of Lorton.

LORTON, Cumbria

Enjoying a pastoral situation beside the River Cocker in the Vale of Lorton, this village includes a church displaying a fine stained-glass window. The 17th-century Lorton Hall (not open) retains the ancient pele tower in which Malcolm III of Scotland and Queen Margaret stayed in 1089. Charles II visited Lorton Hall in 1650.

By the nearside of the village turn right, SP 'Keswick'. At High Lorton turn left into the village and at the end turn right, then at the T-junction turn right again on to the B5292. Continue across the Whinlatter Pass and at the bottom of the descent keep left to enter Braithwaite.

BRAITHWAITE, Cumbria

At the north-eastern end of the Coledale valley and the start of the Whinlatter Pass, this picturesque village is conveniently situated for the tourist. It enjoys great popularity among climbers as the starting point for an attack on Grisedale Pike, one of the northern peaks in the Grasmoor mountain group.

In Braithwaite turn left, SP 'Cockermouth (A66)', then turn left again to join the A66 and continue alongside the shore of Bassenthwaite Lake. At the north end the road veers away from the lake and continues through a wide valley. In 5½ miles turn right on to the A5086 for the return to Cockermouth.

BESIDE THE SOLWAY FIRTH

A coastal tour through small towns and hamlets not widely known, tracing the footsteps of Charles Dickens and his companion Wilkie Collins. Roman forts, Norman buildings and ecclesiastical art abound, a pleasing but complementary contrast to the dramatic coastline and marshlands along the Solway Firth.

Carlisle's priory church became a cathedral in 1133

CARLISLE, Cumbria

Since early times Carlisle has been a strategically important city because of its position on the Anglo-Scottish border. The Romans occupied the town, calling it *Lugavalium*, and finding themselves repeatedly attacked by the Picts, they built Hadrian's Wall, parts of which can still be seen east of the city. Carlisle Castle (AM) was built by the Normans for the same reasons. It was founded in 1092 by William Rufus, strengthened by David I, and was for centuries the kingpin of conflicts between the Scottish and English, each often gaining the city, but never for long. Eventually, in 1745, the Scottish were finally ousted when Bonnie Prince Charlie's troops were driven from the town. Maintaining its military tradition, the castle's keep houses the former Border regiments' museum. Today Carlisle, known locally as 'Carel', is the chief administrative and agricultural centre of Cumbria and although the suburbs are industrialised, the centre has retained its ancient character. The red sandstone cathedral, where Sir Walter Scott was married in 1797, is England's 2nd smallest cathedral. Begun in the 12th century and rebuilt in the 13th century, it preserves one of the finest east windows in the country, superb carved choir stalls and a painted barrel-vault ceiling. Tullie House, the city's museum and art gallery, occupies a magnificent Jacobean mansion and contains Roman relics excavated from forts along Hadrian's Wall. The 15th-century Guildhall (OACT), a charming town house which became the meeting place for Carlisle's 8 Trade Guilds, is now a museum of Guild, Civic and local history. Exhibits include the great bell, pillory and stocks from the medieval castle.

Leave Carlisle on the A595 Workington road and ½ mile beyond the castle turn right on to the B5307. In 1 mile branch right into Burgh Road, SP 'Kirkandrews'. Pass through Kirkandrews-on-Eden and Monkhill to reach Burgh-by-Sands.

BURGH-BY-SANDS, Cumbria

Burgh-by-Sands boasts the strongly-fortified church of St Michael, built almost entirely from Roman stone. A monument to Edward I, who died in 1307 on his way to attack the Scots and lay in state here, may be found north of the village.

At the village end bear right, SP 'Port Carlisle'. NB: between here and Cardunock the road is liable to tidal flooding. Cross unfenced marshland, with views across the Solway Firth to reach Port Carlisle.

PORT CARLISLE, Cumbria

This was the brainchild of the Earl of Lonsdale, who built the harbour in 1819, and the canal to Carlisle in 1823. Unfortunately for him the harbour did not flourish and never grew beyond the row of terraced cottages and single detached house there is today. Over 140 acres of the Solway Firth lands here make up the Glasson Moss National Nature Reserve.

Continue to Bowness-on-Solway.

BOWNESS-ON-SOLWAY, Cumbria

The village of Bowness-on-Solway is situated on a low promontory overlooking the Solway Firth. At one time an iron trestle viaduct spanned the Firth here and carried a railway linking the iron manufacturing industries of west Cumbria with Annan and southern Scotland. The village is built on the site of a Roman settlement at the western end of Hadrian's Wall. The church, dedicated to St Michael, has 2 late-Norman doorways and in the porch rest 2 church bells, one of which is dated 1612. These were stolen from Scotland in the days of the Border raids by an English raiding party as reprisal for 2 bells removed from Bowness Church.

Continue forward, passing the embankment of the dismantled railway viaduct. Continue round the headland and through Cardurnock. 2 miles beyond Anthorn turn right SP 'Kirkbride', and cross the river. At the edge of Kirkbride turn right on the B5307 for the village centre.

KIRKBRIDE, Cumbria

Kirkbride is a pretty village, set amid trees on the tidal creek of the Wampol. Its ancient church, dedicated to St Bridget, is of Norman construction built with material from a Roman fort which stood in the area. There are wide areas of moss land in the parish which provide peat for many local hearths. On the marshes of Kirkbride and Whitrigg there grows a turf of remarkably fine quality which is cut and marketed to provide top-class bowling-greens.

Continue to Abbey Town.

ABBEY TOWN, Cumbria

The village of Abbey Town retains vestiges of a great ecclesiastical past. In approximately 1150, the Cistercian order founded Holme Cultram Abbey here, which soon prospered through the farming skills of its monks. However, over the years the abbey suffered considerably at the hands of Scottish raiders, and now all that remains is the 12th-century nave which forms the basis of today's parish church of St Mary. Abbot Robert Chambers built the west porch in the 16th century, and the church itself was restored many times during the 16th and 17th centuries.

At the crossroads go forward on to the B5302, SP 'Silloth' and 'Skinburness'. In 3¼ miles turn right, SP 'Skinburness', and shortly cross Skinburness Marsh. At Skinburness keep left and follow the coastal road to Silloth, joining the B5302 on entering the town.

SILLOTH, Cumbria
In the middle of the last century Silloth was transformed from a drowsy hamlet in to a busy port by the construction of the docks here, and today its pleasant lawns, putting green, children's amusements and sea-wall promenade (2 miles long), fill the town with holidaymakers during the summer months. West Beach, backed by sand dunes, is a fine expanse of sand where bathing and fishing are popular pastimes. The name 'Silloth' comes from a tithe barn built here by the monks of the great Cistercian abbey of Holme Cultram known as the 'sea lath'. From Silloth there are magnificent views of the Scottish hills across the Solway Firth.

At the crossroads turn left on to the B5300, SP 'Maryport', and shortly bear right. Continue through Greenrow and Blitterless to reach a pleasant coastal stretch with sand dunes, parking and picnic areas. Pass through Beckfoot and Mawbray to reach Allonby. Continue along the B5300 and in 4½ miles turn right on to the A596 for Maryport.

MARYPORT, Cumbria
Maryport was developed during the Industrial Revolution, and rose to prominence through coal mining, coal export and the great

Above: Scottish hills silhouetted against the Solway Firth

Right: the west door of Abbey Town's parish church, where an abbey once stood

iron-making boom. The lord of the manor, Colonel H. Senhouse, was chiefly responsible for this development in 1748-9, and he named the port after his wife, Mary. The sea is Maryport's greatest attraction; miles of beach stretch north and south of the town and there is ample opportunity for sailing, fishing and safe bathing. On high ground to the north of the town are the remains of a Roman fort. This was defended by a double ditch which encloses 4½ acres. Outside the fort boundary there have been found the remnants of a considerable civilian settlement, with shops, workshops and taverns.

At the road junction by the church turn left on to the A594, SP 'Cockermouth'. In 6 miles, at a roundabout, take the 2nd exit and descend to cross the River Derwent into Cockermouth.

COCKERMOUTH, Cumbria
Cockermouth, famous as the birthplace of William Wordsworth, is a pleasant rural town that makes an ideal centre for touring the Lake District. See tour 64.

Turn left into the main street and then keep forward. At the end bear left passing the castle (left) then turn left, SP 'Isel'. After 3¼ miles turn left again, SP 'Blindcrake, Isel'. Descend to cross the river then turn left. In ½ mile turn right, SP 'Bothel Sunderland'. Isel Hall,

Elizabethan, with a pele tower, is seen to the left at this point. In 1 mile turn left, continuing through Sunderland and in 1½ miles turn left on to the A591. At the roundabout, on the edge of Bothel, take the A595, SP 'Carlisle'. Later pass through Mealgate and in 3¾ miles turn left on to the B5304, SP 'Wigton'.

WIGTON, Cumbria
The town of Wigton, known locally as the 'Throstle Nest', is the market town of a wide area and has been for many centuries. In 1262 permission to hold the market was granted by King Henry III to Walter de Wigton. Popular for its market held on Tuesday; there are also cattle and sheep auctions. The red sandstone parish church of St Mary's was erected in 1788 on the site of an earlier church. The monument chest inside the

church is thought to be pre-Reformation, and the church Registers date back to 1604. In the centre of the town is the memorial fountain erected in 1872 by George Moore, a merchant and philanthropist, in memory of his wife. The old parish pump and tall gas lamp which are to be found in West Road were immortalised by Charles Dickens in his book The Lazy Tour of Two Idle Apprentices. Dickens visited Wigton and the surrounding area with his friend Wilkie Collins, and as the many interesting nooks and crannies to be found in the town remain unchanged, it is easy to picture Wigton as he must have seen it.

In the town centre turn right on to the A596, SP 'Carlisle', and in 5¼ miles go forward on to the A595. In 5 miles re-enter the suburbs of Carlisle and keep forward for the castle and city centre.

HADRIAN'S WALL

Along the length of the great wall the Emperor Hadrian
built to protect England from the fierce Picts is a wealth of
Roman remains; temples to the god Mithras, great forts
and little townships, all set in a magnificent countryside of
sweeping views and desolate quiet.

HEXHAM, Northumb
Hexham grew up around the
entrance to the abbey which St
Wilfred founded in 674, and the
buildings nearest the abbey are
therefore some of Hexham's
oldest. Opposite the abbey church
is the Moot Hall, originally the
gatehouse to a 12th-century castle.
In its time this has served as a
Bishop's Palace, and up until 1838
was the town court: now it is the
borough library. The archway
beneath the Moot Hall leads to
the Manor Office. This former
medieval prison dealt with all the
business of the Manor of Hexham
from Elizabeth I's reign up until
about the 1870's. Close by,
overlooking the Tyne valley, is an
attractive whitewashed building
which was the old grammer
school. The plight of its predecessor was an unhappy one, for in
1296 200 scholars were burnt
alive by Scottish raiders, who also
destroyed the abbey. St. Wilfred's
Church was built from Roman
stones taken from *Corstopitum*,
near Corbridge, and of this
original church the foundations of
the apse, piers of the nave and the
crypt remain. An Augustinian
priory took over the church from
the Saxon bishops in 1116, and
they built the beautiful choir and
transept, including the survival of
the almost unique canon's Night
Stair to the dormitory. The nave,
destroyed by the Scottish raid,
was not rebuilt until 1908.
Treasurers of the past within the
church include the Frith Stool,
thought to be the throne upon
which Northumbrian kings were
crowned, later also used as a
sanctuary stool. In the south
transept is a remarkable Roman
memorial to Flavinius, a standard-
bearer, depicted mounted upon a
horse astride a cowering Briton
with a drawn dagger.

*Leave Hexham on the A6079, SP
'Carlisle', and cross the Tyne. At the
roundabout take the A69 then in
¾ mile turn right on to the A6079,
SP 'Rothbury', and pass the edge of
Acomb to Wall. In 1 mile, at the
crossroads, turn left on to the
B6318, then recross the Tyne for
Chollerford.*

CHOLLERFORD, Northumb
Chollerford's fine bridge dating
from 1771 lies with the rest of the
village near the site of *Cilurnum*,
an important Roman station on
the banks of the North Tyne. It

stands in Chesters Park (not open),
a stately mansion which was once
the home of John Clayton,
archaeologist and antiquary, who
pioneered the excavation of
Cilurnum. Today most of the plan
of the camp has been unearthed,
and at the entrance to the site is a
fascinating museum. Artefacts
which have been recovered from
this site are displayed within, as
well as relics found along
Hadrian's Wall, ranging from coins
to mill-stones and including
jewellery and everyday objects of
Roman life.

*At the roundabout take the 1st exit,
SP 'Carlisle', and pass Chesters Park
(left). Follow the line of Hadrian's
Wall to Carrawbrough.*

HADRIAN'S WALL, Northumb
Stretching across the width of
Britain between Solway and Tyne,
Hadrian's Wall was begun in
AD122 by Emperor Hadrian to
keep the barbarians from the north
at bay. It took 7 years to build and
required some 15,000 men to
defend it. On the north side of the
wall a steep ditch was constructed
and to the south a flat-bottomed
ditch and a road. The southern
defence was found necessary to
prevent the conquered tribes
pilfering from the well-fed Roman
soldiers. Further fortification was
provided by small forts, called
milecastles, at 1 mile intervals, and
watch-turrets at every ⅓ mile. In
addition, 17 auxiliary forts were
placed on or near the wall. The
skill of the Roman engineers in
taking advantage of the lie of the
land resulted in the wall crossing
some splendid countryside, with
magnificent views from the many
walks which can be taken along its
length.

CARRAWBROUGH, Northumb
Although this fort was a later
addition to the fortifications of
Hadrian's Wall, there is little left to
see apart from the grassy
ramparts. However, what has been
uncovered is a Mithraeum temple.
For some reason the deity of
Mithras was especially popular
among soldiers, but although it
was a wide-spread religion, the
groups of its followers were small,
and so the temple buildings were
small. Carrawbrough is no
exception, the whole building
measuring no more than 35ft by
15ft. The central passage is
guarded by statues of lesser gods,

leading up to the 3 main carved
alters. Angry Christians destroyed
the temple, not so much disturbed
by the morality of the religion as
by its close parallels with Christian
rites, such as its similar baptism
and communion.

*Continue on the B6318 and in 5
miles reach the car park for
Housesteads.*

HOUSESTEADS, Northumb
This was the ancient Roman fort
of *Vercovicium*, set astride a ridge
in wild frontier country with
magnificent views to the north and
south. What has been excavated
within the fort walls show that
here were granaries, a
commandant's house, military
headquarters, a hospital, latrines,
baths and barracks — a miniature
town in fact. Outside the walls a
civilian settlement grew up, and
here are the remains of long
narrow shops and inns, which had
sliding shutters to the street fronts.
In one of these the bodies of a
man and a woman of the 4th
century were found. A dagger was

embedded in the man's ribs, which
prompted the excavators to name
the house Murder House. The site
museum contains many finds from
the excavation.

*Continue on the B6138 and after 3
miles pass a Northumberland
National Park Information Centre,
next to the Twice Brewed Inn. In
another 2½ miles, at a crossroads,
turn left, SP 'Haltwhistle'. A mile
farther descend into the South
Tyne valley then turn right into
Haltwhistle.*

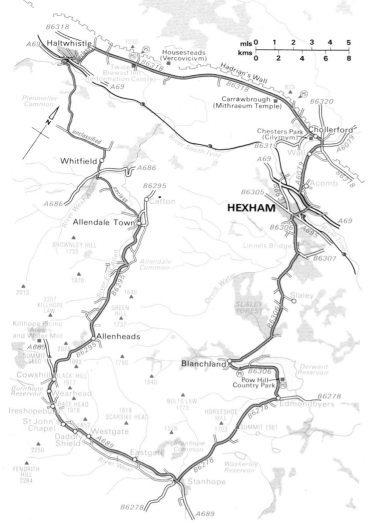

HALTWHISTLE, Northumb

This small industrial town lies between the junction of Haltwhistle Burn and the South Tyne, and is an excellent touring centre for Hadrian's Wall, which lies a little to the north. The towerless Holy Cross Church, hidden by trees and surrounded by houses, is considered a superb example of early English architecture.

Continue through the town and turn left, SP 'Carlisle', then turn right on to the A69. In ½ mile turn left on to the Plenmeller/ Whitfield road. Cross the River Tyne and turn left. After 4 miles turn left and 2¼ miles farther turn right, then descend into West Allen Dale for Whitfield.

WHITFIELD, Northumb

In all Allendale there is no prettier village than Whitfield, set amid trees by the banks of the West Allen River. Whitfield has 2 churches, known as the 'Old' and the 'New'. The 'Old' is St John's, a Georgian building with Victorian alterations, which lies hidden off the main road; the 'New' is all Victorian, rather out of character in the dales, looking as though it has been transplanted from the gentler landscape of southern England.

Turn right on to the A686, SP 'Alston', then in ¼ mile turn left, SP 'Allendale'. Cross the West Allen River and in 3½ miles go forward to join the B6295. In ½ mile cross the East Allen River and ascend to Allendale Town.

ALLENDALE TOWN, Northumb

A sundial, set in a wall near the 14th-century church high up on the wooded banks of the River East Allen, records longditude and latitude, for Allendale claims to be the centre of Britain. The solid little town has a stone-built market place, and an attractive main street enhanced by trees and greens. The many boarding houses and hotels attract the same visitors every year, for this pleasant village is set in fine hill and dale country, and is superbly situated as a touring centre. New Year's Eve is a big occasion here. It is celebrated with a huge bonfire at midnight, and by a procession of costumed men parading the streets carrying tubs of blazing tar on their heads — a curious custom thought to have originated from a form of fire worship introduced by the Norsemen.

Turn right on to the the Allenheads/ Cowshill road and follow East Allen Dale over the lofty and bleak Allendale Common to reach Allenheads.

Remains of the bath house at the Roman fort of *Cilurnum*. It was a complex of rooms consisting of changing rooms and a series of hot and cold baths

ALLENHEADS, Northumb

At one time a seventh of all lead mined in the Kingdom once came from near Allenheads, although now the workings are all long grown over, in some areas producing a strange irregular landscape. The hamlet of Allenheads lies snugly in a pine-covered enclave surrounded by bare moorland criss-crossed by stone walls at the head of wide East Allendale.

Continue on the B6295 and in 1½ miles, at the summit (1,860ft), enter the county of Durham. Descend and in 1¾ miles join the A689 Durham/Stanhope road. Continue through Cowshill, Wearhead and St Johns Chapel then Daddry Shield, Westgate and Eastgate. At the Grey Bull PH at the edge of Stanhope turn left on to the B6278, SP 'Edmondbyers'. In ½ mile a steep climb leads to Stanhope Common and 2 miles farther bear right. Later turn left on to the B6306, SP 'Blanchland', and after 1 mile a side road (right) leads to Pow Hill Country Park.

POW HILL COUNTRY PARK, Durham

This delightful park is set in beautiful countryside in a sheltered valley above Derwent Reservoir. Waders and waterfowl can be seen here, which are best observed from a specially constructed hide beside the reservoir. Car parks, a picnic area and other amenities have been provided for the convenience of visitors and the protection of the wildlife.

Continue on the B6306 and in 3½ miles cross the River Derwent to re-enter Northumberland and continue to Blanchland.

BLANCHLAND, Northumb

Blanchland has a neat, orderly appearance, its grey-stone cottages arranged around an L-shaped, gravelled 'square'. The village occupies the site of a 12th-century abbey; the square was previously the abbey courtyard and the Lord Crewe Arms was part of the abbey's guesthouse; the monastery gateway is still one of the entrances to the village. Hidden deep in wild moorland, a story tells of how in 1327 Scottish raiders bent on sacking the abbey got lost in a mist, and decided to return home. The monks, hearing of this, were so joyous they rang the abbey bells in celebration. Unfortunately the Scots heard the bells too and, guided by their sound, returned.

Turn right, SP 'Hexham', then ascend. There are more views of the Derwent Reservoir to the right. After 2 miles keep left and continue past the edge of Shaley and cross the Devil's Water at the narrow Linnels Bridge (care needed) before the return to Hexham.

MORPETH, Northumb

Quiet prosperity came to Morpeth in the early 18th century as it was the last market in Northumberland on the cattle route down to the south. Although the railway age subsequently made such markets largely redundant, Morpeth has remained a busy country town. In the old market place there stands a 17th-century tower whose curfew bell is rung at 8 o'clock every evening. The town hall, an elegant structure dating from 1718, was designed by the architect Vanbrugh. The imposing bridge was built at a later date, 1831, across the River Wansbeck which intersects the town. It leads to the parish church, set well away from the town centre on high ground. The church has a refreshingly plain 14th-century interior and in the churchyard is a little watch tower, built in 1831 to help restrict the practice of body-snatching. Behind the church lie impressive earthworks of the castle which was built after the Conquest but little masonry is left of the noble fortress which looked over the river and town. Around Morpeth the banks of the river are pleasantly wooded, and in the town itself a park runs along part of it. Every year Northumberland miners mix pleasure and politics at the gala held in the park.

Leave on the A192, SP 'Alnwick'. In 1½ miles, at the roundabout, join the A1, then in ¼ mile branch left on to the A697, SP 'Coldstream'. Pass through Longhorsley and in 2¾ miles turn left on to the B6344, SP 'Rothbury', to enter the Coquet valley. In 1½ miles a short detour to the left leads to Brinkburn Priory.

BRINKBURN PRIORY, Northumb

Within a loop of the River Coquet in charmingly wooded parkland stands a possible rival in grandeur to the abbeys of Fountains and Tintern. Although Brinkburn (AM) is a 12th-century church, it has all the hallmarks of a great cathedral. It was a roofless ruin by 1858, but the architect Thomas Dobson restored it superbly in that year.

Continue along the B6344 and in 3½ miles pass the fine hillside grounds of the Cragside Estate on the right.

CRAGSIDE ESTATE, Northumb

The 1st Lord Armstrong commissioned architect Norman Shaw in 1863 to design this delightfully romantic house. However, the real attraction to Cragside (NT) is the gardens. The house is built high above the River Coquet on a plateau where rock gardens, artificial lakes and masses of rhododendrons and azaleas create an enchanting landscape. The house itself claims its place in history as being one of the first houses in the world to be powered by electricity.

NORTHUMBERLAND'S QUIET LOWLANDS

'Northumberland may claim to the least spoiled, least known, county of England' and this proves true as the tour travels through the remote countryside between the Cheviots and Hadrian's Wall, by way of peaceful valleys and stone-built villages.

Shortly join the B6341 to enter Rothbury.

ROTHBURY, Northumb

Hill and river country surrounds the little town of Rothbury, whose name means a clearing in the forest. It is typical of the Border towns; solid, stone-built houses lining, in this case, a steep wide street where the verges are planted with trees. This was a lawless town, and at the time of the Reformation thieving by the inhabitants of Rothbury was such an art that 'they could twist a cow's horn or mark a horse so that its owner would not know it'.

Keep forward through the town on the B6341, SP 'Otterburn', to Thropton.

THROPTON, Northumb

Built on either side of the River Coquet, Thropton lies in the stunning countryside of Simonside. This pretty but straggling village is dominated by Simonside itself, the 1409ft-high peak giving its name to the whole range of sandstone hills, which, it is said, can be seen from every corner of Northumberland. Here the heather-clad hills contrast strongly with the gentle arable land of the lower reaches of Coquetdale, especially in August when the hills are purple with the flowering heather and the lower fields are a carpet of golden corn.

Continue on the B6341 for 2¼ miles then turn right, SP 'Harbottle'. In 3 miles descend and cross the River Coquet, then turn left for Holystone.

7 million trees were planted on the Cragside Estate in the 19th century, which helped transform it from a barren hillside into a magnificent garden

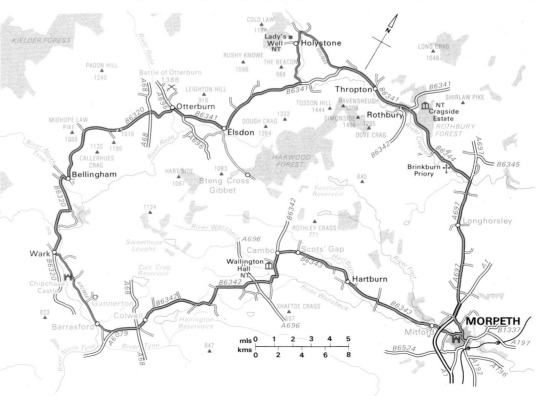

HOLYSTONE, Northumb

In the upper reaches of Coquetdale is the pleasing village of Holystone. Set within a circular enclosure surrounded by trees is the Lady's Well (NT), closely connected with St Ninian and St Paulinus. Paulinus is said to have come here to baptise the heathen Northumbrians and legend has it that on one Easter Day he baptised 3,000 souls. His statue stands in the centre of the well. Today the village has the holy water on tap, for the well supplies Holystone with its drinking water. Little remains of the priory that was built here for Augustinian canonesses, but the village, with its inn, church, and good stone houses, is one of the most attractive in Coquetdale.

Turn left at the edge of Holystone and continue along the valley, and in 2½ miles turn right to rejoin the B6341. Proceed through open and wilder countryside to reach Elsdon.

ELSDON, Northumb

Set among the rolling hills of Redesdale, Elsdon has a large triangular green with a few 18th-century houses gathered about it. By the church is a rare 14th-century fortified rectory, a reminder of more violent days, as is the Norman castle, c1080, nearby. When the chuch was restored 100 skeletons were found, and they are thought to be those of men who died at the Battle of Otterburn in 1388. Up above the village, on Steng Cross, are the remains of a gibbet. Here the body of one William Winter was hung after his execution in Newcastle for the murder of an old woman of Elsdon in 1791. In the hills hereabouts are many remnants and remains of prehistoric peoples — cairns, earthworks and hut circles.

Bear right through the village and in 2½ miles turn right on to the A696 for Otterburn.

OTTERBURN, Northumb

At the east end of Otterburn is Otterburn Tower — a largely Victorian building incorporating the remains of an old pele tower which withstood an assault by the Scottish army on its way to the Battle of Otterburn. This was fought 1½ miles north-west of the village in 1388 and was one of the many encounters between Scottish and English armies over this disputed territory. Today Otterburn is known for the textile mill by the bridge, where the famous Otterburn tweeds are made.

Turn left on to the B6320, SP 'Bellingham', and shortly cross River Rede. In 1½ miles cross the main road and ascend on to the moors, reaching 1,019ft before the long descent into the North Tyne valley and Bellingham.

BELLINGHAM, Northumb

Bellingham is a small market town, important in its own way as the capital of the North Tyne countryside and Redesdale. Its position also makes it an excellent base from which to explore this beautiful countryside. The church here has an unusual early stone roof. The story goes that the Scots, raiding from over the border, burnt the place so often it was decided a permanent, fireproof roof would be more economical in the long run. The inhabitants of this border country appear to have spent most of their time raiding the herds of their enemies over the border. Today, the farmers, many of them descendants of these lawless men, meet at Bellingham in autumn in a far more friendly fashion for the lamb sales, and again in September for the agricultural show.

Continue on the B6320, SP 'Hexham', and in ¼ mile turn left to cross the North Tyne River. In 5¼ miles enter Wark.

The kitchen at Wallington Hall is kept as if in daily use as it would have been at the turn of the century

WARK, Northumb

Now a few pleasant streets and a quadrangle of houses around a green, Wark was in medieval times the capital of North Tynedale; at the time this was a part of Scotland. It stands on a lovely stretch of the North Tyne River, near both Wark Forest and the Border Forest Park.

Turn left, SP 'Barrasford', recross the North Tyne and turn right. In 1½ miles pass (right) the 14th-century Chipchase Castle. Pass through Barrasford and in ½ mile turn left, SP 'Colwell'. In ¾ mile turn left again on to the A6079, SP 'Rothbury'. In 1½ miles bear left over the crossroads on to the B6342. Shortly pass the edge of Colwell. In 7½ miles turn right then immediately left across the A696. In 2 miles cross the River Wansbeck and pass through the grounds of Wallington Hall.

Tweed, being woven here at Otterburn Mill, is traditionally made with 2 or more colours of the same quality yarn

WALLINGTON HALL, Northumb

The exterior of Wallington Hall (NT) has hardly altered since Sir William Blackett built it in 1688. The house which he demolished to make way for his building belonged to Sir John Fenwick, who was executed for treason by William III. However, Fenwick's famous house, which the king kept, brought him revenge when it stumbled on a mole hill and threw the sovereign, who consequently died. The modest façade of the Hall hides a sumptuous interior remodelled in the mid-18th century, when, among other things, the wonderful plaster decoration was added by Italian craftsmen. A century later, the architect John Dobson was employed to roof over the central courtyard to create the magnificent central hall. The gardens can be divided into 3 areas: the peaceful lawns and flowerbeds around the house, woodland and lakes, and an L-shaped walled garden and conservatory.

In 1 mile at Cambo turn right on to the B6343, SP 'Morpeth', and continue past Scots' Cap to Hartburn.

HARTBURN, Northumb

Hartburn lies in a superb position with steep, dramatic waterfalls on either side that drop down to the Hart Burn. In the village is a curious building known as Dr Sharpe's Tower. It is a castellated tower that was built to house the village schoolmaster on an upper floor reached by an exterior staircase, with a schoolroom below and stables for the village hearse. Next to it is the schoolhouse of 1844. There is also an elegant Georgian vicarage which has a 13th-century pele tower incorporated in to it. The church has a squat tower dating from the late 12th-century, and carved on a doorpost are 2 daggers and a Maltese cross.

Continue along the B6343 following the Wansbeck valley for the return via Mitford to Morpeth.

Scotland

THE MACHARS OF WIGTOWNSHIRE

Along the coast from Newton Stewart breathtaking views of the Isle of Man and over the Solway Firth to the distant mountains of the Lake District introduce the sandy rock-strewn shores of the lovely Bay of Luce and, inland, across the lonely moors and the high hills of Galloway.

NEWTON STEWART, Dumf & Gall

The mountainous wooded landscape of the distant Galloway Hills provides the magnificent setting of this busy little market town. Newton Stewart grew up around an ancient ford and was founded by William Stewart, son of the Earl of Galloway, in 1677. He gave the town its name and obtained its charter as a burgh of barony from Charles II. In the next century it was bought by Sir William Douglas, who established the weaving industry and attempted unsuccessfully to change the name to Newton Douglas. Many of the old houses lining the attractive main street stand so close to the river that they look almost Venetian. The 5-arched granite bridge over the Cree, that connects Newton

Stewart to the neighbouring village of Minnigaff, was built in 1813 by the famous engineer John Rennie.

From the bypass roundabout at the south end of the town follow SP 'Wigtown A714'.

WIGTOWN, Dumf & Gall

Where Wigtown's broad main street opens out into a spacious green, cattle were once herded for safety at night. The more ornate of the town's 2 mercat crosses was erected in 1816 to commemorate the Battle of Waterloo; the other, incorporating a sundial, is older and dates from 1738. In the churchyard and on the crest of Windy Hill, the highest point in the town, stand memorials to the 5 Wigtown Martyrs; 3 men and 2 women, executed in 1685 for adhering to their Presbyterian faith. The women, Margaret

McLauchlan, aged 63, and the 18-year-old Margaret Wilson suffered a terrible fate: they were tied to stakes in the estuary and slowly drowned by the incoming tide.

Turn right through the Square and pass the memorial, then turn left, SP 'Whithorn', for Bladnoch.

Roland, Lord of Galloway, founded Glenluce Abbey in 1190 as a Cistercian house and daughter house of Dundrennan Abbey

Port William overlooking Luce Bay

BLADNOCH, Dumf & Gall

Bladnoch Water runs by the little village and out to the sea above Baldoon Sands. Overlooking the estuary stands ruined Baldoon Castle, home in 1669 of David Dunbar on whom Sir Walter Scott modelled the bridegroom in his tragic novel *The Bride of Lammermoor*. The events on which he based his story were true: Lady Dalrymple, wife of Lord Stair of Glenluce, obliged her daughter Janet to marry Dunbar although she loved the penniless Lord Rutherford. The marriage took place at Glenluce, but Dunbar had scarcely arrived home with his young wife when she fell ill and died within the month.

Turn left and cross the River Bladnoch and in 1¼ miles go forward on to the A746. A mile beyond Kirkinner branch left on to the B7004, SP 'Garlieston'. In 4 miles reach the edge of Garlieston and turn right, SP 'Whithorn', (for the village centre turn left).

GARLIESTON, Dumf & Gall

Founded in the 18th century by Lord Garlies, 7th Earl of Galloway, the village, with its pretty cottages, peaceful bowling green and old mill, lies at the head of a delightful bay on the east coast of the Machars peninsula. The bay is sheltered by the low, rocky promontory of Eggerness Point and at low tide all the upper part of the beach is left high and dry, revealing a multitude of delightful rock pools to explore.

In ½ mile turn left and in 4 miles further turn left on to the A746 for Whithorn.

WHITHORN, Dumf & Gall

In the bleak countrysde of the Machars lies one of the earliest centres of Christianity in Britain. St Ninian landed on this remote western shore in AD397 and built his simple oratory at Whithorn —

the name comes from hwit aern, meaning 'white house'. The priory, today in ruins, was founded in the 12th century by Fergus, Lord of Galloway, and soon became a place of pilgrimage, being visited by many of the Scottish sovereigns. The last royal visitor, before the priory was finally dissolved, was Mary, Queen of Scots in 1563. The entrance to the priory lies through a graceful 17th-century gateway, emblazoned with the royal coat of arms, known as the Pend. The town museum contains a notable collection of early Christian relics, including the Latinus Stone dating from the 5th century.

From the southern end of the main street a detour to Isle of Whithorn can be made by turning left on to the A750.

ISLE OF WHITHORN, Dumf & Gall
This quiet, lonely little village, perched almost on the tip of the peninsula, lays claim to be the most southerly village in Scotland. The isle has long been joined to the mainland by a causeway. On a rocky headland looking out to sea stands a ruined 12th-century chapel dedicated to St Ninian. This was originally thought to be the site of his oratory, but excavation has shown that Whithorn Priory is the more likely place. In St Ninian's Cave further round the coast numbers of crosses and other relics dating from the Celtic period have been found, showing that the cave was used as a hermitage for Whithorn Priory.

From here the detour returns along the A750 for 1½ miles then goes forward on to the A747 Port William road across windswept countryside. The main tour from Whithorn continues on the A746 Port William road and in 1½ miles turns right on to the A747 for Monreith.

MONREITH, Dumf & Gall
In earlier times the splendid sands of Monreith Bay saw the secret landing of many a cargo of contraband from Ireland or the Isle of Man run in by local smugglers. The strangest landing however occurred in 1760, when villagers were astonished to find on the shore the body of a French naval officer in full dress uniform, wrapped in a velvet carpet. He was identified as Captain Thurot, commander of a French squadron that had captured Carrickfergus Castle, only to be defeated by the British in the Bay of Luce.

Follow the coast round Barsallock Point to Port William.

PORT WILLIAM, Dumf & Gall
A seaside village whose pretty cottages look out across Luce Bay, Port William was founded beside an attractive sandy beach in 1770 by Sir William Maxwell whose family home, Monreith House, stands a little way inland beside the White Loch of Myrton.

At the roundabout take the 1st exit, SP 'Glenluce'. Continue along the coast for 10 miles, with views across Luce Bay, then turn inland across a stretch of bleak Machars countryside. Later turn left on to the A75, SP 'Stranraer', into Glenluce.

GLENLUCE, Dumf & Gall
Glenluce, one of the prettiest villages in the region, lies on the east bank of the Water of Luce, surrounded by lovely wooded countryside. The Castle of Park, built in 1590 by Thomas Hay, looks down over the village, where, in 1654, a famous poltergeist took up residence in a weaver's cottage and defied all efforts at exorcism for 4 years, at the end of which time the phenomenon mysteriously ceased.

At the end of the village, on a sharp left-hand bend beneath the railway viaduct, take the 2nd unclassified road to the right, SP 'Glenluce Abbey'. In 1¼ miles pass Glenluce Abbey.

GLENLUCE ABBEY, Dumf & Gall
Founded in 1190, the ruined abbey (AM) occupies a superb site in the beautiful Vale of Luce. Its vaulted 15th-century chapter house remains almost intact and, for its period, a remarkably efficient medieval drainage system has been excavated. This consists of skilfully jointed stone channels and interlocking earthenware pipes that could still be functional today. The abbey is associated with the 13th-century wizard Michael Scott, who is said to have stopped an outbreak of plague in the area by luring it to the abbey and walling it up, thus starving it to death. A little to the east of this site stand the gaunt remains of Carscreugh Castle, home of Janet Dalrymple, whose tragic death in 1669 inspired Sir Walter Scott to make her the heroine, Lucy Ashton, of *The Bride of Lammermoor*.

Continue alongside the Water of Luce for 4 miles to New Luce.

NEW LUCE, Dumf & Gall
The village, known as the 'capital' of the moors district of Galloway, lies high up in the Vale of Luce at the point where the Cross Water and the Main Water of Luce join forces to form the Water of Luce. Behind the village rises a bleak expanse of moorland.

Keep forward SP 'Barrhill' on to a narrow, hilly road crossing bleak moorland. Later rejoin, and then turn right to cross the Cross Water of Luce, following the Ayr-Stranraer railway line on the opposite side of the valley. Several miles after leaving the railway enter the Arecleoch Forest (Forestry Commission) before descending into the Duisk valley and Barrhill.

BARRHILL, Strathclyde
In the days of the stagecoach this remote village on the River Duisk was a welcome staging post on the road from Girvan to Newton Stewart. Two roads meet at Barrhill and take a separate path across the lonely moors, merging again just outside Newton Stewart. The more northerly one crosses the fringe of Galloway Forest Park; the other ascends to 3 high mountain lakes, Lochs Dornal, Ochiltree and Maberry.

Turn right on to the A714 and at the end of the village right again on to the B7027, SP 'Newton Stewart via Knowe'. This road passes through open moorland with many lochs and rivers and fine views of the high Galloway Hills to the east. At Challoch turn right on to the A714 for the return to Newton Stewart.

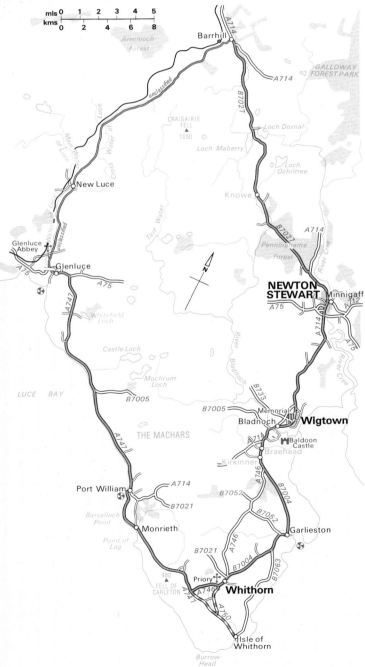

QUEEN OF THE SOUTH

From Dumfries, where Robert Burns, Scotland's national poet, made his final home, travel on to visit the romantic ruins of Sweetheart Abbey, the riches of Maxwelton House, a glorious garden on the shores of the Solway Firth and the sylvan expanses of the Forest of Ae.

DUMFRIES, Dumf & Gall

Queen of the South is the title of this ancient burgh with its old red sandstone buildings and well-tended parks beside the broad waters of the River Nith. The town received its first charter in 1393 from Robert III, and it was here that Robert the Bruce assassinated the Red Comyn, the representative of the English Crown, in 1306, so precipitating the Wars of Independence. Bruce declared himself King of Scotland shortly afterwards, and soon returned to Dumfries to capture the castle in his first victory over Edward I. The remains of the castle (AM) lie in wooded parkland at Castledykes. Dumfries' centre point and landmark is the Mid Steeple. This was built in 1707 to act as a court house, prison and administrative centre. Robert Burns is Dumfries' hero. He lived in the town from 1791, until his death in 1796, in a house in Mill Vennel, now called Burns Street. His house is open to the public and contains many precious relics of this celebrated national poet. The Globe Inn, Burns' favourite pub, also holds tangible memories of him, including the chair he used to sit in and a window pane on which the poet is believed to have scratched some verse with a diamond. Dumfries Burgh Museum is an 18th-century windmill that had a camera obscura built into it in 1836 which projects a living panorama of the town on to a table. The museum specialises in local history and personalities of the past. At one end of the medieval stone bridge over the Nith is Old Bridge House. Here each room has been furnished to illustrate a period of history — it has, for example, an 1850s kitchen and a Victorian child's room. Below the old bridge is the Caul — a weir built to power the riverside grain mills in the 18th century.

Leave on the A75 Stranraer road and cross the Buccleuch Street bridge into the adjoining town of Maxwelltown. In ½ mile turn left on to the A710, SP 'New Abbey' and 'Solway Coast', and in 6½ miles enter New Abbey.

NEW ABBEY, Dumf & Gall

The slopes of Criffel (1,866ft) tower above the picturesque village of New Abbey with its low, whitewashed cottages and charming 18th-century water-mill

on the banks of the New Abbey Burn. However, it is Sweetheart Abbey that dominates the village. A great precinct wall, built of giant boulders, enclose some 30 acres in which stand the hauntingly-beautiful ruins of this Cistercian abbey (AM). It was founded in the 13th century by Lady Devorgilla, wife of John Balliol, regent of Scotland. The good lady was buried in front of the high altar in 1289 with the embalmed heart of her husband, in whose memory she built the abbey. Her devotion is thought to have given the abbey its name. The ruins from the 13th and 14th centuries consist of a 90ft central tower, much of the nave and transepts, and a choir with a huge rose window, all built of red sandstone.

Continue on the A710, passing through Kirkbean, and Mainsriddle and at Caulkerbush keep forward, SP 'Rockcliffe'. At Colvend, next to White Lock, a short detour can be made to Rockcliffe by turning left on to an unclassified road.

ROCKCLIFFE, Dumf & Gall

This quiet resort on the Rough Firth was more dangerous in the 18th century when smugglers of wine and tobacco used the narrow inlets and bays nearby for their illegal, but prosperous, trade. Today the bays and the mild climate are enjoyed by tourists. A hill walk to nearby Kippford passes the Mote of Mark (NTS), an ancient hill fort occupied C AD600. It overlooks another NTS property, Rough Island, a 20-acre bird sanctuary which can be reached by foot over sands at low tide from Rockcliffe.

Above: Mid Steeple, behind the statue, was a courthouse and prison until 1867

Right: the roofless red sandstone ruins of Sweetheart Abbey

Continue on the A710 Dalbeattie road through Colvend and past the wooded hills of Dalbeattie Forest. After 2¼ miles a 2nd detour can be made by turning left to Kippford.

KIPPFORD, Dumf & Gall
A village of whitewashed cottages on the rugged and beautiful estuary of the Urr — the Rough Firth. In days gone by its livelihood was gained from fishing and smuggling, but in this century tourism and yachting provide the villagers with a living. There is also a 9-hole golf course here.

The main tour continues on the A710 through the Urr valley to Dalbeattie.

The tiny village of Kippford is a popular holiday resort on the Solway Firth

DALBEATTIE, Dumf & Gall
Lying in the wooded valley of the Urr, Dalbeattie is built of the shiny grey stone which brought it wealth and prosperity in the 19th century. This granite was used for building all over the world, and even today stone chips from the Craignair quarries are used for road surfacing, but the once crowded harbour is now deserted.

At the crossroads go forward on to the B794 Haugh of Urr road. Follow the Urr Water northwards and pass, after 2½ miles, the Motte of Urr across the valley. Bear left into Haugh of Urr then keep forward and in 1 mile turn left on to the A75 Stranraer road. In 1¾ miles turn right on to the B795, SP 'Laurieston'. At Townhead of Greenlaw turn right on to the A713, SP 'Ayr', to Crossmichael.

CROSSMICHAEL, Dumf & Gall
Crossmichael owes its name to the Cross of St Michael which once stood here and where the Michaelmas Fair was held at Christmas. In the churchyard lies the martyr's grave of 'William Graham, shot dead by a party of Claverhouse's troop, for his adherence to Scotland's Reformation Covenants, 1682.' The River Dee widens here to form a reservoir, of which Loch Ken is now an extension.

Continue alongside the shores of Loch Ken to pass through Parton and in 6½ miles turn right on to the A712 Corsock and Crocketford road. In ½ mile turn left on to the A769 (no SP), and 2 miles further turn right on to the A702 for Moniaive.

MONIAIVE, Dumf & Gall
Cairn Water is formed here by the confluence of the Craigdarroch and Dalwhat waters and the Castlefairn Burn. The village itself was chartered as a burgh in 1636, though all that remains of such grandeur is the 17th-century mercat cross that still stands as the centrepiece. James Renwick, the last Covenanter to be executed, was born in Moniaive, and died in Edinburgh in 1688 at the age of 26.

Turn right, SP 'Thornhill', and cross the river bridge then turn right again. In 2¼ miles a short detour can be made to Maxwelton House by turning right on to the B729, then turning left after 1 mile.

MAXWELTON HOUSE, Dumf & Gall
During the 14th and 15th centuries the house (OACT) was the stronghold of the Earls of Glencairn. In the 17th century it became the home of the Lauries, one of whom, Annie Laurie, is immortalised in the famous Scottish ballad named after her. The author was Douglas of Fingland, deemed by Annie's father to be an undesirable suitor. The house has recently been restored and contains an interesting museum of early agricultural and domestic life.

The main tour continues along the A702 to Penpont. 1 mile beyond the village an unclassified road to the left leads to Drumlanrig Castle.

DRUMLANRIG CASTLE, Dumf & Gall
William Douglas, 1st Earl of Queensberry, built this magnificent house (OACT) of rose-red sandstone between 1679 and 1691. The vast formal gardens he laid out have disappeared, but the house remains, grandiose and impressive. Richly decorated within, it is filled with world famous art treasures, including a Rembrandt painting, outstanding silver, and superb furniture given to the house by Charles II. A carved winged heart surmounted by a crown frequently occurs on the stonework and this, with the word 'FORWARD', is the Douglas Crest. It originated thus: when Robert Bruce died in 1329 without achieving his ambition of going on a crusade to the Holy Land, his embalmed heart was entrusted to Sir James, 'The Black Douglas', who went to Spain to fight the muslims. As Sir James, mortally wounded in battle, fell, he threw the silver casket containing the heart at the unbelievers, shouting, 'Forward, Brave Heart'. After 13 generations the Douglas line died out, and the house and title went to the Dukes of Buccleuch in 1810, who own the house today.

The main tour continues over the River Nith then bears left and shortly right. At the T-junction turn right on to the A76, SP 'Dumfries', for Thornhill.

THORNHILL, Dumf & Gall
This small town on an attractive stretch of the River Nith is known as the 'ducal village', because of its long association with the Dukes of Queensberry and Buccleuch. North Drumlanrig street has an avenue of lime trees planted in the 19th century by the 6th Duke of Buccleuch, and a tall column crowned by a statue of a winged horse — the emblem of the Queensberrys — stands in the town centre. Drumlanrig Castle is closely associated with both families.

Follow the Dumfries road south and ¾ mile beyond Closeburn turn left, SP 'Loch Ettrick'. In ¾ mile turn left again to reach Loch Ettrick. Shortly beyond it turn right, SP 'Ae', to enter the Forest of Ae. In 4 miles, at the crossroads, branch right to skirt (left) the village of Ae.

AE, Dumf & Gall
Set in the Forest of Ae, the village was built by the Forestry Commission in 1947 to house its workers. Experiments carried out here have given rise to notable advances in forestry techniques; trees can now be grown well above the normal tree line and can be planted in peat bogs — thought previously to be impossible. The forest itself is mainly sitka spruce, with some larch, Scots pine and Norway spruce. Ornamental trees have been planted along the road from Closeburn, and nature trails and marked walks have been laid out, beginning from the picnic area on the banks of the Water of Ae. Roe and fallow deer live in the forest, and the sparrow hawk may sometimes be seen.

Continue through open countryside and in 3¾ miles, at the crossroads, keep forward. In 2½ miles at Locharbriggs turn right on to the A701 for the return to Dumfries.

MOFFAT, Dumf & Gall

Moffat lies in the deep valley of the River Annan, overshadowed by the steep Lowther Hills. This is sheepfarming country, its importance celebrated by the conspicuous bronze ram that stands proudly on top of the Colvin fountain at the end of the town's broad High Street. In the 17th century sulphur springs were discovered a short distance away from Moffat, and it remained popular as a spa throughout the 18th and 19th centuries. Holiday-makers today find it an ideal base from which to explore the beauties of Annandale. Famous people associated with Moffat include road engineer John Macadam, who was buried in the churchyard in 1836, and James Macpherson, who launched his Ossianic Fragments at Moffat House, now an hotel, in 1759. These fragments purported to be ancient Gaelic poems which Macpherson claimed to have discovered, to the great excitement of the literary world of his day, but later their authenticity was disputed in a storm of controversy.

Follow SP 'Selkirk A708', and shortly enter the valley of the Moffat Water. After the Craigieburn Plantation the valley narrows considerably, with hills rising to over 2,100ft on both sides. Near the summit of the climb pass (left) the Grey Mare's Tail waterfall.

GREY MARE'S TAIL, Dumf & Gall

Emptying out of Loch Skene, the Tail Burn cascades 200ft over the rockface in a breathtaking fall of white water aptly christened the Grey Mare's Tail. There are 2 other falls with the same name in the south-west, but neither is as magnificent as this one. The countryside around the burn, now owned by the National Trust for Scotland, is famous for its profusion and variety of flowering plants, and goats inhabit the rocky hillsides.

After reaching 1,100ft the route descends to Loch of the Lowes and Tibbie Shiel's Inn.

TIBBIE SHIEL'S INN, Borders

St Mary's Loch, set among a superb landscape of steep hills, is joined to the tiny Loch of the Lowes by a neck of land on which, strategically placed, stands Tibbie Shiel's, a famous fishermen's inn. Nearby is the statue of the Ettrick Shepherd, as the vernacular poet James Hogg (1770-1835) was known. Many of his poems describe St Mary's Loch.

Continue alongside St Mary's Loch for 1½ miles then cross the Megget Water and shortly turn left, SP 'Tweedsmuir', along the Megget Water valley. The road ascends to a 1483ft summit at the Megget Stone before descending steeply to the shores of Talla Reservoir. Continue to Tweedsmuir.

TWEEDDALE AND CLYDEDALE

Scotland's great Lowlands rivers, the Tweed and the Clyde, roll majestically east and west through the green hills of the wild Borders country, where centuries of family feuds and bitter skirmishes with the marauding English found their most lyrical expression in the haunting sadness of the Border Ballads.

Talla Reservoir, completed in 1905, provides Edinburgh with its water and the angler with brown trout

TWEEDSMUIR, Borders

This delightful village with its single-arched stone bridge spanning the River Tweed, was made famous by John Buchan, best known for his novel of adventure *The Thirty Nine Steps*. Many of the exciting episodes described in his books are set in the wild Borders country of his boyhood home. When, as Governor General of Canada (1935), he was raised to the peerage, he chose the title of Baron Tweedsmuir. This was strong Covenanting country and several victims of the 17th-century persecution of the staunchly Presbyterian Covenanters lie buried in the graveyard of Tweedsmuir Church.

Turn right on to the A701 Edinburgh road and descend through Tweeddale. After 7 miles turn right on to the B712 Peebles road. Shortly enter Drumelzier.

RIVER TWEED, Borders

The source of the Tweed lies close to that of the other great Lowland river, the Clyde. Instead of flowing westwards, however, it makes its way eastwards and for some distance is used as the border with England, flowing out to the North Sea at Berwick, 97 miles away. The Tweed has inspired many of the most beautiful Border ballads and the works of some of the most famous of Scotland's writers, in particular Sir Walter Scott. Many weaving towns are scattered through the valley, but the world-renowned cloth obtained its name through a Sassenach misunderstanding. Londoners read the local technical term 'tweel' as tweed, and the name has stuck ever since. Salmon, sea trout and brown trout all live in the river.

DRUMELZIER, Borders

High above Tweeddale, north-east of the village, the ruins of Thines Castle, destroyed by James VI in 1592, and by tradition the burial place of the Arthurian wizard Merlin, overlook the confluence of the River Tweed and Drumelzier Burn.

In 2 miles pass (right) the grounds of Dawyck House (not open) and Arboretum.

DAWYCK BOTANIC GARDEN, Borders

These beautiful gardens (OACT) specialising in trees and flowering shurbs, were created in the 18th century by Sir James Naesmyth, acting on the advice of his teacher, the great Swedish botanist Linnaeus, to whom we owe the scientific classification of plants. Sir James is credited with being the first person to introduce the larch to Scotland (1725). The gardens are famous for their rhododendrons, magnificent Douglas firs, pinetum and avenues of lime trees and silver firs.

Cross the River Tweed and in 2 miles reach Stobo.

STOBO, Borders

In the barrel-vaulted porch of Stobo's Norman church are preserved a set of jougs, the Scottish equivalent of stocks. These were a type of iron collar in which wrongdoers were confined.

In 2½ miles cross the Lyne Water then turn left on to the A72, SP 'Glasgow'. Follow the Lyne Water and then Tarth Water for 6½ miles then keep left, SP 'Biggar'. In 5½ miles enter Skirling.

SKIRLING, Borders

A wealth of wrought iron work decorates Skirling's houses, attractively arranged around the village green. Scattered here and there are painted figures of beasts and birds. The idea was Lord Carmichael's who built his own house here and died in 1926.

Continue on the A72 and in 2 miles turn left on to the A702 to enter Biggar.

BIGGAR, Strathclyde

The crowning in July every year of the Fleming Queen commemorates Mary Fleming, one of the 'Queen's 4 Marys' of the folk song, who was born at Boghall Castle, now ruined. Mary Fleming, Mary Seton, Mary Beaton and Mary Livingstone were all Ladies-in-Waiting to Mary, Queen of Scots. Biggar's broad main street lies alongside Biggar Water, ending at Cadger's Bridge, which has preserved this name ever since William Wallace, hero of the 13th-century Scottish Wars of Independence, crossed it disguised as a cadger (pedlar) to lead his army to victory over the English at a battle south of the town. The Gladstone Court Museum, a

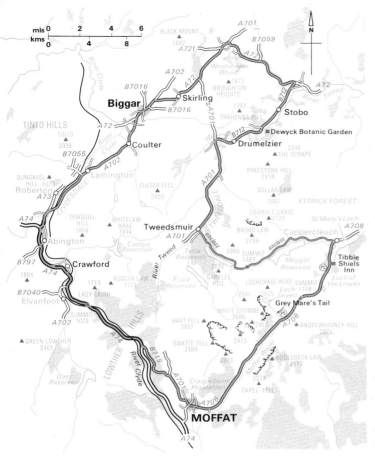

converted 19th-century coachworks, has a fascinating reconstruction of an old-world village street, complete with authentic shop signs and advertisements. Among the premises on display are an old bank and telephone exchange. An outdoor extension will eventually house agricultural buildings and a Victorian gasworks. The museum is named after William Gladstone, whose family came from this area.

Keep forward on the A702, SP 'Carlisle', entering the Clyde valley. After 3 miles pass through Coulter.

COULTER, Strathclyde
This pretty village stands beside the Coulter water, well shaded by trees. By the former railway station, Coulter Motte Hill is an early medieval castle mound and would originally have had a moat and a timber tower and palisade. Tinto Hill rises up to 2,335ft in the distance.

Across the valley to the right there are further views of Tinto as the tour approaches Lamington. Shortly beyond Lamington the road joins the River Clyde and the electrified Glasgow railway line, running alongside the latter for 3 miles before crossing the valley and turning left on to the A73. In 1¼ miles turn left to join the A74.

RIVER CLYDE, Strathclyde
The Clyde rises as a mountain stream in the hills south-west of Crawford and flows westwards for 106 miles. In its upper reaches the

Clyde is famed for its limpid waters, populated by the wary brown trout. The stream is so clear that local anglers would only use horse-hair lines because gut and nylon were held to be too coarse, and the fish would not rise to the bait. The fertile Clyde valley is the home of the celebrated Clydesdale heavy horses, and is also noted for its fruit orchards.

Follow the railway and river up the valley to Crawford.

CRAWFORD, Strathclyde
On the opposite bank of the Clyde from the village, Crawford Castle (not open) has stood as guardian since the 13th century, when it belonged to the powerful Border family — the Lindsays. It was restored and reconstructed in the 17th century when it passed into the hands of the Douglases. Crawford makes an excellent centre from which to explore the green lowland hills. The curious stone pillar in the village street was, in fact, destined to be a tombstone for the Cranston family who ran the last mailcoach in the area.

In 9 miles, on the winding descent through the forested Lowther Hills, branch left on to the B719 Moffat road. Climb again through woodland before descending into the upper Annan valley and turning right on to the A701 for the return to Moffat.

Grey Mare's Tail waterfall cascades down 200ft into Moffat Water

SIR WALTER SCOTT'S COUNTRY

This is where Scott, the great romantic novelist, chose to live; first at Ashiesteel House, and then at Abbotsford, where the wrote the *Waverley* novels. Scott was fascinated by Scottish history, and in these borderlands reflecting centuries of clan feuds and Anglo-Scottish rivalry he found much to inspire him.

GALASHIELS, Borders

Galashiels was granted a charter in 1599. A pageant that is still celebrated and illustrates the town's history is the 'Braw Lads' gathering in early summer. The focal point for this event is the Mercat Cross, dating from 1695. Woollen mills have operated in the town since 1622, but the industrialisation of the 19th century brought both the industry and the town to the forefront. The Scottish College of Textiles, founded here in 1909, is the centre of wool studies in Scotland. In the town centre in front of the clock tower is the splendid war memorial, designed by Robert Lorimer — a statue of a mounted Border Reiver or moss-trooper — a bandit who raided the borderlands between the 16th and 18th centuries. Old Gala House, new headquarters of the Galashiels Art Club, dating from the 15th and 17th centuries, is one of the oldest buildings in the town and houses a unique 17th-century Scottish painted ceiling.

Leave on the B6374 Melrose Road for Lowood, passing in 1½ miles, at Langlee, a tablet recording Sir Walter Scott's last journey from Italy to Abbotsford House shortly before his death. In 1½ miles go forward on to the B6360. Pass through Gattonside and in 2¼ miles follow SP 'Edinburgh' to join the A68 for Lauder.

LAUDER, Borders

Old Berwickshire's only royal burgh, Lauder, was granted its charter in 1502, although it claims to have been a burgh since William the Lion's reign. Situated on the Leader Water in Lauderdale, the town is an excellent angling centre. The Lauder Common Riding, held late summer, is one of the oldest horse riding festivals in the country.

Continue on the A68 Edinburgh road through the broad valley. In 2 miles reach the famous Soutra Hill viewpoint (1,130ft). On the descent pass Fala village, and in 1¼ miles turn left on to the B645. In 2½ miles at Tynehead go forward on to the B6367 and 1¼ miles further turn left on to the A7, SP 'Galashiels'. Shortly enter the Gala Water valley and follow it to Stow.

STOW, Borders

The area around Stow is steeped in early history, and legend tells how King Arthur routed the Saxons here then built a church in thanksgiving. The old church of St Mary's was first consecrated in 1242 but is now a ruin, and the modern church which has replaced it, a pleasing 19th-century Gothic building, bears a 140ft-high spire. Opposite, a packhorse bridge dating from 1655, spans the Gala Water. These bridges are extremely rare, and are known as packhorse bridges because of the low parapets built to prevent heavily laden packhorses falling into the river.

Continue on the A7 and in 3¾ miles turn right on to the B710 for Clovenfords.

CLOVENFORDS, Borders

Sir Walter Scott frequently stayed at Clovenfords, although the inn he used has now been replaced. The great novelist stayed here on visits while he was Sheriff of Selkirk, before he bought nearby Ashiesteel where he lived from 1804 to 1812, and wrote *Marmion*, *Lady of the Lake* and *The Lady of the Last Minstrel*. Wordsworth also stayed here in 1803.

At the crossroads turn right on to the A72. Descend to the Tweed valley and turn right. Ashiesteel House can be seen across the river at this point. Continue for 5 miles to Walkerburn.

WALKERBURN, Borders

This village was created by Henry Ballantyne in 1854, when he and his sons built the first wool mill in which new wool went in one end, and finished cloth came out the other. He was the 7th generation of weavers in his family, and the 12th generation continue the business today. The Scottish Museum of Wool Textiles (OACT) is sited here, which illustrates the history of spinning and weaving from its beginnings to the present day.

Continue on the A72 and in 2 miles enter Innerleithen.

INNERLEITHEN, Borders

Innerleithen was no more than a hamlet before 1790, when Alexander Brodie — a Traquair blacksmith who made his fortune in London — built the first wool mill here, a step which has developed into an important wool, spinning and knitwear industry. The early 19th century saw the growth of Innerleithen as a spa town because the mineral spring called Doo's Well was thought to have curative properties similar to the waters at Harrogate. Lord Traquair supplied a pump room in 1824, along with reading rooms and a verandah. Border games are held in the town annually, and a pageant known as the Cleikum Ceremony has been performed since 1900; it represents St Ronan ridding the town of the devil.

Turn left on to the B709, and shortly cross the River Tweed, in ½ mile pass (right) the entrance to Traquair House.

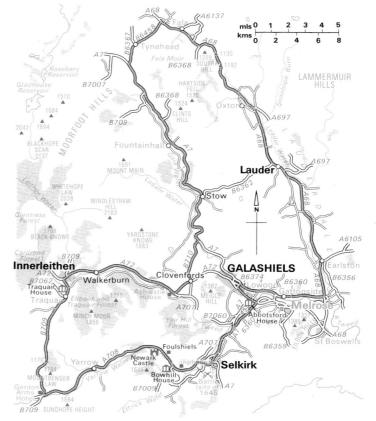

Above: this 16th-century calculator at Traquair House was invented by Napier and called 'Napier's Bones'

Left: Borders countryside near Galashiels

TRAQUAIR HOUSE, Borders
Traquair House (OACT) is said to be the oldest inhabited house in Scotland. It was originally a hunting lodge for Scottish kings; the first recorded royal visit was made in 1107. The oldest part of the house contains the remains of a 14th-century pele tower but the present house was mainly built in the 16th century, although the entrance porch was added during the last century. Twenty-seven monarchs have stayed here over the years, including Mary, Queen of Scots. Examples of her embroidery are among the delightful treasures within the house, but of all these the visitor must not miss the Brew House, where the potent Traquair Ale is traditionally brewed in the old vats.

Continue through Traquair village up the narrow valley of the Paddock Burn to a summit of 1,170ft before descending to the Gordon Arms Hotel on the Yarrow Water. At the crossroads turn left on to the A708 and in 9 miles pass (left) Foulshiels.

FOULSHIELS, Borders
On the banks of the Yarrow Water stands Foulshiels, where the celebrated explorer Mungo Park was born in 1771. He studied medicine at Edinburgh and became an assistant ship's surgeon on the *Worcester*, bound for Sumatra. He joined the African Association in 1795 and set out on a journey which lasted 19 months, and included his capture by an African chief and his subsequent escape. He returned to Peebles and settled as a doctor, but in 1805 the wanderlust overcame him again and he once more set off into the African interior where he met his death in a fight with natives on the Niger.

To the right, on the opposite side of the river, stands Newark Castle.

NEWARK CASTLE, Borders
This massive Border stronghold crowning the steep banks of the River Yarrow, was built during the mid 15th century. Though now a ruin, it was a royal hunting-seat, as the surrounding Ettrick Forest was famous for its abundance of game. In 1548 the castle was the scene of a seige by the English under Lord Grey, and in 1645 100 men in Montrose's army were executed here after the Battle of Philiphaugh.

In 1¼ miles pass (right) the B7039 which leads to Bowhill House.

BOWHILL HOUSE, Borders
Sir Walter Scott called it Sweet Bowhill, for this great, rambling house (OACT) has an easygoing, comfortable atmosphere attributable, perhaps, to those who lived here. However, it was the 4th and 5th Dukes of Buccleuch who left their mark most distinctly. The former was a close friend of Sir Walter Scott, and the latter was a notable agriculturist and among the most enlightened of Victorian landowners. Yet despite the impression of a family home these 2 congenial men imparted to the house, it contains many art treasures worthy of a museum or art gallery. Among these are 3 superb Mortlake tapestries, works by the painter Lely and artists of the Van Dyck School, and beautiful French furniture. There are also many curious relics of history, such as the white linen shirt in which the Duke of Montrose was executed.

In 2 miles bear right, then turn right to cross Ettrick Water into Selkirk.

SELKIRK, Borders
Selkirk's position on the borderlands put it in the front line of Anglo-Scottish wars for 3 centuries, but in 1513 the town was burned by the English forces after the Battle of Flodden. A statue of a standard-bearer, representing the sole survivor of this defeat, stands in the market place and the town hall, with its 100ft spire, still sounds a nightly curfew. Halliwells House museum, in the town's oldest surviving building recreates its past roll as a house and ironmongers shop.

Leave Selkirk on the A7 Galashiels road and in 2¾ miles turn right on to the B6360 for Abbotsford. Follow the River Tweed to Abbotsford House.

ABBOTSFORD HOUSE, Borders
In 1811 Sir Walter Scott was successful enough in his writing to buy a modest farmhouse and farm of about 110 acres in this countryside he loved so much. Here the *Waverley* novels were written, bringing sufficient wealth to enable Scott to knock down the farmhouse and build Abbotsford House (OACT) in 1822. The house is of Tudor design and covered in Gothic detail which sparked off the distinctive baronial style seen in so many Victorian houses. Ruskin condemned it, Queen Victoria referred to it as rather gloomy, but Scott loved it. His personality dominates the house with its dark panelling, moulded ceilings and great pseudo-medieval firegrates. Scott's study is just as he kept it. Gifts from the great, including Goethe's medallion portrait, keep company with the fascinating objects Scott collected himself — an engraved tumbler which belonged to Robert Burns and a lock of hair belonging to Prince Charles Edward, are among his treasures.

In ½ mile, at the roundabout, take the A6091 for the return to Galashiels. Cross the River Tweed and at the next roundabout take the A7 for the town centre.

A detail of a window in Selkirk town hall to those who died at Flodden

DUNBAR, Lothian

An old fishing port which became a royal burgh in 1370, Dunbar lies between the fishing grounds of the North Sea and the rich farmland of its hinterland, renowned for the redness of its soil in which grows the Dunbar Red potato. The town's long civic history is epitomised by the Town House. This features a 6-sided tower, dates from 1620, and is said to be the oldest public building in Scotland to have been in continuous use; the old market cross stands close by. The parish church, situated on high ground with a tower 180ft high, is a landmark for local fishermen. Much of the town's history is tied up with its castle, another landmark, high up on a rocky headland. The castle was eventually destroyed by the Regent Moray after the Battle of Carberry, which resulted in the downfall of Mary, Queen of Scots. Close to the town a country park of some 1600 acres conserves the natural beauty of the area. It is named after conservationist John Muir, born in Dunbar in the mid 19th-century.

Leave on the A1087 Berwick road shortly passing through the hamlet of Broxburn. In 1 mile turn left on to the A1 and continue south-east, passing close to the cliff-edge on the approach to Cockburnspath.

COCKBURNSPATH, Borders

Cockburnspath lies on the edge of the Lammermuir Hills near the rocky North Sea coast. The pretty 14th-century church has a distinctive round 16th-century beacon-tower and the early 17th-century mercat cross is crowned by a stone thistle. Just to the east of the village is the sandy beach of Pease Bay, which lies at the edge of the steep Pease Dean valley. Spanning this is a bridge nearly 130ft high and 300ft long which was built in 1786.

½ mile south of the village turn right off the A1 on to an unclassified road, SP 'Abbey St Bathans'. Follow SP 'Preston' and 'Duns', and later turn right on to the A6112 for Preston. Turn right into the village and at the end turn right again on to the B6355. Shortly cross the Whiteadder Water and in ¾ mile turn right. Later recross the Whiteadder at Ellemford Bridge and follow its valley to Cranshaws.

CRANSHAWS, Borders

At the heart of the Lammermuir Hills, set beside the Whiteadder Water, the hamlet of Cranshaws possesses probably the best preserved of the Border pele towers. It has been identified as Ravenswood of Sir Walter Scott's *The Bride of Lammermoor;* Scott heard the original story from his great aunt Margaret Sirenton, who almost certainly knew the Cranshaws.

Continue on the B6355 to Gifford.

DUNBAR AND THE LAMMERMUIR HILLS

Bounded to the north by a rocky coast dotted with pleasant villages and seaside resorts overlooking the Firth of Forth, this corner of Lothian is dominated by the great rolling summits of the windswept Lammermuir Hills which shelter such treasures as Dunbar Castle and Haddington's abbey church.

Above: the remains of Dirleton Castle date from the 13th century when it was built by the Norman de Vaux family

GIFFORD, Lothian

This neat, well-planned, 18th-century village once had many small industries, notably linen-weaving and papermaking — Scottish banknotes were printed on Gifford paper in the early 18th century. Today, however, the industry has gone, nor are the village's 3 annual livestock fairs held any more. It has become a charming, old-world backwater, ideal as a walking and pony-trekking centre for the Lammermuir Hills.

Turn right on to the B6369 and in 4¼ miles turn right again on to the A6137 to enter Haddington. Shortly turn left, SP 'Edinburgh', to reach the town centre.

HADDINGTON, Lothian

Haddington is one of the country's most beautifully restored and preserved towns, and an outstanding example of Scottish burghal architecture. It has a distinct medieval street plan and many buildings are scheduled as special architectural or historic interest. The best illustration of the kind of extensive restoration undertaken is the Parish Church of St Mary. This red sandstone church, known as the Lamp of the Lothians, was built in the 14th century to replace an earlier church. By 1540 it became known as an important collegiate church, but shortly after this period of prosperity fighting between the English, Scots and French came to the town and the church and town were severely damaged. The citizens of Haddington have, through various societies, rebuilt the chancel and completely restored this building where John Knox worshipped as a boy. Other notable buildings include the Town House, which like many other houses here, was designed by the famous architect William Adam. Poldrate Mill, a 3-storey corn-mill with an undershot water-wheel, is now an arts and community centre and 17th-century Haddington House, the oldest domestic building in the town, is now used as a library, meeting rooms and administrative centre for the Collegiate College.

Leave on the B6471 Edinburgh road and in 1½ miles turn left on to the A1. In 2¼ miles pass through Gladsmuir then in ¼ mile, at the crossroads, turn right on to the B6363. In 2 miles turn right on to the A198 into Longniddry. Shortly bear left with the A198 to reach Gosford Bay and skirt the grounds of Gosford House (not open). In 1 mile enter Aberlady.

Below: Preston Mill, now restored, is one of the oldest and smallest watermills left in Scotland

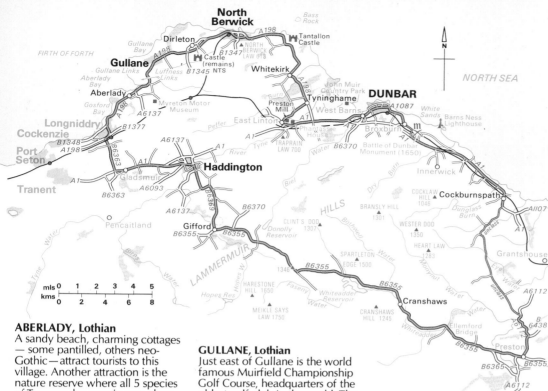

ABERLADY, Lothian
A sandy beach, charming cottages — some pantilled, others neo-Gothic — attract tourists to this village. Another attraction is the nature reserve where all 5 species of Tern can be seen in one place (many species of birds have been recorded here). A collection of historic motor cars dating from 1896, motorcycles from 1903 and many other types of vehicle, are displayed in the Myreton Motor Museum (OACT) on the outskirts of the village.

Turn left then bear right and skirt the inlet of Aberlady Bay before crossing the Luffness and Gullane Golf Links to enter Gullane.

GULLANE, Lothian
Just east of Gullane is the world famous Muirfield Championship Golf Course, headquarters of the oldest golf club in the world. The view over the Firth of Forth from Gullane Hill reaches over the water to the Fife coast, and beyond that to the distant Lomond and Ochil Hills. The 12th-century Church of St Andrew is now a roofless ruin — it is said James VI dismissed the last vicar for smoking tobacco.

Continue on the A198 to Dirleton, turning left on to the B1345 to enter the village.

DIRLETON, Lothian
This is claimed by many to be the most beautiful village in Scotland. Three sides of a green are lined by 17th- and 18th-century houses, the fourth side is taken up by the castle (AM) and its grounds; trees surround it all and complete a scene of well-matured unity. The castle last stood seige against Cromwell's troops, and was rendered indefensible by General Lambert in 1650. Today it is surrounded by flower gardens. The castle's own gardens are hemmed in by ancient yew trees, and include a 17th-century bowling green, still in use, and a 16th-century circular dovecot.

At the end of the village turn left to rejoin the A198, shortly entering North Berwick, and keep forward on the B1346 for the sea-front.

NORTH BERWICK, Lothian
An ancient burgh, fishing village, and popular resort, North Berwick boasts 2 golf courses and 2 sandy beaches which are divided by an attractive harbour with a heated open-air swimming pool set into the rocks beside it. The ruins of a 12th-century church can be explored near the harbour, a place where, in 1591, it is said the devil appeared before a group of local witches and wizards. This story is related in the local records of the witches' trial. Boats from North Berwick take visitors around the fascinating Firth of Forth islands which stand just off the coast.

Follow SP 'Berwick B1346' and shortly rejoin the A198. In ¾ mile, at the roundabout, take the 1st exit. In 2 miles pass (left) the track leading to Tantallon Castle.

TANTALLON CASTLE, Lothian
Perched upon a headland, defended by 100ft-high cliffs on 3 sides and by a moat on the other, Tantallon Castle (AM) was a stronghold for the Douglas clan for centuries. An old saying hereabouts likened an impossible task to 'knocking down Tantallon or building a bridge to Bass'. Built in 1375 Tantallon was however, knocked down after a siege by James V in 1528, and General Monk reduced it to rubble after heavy bombardment in 1651. Walls, towers and earthworks survive, and a 17th-century dovecot stands between the 2 inner ditches.

In 2¾ miles enter Whitekirk.

WHITEKIRK, Lothian
A massive square tower topped by a wooden spire was the target of suffragettes in 1914 — the church was completely gutted and although arson was suspected, it was never proved. National subscription, however, enabled it to be rebuilt in 1971, and the church remains one of the finest examples of Gothic parochial architecture in Scotland. A long, narrow, bare building behind the church is one of the last tithe barns in Scotland, and it is said monks from Holyrood in Edinburgh stored grain here.

Turn left and shortly pass through the grounds of the Tyninghame Estate on the approach to Tyninghame.

TYNINGHAME, Lothian
A delightful estate village, Tyninghame is built of the characteristic local red sandstone. The first church here, however, was founded by St Baldred (who died in 756), but was destroyed by Anlaf the Dane in 941. Today the remains, 2 12th-century Norman arches, are used as the burial chapel of the Earls of Haddington, who own nearby Tyninghame Manor (not open).

Turn right on to the B1407 and in 1½ miles pass Preston Mill.

PRESTON MILL, Lothian
Preston Mill (NTS) is the only watermill surviving on the Tyne now; for centuries there were several grain mills along the river. The 16th-century mill has been restored to working order, and is complete with all its attendant outhouses, tools and machinery. The buildings, which include the curious conical roof of the drying kiln, provide a scene much favoured as a subject by artists.

Turn left into East Linton then bear left, SP 'Dunbar', to cross the River Tyne and shortly turn left (next to Phantassie House (not open) on to the A1. In 3 miles, at the roundabout, take the A1087 for the return through West Barns to Dunbar.

WHERE ROB ROY LIES

Deep lochs and dour mountains, swift-flowing and bubbling streams, glittering waterfalls and hillsides covered in dark green pine — all the elements of a highland landscape within a day's drive. In these picturesque surroundings the romantic life of Rob Roy unfolded, his deeds the subject of many a legend and ballad.

CALLANDER, Central

Almost English-looking meadows flank the River Teith as it flows toward the town, whose main street and simple square are surrounded in turn by Regency-style houses, some with picturesque first floor bow-windows which overhang the pavement below. This comfortable town was originally built by the Commissioners for the Forfeited Estates on the Drummond lands after the 18th-century Jacobite risings. Callander is especially fortunate in having several beauty spots within reach of the walker, such as the Falls of Bracklinn, the Pass of Leny and its Falls, and Ben Ledi. In the town is the fascinating Kilmahog Woollen Mill, which at one time was famous for its handwoven blankets and tweed. Parts of the old structure are preserved along with an old water wheel which is still in working order and traditional woollens can be bought in the shop. Callander is better known as 'Tannochbrae' in the BBC series *Dr Finlay's Casebook*.

Leave on the A84 Stirling road and pass in 6¾ miles (left) the road to the Doune Motor Museum.

DOUNE MOTOR MUSEUM, Central

An attractive 16th-century house Newton Doune, houses the Doune Motor Museum (OACT), where vintage and post-vintage cars are displayed and motor racing hill climbs are held.

Shortly turn left on to the A820, SP 'Dunblane', to enter Doune.

DOUNE, Central

This proud, old-fashioned town took its importance from the castle, which was once a royal palace and is still the property of the Earls of Moray. At the western end of Doune is the small, triangular market place, an old mercat cross at its centre, where cattle and sheep fairs were held. The double-arched bridge was built in 1535 by the wealthy Robert Spittal, tailor to James IV. Doune was long famous for the manufacture of pistols, and today they are highly prized by collectors. Sporrans were also made here, but after the rebellion of 1745 Highland dress was banned. Cotton-milling became the new industry of Doune at Deanston Mills half a mile away, where there is also a distillery. Doune Castle is one of the best preserved medieval castles in Scotland open to the public. It stands at the junction of the Rivers Ardoch and Teith. Two great keeps are connected by low buildings, which include the great hall, to make one side of a quadrangle, and the other 3 sides are enclosed by massive 40ft walls, 8ft thick and capped by a parapet and wall-walk. Dating from the early 15th century, the castle was built by the Dukes of Albany, and passed into the hands of the Stuarts of Doune, Earls of Moray, in the 16th century.

From Doune a detour can be made to visit Scotland's Safari Park at Blair Drummond House 2 miles south. Turn right, following SP 'Stirling A84', and shortly cross the River Teith. In 2¾ miles, at the crossroads, turn left for Blair Drummond House.

BLAIR DRUMMOND HOUSE, Central

Two lairds of Blair Drummond have, through their own initiative, brought repute to this ancient property. A celebrated judge, Henry Home, married the Drummond heiress in 1741, and when his wife came into property in 1767 he carried out a scheme to convert soggy peat land into fine arable land. He built a series of sluices and channels which eventually led down to the River Forth. The peat was cut out and dumped into the channels which periodically flooded and so washed the peat away. The project created 1,500 acres of fine agricultural land, which is still farmed today. Today the park around the house has been turned into a wildlife safari park by the joint efforts of the present laird, a neighbouring laird, and Chipperfield's Circus. This popular park features wild lions, giraffes, buffalo, eland, zebras, camels and elephants among its collection, which wander freely about 100 acres of woodland tended by gamekeepers.

Return to Doune and on entering the town turn right on to the A820 Dunblane road and in 3¼ miles enter Dunblane. On reaching the A9 turn right, SP 'Stirling', and in 1 mile, at the roundabout, take the 1st exit. SP 'Bridge of Allan' and 'Stirling'. Off the B824 to the right lies Keir House Gardens. The main tour continues to Bridge of Allan.

During the summer months salmon may be seen leaping up the rapids of the Falls of Leny — a popular beauty spot

Loch Earn is a well-known yachting and water-skiing centre

BALQUHIDDER, Central
Salmon, trout and the rare char live in the cold waters of Loch Voil, and at its eastern end stands the 2 churches of Balquhidder (pronounced Balwhidder). One is mid-19th century, and now a roofless ruin. However, in the churchyard is the grave of the great Scottish hero, Rob Roy. He was born into the MacGregor clan in 1660, and inherited the chieftainship. He was a staunch Jacobite and a great rebel who was outlawed after the failure of the rebellion of 1715. Although a man of action, Rob Roy died peaceably at Kirton, Balquhidder, in 1740, aged about 80 years old. Sir Walter Scott in his novel *Rob Roy*, describes the legends, stories and fact which accompany this charismatic figure.

From Kingshouse continue on the A84 southwards into the thickly forested Strathyre.

STRATHYRE, Central
Strathyre, a village in the Strath of the same name through which flows the River Balraig, has 2 functions — to cater for the visitor, and to act as a forestry centre for Strathyre Forest. It has always attracted tourists (Wordsworth stayed here in 1803) and is a convenient touring centre for the southern Highlands. The Forestry Commission established Strathyre Forest in the 1930s, and now the entire valley is clothed in dark pines, although in 1968 80,000 trees were blown down in a fearsome storm; however, 8,000,000 survived, which gives an idea of the extent of the forest. The Strathyre Forest Centre contains a museum, demonstration room and exhibition room, where information of forest trails and walks can be found.

A mile south of the village the road reaches the eastern shore of Loch Lubnaig.

LOCH LUBNAIG, Central
A place of poetical beauty, Loch Lubnaig stands at the foot of Ben Ledi (2,883ft) and stretches 5 miles north to south. Near its head are the remains of a crannog, or artificial island refuge. From the road the view to the opposite side makes a fine spectacle, the great mountain clothed in trees with streams pouring down the steep side in numerous waterfalls. St Bride's derelict churchyard stands, where the loch pours out as the River Leny, overgrown and romantic, on a most beautiful site. A mile below, in the Pass of Leny, are the Falls of Leny — actually a series of rapids rather than a waterfall.

At the southern end of the loch the road enters the narrow Pass of Leny before the return to Callander.

KEIR HOUSE GARDENS, Central
Sir William Stirling Maxwell laid out these 40 acres of woodland and formal gardens (OACT) around Keir House in the 1860s, and the layout remains largely true to the original plan. Special features include a yew tree-house, a water garden and a pond which was cleared and replanted in the 1960s, magnificent rhododendrons, flowering shrubs and herbaceous borders. Perhaps the most important element in these beautiful gardens is the trees; an arboretum of rare conifers and a woodland of large rare trees draw enthusiasts from all over the world.

BRIDGE OF ALLAN, Central
For 150 years this was a spa town, and the fine villas found here date from about 1810 when the properties of the mineral waters of the Arthog springs were discovered. The baths and pump room which were built still stand. The small town now benefits from its proximity to Stirling University.

Left: Rob Roy's grave at Balquhidder

At the end of the town turn left, SP 'Sheriffmuir', passing the grounds of Stirling University then, on the ascent, bear right. Ascend onto the edge of the Ochil Hills, later crossing the Wharry Burn. Shortly keep forward on the Blackford road to cross Sheriff Muir, reaching a height of 1,031ft. In ¾ mile, on the descent, turn left, SP 'Greenloaning'. At the A9 turn left then right, SP 'Braco', and in ¼ mile right again on to the A822 for Braco.

BRACO, Tayside
In the grounds of Ardoch House (not open) lie the substantial and exceptionally well-preserved remains of a Roman fort. Coins have been found here, and this, with the Roman Great Camp to the north-west, could house 40,000 troops at any one time.

Continue on the A822, cross the River Knaik and in ¾ mile turn left on to the B827, SP 'Comrie', to follow the river through moorland before descending to Comrie.

COMRIE, Tayside
The Earn, the Lednock, the Ruchill Waters and the glens of Lednock and Arthog, all meet at Comrie, which stands on the Highland Boundary Fault — the 20,000ft-deep fracture in the earth which divides the Highlands from the Lowlands. Comrie therefore has more recorded earthquake tremors than anywhere else in Britain, although none have caused more damage than cracks in the walls of a few houses. It is possible that the New Year custom of the Flambeaux procession is in some

way connected with the tremors — a torchlight procession parades around the town, and there is dancing around a bonfire, ostensibly to drive away evil spirits. All around the town wooded hills rise, and there are delightful walks to the Devil's Cauldron, Spout Falls, and other waterfalls at Glen Turret and Glen Boltachan.

Leave on the A85 Crianlarich road and continue to St Fillans.

ST FILLANS, Tayside
Set at the eastern tip of the long and beautiful Loch Earn, St Fillans is a favourite haunt of those who love fishing, sailing, mountaineering, walking, or just admiring scenery. To the south rises wooded Dunfillan Hill (2,011ft) on top of which perches a rock known as St Fillans Chair, a site once fortified by the Picts.

Beyond the village the road takes the north bank of Loch Earn and at the western end stands the village of Lochearnhead.

LOCHEARNHEAD, Central
Lochearnhead, gazing eastwards from the green slopes above Loch Earn at the foot of Glen Ogle, is a pleasing, scattered village, with ample hotels for the many tourists who come here to enjoy the water-skiing and yachting available on the loch. The surrounding country, ablaze with wild nasturtiums in the summer, offers fine hill-walking.

Turn left on to the A84 Stirling road and proceed to Kingshouse. From here a detour can be made to Balquhidder and Loch Voil by turning right on to the unclassified road.

GLASGOW, Strathclyde

Glasgow owed its tremendous growth to the Industrial Revolution, during which time it became one of the major ship building and heavy engineering centres in the world. The centre of the city contains many gracious and imposing Victorian buildings, including, in George Square, the palatial City Chambers (OACT), which were opened by Queen Victoria in 1888. Glasgow Cathedral stands on the site of a church built in AD534 by St Mungo — the traditional founder of the city. A good deal of 12th and 13th century work survives in the cathedral, especially in the magnificent crypt, which now serves as Glasgow's parish church. The city is richly endowed with museums, art galleries, parks and gardens. The Glasgow Art Gallery and Museum, in Kelvingrove, contains the finest municipal art collection in the United Kingdom as well as extensive collections covering archaeology and natural history; Pollok House is a lovely 18th-century mansion, set in beautiful gardens, which houses paintings by such artists as El Greco, Goya and William Blake. Haggs Castle, in St Andrew's Drive, was built in 1585 and is now a museum, created especially for children, whose theme is the exploration of time. One of Glasgow's most famous buildings is the School of Art (OACT). It was designed in a brilliantly original style, by C.R. Macintosh and completed in 1909. Other museums in Glasgow include the Royal Fusilier's Regimental Museum, the Hunterian and the Peoples Palace, which contains a visual record of the people and life of Glasgow, and the Transport Museum. Of Glasgow's hundreds of acres of splendid parks and gardens perhaps the most exciting is the Botanic Gardens. The astonishing Burrell Collection — with its paintings, pottery porcelain, precious metalwork, stained glass, etc — is housed in a special gallery in Pollok Country Park.

Leave Glasgow on the A82 Great Western Road, SP 'Dumbarton Crianlarich'. In 12 miles follow SP 'Crianlarich' to skirt Dumbarton. Cross the Leven Valley and pass Alexandria. At the roundabout junction with the A811, at the end of the by-pass, turn off to visit Balloch.

BALLOCH, Strathclyde

Its position on the banks of Loch Lomond has made this little village popular with holidaymakers and yachtsmen. Balloch Castle Country Park (OACT) is an extensive area of grassland surrounded with woods which includes among its attractions a walled garden and a nature trail. From the village a visit can be made to Cameron Loch Lomond Wildlife Park.

TOUR 74 — 79 MILES

THE GARDEN OF GLASGOW

Within a few short miles of Scotland's largest city and seaport is the natural beauty of the loch country, the queen of which is Loch Lomond, largest of Britain's waters — and one of the prettiest. Glasgow too has its treasures; buildings, museums and art galleries which rank among the best in the world.

Glasgow Cathedral is the only complete medieval cathedral in Scotland

CAMERON LOCH LOMOND, WILDLIFE PARK, Strathclyde

Among the many creatures which roam the parkland here are bears, bison, yak and deer. Also in the park is a childrens' zoo, a water-fowl sanctuary and numerous leisure facilities. Cameron House (OACT) is a beautiful and historic family home that is particularly associated with the 18th-century novelist Tobias Smollett.

The main tour continues northwards, on the A82, SP 'Crianlarich', to Rossdhu House.

ROSSDHU HOUSE, Strathclyde

This charming Georgian mansion (not open) is the home of the chiefs of Clan Colquhoun. It was built near the loch-side site of the original 15th-century castle, and the grounds include a sweep of beach that is ideal for picnics and walks.

Continue on the A82, passing Loch Lomond on the right.

LOCH LOMOND, Strathclyde

Often described as the Queen of Scottish Lakes, Loch Lomond is the largest area of land-locked water in Britain and stretches some 23 miles from Ardlui in the north down to Balloch in the south. The tremendous beauty of the loch is enhanced by the many islands which are dotted across its southern waters. Five of the islands form part of the Loch Lomond National Nature Reserve.

Continue to Luss.

LUSS, Strathclyde

Luss is beautifully set at the mouth of Glen Luss and looks over a group of wooded islands towards the distinctive summit of 3,192ft Ben Lomond. Sir James Colquhoun built the church in 1875 in memory of his father, who drowned in the loch. In the churchyard is an ancient effigy of St Kessog, one of many missionary saints who lived in the Loch Lomond area during the 5th and 6th centuries, and an ancient stone font.

Continue north on the A82 turning left on to the A83 at Tarbet, then continue to Arrochar.

ARROCHAR, Strathclyde

This little touring and yachting centre is set at the head of Loch Long and makes a superb base from which to visit the rugged mountains and wooded expanses of the Argyll Forest Park. Away to the north-west is 2,891ft Ben Arthur, popularly known as the Cobbler from its Gaelic name An Gobaileach; and to the west, in the heart of Ardgarten Forest, is 2,580ft Brack.

Turn sharp left on to the A814, SP 'Helensburgh', to pass Loch Long.

LOCH LONG, Strathclyde
Stretching like a long, thin finger from the Clyde estuary up to Arrochar, this sea loch is increasingly popular with yachtsmen from Glasgow. The whole of its western shore is bounded by the huge Argyll Forest Park (see tour 75), which includes the line of hills known as Argyll's Bowling Green.

Continue along the A814 past Garelochhead.

GARELOCHHEAD, Strathclyde
Yachts and many other pleasure craft ply up and down Gare Loch during the holiday season, and large ships are frequently to be seen laid up in the loch's waters. Garelochhead itself is a well-known resort with a green back-drop bordered by the long ridges of Argyll's Bowling Green. Away to the east is a range of lonely hills whose highest point is 2,339ft Beinn Chaorach.

For a detour to the Rosneath Peninsula (adds 29 miles if Coulport is visited) turn right on to the B833, SP 'Kilcreggan'.

Inset: Loch Long, over 17 miles long and one of the deepest lochs in Scotland, is used for submarine trials

KILCREGGAN, Strathclyde
Situated at the tip of the Rosneath Peninsula, where many Clyde businessmen have their homes, Kilcreggan is linked by ferry to Gourock, across the Clyde estuary. The peninsula figures in Sir Walter Scott's novel *The Heart of Midlothian,* in which Knockderry Castle, 3 miles north-west of Kilcreggan, is called Knock Dunder. The road which runs round the tip of the Rosneath Peninsula ends at Coulport, which stands on the east shore of Loch Long and looks across to the Cowal Peninsula and Argyll Forest Park.

The main tour continues on the A814 Helensburgh road from Garelochhead to Rhu.

RHU, Strathclyde
A notorious smuggling centre during the 18th and 19th centuries, Rhu is now used by respectable yachtsmen. Henry Bell, who launched the pioneer Clyde steamboat *Comet* in 1812, is buried in the churchyard. Glenarn Gardens (OACT), on the outskirts

Helensburgh was developed on the lower Clyde in about 1776 by Sir James Colquhoun

of the village, contain a large variety of shrubs and are particularly notable for their remarkable collection of rhododendrons.

Continue along the A814 to Helensburgh.

HELENSBURGH, Strathclyde
The flywheel from the *Comet,* Europe's first steam-driven ship, along with an anvil used in its construction, are preserved in Helensburgh's Hermitage Park. Henry Bell, who designed and built the craft, is commemorated by an obelisk in the town. Another famous inventor, John Logie Baird, who pioneered television, was born here. Helensburgh is set in magnificent mountain scenery, and the road which leads northwards into Glen Fruin is particularly notable.

Continue on the A814 to Dumbarton.

DUMBARTON, Strathclyde
Dumbarton Rock, a magnificent 240ft crag rising above the confluence of the Rivers Leven and Clyde, has dominated Dumbarton's history since at least as early as the 5th century. It was at the centre of the independent kingdom of Strathclyde, and a royal castle stood on the rock until the Middle Ages. Little survives of the medieval castle, but considerable portions of the fortifications built during the 17th and 18th centuries still stand (AM). Preserved in the castle is a sundial presented to the town by Mary, Queen of Scots during her brief stay at the castle in 1548. One of the oldest buildings in the town is Glencairn House, which dates from 1623. Boat-building, which included the construction of the famous clipper *Cutty Sark,* was once the town's principal industry, but today Dumbarton is mainly concerned with the blending and bottling of whisky.

Leave on the A814 Glasgow road and in 2 miles turn right on to the A82. In 11 miles re-enter Glasgow along the Great Western Road.

THE COWAL PENINSULA

Bordered by the waters of Loch Fyne, the Firth of Clyde and the Kyles of Bute, the Cowal Peninsula is a natural holiday ground for nearby Glasgow. Yet despite its popularity, this wooded, hilly country retains a remoteness and wildness surprising for a place so near Scotland's largest city.

DUNOON, Strathclyde

By the terms of the charter of 1471 the Campbells had to pay a fee of 'one red rose when asked for' to the crown for the keepership of Dunoon Castle. Traces of the old 13th-century castle can be seen on Castle Hill above the pier where, in 1646, the Marquess of Argyll brought 200 prisoners and had them massacred and thrown into mass graves after a raid by the Campbells on Lamont territories. The present castle, Castle House, was built as a villa in 1822 for James Ewing, Provost of Glasgow, and is now used for municipal purposes. At the foot of Castle Hill is a statue of Burns' sweetheart, 'Highland Mary', who was born near Dunoon on the site of the farm at Auchnamore. Up until the beginning of the 19th century, when tourism became a fashion, Dunoon remained a quiet village, but now it is a thriving holiday resort. It boasts 2 fine bays which are popular with yachtsmen. At the end of August the Cowal Highland Gathering is staged in the town's sports stadium, after which the stirring March of a Thousand Pipers takes place in the streets.

Leave Dunoon on the A815 following the shoreline through Kirn to Hunter's Quay.

HUNTER'S QUAY, Strathclyde

Hunter's Quay, the headquarters of the Royal Clyde Yacht Club (the first to be founded in Scotland), stands at the entrance of Holy Loch. Its busiest time is in July when the Clyde Yachting Fortnight takes place. The name of this little resort comes from the Hunter family, of Hafton House, which stands north-west of the town. The loch is said to take its name from an incident which occurred during the building of Glasgow Cathedral. A ship loaded with earth from the Holy Land, which was to be laid beneath the foundations, became stranded here. Today the loch is used by the Polaris submarines.

Continue on the A815 into the village of Holy Loch and in 2 miles enter Sandbank.

SANDBANK, Strathclyde

Sandbank, set in beautiful countryside on the banks of Holy Loch, is a popular holiday resort. Several Americas Cup challengers

have been built in the shipyards in this little town and the tradition of boat-building here is a long and famous one.

Turn right, remaining on the A815 and in 1½ miles bear right. At the head of the loch cross the River Eachaig and enter Strath Eachaig, passing in 2 miles the entrance to the Younger Botanic Garden, which occupies the valley.

Right: Dunoon's pier, from which steam cruises can be taken to nearby waters

Below: the Kyles of Bute separate the Isle of Bute from the mainland

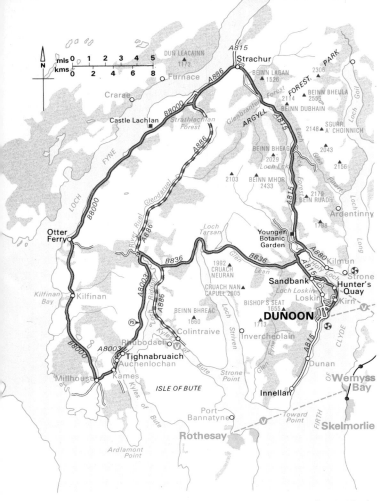

CASTLE LACHLAN, Strathclyde
Overlooking the waters of Loch Fyne this ruined tower is possibly part-12th or 13th-century, but dates mostly from the 16th century. It was destroyed after the defeat of the Scots at Culloden.

Continue along the shores of Loch Fyne to Otter Ferry.

OTTER FERRY, Strathclyde
Otter Ferry sits at the shoreward end of a mile-long sand spit, which stretches out into Loch Fyne. This little township takes its name from its position — oitr means sand spit in Gaelic. Across the loch rise the green rounded hills of Knapdale.

Turn left and continue through Kilfinan and in 6¼ miles, at Millhouse crossroads, turn sharp left. At the edge of Kames turn left. Shortly pass through Auchenlochan and in ¼ mile turn left on to the A8003 Glendaruel road. For the centre of Tighnabruaich keep forward on the B8000.

TIGHNABRUAICH, Strathclyde
Cruise steamers call at the pier here, which reaches out into the Kyles of Bute, the Isle of Bute being only half a mile away across the water. Tighnabruaich means house on the brea, and is a reminder of the days when one solitary house stood here. Nowadays Tighnabruaich is a popular little resort. Two miles away is the Tighnabruaich Wildlife Centre and Forest Trail. A feature here are the photo-safari hides which overlook a small lochan, where wild ducks, roe deer, Soay sheep and blue hare may be viewed.

Climb out of Tighnabruaich on the A8003 to pass high above the Kyles of Bute.

ISLE OF BUTE, Strathclyde
The Isle of Bute, a 15 mile-long island, dovetails into the cloven coastline of the Cowal Peninsula, from which it is separated by the beautiful stretches of water known as the Kyles of Bute. Where now a car ferry crosses from Colintraive on the mainland to Rhubodach on the island, cattle were made to swim in the days when there was no ferry. The northern half of the island is hilly, the south flatter and more fertile. The main town is Rothesay, a favourite resort, with sandy bays and the remains of a 13th-century castle (AM), surrounded by a deep moat. The fortress was destroyed by Cromwell in the 17th century. Also of interest is ruined St Mary's Chapel and the Bute Museum where the island's past is recorded.

Continue past the shores of Loch Riddon. Later descend to the River Ruel at the head of the Loch and in 1½ miles turn right on to the A886. In 1½ miles turn left on to the B836. For a detour to Colintraive (5¼ miles), where the car ferry leaves for Rhubadach on the Isle of Bute, continue on the A886. The main tour continues on the B836 passing round the head of Loch Striven, before skirting Loch Tarsan reservoir. After passing through Glen Lean return to Holy Loch and turn right on to the A815. At Sandbank turn left, returning along the Clyde shores through Hunter's Quay to Dunoon.

A short excursion can be made to Innellan by taking the A815 southwards out of Dunoon.

INNELLAN, Strathclyde
This Cowal Peninsula holiday resort has a climate so mild that palm trees grow in some of the gardens. A steamer pier links Innellan with Wemyss Bay across the Firth of Clyde, and there is also a fine view of Clyde shipping from here. Delightful villas, built on terraces at the turn of the century by wealthy Greenock merchants, enjoy the view. The road through Innellan continues past Toward Point and round to the remote settlement of Inverchaolain on the shores of Loch Striven. Ruined Castle Toward is passed before this last outpost of civilisation is reached, and shows a good 15th-century tower, 3 storeys high, backed by the 165ft-high Bishop's Seat.

Tighnabruaich — a small resort with a steamer pier facing the Isle of Bute

YOUNGER BOTANIC GARDEN, Strathclyde
An impressive avenue of 130ft-high sequoias leads from the entrance of the gardens to Benmore House, which is now used as an adventure centre for Glaswegian children. The trees were planted by James D. Duncan, a wealthy sugar refiner, who owned the Benmore estate in the latter half of the 19th-century, and planted some 6 million trees between 1870 and 1883. The last private owner, H. G. Younger of the Scottish brewing family, donated the gardens and woodlands (OACT) to the nation in 1928. It is now an annexe of the Royal Botanic Gardens, Edinburgh. Apart from conifers and hardwoods, the botanic gardens offer beautifully laid-out flower beds and shrubberies, and among the less usual plants is the Chilean fire bush. The Golden Gates at the rear of the park were originally made for the Great Exhibition of 1851, and were brought here by James Duncan.

ARGYLL FOREST PARK, Strathclyde
In 1935 the Argyll Forest Park was created, the first of its kind in Britain, 10 years before the Dower Report advocated the formation of the larger National Parks. It consists of large stretches of forest, mountain and moorland; some 60,000 acres in all. It is ideal country for the keen walker or rambler, and the astonishing variety of animals and plants can be appreciated by everyone. The tour takes in the southern part of the park between Dunoon and Loch Ech, known as Benmore Forest.

Continue on the A815 for 6½ miles with views to the left of Beinn Mhor (2,433ft) before entering Strachur.

STRACHUR, Strathclyde
Lying near the shores of Loch Fyne, which reaches a depth of some 600ft here, Strachur has become a small but popular resort. It was originally the seat of the McArthur Campbells, whose mansion, Strachur Park (not open), dates from about 1783. Nearby Argyll Forest Park provides Strachur with an important saw-milling and wood-working industry.

Turn left on to the A886, SP 'Colintraive', to follow the shores of Loch Fyne. Ater 3½ miles turn right on to the B8000 Otter Ferry road (a short cut, saving 19 miles, can be taken by continuing on the A886 through Glendaruel). Descending through Strathlachan, the road rejoins Loch Fyne with views of Castle Lachlan to the right.

GLENCOE AND THE PASS OF BRANDER

A corner of Scotland steeped in a history as wild and dramatic as the landscape in which it took place: Glencoe and the Pass of Brander — scenes of bloody warfare; Dunstaffnage Castle, where the Stone of Destiny first rested on Scottish soil; and from this century the subterranean power station beneath Ben Cruachan.

Oban, easily accessible by sea and land, is a busy fishing port and market town

OBAN, Strathclyde

Oban, situated at the centre of Scotland's western seaboard, is at the hub of the tourist industry. There are sea trips from the bustling harbour to the many nearby islands along the coast, such as Mull, Tiree, Coll, Barra and South Uist. The town has many hotels and guesthouses, for it is a beautiful and romantic place in its own right, looking over an almost landlocked bay and surrounded by hills and mountains in every direction. A strange relic of yesteryear stands on top of Oban Hill and dominates the townscape. This is Macaig's Folly. Macaig was a wealthy banker, who began building this Colosseum-like structure to help solve the local unemployment problem, and to provide a museum which would also serve as a memorial to his family. Unfortunately he died before its completion and the scheme was abandoned; today it remains an empty shell. The Corran Hall on the esplanade houses a museum and the country library, and is also the venue for much traditional dancing and music. Macdonald's Mill (OACT) houses an exhibiton called the Story of Spinning and Weaving, and demonstrations of this ancient craft are given on the premises. On the northern outskirts of Oban stands ruined Dunollie Castle (not open) which belonged to the MacDougalls, an ancient and powerful family who once owned as much as a third of Scotland.

Leave Oban on the A85, SP 'Connel' and 'Crianlarich', and continue to Taynuilt.

TAYNUILT, Strathclyde

This small resort lies at the point where the Pass of Brander meets Loch Etive, overlooked by the impressive and beautiful Ben Cruachan (3,689ft). Near Muckairn Church stands a large stone of unknown antiquity, re-erected here by workmen to commemorate Lord Nelson in 1805, the year of Trafalgar. It was the first of the many monuments to be raised in Nelson's honour all over Britain.

Remain on the Crianlarich road and enter the Pass of Brander, then continue alongside Loch Awe to Cruachan Power Station.

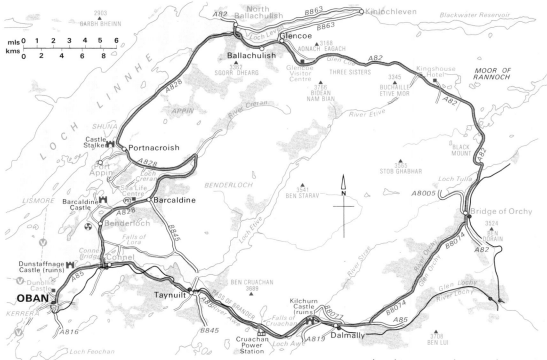

CRUACHAN POWER STATION, Strathclyde

Above the Pass of Brander towers 3,689ft-high Ben Cruachan. In the shoulder of the mountain lies the Corrie Reservoir and at its foot Loch Awe. During the day water from the Corrie drives the turbines of the power station (OACT) housed in a man-made cave the size of Coventry Cathedral 1,000ft beneath the mountain. At night water is pumped back up the mountain from Loch Awe, to replenish the head of water in the reservoir. Visitors are taken into the power station via a tunnel nearly a mile long, carved out of solid granite.

Continue on the A85 to the village of Lochawe. At the north-east extremity of Loch Awe is Kilchurn Castle.

KILCHURN CASTLE, Strathclyde

This was the seat of the Glenorchy Campbells and at one time stood on an island, but as Loch Awe has dropped its water level by 10ft, the castle (AM) is now surrounded by marshland instead. The keep is 15th century, 3 storeys high and surmounted by a parapet and wall-walk. The north and west extensions were added a century later. There are round towers at 3 corners of the courtyard with extensive lean-to buildings where the troops were housed. Strangely, there is only one entrance to the castle, and to reach the courtyard the soldiers had to tramp through the kitchen.

The tour enters the Strath of Orchy to reach Dalmally.

DALMALLY, Strathclyde

Dalmally is a pleasant place scattered over the floor of a wooded valley, where the River Orchy flows into Loch Awe. The large hotel here, formerly an ancient inn, is particularly popular with anglers, who come here for the excellent sport provided by the river, the loch, and the many streams hereabouts. Opposite the hotel is a strangely-twisted stone known as Bruce's Stone. Bruce passed through the village twice; once in 1306 after his defeat at Methven, and again in 1308 before his victory at the Pass of Brander.

In 2¼ miles turn left on to the B8074 and follow a single track road through Glen Orchy. After 10 miles turn left on to the A82 for Bridge of Orchy. Beyond the village pass Loch Tulla and climb on to the Moor of Rannoch.

MOOR OF RANNOCH, Strathclyde & Tayside

Famous as the largest moor in Scotland, the Moor of Rannoch is an exhilaratingly desolate area of some 60 square miles of bog, moor, lochans and mountains. A railway crosses the moor, and as the peat over which it travels is often boggy and up to 20ft deep, the line used to be supported on brushwood. The north-east corner of the moor is a Nature Reserve, where several rare species of bog flora grow, and a patient observer may be rewarded by the sight of red deer or a lone golden eagle.

The menacing crags that tower up above Glencoe provide some of the most famous rock and ice climbs in Britain

Beyond the Moor of Rannoch the tour enters the Pass of Glencoe.

GLENCOE, Highland

Both history and magnificent scenery have made Glencoe one of the most celebrated glens in Scotland. It drops some 10 miles from the Moor of Rannoch to the saltwater Loch Leven, a total descent of about 1,100ft. Great rocky mountains rise on either side — Bidean nam Bian (3,766ft) is the highest summit in Argyll. Some 14,500 acres of the countryside are now owned by the National Trust for Scotland, but this does not include the lower part of the valley where the notorious massacre of the Macdonalds occurred in 1692. After the Jacobite Rising of 1689, William III pardoned all clan chiefs, provided they signed an oath of allegiance by January 1692. Maclean of Glencoe was prevented from signing by his old rivals the Campbells. As a result soldiers under Campbell of Glenlyons were billeted on the MacDonalds as a punishment. They were entertained and fed for 12 days during this, an exceptionally hard winter. However on the 12th day, under government orders, the Campbell soldiers rose and slew

men, women and children without warning. Some escaped only to perish on the freezing hillsides. A monument in the form of a tall Celtic cross beside the Bridge of Coe at Carnoch commemorates the dead chief and his people. Close to the site of the massacre is a Visitor Centre, which provides a Ranger Naturalist Service. In the main street of Glencoe itself is the Glencoe and North Lorn Folk Museum (OACT) housed in 2 heather-thatched cottages, which displays Macdonald relics, local domestic and agricultural exhibits, Jacobite relics, costumes and embroidery.

Gradually descend through the Glen to the edge of Glencoe village and follow the shoreline of Loch Leven past Ballachulish.

BALLACHULISH, Highland

This scattered village at the sea entrance to Loch Leven was the scene of a notorious murder trial known as the Appin murder case. A granite memorial near the new bridge over the loch marks the spot where James Stewart of the Glen was wrongly hanged for the shooting of Colin Roy Campbell of Glenure — 11 of the jury were Campbells. The identity of the true murderer was never discovered. Slate used to be quarried nearby, and Ballachulish is mainly composed of stone quarrymen's cottages.

In 1 ¾ miles, at the roundabout, take the A828, SP 'Oban', and pass beneath the Ballachulish Bridge. Continue southwards and follow Loch Linnhe to reach Portnacroish.

PORTNACROISH, Strathclyde

This little community at the western edge of the Strath of Appin takes its name from the episcopal Church of St Cross. Upon a wooded rise nearby stands a monument commemmorating the Battle of Stalc between the 1st Stewart of Appin and a Campbell, MacDougall and Macfarlane alliance. The Stewart's victory here avenged the murder of his father, slain at his second wedding. The battle was fought in 1468, and the Hollow of Treachery, close by, is where the slaughter took place.

Opposite Portnacroish is Castle Stalker.

CASTLE STALKER, Strathclyde

Artists and photographers delight in recording the image of this strong and tall rectangular keep stood upon its tiny rock at the mouth of Loch Laich. It dates from the 15th century, although the upper parts were altered in 1631. It has 9ft-thick walls, is 4 storeys high, and is topped by a parapet and a wall-walk. The basement is vaulted, and there is a dungeon reached only by a trap door at the foot of the stairway. The castle (OACT) was erected by Duncan Stewart the 2nd of Appin, later made Chamberlain of the Isles by James IV, who used it as a hunting lodge.

Continue on the A828 around Loch Creran to Barcaldine.

BARCALDINE, Strathclyde

South-west of the hamlet is the Sea Life Centre, where the largest collection of marine life in Britain is kept on display in a way designed to enable a greater understanding of the underwater world. Further along the shores of

Loch Creran is Barcaldine Castle. (open by appointment). This baronial-style 16th-century castle, commanding magnificent views over Loch Cleran to Glencoe, was built by Duncan Campbell of Glenorchy. It remained in that family's hands until 1842 when it was sold. It was later bought back, roofless, and restored by the family between 1896 and 1910, and is still lived in to this day. It is an L-shaped tower-house of 3 storeys, with a stair tower and 4 angle-towers at the corners.

Remain on the A828 to Benderloch, then in 2½ miles cross Loch Etive by the Connel Bridge and at the A85 turn left. 1½ miles farther, across Dunstaffnage Bay (right), stands Dunstaffnage Castle.

DUNSTAFFNAGE CASTLE, Strathclyde

Almost islanded on its high promontory, Dunstaffnage (AM) stands in an excellent strategic position at the mouth of Loch Etive. This was the first resting place on Scottish soil of the Stone of Destiny when it first arrived from Ireland. In the 9th century the stone was removed to Scone, where kings of Scotland were crowned on it for many years. Robert the Bruce took the castle after his victory over the MacDougall clan at the Pass of Brander in 1308, and it was given to the Campbells. In the 15th century Alexander II had the castle enlarged in preparation for his attack on the Norsemen occupying the Hebrides. Flora MacDonald was held captive here in 1746, but the castle has not been lived in since 1810, when it was destroyed in a fire.

Continue on the A85 for the return to Oban.

Ben Cruachan rises up behind Loch Etive — a narrow sea loch stretching from the Firth of Lorne to the foot of Glen Etive

BRAEMAR, Grampian

The royal and ancient Highland Games for which Braemar is most famous are held in early September every year. Tradition has it that the originator of the Gathering was King Malcolm Canmore, who ruled much of Scotland at the time of the Norman invasion. He called the clans to the Braes of Mar so that he might 'by keen and fair contest, select his hardier soldiers and fleetest messengers'. Visitors, often including the Queen and other members of the Royal Family, come from all over the world to listen to the piping and to watch the athletic events, which culminate in tossing the caber. Braemar itself is a pretty little place, with a number of guest houses and hotels. One of these, the Invercauld Arms, stands on the spot where, in 1715, the Standard was raised which marked the beginning of the blood-thirsty futile Jacobite rebellions. Opposite the Invercauld Galleries is the house where Robert Louis Stevenson wrote *Treasure Island* in 1881. Braemar Castle (OACT) was originally built by the Earl of Mar in 1628, but after the Jacobite Rising of 1715 it became a barracks for English troops, who were moved here in an attempt to keep the Highlanders in check. During the latter part of the 18th century the castle was strengthened and extended.

Leave on the A93 Perth road and proceed along Glen Clunie, gradually ascending to the Cairnwell Pass.

CAIRNWELL PASS, Tayside & Grampian

The summit of this awe-inspiring pass reaches to 2,199ft, making it the highest classified road in Britain. Glenshee, of which the Cairnwell Pass forms part, has been one of the most important mountain passes in Scotland since as early as Roman times. The Glenshee Chairlift, to the west of the pass, runs to the summit of the 3,059ft Cairnwell Mountain.

Continue down Glen Beag to Spittal of Glenshee.

SPITTAL OF GLENSHEE, Tayside

Until recently no more than a scattered community in the wild heart of the Grampian Mountains, Spittal of Glenshee is now a flourishing ski-centre, complete with hotel, ski-school and ski-hire shop. Its peculiar name is derived from the hospital that once stood here and provided shelter for travellers in the remote Highlands.

Continue on the A93, following Glen Shee for 5¼ miles, then turn sharp left on to the B951, SP 'Kirriemuir, Glenisla'. Shortly cross the Shee Water and in ¼ mile, at Cray, bear right. In 2½ miles bear right again into Glen Isla. In 4 miles enter Kirkton of Glenisla.

THE GRAMPIAN MOUNTAINS

Beautiful Highland scenery greets the traveller at every turn in the glens and mountains of Grampian. At Balmoral the Royal Family spend their holidays and every year thousands follow suit — to see the Highland Games and Pipers at Braemar, to ski, to walk, to climb and to admire.

Left: Glen Isla, 20 miles long, forms a natural route into the lonely Grampians

KIRKTON OF GLENISLA, Tayside

Exceptional Highland scenery stretches many miles north of this attractive village. Nearly 12,000 acres are covered by the plantations of the Braes of Angus Forest, which was established in 1945. Boating and other water sports can be enjoyed on the Blackwater Reservoir, 3 miles east of the village. Glen Isla itself runs northwards through increasingly splendid countryside towards Caenlochan Forest, parts of which are the National Nature Reserve.

Continue on the B951 and in 1½ miles leave the glen to enter the Melgam Water valley, Shortly pass the Loch of Lintrathen, and 3½ miles farther enter Kirkton of Kingoldrum. Continue on the B951 and in 3 miles turn left on to the A926 and shortly sharp right to enter Kirriemuir.

KIRRIEMUIR, Tayside

Peter Pan's creator, Sir James Barrie, was born in Kirriemuir in 1860. In his novels he called the town Thrums, and in the suburb of Southmuir is the cottage in which Barrie described *A Window in Thrums*. His birthplace, 9 Brechin Road, is a modest 2-storey cottage that has been transformed into a museum (NTS) containing original manuscripts, momentoes and some of the original furnishings. In a pavilion behind the cemetery of New Church, where Barrie is buried, is a camera obscura (OACT), which gives panoramic views of the surrounding scenery.

Leave on the B957, SP 'Brechin', and after 5½ miles cross the River South Esk to reach Tannadice. In 1½ miles turn left on to the A94. In 5½ miles turn right on to the A935, SP 'Brechin', for Brechin.

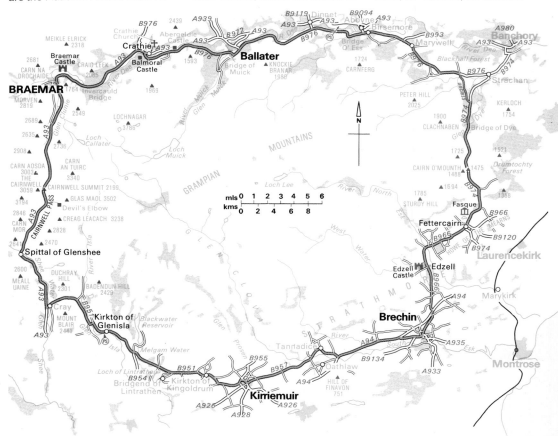

The modern Gathering, held in Braemar's Princess Royal Park, dates from 1832

Leave on the B974 Strachan Banchory road. After 4 miles the road starts the long climb (1 in 5 in places, with hairpin bends) to the summit which, at 1,475ft, is a fine viewpoint. Descend towards Deeside and later cross the Bridge of Dye (1680). In 2 miles, at AA Box 753, turn left, SP 'Aboyne'. After 2¼ miles turn left on to the B976, rejoining the Dee valley after 6 miles. In 3 miles, at Birsemore, keep forward, SP 'Ballater', and continue for 11¼ miles to the edge of Ballater.

BALLATER, Grampian
Ballater was not established until 1770, when a Farquharson laird decided to cater for the tide of people who came to try the mineral wells discovered at Pannanich, 2 miles south-east. Although the wells no longer flourish, the town is still a popular holiday centre. There are numerous sporting facilities in the area, and the Ballater Highland Games are a highlight every August.

At the edge of the town keep forward on the B976, SP 'Balmoral', and in ½ mile bear right to cross the River Muick, SP 'Breamar'. In 5½ miles pass (right) Abergeldie Castle (not open), residence of King Edward VII whilst Prince of Wales. In 2 miles pass the entrance to Balmoral Castle.

BALMORAL CASTLE & CRATHIE CHURCH, Grampian
Queen Victoria spent her first holiday at Balmoral in 1848, and instantly fell in love with the house and its surroundings. Prince Albert purchased the estate in 1852 and immediately set about transforming the original castle into a large Scottish baronial-style mansion. Today Balmoral remains the much-loved holiday home of the Royal Family. Although the castle is not open to the public, the grounds are open for several months during the summer. Crathie Church stands across the Dee from Balmoral, and is the church used by the Royal Family when they are staying at the castle. Queen Victoria laid the foundation stone of the present church in 1895, and it contains several memorials to members of the Royal Family. In the churchyard is a monument to John Brown, Queen Victoria's famous servant.

After crossing the River Dee turn left at the edge of Crathie on to the A93. Follow the north bank of the Dee, passing through more pine forests with fine views of the most eastern Cairngorm Mountains. Later recross the River Dee at Invercauld Bridge and after 2¼ miles pass the entrance (right) to Braemar Castle (see Braemar) before the return to Braemar.

watchtower and as a place of refuge during periods of danger and unrest. Near the church is 18th-century Brechin Castle (not open), the seat of the Earl of Dalhousie, which stands on the site of a very much earlier fortification.

Leave on the B996, SP 'Aberdeen'. In 2 miles turn right on to the A94, then in ¼ mile turn left on to the B966. In 3½ miles enter Edzell.

EDZELL, Tayside
Set on the River North Esk in the fertile Howe of Mearns, Edzell is a neat little village whose origins go back to the 16th century, but which was largely rebuilt in 1839. Edzell Castle (AM), lying a mile west of the village, was once said to be the finest castle in Angus. Its oldest part is the 16th-century tower house, to which a large quadrangular mansion was added a few years later. In 1602 Sir David Lindsay, Lord Edzell, added the castle's most famous feature, the extraordinary walled garden. The wall itself is unique in Britain, being decorated with a wealth of heraldic and symbolic motifs.

Continue on the B966 to Fettercairn.

FETTERCAIRN, Grampian
In 1861 Queen Victoria and Prince Albert paid an incognito visit to Fettercairn, and 3 years later the imposing turreted arch which forms an entrance to the village was built to commemorate the occasion. In the picturesque little square is part of the town cross from the ancient town and royal residence of Kincardine. Of Kincardine itself nothing survives except the neglected churchyard of a small chapel. North of the village is Fasque, a large mansion (OACT) which has been the home of the Gladstone family since 1829. The contents of the house reflect the lives of the family, who included William Gladstone, 4 times Prime Minister of Britain.

BRECHIN, Tayside
Many buildings of local red sandstone give the old streets of this town a pleasing and harmonious character. A background of green hills rising towards the eastern Grampians, and the sparkling waters of the River South Esk, add to the charm of the setting. Brechin Cathedral, which now serves only as the parish church as it is no longer the

The interior of J. M. Barrie's birthplace in Kirriemuir has been refurbished as a museum to his life and work

bishop's seat, was originally built in about 1170, but was entirely restored from 1900 onwards. The 87ft-high round tower (AM) attached to the church is Brechin's greatest treasure. Thought to date from the 10th or 11th century, it has functioned both as a

BANCHORY TO HUNTLY

From wooded Deeside the route crosses the valley of the River Don, then over the Correen Hills and along the River Bogie to the magnificent castle at Huntly, formerly known as the Palace of Strathbogie. The return journey takes in Craigievar Castle, the loveliest and most perfectly-preserved of Scotland's castles.

BANCHORY, Grampian
Banchory is a popular and well-favoured holiday town built of silvery granite and surrounded by forests of pine. The arrival of the railway brought new prosperity to Banchory and encouraged a great deal of new building in what had been little more than a village. Its history, however, stretches back to the 5th century, when St Ternan founded a monastery here on the banks of the Dee. The oldest part of the town, Kirkton, is at the east end. Here can be found the old churchyard of St Ternan's, although the church has long since disappeared. A 2-storeyed circular morthouse, built to guard against body snatchers, stands in the churchyard. Banchory has 3 parks and also boasts a most unusual local industry — a lavender farm and lavender-water distillery (OACT). Banchory Museum, in the Council Chamber, has an exhibition of local history and bygones.

Leave Banchory on the A93 Aberdeen road and in ½ mile turn left on to the A980. In 2¼ miles turn left, skirting the Hill of Fare (1,545ft), to reach Torphins.

TORPHINS, Grampian
Torphins is a substantial little residential town which now quietly thrives on the tourist industry. Large, granite Learny House (not open) was built in 1898 by Colonel Francis Innes, and down a nearby side street is a row of old almshouses which the Colonel's father converted into a single residence for himself. A small entrance tower built as a porch and decorated with the Innes arms, has been added to it since.

Turn right on to the B993 and in 3½ miles, at the junction with the B9119, turn left then right. In 4½ miles turn left on to the A944 Alford road. In 1¾ miles turn right to rejoin the B993. After 3¼ miles turn left to enter Monymusk.

MONYMUSK, Grampian
The great attraction in this village is the church. In 1170 the Earl of Mar built a priory here, but after the Reformation the priory chapel was turned into the parish church. This handsome building has a great square crenellated tower at one end, and is built of pinkish granite with facings of Kildrummy sandstone.

Continue through the village and in 1 mile, at the crossroads, turn right, SP 'Chapel of Garioch', then cross the River Don and in ¼ mile turn left. In ¼ mile turn left again, SP 'Keig via Lord's Throat'. Follow this road for 6¼ miles, later climbing through the My Lord's Throat Pass, then turn right on to the B992. In 4 miles pass through Auchleven, then in 2¼ miles turn right on to the B9002. Go over a level-crossing then immediately turn left on to the B992 to enter Insch.

INSCH, Grampian
Now a large village, with a fine parish church at its centre dating from 1883, Insch was a burgh of barony in the 16th century. A lonely gable supporting an empty belfry in the churchyard is all that remains of the original church. At the base of the gable is an ancient stone marked with Pictish symbols and a small wheel cross, possibly even earlier than the date 1199 accredited to it.

Pass the telephone box and turn left into Western Road. Shortly pass beneath Dunideer Castle.

DUNIDEER CASTLE, Grampian
The ruins of Dunideer Castle (not open) perched on an isolated conical hill 876ft high are an impressive landmark. They consist of a great wall with a rough arch in the middle and the remaining gable of a rectangular keep measuring 220ft by 90ft. Forming an outer ring around the castle are the remains of an Iron-Age vitrified fort — so called because the stones have been converted into a vitreous substance through the action of fire. This in turn is enclosed by a multiple earthwork, the origins of which are unknown.

The cattle bred in Scotland are said to produce the finest beef in the world

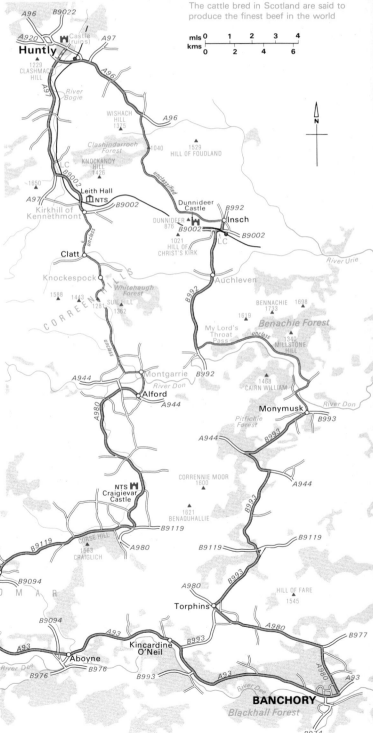

At the junction with the A96, turn left, SP 'Huntly'. Continue for a further 4¾ miles, at the roundabout, take the 3rd exit for Huntly town centre.

HUNTLY, Grampian

This pleasant little market town is built on an 18th-century grid-iron pattern, based on 2 long, narrow, straight streets which intersect at the market place. From here Castle Street leads beneath the arch of the Gordon Schools — founded in 1839, and built on the site of the castle gate-towers — to the wooded drive of the magnificent castle (AM). This grew from a Norman fortress to a 17th-century Renaissance palace under the ownership of the powerful Gordons. After 1752 the family seat was moved to Gordon Castle, and Huntly was abandoned to fall into decay. Huntly Museum in the square displays exhibits of local historical interest.

Leave on the A97, SP 'Rhynie', following the road southwards through Strathbogie. After 6 miles turn left on to the B9002 and in 1¾ miles pass (left) the entrance to Leith Hall.

Craigievar Castle, which fortunately never saw action, represents the zenith of traditional Scottish architecture

LEITH HALL, Grampian

James Leith, a member of a wealthy land-owning and shipping family, bought land here, and in 1649 his son laid the foundations of Leith Hall House (NTS) — a rectangular block, 4 storeys high and just one room deep. Domestic offices and stables were built in later years, and 50 years after their completion a new suite was added, which doubled the size of the house. A final wing, completely enclosing the courtyard, was added in 1868. The treasures within are not spectacular, but they chart the fortunes of a typical Scottish laird's family, including relics and keepsakes connected with Bonnie Prince Charlie, the Peninsula War, the Crimea, and the Indian Mutiny. In the grounds is a rock garden.

In ¾ mile, at the end of Kirkhill of Kennethmont, turn right, SP 'Clatt'. In 2 miles enter Clatt.

CLATT, Grampian

The name of this little village is derived from 'cleith', which means concealed. This it is, for it hides away in the Gadie valley beneath the Correen Hills of the Garioch. The church is a plain building of 1799, rough-plastered, narrow and long. Within is a small, laird's gallery and an old stone font.

Keep forward on the Knockespock road and in ½ mile bear right. Beyond Knockespock climb to cross the Correen Hills. In 4 miles turn left to reach Montgarrie. Here turn right then cross the River Don and continue to Alford.

ALFORD, Grampian

A thriving little town, Alford is the centre of a prosperous agricultural area where cattle markets are held and the local people come in from the country to meet. A hill west of the town was the scene of a famous victory by Montrose, supporter of Charles I, over Convenantor General Baillie in 1645. In Haughton Park is the Alford Valley Railway — 1½ miles of narrow-gauge are laid out through nature trails in delightful countryside.

Turn right on to the A944 and in 1 mile keep forward on to the A980. After 5½ miles pass the entrance to Craigievar Castle.

CRAIGIEVAR CASTLE, Grampian

This isolated, romantic castle, set in a green, hilly countryside and surrounded by tall, mature trees, is one of Scotland's most picturesque buildings (NTS). The L-shaped tower house, built in 1626 by William Forbes, a wealthy Aberdeen merchant, rises up 7 storeys, smooth-walled and clean-lined, to a fairytale skyline of turrets. It has hardly altered since the day building was completed, and the magnificent plaster ceilings, the work of London craftsmen, remain intact. One of the bedrooms, called the 'Queen's' bedroom, has a most elaborate plaster ceiling and a splendid canopied bed. The great hall, overlooked by a charming minstrels' gallery, has a grand fireplace surmounted by an immense armorial tablet of the Royal Arms.

In 2½ miles turn right on to the B9119, skirting the base of Corse Hill. In 3 miles the road starts to descend into Tarland.

TARLAND, Grampian

Tarland, lying in the middle of the Howe of Cromar, is an ancient market town where herds of pedigree cattle — Aberdeen Angus, British Friesian, Highland and Galloway — and valuable flocks of sheep, are bought and sold. Alastrean House, formerly the House of Cromar, passed from the Marquess of Aberdeen to the MacRobert family in 1934. Two sons of the family died fighting with the RAF in World War II, and in 1943 Lady MacRobert gave the house to the RAF as a guest and rest house for RAF officers.

Continue on the B9119 for 3 miles then turn left at the crossroads, remaining on the B9119. At Dinnet, on Deeside, turn left on to the A93 and follow the river to Aboyne.

ABOYNE, Grampian

In 1650, Charles Gordon, 1st Earl of Aboyne, was granted a charter to build a burgh of barony close to Aboyne Castle (not open) and so began the history of this popular Deeside resort. Actually named Charlestown of Aboyne, the scattered village is grouped about a green, where the famous Aboyne Highland Games are held. Old Scots pines still grow in the built-up areas, creating a most pleasant shopping centre.

Continue along the A93 to Kincardine O'Neil.

KINCARDINE O'NEIL, Grampian

This was once an important place, for here the Cairn-O'-Mount road, the main highway between Strathmore and Moray, crossed the River Dee. Thomas the Durval built a wooden bridge here in the 13th century, and before then there was a pass and a ferry. His son erected a church and a hospice for wayfarers; the church remains, roofless, standing among the old table-top tombs of the graveyard. In the 18th century the churchyard was used as a market place, the tombs serving as stalls. The present church dates from 1865.

The final stretch back to Banchory runs alongside the river and through pleasant pine woods.

THE ROCKY NORTH SEA COAST

Many of the villages on this tour were founded by enlightened landlords of the 18th and 19th centuries in an attempt to encourage new industry and better the lot of their tenants. Inland, weaving was introduced, and on the coast harbours were built. The neat, tidy towns and villages remain, but the cottage looms have gone and North Sea oil dominates the area's future.

FRASERBURGH, Grampian
Alexander Fraser, 7th Laird of Philorth, was granted a charter in 1546 which enabled him to build a harbour and from this grew Fraserburgh. The old town huddles around the harbour complex, with all its attendant warehousing, boatbuilding, fish processing, cold storage and other maritime industries. On Kinnaird Head overlooking the town stands a 16th-century castle. The massive whitewashed keep has walls 6ft thick, and is 4 storeys high — the roof has been made flat and the caphouse for the turnpike stair converted into a lighthouse. About 50yds away stands an original tower known as the Wine Tower. Its purpose is unknown, but it has 2 storeys connected only by a trapdoor and dates from c 1560.

Follow the A98 Inverness road for ¾ mile then turn right on to the B9031, SP 'Rosehearty'.

ROSEHEARTY, Grampian
Rosehearty, a sturdily-built fishing village, stands on old Aberdeenshire's northern-most point. It was allegedly founded in the 14th-century by shipwrecked Danes. The streets are regularly set out with brightly-painted cottages. The oldest building here is the Dower House of Pitsligo, which dates from 1573 and now stands, sadly, as a roofless shell.

Continue on the B9031, SP 'New Aberdour'. In 2½ miles turn left on to the B9032, SP 'Rathen'. In 1½ miles, at the crossroads, turn right on to the A98 then in ¼ mile turn left on to an unclassified road, SP 'Strichen'. In 4¼ miles turn right on to the A981 for Strichen.

STRICHEN, Grampian
Lord Strichen of Session laid out this little plain stone town in 1766, in an attempt to provide better housing and employment for his tenants: today it is a thriving community. A stream, crossed by several little bridges, flows along one side of the village.

At the far end of Strichen turn right, SP 'New Deer', pass under a bridge, then branch left on to an unclassified road, SP 'Old Deer'. After 4 miles turn left on to the A950, then 1¾ miles further turn right on to the B9030, SP 'Auchnagatt', to enter Old Deer.

Right: traditional fishing boats in the harbour at Peterhead

Below: Pitmedden Gardens had fallen into ruins until acquired by the NTS in 1952 who recreated them exactly as they would have been in the 17th century

OLD DEER, Grampian
This small village lying in the wooded valley of the South Water of the Agie was an important ecclesiastical centre long ago. Its history begins in AD520, when St Dristan, a Pict, established a monastery beside the river. By the end of the 12th century this first foundation dwindled, and the buildings became ruined. However, in 1218 William Comyn founded a new Cistercian abbey (AM) on the opposite banks of the River Agie, which became the administrative centre of the area. The ruins which remain of this latter community comprise the church, cloister, kitchen, refectory, warming room, abbot's house and infirmary.

Continue on the B9030 to Stuartfield.

STUARTFIELD, Grampian
In 1772 John Burnett, Laird of Crichie, created this village and named it in honour of his grandfather, Captain John Stuart. At this time landowners were

becoming increasingly aware of their tenants welfare and it was built specifically as a weaving community — each house possessing its own loom.

Continue on the B9030 and at the end of the village bear right. At Auchnagatt turn right on to the A948, then cross the bridge and turn left on to an unclassified road (no SP). In 2 miles keep forward on the Methlick road and in 3½ miles turn left on to the B922 to Methlick.

METHLICK, Grampian
Methlick has rather grander buildings than most of its neighbours, and among these are the Beaton public hall of 1908, and the fine Gothic parish church with gabled clock tower, which stands on its own green.

Continue on the B9170 Old Meldrum road. After 2¾ miles turn left on to the B999, SP 'Tarves'. 1¾ miles farther, at a crossroads, turn left to reach Tarves.

TARVES, Grampian
Set on a slight ridge, Tarves is centred around what used to be a small green, but is now covered with tarmac. At one end stand the old church and a war memorial cross. In the church is the tomb of the Forbes family, which William Forbes built in 1589; it is a splendid Gothic piece with Renaissance trimmings. Arched recesses contain beautiful carved figures of William and his wife — enlightened and popular people who endowed a poorhouse for paupers in the village.

Continue on the B999 passing a road (right) to Tolquhon Castle.

TOLQUHON CASTLE, Grampian
In a remote position in a pleasantly-wooded dell stands handsome Tolquhon (AM), a courtyard castle that was originally just a single keep, built by the Prestons of Craigmillar in the 13th century. The castle passed to the Forbes family by marriage in 1420. In 1584-9 William Forbes had architect Thomas Leiper build the large quadrangular mansion and gatehouse seen today. It has inner and outer courts with both circular and square towers; one of them, Preston Tower, was built in the 15th century by the 1st Forbes Laird, Sir John.

Return to the B999, cross over the A920, and pass (right) the entrance to Pitmedden Gardens.

PITMEDDEN GARDENS, Grampian
Here are the magnificent formal gardens first laid out by Sir Alexander Seton, who inherited Pitmedden (NTS) in 1675. They are laid out on 2 levels — to the north an upper garden with terraces and to the south the Great Garden. This consists of 4 parterres; 2 are replicas of designs known to have existed in Charles I's garden in 1647. The parterres are separated by lawns and yew and box hedges, and each garden has a fountain.

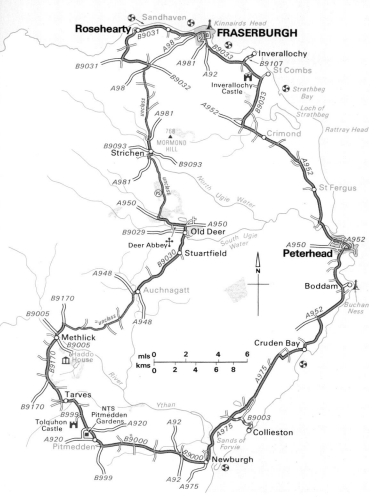

Continue on the A975, SP 'Cruden Bay'. In 3½ miles (right) is the B9003 leading to Collieston.

COLLIESTON, Grampian

Picturesque Collieston perches upon clifftops around a deep rocky bay known as St Catherine's Dub; so called because in 1594 a Flemish galleon, called the *St Catherine,* was wrecked here. The indented coastline with its many caves made Collieston as popular with smugglers in the past as it is with holidaymakers today.

Continue north on the A975 to Cruden Bay.

CRUDEN BAY, Grampian

A small town and its fishing harbour, Port Errol, lie in a bay with 2 miles of sands flanked by links, which have helped to make Cruden Bay a renowned golfing centre. The 19th Earl of Errol created the harbour in the 19th century to take advantage of the fishing grounds and coastal trade along the coast. Today, the pleasant fishermen's cottages make delightful holiday homes, and the golf course is as popular as ever.

Continue on the A975 Peterhead road. After 2¾ miles turn right on to the A952 and then in 2½ miles pass the B9108 (right) leading to Boddam.

BODDAM, Grampian

Buchan Ness is the most easterly point of the Scottish mainland, and by it stands the pink granite village of Boddam, overlooking its large double harbour. It is a fishing port, though not as prosperous as it once was, and has a large school and a 130ft-tall lighthouse which was built by Robert Stevenson in 1827.

Continue on the A952 to Peterhead.

PETERHEAD, Grampian

George Keith, 5th Earl of Marishal, founded Peterhead in 1593 with 56 inhabitants. Since then the town has prospered to become a sizeable place clustered around the harbour. For a while at the end of the 18th century, it was a popular spa town, but this was short lived and when the whaling industry was in full swing Peterhead became Scotland's whaling 'capital'. When this declined the herring boom followed, now replaced by more modern fish-processing plants. Peterhead's latest main concern is oil, and a huge harbour has been built to accommodate North Sea oil vessels. The Arbuthnot Museum and Art Gallery (OACT) specialises in local exhibits, especially those connected with the fishing industry.

Leave Peterhead on the A952, SP 'Fraserburgh', to pass through Saint Fergus and Crimond. 1½ miles beyond Crimond turn right on to the B9033, SP 'St Combs'. After 3¼ miles turn left, SP 'Fraserburgh', then 1½ miles farther pass the B9107 (right) leading to Inverallochy.

INVERALLOCHY, Grampian

This is a small, typical fishing village with close-set rows of cottages packed gable-end towards the narrow streets. There is no harbour — the boats were landed on a shingly beach — and now the fishermen work out of Fraserburgh. Inverallochy Castle is a crumbling ruin (not open), consisting of a lofty tower and remnants of a curtain wall 30ft high. It was an important stronghold of the notorious Comyn family.

Continue on the B9033 and then the A92 for the return to Fraserburgh.

From Pitmedden village continue on the B999 Aberdeen road, then in ½ mile turn left on to the B9000, SP 'Newburgh'. In 5 miles turn right on to the A92 then turn left to rejoin the B9000 for Newburgh.

NEWBURGH, Grampian

A large village and once a busy fishing port, Newburgh stands at the mouth of the Ythan estuary — the largest on the Aberdeen coast. Although the river which flows through it is not much more than a stream, when the tide is in the waterway stretches 700 yards across.

View from Boddam Lighthouse of the coast to the south of Peterhead

ELGIN, Grampian

Set in a richly fertile agricultural district known for hundreds of years as the Garden of Moray, Elgin stands on the meandering loops of the River Lossie and retains many of its fine old 18th- and 19th-century buildings. Its greatest treasure is the ruined cathedral (AM), founded by Andrew, Bishop of Moray in 1224, which stands today as one of the most beautiful ecclesiastical buildings in Scotland. Despite centuries of neglect and vandalism a great deal of 13th-century work survives in the cathedral, notably in the choir. The Panns Gate, or East Gate, is the only surviving gate from the cathedral precincts, and a wing of the 16th-century Bishop's House (AM) still stands. Other notable buildings in the town include St Giles Church, a classical structure dating from 1828, the Greyfriars Chapel, which incorporates fragments from an abbey founded by Alexander II. The town museum displays collections of fossils and prehistoric artefacts. At the west end of the town is Lady Hill, crowned by a 19th-century statue to the Duke of Gordon.

Leave Elgin on the A941, SP 'Lossiemouth'.

BETWEEN THE MORAY FIRTH AND STRATH SPEY

Castles and cathedrals, beaches and bays, an enigmatic monument made by the ancient Scots, and one of the most beautiful bridges in Britain are all encountered on this tour through the forests and valleys of the old county of Morayshire.

LOSSIEMOUTH, Grampian

Long, sandy beaches and a host of recreational facilities make this prosperous fishing village popular with holidaymakers. James Ramsay MacDonald, Britain's first Labour Prime Minister, was born here in 1866. Fascinating caves and rocks may be found 2 miles west at Covesea, where there is also a lighthouse.

From the seafront follow the B9040, SP 'Hopeman, Burghhead'. After 5½ miles, for a detour to Duffus, take the B9012 on the left.

The pleasant, open countryside around Craigellachie is characterised by large conifer plantations. Ben Aigan rises to 1,544ft in the distance

DUFFUS, Grampian

A couple of miles south-east of Duffus is one of the finest examples of a motte-and-bailey castle (AM) in Scotland. Its earthen mound is surmounted by the remains of a 14th-century tower which eventually collapsed because the mound could not support its massive weight. Nearly 8 acres are enclosed by the castle's precinct ditch. Duffus Church (AM) retains the base of a 14th-century tower, a vaulted 16th-century porch and a number of interesting tomb-stones. Also of the 14th-century is the village's tall parish cross (AM).

The main tour continues on the B9040 to Hopeman. Continue on the B9012 and after 1½ miles, a turning (right) leads to Burghead.

BURGHEAD, Grampian

This busy little port stands on a headland still protected by the ramparts of an ancient hill fort. Within the fortifications is the so-called Roman Well (AM), which is neither Roman nor a well. It is a rock-cut chamber approached down a flight of steps at the bottom of which is a cistern surrounded by a ledge. The structure is unique and is thought to be an early Christian baptistry. Burghead's museum has displays which illustrate the archaeology of the Laich of Moray. An extremely ancient ceremony called Burning the Clavie is enacted in the village on 11 January, the old New Year's Day. A lighted tar barrel is first paraded round the burgh, then cast from the top of Dourie Hill to ward off evil spirits.

The main tour continues on the A9089 Forres road to Kinloss. The B9011 (right) leads to Findhorn.

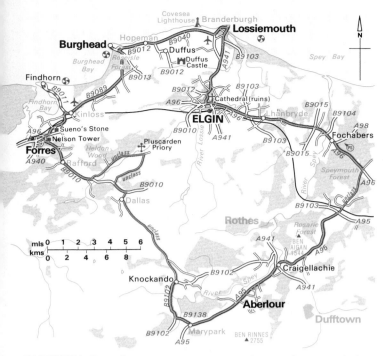

FINDHORN, Grampian

Findhorn Bay was formed by the River Findhorn as it tried to find a way through the drifting expanses of the Culbin Sands. Formerly the largest area of dunes in Britain, much of Culbin Sands was stabilised and afforested by the Forestry Commission between 1922 and 1966. Beyond the forest is The Bar, where marshes and dunes combine to form a haven for myriads of birds and a great variety of wild flowers. The village is a popular seaside resort, ideal for bathing and fishing. Findhorn is world-famous for the Findhorn Foundation, which was begun in 1962 as a community devoted to bringing fertility to the barren sands by spiritual methods. It has now grown into a highly successful and efficient enterprise, complete with pottery, weaving, candle-making shops and a printer.

The main tour continues on the B9011 to Sueno's Stone.

SUENO'S STONE, Grampian

One of the most remarkable monuments (AM) of its kind in Europe, this slender, 20ft-high sandstone pillar is sculpted on all 4 of its faces. On one of the 2 broad sides is a tall cross surrounded by elaborately carved figures, and on the other are groups of figures depicting hunting and fighting scenes. The stone possibly commemorates victory of Sueno, son of the King of Denmark, over Malcolm III, which would date the stone at 1008.

Turn right on to the A96 to enter Forres.

FORRES, Grampian

Beautiful Highland scenery surrounds this ancient royal burgh. The town's royal connections can be traced back to the 10th century, and it is especially associated with characters immortalised in Shakespeare's play *Macbeth*. King Duncan held his court at Forres in the early 11th century, and it was here that Macbeth and Banquo were confronted by the 3 'weird sisters'. The town's standing as a royal residence was brought to an untimely end when the Wolf of Badenoch burned it in 1390. Today Forres is a quiet little town, with only a castle mound to serve as a tangible reminder of its famous past. It is marked by a tall granite memorial to Dr Thomson, who died in the Crimean War tending the wounded. In the Falconer Museum is a splendid collection of fossils, many of them recovered from Culbin Sands. Nelson Tower, built on Cluny Hill in 1806 to commemorate Lord Nelson, serves as a splendid viewpoint from which to enjoy the lovely countryside along the River Findhorn.

Leave Forres on the B9010, SP 'Dallas'. After 4½ miles branch left, SP 'Elgin', to reach Pluscarden Priory.

PLUSCARDEN PRIORY, Grampian

Overlooked from the north by the dark mass of Monaughty Forest, Pluscarden Priory stands beside the Black Burn. Originally founded by King Alexander II in 1230, the priory was deserted from 1560 to 1948, when it was re-colonised by monks from Prinknash Abbey near Gloucester. Through the labour of the monks and many charitable gifts, the priory has been restored and is now the hub of a thriving community. Visitors — who are made very welcome — enter the priory through a door in the 13th-century tower and can see ancient wall-paintings, modern stained glass, and the lovely Lady Chapel, which has been preserved almost intact.

A window depicting the Visitation in the public chapel of Pluscarden Priory

Continue towards Elgin then after ¼ mile, at the church, turn right. After 3¼ miles turn left to rejoin the B9010, then in 1 mile turn right, SP 'Knockando', to reach Dallas. At the end of the village turn left and cross the River Lossie. The scenery becomes increasingly wild and desolate on the long run down to Knockando.

KNOCKANDO, Grampian

The church here has an internal gallery, and ancient carved slabs can be seen in the churchyard. To the south, beyond the beautiful Spey valley, is the 2,755ft peak of Ben Rinnes. Elchies Forest, to the north of the village, covers some 3,500 acres and forms the main mass of Craigellachie Forest.

Turn right on to the B9102, SP 'Grantown'. After 3 miles turn left on to the B9138, SP 'Marypark'. Cross the River Spey, then at Marypark turn left on to the A95 and later enter Aberlour.

ABERLOUR, Grampian

Correctly named Charlestown of Aberlour, from its founder Charles Grant of Aberlour, this long village was planned in 1812 and retains its pleasing uniformity of style. A footpath leads from the village to a pretty footbridge over the Spey. Many riverside, woodland and hill walks start from the village, which is also a noted salmon angling centre.

Continue to Craigellachie.

CRAIGELLACHIE, Grampian

Thomas Telford's graceful bridge over the Spey lends distinction to this lovely village. It was built in 1812 at the foot of a precipitious crag called Craigellachie Rock. Part of the crag had to be blasted away to make an approach road to the bridge, which is a single iron span with twin stone towers at either end. The bridge survived devastating floods in 1829, but the southern bank was swept away.

Continue on the A95 Keith road and after 6½ miles, at a crossroads, go forward on to an unclassified road. After 3¾ miles turn left on to the A96 to reach Fochabers.

FOCHABERS, Grampian

In 1798 Fochabers was built in its present position after the original village had been demolished so that Gordon Castle could be enlarged. Much of the castle itself, which stands to the north and was once one of the biggest buildings in Scotland, has now been demolished. Speymouth Forest stretches away to the east, and has several car parks, picnic sites and forest walks. Some of the pine trees on the hills above Fochabers were planted over 200 years ago by the Dukes of Gordon.

Continue on the A96 Inverness road and pass through Lhanbryde before returning to Elgin.

CAPITAL OF THE HIGHLANDS

Between Loch Ness and the cold North Sea lies Inverness, now dubbed Capital of the Highlands. South and east is a land of high mountains and deep glens, glamorous ski-resorts and bleak battlefields — among them Culloden, where Bonnie Prince Charlie was finally defeated.

The house on Culloden Moor that is reputed to have been used by the Duke of Cumberland during Culloden

INVERNESS, Highland

King David I proclaimed Inverness a royal burgh in the 12th century, and it is he who first built a stone keep on Castle Hill. The present castle was built in 1834, and is now a courthouse and administrative centre (Inverness is the headquarters of the Highland Region). Within is an exhibition illustrating the history of the Gael, a Highland craft shop and an information centre. A statue of Flora MacDonald stands on the castle esplanade. Erected in 1899, it looks towards the hiding place where she hid Bonnie Prince Charlie after his defeat in 1746. Little of the old town which huddled under David's royal castle is left, and the town centre is a new development of the 1960s. Reminders of the past do remain, such as Abertarff House, the headquarters of the National Trust for Scotland. This dates from 1593 and has a rare turnpike stair — a medieval spiral staircase. The Tolboothe Steeple in Church Street, built in 1791, is where dangerous criminals were kept. St Andrew's Cathedral, with its fine carved columns, is also worth a visit. Inverness, a city of much greenery and many trees, sits astride the River Ness which flows between tree-lined banks and deserves the title Capital of the Highlands.

Leave on the A9 Perth road then shortly turn left, SP 'Croy', on to the B9006 to reach Culloden Moor.

CULLODEN MOOR, Highland

Upon this field (NTS) on 16 April, 1746 the Jacobite cause was finally quelled and the English finally conquered the Scots. The Jacobite army had retreated from England and returned to the Highlands, where the English army, under the Duke of Cumberland, caught up with them. The night before the battle Bonnie Prince Charlie had attempted a surprise attack on the English, but before they were within 2 miles of the camp the English sounded the alert — they had been discovered. They returned to Culloden House where they were billeted, only to find Cumberland hot on their heels and ready for battle the next morning. After the Jacobite's crushing defeat, Cumberland took no prisoners and gave no quarter; the wounded were murdered, prisoners shot, retreating Jacobites chased and cut down. This, and the reign of terror created by Cumberland in the aftermath, earned him the nickname 'Butcher' Cumberland. Prince Charles escaped, eventually to France, but his followers were persecuted to destruction. Today the battlefield is marked by a cairn erected in 1881 which stands 20ft high. Old Leanach Cottage, which survived the battle that had raged around it, is now a museum, housing a display of historical maps and relics of the battle; other features of the field are pointed out here, and a topographical battle plan shows how the battle was fought. There is also a Trust Visitor Centre with a museum and an exhibition.

¼ mile beyond the Visitor Centre turn right, SP 'Clava Cairns'. At the next crossroads the road ahead leads to Clava Cairns and Standing Stones (AM) dated at 1800-1500 BC. The Cairns were originally domed and used as burial chambers, and are among the most complete in Scotland. The main tour continues on the B851 Daviot road. After 3¾ miles turn left on to the A9, SP 'Perth'. In 9 miles an unclassified road (right) leads to Tomatin.

TOMATIN, Highland

This Strath Dearn village is situated on the River Findhorn, which has its source in the lonely wilderness of the Monadhliath range of mountains, to the south-west. The district has many distilleries, the peaty streams providing water ideal for the brewing of whisky. The streams and rivers also attract large numbers of anglers, for whom Tomatin caters admirably. The village was once a royal hunting ground belonging to Inverness Castle.

Later pass Slochd Mor (1,332ft) and 3½ miles farther branch left on to the A938, SP 'Grantown', to reach Carrbridge.

CARRBRIDGE, Highland

Carrbridge is a popular skiing resort in the Cairngorms, and here the tourist season is a long one — skiing in the winter, fishing and touring in the summer — so there are several hotels and guesthouses. The Landmark Visitor Centre here provides a superb introduction to the area. A multi-screen slide show tells, in sound and vision, the story of the Highlands from the last Ice Age to the present day, and in the evenings film shows are given, often about natural hisory. Also to

be found here is a craft and book shop, a nature trail and an open-air sculpture park, the whole complex beautifully set in delightful countryside beside a small lochan.

Continue on the A938 and after 1¾ miles turn left on to the B9007, SP 'Forres'. After 6¾ miles turn right, SP 'Lochindorb', to reach Lochindorb Castle.

LOCHINDORB CASTLE, Highland

The ruins of Lochinbord Castle lie on a small island in a loch of the same name, 969ft above sea level, in the middle of desolate Dava Moor. The castle was a hunting seat for the powerful Comyns, and was occupied for 3 months by Edward I in 1303 during his Scottish campaign. During the latter half of the 14th century it became a stronghold of the Wolf of Badenoch, who terrorised the surrounding countryside, and is notorious for his burning of Elgin Cathedral in 1390. The castle was destroyed during the reign of James II.

Continue along the unclassified road and after 3¼ miles turn left on to the A939, then turn right on to the A940 to reach Forres.

FORRES, Grampian

This is the ancient burgh where King Duncan held court and, in Shakespeare's play Macbeth, the place to which Macbeth and Banquo were travelling when they met the 3 'weird sisters'. See also tour 80.

Continue on the A96 Inverness road to Brodie.

BRODIE, Grampian

The land belongs to the Brodie of Brodie, whose family is one of the oldest untitled families in Britain, and has owned the lands here since the 11th century. It is

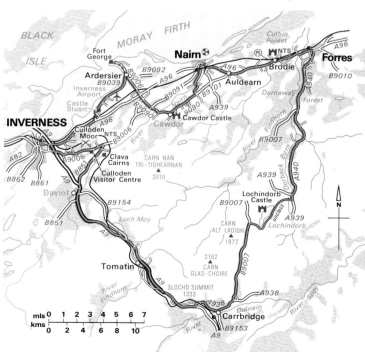

Inverness's Victorian castle occupies the same strategic site as its predecessor

Scottish courtesy to call the head of the family simply 'Brodie'. The castle (NTS), which stands north of the village dates from the 15th century with 16th-century additions. It was burnt down in 1645 by Lord Gordon on behalf of Montrose during the campaign for Charles I. However, some parts survived and were rebuilt, then added to again in 1840. There is a magnificent private collection of Dutch, Flemish and English paintings in the castle.

Continue on the A96 Inverness road to Auldearn.

AULDEARN, Highland
Auldearn is chiefly remembered for a battle fought here in 1645 between Montrose, for Charles I, and the Covenanters. Montrose defeated the enemy, who outnumbered his force 2 to 1, by what is considered his most brilliant tactical display. A royal castle once stood here, but now all that overlooks the battlefield is the peaceful 17th-century Doocot of Broath (NTS) — a circular dovecot which must have housed a considerable number of birds within its superb masonry.

Continue on the A96 to Nairn.

NAIRN, Highland
Nairn is a popular resort on the Moray Firth, sometimes referred to as the Brighton of the North. It is easy to see what has made this town so popular, with its surprisingly dry and sunny climate, splendidly wooded countryside and dramatic river valleys around it. There are also fine sands with good bathing and 3 golf courses. The harbour was built to plans by Thomas Telford in 1820, but has since been enlarged.

Leave on the B9090, SP 'Cawdor', and after 2¾ miles turn right to reach Cawdor Castle.

CAWDOR CASTLE, Highland
A great castle (OACT) dominates the little village of Cawdor gathered at its feet. The tower keep of the castle dates from 1454, although there is some stone work which dates back to 1386. This once stood on its own, surrounded by a dry ditch and entered by a drawbridge and portcullis. The tower is 4-storeys high with turrets at each corner. In the 16th century a curtain wall and extra living space was added, and in the 17th century the north and west wings were enlarged, giving the castle the shape and form seen today. It was inhabited by the Thanes of Cawdor until 1510, and then by the Campbells of Cawdor until the 1745 uprising.

Continue on the B9090 and after 1¼ miles turn right, SP 'Inverness'. After ¾ mile, at a crossroads, go forward, SP 'Ardersier', and after 3½ miles reach Ardersier.

ARDERSIER, Highland
Known as Ardersier, the village is often called Campbelltown because these lands were acquired by the Campbells of Cawdor in 1574. A charter of 1623 enabled them to erect a burgh of barony called Campbelltown, which was to have a weekly market. The Campbells intended great things for their burgh, but it never became more than a village. It had a small fishing industry, and for a long time was a charming, quiet fishing village. However, in recent years the oil industry has changed all that, and Ardersier is widely known as the base for the construction at Whiteness Head of huge platforms for the oil fields under the North Sea.

Continue on the B9006 to Fort George.

The old kitchen, complete with its original utensils, at Cawdor Castle

FORT GEORGE, Highland
Considered to be the finest example of late artillery fortification in Europe, Fort George (OACT) was built to replace an earlier fort of the same name which had been blown up by the Jacobites in 1746. The architect was Robert Adam, and the irregular polygonal shape was erected between 1748-63 at a cost of £160,000. It covers 12 acres, and stands on a narrow spit of land where Inner and Outer Loch Moray meet. Today the fort is garrisoned by the Queen's Own Highlanders, but the Regimental Museum and some parts of the fort are open to the public, and is rather more pleasant than the grim exterior might suggest.

The main tour continues from Ardersier on the B9039 and passes, after 4 miles, Castle Stuart. In ¾ mile turn right on to the A96 for the return to Inverness.

LOCHCARRON, Highland

Perhaps the most pleasant village in all of Wester Ross, Lochcarron lies scattered along 4 or 5 miles of road; bright, neat houses with bright, neat gardens look over the loch towards the ranks of mountains beyond. The part of the village by the old harbour is called Slumbay, which means Safe Bay, a name harking back to the days when hundreds of boats would shelter in Loch Carron when herring were plentiful. The main part of the village, known as Jeantown, grew up in the 19th century, although the commercial herring fishing died away by the turn of the century. This beautifully-placed village has several guest houses and shops, and is a delightful, quiet place for those who enjoy boating and fishing and walking.

Leave Lochcarron on the A896, SP 'Applecross and Shieldaig'. Ascend on to higher ground and later descend to the shore of Loch Kishorn. In 1½ miles turn left, SP 'Applecross'. Cross the mountains via the 'Pass of the Cattle', a fine viewpoint at 2,053ft, and descend to Applecross.

APPLECROSS, Highland

Applecross is one of the most inaccessible places in Scotland and can only be reached by a tortuous road which zig-zags up from sea-level to 2,054ft. St Maelrhuba founded one of the earliest Christian churches in the north here. He came here in 673 from Ireland, and went about his missionary work throughout the Applecross Peninsula until his death in 722. The saint is said to have been buried in the old churchyard some 1,000 years before the present church was built and the people of Applecross used to carry a pinch of soil taken from near his grave as a safeguard on long or dangerous journeys. Applecross was also a place of sanctuary for fugitives hundreds of years after the saint's death. The church was delapidated for many years until the West Highland School of Adventure had it completely restored to act as a chapel for the school, which is based at the former shooting-lodge of Harefield. The main part of the village lies on the east side of the bay, and was built by crofters at a time when, inland, the estates were being made into deer parks where wealthy landlords could shoot deer. It is little more than a line of houses called The Street, overlooking the sea.

Leave on the unclassified Shieldaig road, and follow the coast through remote, rugged country with views across the Inner Sound to the islands of Skye, Raasay and Rona. Beyond Fearnmore the tour turns eastwards alongside Loch Torridon. On reaching the A896 turn left for Shieldaig.

THE APPLECROSS PENINSULA

Shaped like a fish's tail, the peninsula has a unique beauty — one of strong bare rock and wide skies. There are no fences or apparent restrictions, and the fishing and crofting hamlets of this sparsely populated region seem to belong to another, less hurried age.

Above: Shieldaig village between the loch and high mountain of the same name

Right: Loch Torridon

SHIELDAIG, Highland

A bright, tidy village which looks westward over the bay of Loch Shieldaig towards the lofty hills of North Applecross. The village was created solely for the purpose of encouraging young men to settle here as fishermen and provide a steady supply of manpower for the Royal Navy, if and when needed. Official grants were provided for boat-building, there were guaranteed prices set for the fish caught, duty-free salt was supplied for the curing of the fish, and plenty of land was provided for the tenants on which to build and grow food. Perhaps most important of all, a new road was constructed, giving Shieldaig access to the outside world. The people prospered for many years, until the estates passed to the Duchess of Leeds, who had no interest in her tenants and seemed to consider them less important than sheep. Poverty came to Shieldaig when all their special privileges were stripped away. By the 1860s only one boat remained and the villagers were so poor that they could not operate it.

Follow the Torridon road to Annat.

ANNAT, Highland

This scattered settlement is approached along a pleasant road above which lie unexpected banks of rhododendrons and pine trees. There are old houses here with sheep pens beside the rocky seashore, and the strips of cultivated land beside the road are tended much as they have been since the days when these crofts were self-sufficient.

Continue on the A896 and after 1 mile (left) is the road for Torridon.

TORRIDON, Highland

'Glen Torridon, its loch and the mountains on either side exhibit more beauty than any other district of Scotland, including Skye'. So said W. H. Murray in his assessment of the Highland landscape, which he made for the National Trust for Scotland in 1961. The mouth of the great sea loch of Torridon faces the north-east of Skye, and as it progresses inland it splits into upper Loch Torridon and Loch Shieldaig. At the north end rise red sandstone mountains, some capped with white quartzite, which make an unforgettable sight when caught in the rays of sunset. One of these is Liathach (3,456ft) and beneath its precipitous scree slopes is Torridon village, which stands at the head of the loch. The sandstone from which this impressive range is sculpted is 750 million years old. Some 16,000 acres of the Torridon area is owned by the National Trust for Scotland and apart from its splendidly rugged scenery, which is of especial interest to geologists, it is also valued for its wildlife. Here live the red and roe deer, mountain goats, the rare golden eagle, the mountain hare and the wildcat. Near Torridon village is a Trust Visitor Centre, where there is a red deer museum and an audio-visual presentation of local wildlife.

Leave Torridon on the A896 Kinlochewe road, and follow Glen Torridon. Later skirt the Beinn Eighe Nature Reserve.

BEINN EIGHE NATURE RESERVE, Highland

Established in 1951, the first National Nature Reserve to be declared in Britain, Beinn Eighe Nature Reserve covers over 10,000 acres, and includes the woodlands of Coille na Gas-Leitire, Kinlochewe Forest and 3,309ft Ben Eighe. Coille na Gas-Leitire — meaning Wood on Grey Slopes — is a remnant of the Caledonian Forest which at one time spread right across the Highlands. These woods are used as a study area for the re-establishment of the ancient woodlands, and, of course, are an important haven for wildlife. Pine marten, wild cat, otter, fox, deer, golden eagle, buzzard and falcon all live here, although some of them are rarely glimpsed.

Continue to Kinlochewe.

KINLOCHEWE, Highland

This small, scattered village lies at the head of beautiful Loch Maree, dominated by the mountain of Slioch, the 'spear', which rises 3,217ft. There is a hotel here which is a splendid base for those who

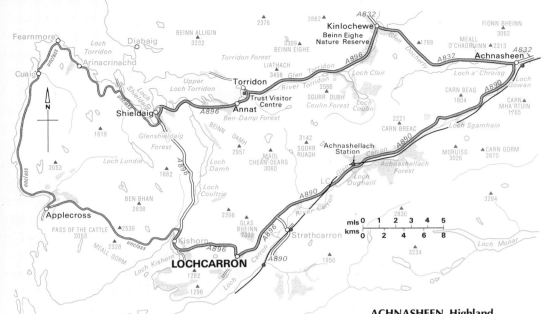

enjoy magnificent mountain scenery, hill-walking, climbing or fishing — the latter is excellent, with sea trout, brown trout and salmon being the best catches.

Turn right on to the A832, SP 'Achnasheen'. The tour then follows Glen Docherty and later runs alongside Loch a'Chrosg to reach Achnasheen.

ACHNASHEEN, Highland
Achnasheen lies between Strath Bran and Glen Carron, dominated to the north by the 3,060ft granite peak of Fionn Bhein. It is a little hamlet in which the hotel is actually part of the old railway

station. The area roundabout is used in the production of hydro-electricity.

Leave on the A890, SP 'Kyle of Lochalsh'. Cross open moorland then pass Lochs Gowan and Sgamhain. Enter the Achnashellach Forest and follow the River Carron before reaching Achnashellach railway station.

ACHNASHELLACH STATION, Highland
Behind Achnashellach railway station a track follows the River Lair to a narrow gorge where the river crashes over waterfalls. Beyond, the track leads to Coire Lair, where the river's source lies. To go further (8 miles) follow the footpath to Lochs Coulin and Clair and so to Glen Torridon. This walk is exceptional — the views from Coulin Woods to Beinn Eighe and Liathall, their feet reflected in the lochs, is not to be missed, for the countryside is the finest in Wester Ross.

Continue on the A890 then keep forward on to the A896 for the return to Lochcarron.

IN WESTER ROSS

This is the gentler corner of Wester Ross where Loch Maree, dotted with pine-clad islands, the sandy bays of Gairloch and the unexpected lushness of Inverewe Gardens soften the harsh landscape of the Torridon rocks that are millions of years old.

Above: beautiful Loch Maree above which soars the 3,217ft snow-speckled mass of Ben Slioch

Left: the River Dromas and the Falls of Measach in Corrieshalloch Gorge

GAIRLOCH, Highland

This village resort on Loch Gairloch has distant views of the Outer Hebrides and the bay provides good fishing and bathing from sandy beaches; boating facilities are also available. Gairloch was once a fishing hamlet dependent on the sea for its livelihood, and fish are still landed here; big salmon in the morning, and in the evening, the little fleet brings home catches of whitefish, prawns, lobsters and crabs. Freshwater trout can be had in the several lochs within easy walking distance of the village. There are hotels and guesthouses here to cater for the visitor, as well as a 9-hole golf course — unusual in this part of north-west Scotland. The most imposing building here is Flowerdale House (not open), an 18th-century mansion which stands between the hotel and the pier. It was once the seat of the Mackenzies of Gairloch.

Leave Gairloch on the A832 Kinlochewe road and follow the River Kerry past the Gairloch Dam and through Slattadale Forest to the shore of Loch Maree.

LOCH MAREE, Highland

This is the largest entirely natural loch in Scotland, for Loch Maree has not yet been dammed or altered in the interests of hydro-electricity. The loch has great visual impact, nearly always viewed as a sweeping whole, a primeval landscape of sombre colours, water, wind and rock. There were great forests hereabouts of ancient oak, but these were destroyed when charcoal burners from the south, banned by Elizabeth I from felling trees in England, came north in search of fuel for their primitive iron-foundries which used local bog-iron to fulfil the demand for metal for canons and firearms. The loch has many wooded islands, among these the Isle of Maree, made famous by Saint Maelrubha who set up his cell here in the 7th century. The island is associated with Druids, as well as Celtic Christianity, and the Druids sacred oaks still grow beside the Christians' holy holly trees. Special powers connected with this place were said to cure lunacy. Salmon and trout are highly prized in this loch, and the whole area is a valuable refuge for wildlife, including black-throated and red-throated divers and golden eagles. At Anancaun there is a Field Station in which there is an Information Centre where a pamphlet can be obtained describing a nature trail taking one hour, which serves as a splendid introduction to the wildlife of Loch Maree.

Beyond Loch Maree pass through Kinlochewe and continue to Achnasheen (see tour 82) then follow Strath Bran to reach Gorstan. Here turn left on to the A835 Ullapool road. Later pass the shores of Loch Glascarnoch.

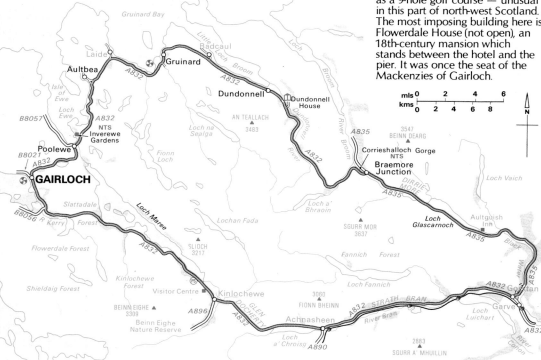

mls	0		2		4		6
kms	0	2	4	6	8		

LOCH GLASCARNOCH, Highland
This is a 'new' loch created by the Scottish Hydro-Electric Board as part of their Conon valley scheme. The waters are held back by a 2,670ft-long, 92ft-high dam. A tunnel carries the water 5 miles, dropping 550ft, to Mossford Power Station on Loch Luichart.

Continue along the A835 to Braemore Junction.

BRAEMORE JUNCTION, Highland
The junction is between the Dundonell and Ullapool roads which converge on their way to Inverness. The breathtaking mountain scenery is typical of the route; to the north-east rise the vertical cliffs of 3,041ft Seana Bhraigh between the forests of Inverlach and Freevater. Southwards brood the remote Fannich Mountains, among them 3,673ft Sgurr Mor, overlooking cold, glassy Loch Fannich.

Turn left on to the A832, SP 'Gairloch', and shortly pass the entrance to Corrieshalloch Gorge.

CORRIESHALLOCH GORGE, Highland
Over countless years water has tumbled into this 200ft box canyon, gradually wearing down the hard metamorphic rocks to create this spectacular and dramatic gorge (NTS). The river itself plunges in a long white plume 150ft over the Falls of Measach. In the crags and crannies in the walls of the canyon grow flora of the Highlands, elsewhere made scarce by the introduction of sheep, which eat it, and the extensive burning during the last century. Five species of fern grow here among plants with charming names such as hairgrass, mountain sorrel, woodmillet, goat willow and bird cherry. Below the falls is a suspension bridge with a viewing platform. The bridge was built by Sir John Fowler (1817-98), joint designer of the Forth Railway Bridge.

The A832 climbs on to higher ground and later follows the Dundonnell River. To visit Dundonnell House turn right on to an unclassified road and cross over the river.

DUNDONNELL HOUSE, Highland
The gardens (OACT) of this 18th-century house are particularly fine. Numerous rare plants and shrubs can be seen, with Chinese and Japanese varieties predominating. There is also a colourful collection of exotic birds in the gardens.

The main tour continues on the A832 to Dundonnell.

DUNDONNELL, Highland
The road to Dundonnell is known as 'destitution road', for it was built as a relief scheme, giving employment to crofters who were suffering terrible hardship as a result of the potato famine in 1847. Dundonnell itself is a climbing centre which lies at the head of Little Loch Broom, in the comparatively lush valley of Strath Beg; above tower the peaks of 3,484ft An Teallach. The name of this bleak mountain means The Forge, and refers to the smokelike mists which seem to perpetually shroud its peak.

Continue alongside Little Loch Broom before rounding a headland to reach Gruinard.

GRUINARD, Highland
The scenery here, is, as often is the case in the Highlands, the outstanding feature. Stattic Point and Rumore Promontory reach with long arms to virtually enclose the islanded bay, and a long strip of golden sand arcs alongside the shore, closely followed by the road. From Gruinard Hill there are views of An Teallach, Ben More Coigeach, and towards the horizon the hills of Sutherland. Gruinard Island has a rather sad story. During World War II scientists came here to experiment with germ warfare; the result is that the island is infected with anthrax and landing on it is prohibited.

Continue along the coast to the hamlet of Laide. Here turn inland and later rejoin the coast again near the outskirts of Aultbea.

AULTBEA, Highlands
Aultbea stands on the shores of Loch Ewe, a safe anchorage used extensively during both world wars by the Home Fleet. It was because of this that Sir Winston Churchill visited Aultbea in his capacity as 1st Lord of the Admiralty in 1939. Today the loch is being further developed by NATO (North Atlantic Treaty Organisation).
Aultbea itself is a small crofting village, sheltered to some extent by the Isle of Ewe opposite. Today the inhabitants are wage earners, but in the past their croftlands — cultivated strips salvaged by back-breaking labour from this most hostile of landscapes — had to support entire communities with only a little fishing to supplement the family income. Today income is boosted by another kind of catch — tourists.

Remain on the Gairloch road alongside Loch Ewe. In nearly 6 miles pass the entrance to Inverewe Gardens.

INVEREWE GARDENS, Highland
This is a truly unexpected delight, a magnificent garden (NTS) of 24 acres in which some 2,500 species of plants, trees and shrubs grow — some of them sub-tropical — on a Highland headland. When Osgood Mackenzie inherited the estate in 1861, this headland of Torridon sandstone had no more growing on its peat hags than some heather, crowberry and 2 dwarf willows. He began planting in 1865, first Corsican and Scots pines to act as a windshield, then gradually as these trees grew, he planted others in their shelter, as well as an astonishing variety of plants. Soil was carried manually in creels — large baskets — to provide a topsoil. Today, through his careful planning and experimentation, the gardens nurture, in subtly-designed surroundings, plants from such far-flung countries as Japan, Tasmania, Chile and South Africa.

Continue into the village of Poolewe.

POOLEWE, Highland
Situated at the head of Loch Ewe, Poolewe is a centre for the excellent salmon and trout fishing to be had in the loch and river. There are 2 hotels to cater for visitors, as well as camping and caravan sites. Stunning views down the entire length of Loch Maree are much photographed and very memorable.

At Poolewe turn inland and pass through rugged country before the return to Gairloch.

Gruinard Bay is a popular feeding ground for many rare birds

LAIRG, Highland

Many of the roads which cross the wild landscapes of the far north-west of Scotland converge at this little village. It is a thriving community with shops, and a market that is particularly busy during the lamb sales. Anglers come here to take advantage of the fishing on Loch Shin, which stretches away to the north-west. At certain times of the year salmon can be seen leaping through a narrow gorge at the spectacular Falls of Shin, 5 miles south of Lairg.

Leave Lairg on the A836, SP 'Tongue'. After 9 miles enter the North Dalchork Forest, then pass the Crask Inn and follow Strath Vagastie to Altnaharra.

ALTNAHARRA, Highland

This angling resort, which consists of little more than a hotel and a cluster of houses, is situated in Strath Naver at the western tip of Loch Naver. It is overlooked from the south by the great mass of Ben Klibreck, whose highest peak reaches 3,154ft. Until the early 19th century, over 1,000 people made their livings on the fertile lands alongside Loch Naver. They were forced to leave their homes during the infamous land 'clearances', when landlords evicted their tenants to free their land for sheep farming and deer hunting, which they found to be more profitable. The homeless peasants settled on the desolate coast where they could eke a meagre living from the sea. The tumbled ruins of their villages can still be seen, as can remains left by earlier builders. Near Klibreck Farm, at the south-west end of the loch, are prehistoric hut circles and a Celtic cross, and further along the loch are the remains of a broch (an ancient stone tower)

AN ANGLER'S PARADISE

This land at the northernmost tip of our island is a fisherman's dream, with numerous lochs and fast-flowing rivers offering some of the best sport in the country. Great mountains of stark, bare rock, deep valleys and cold lochs create an almost lunar landscape — the work of the great glaciers of the last Ice Age.

Kyle of Durness is one of the 3 sea lochs that split the northernmost tip of Scotland into 3 great headlands

known as Dun Creagach. A lovely but narrow road runs north-west from Altnaharra passing lonely Loch na Meadie and reaching Strath More near its junction with Glen Golly.

The main tour continues along the Tongue road through more barren country to reach the shore of Loch Loyal. Beyond the loch there is a short climb on to higher ground before the descent towards the Kyle of Tongue. On reaching the A838 turn left for Tongue.

TONGUE, Highland

Tongue is set beside the sandy shores of the large sea loch called the Kyle of Tongue. On the headland, where the little Allt an Rhian stream enters the kyle, are the ruins of Castle Varrich. This is thought to have been the fortress of an 11th-century Norse king and later became a Mackay stronghold. The kyle was bridged to the north of Tongue in recent years, by means of a causeway, saving a long detour round the head of the loch. During the 1745 Rebellion the naval ship *HMS Hazard* was captured by Jacobites, who renamed it the *Prince Charles,* and loaded it with supplies and money. The vessel was pursued by navy

ships and eventually ran ashore in the Kyle of Tongue. Prince Charles sent a large force to retrieve his lost cash, but both money and men were captured. To the south of Tongue is the mighty granite peak of 2,504ft Ben Loyal, from whose summit there are dramatic views of large areas of northern Scotland.

Leave on the A838 Durness road and cross the Kyle of Tongue by a causeway. After 8½ miles the tour runs alongside Loch Eriboll before reaching Eriboll.

ERIBOLL, Highland

Wild and beautiful Loch Eriboll stretches far into the mountains of north-west Scotland, and the tiny cluster of houses that is Eriboll village clings to the hillside on its eastern side. King Haco of Norway anchored his fleet here in 1263, and was frightened and dismayed by the eclipse of the sun which occured while he was there. The loch was a point of assembly for allied warships during World War II. Seals can sometimes be seen feeding in Loch Hope, which lies to the east of Eriboll.

Continue around Loch Eriboll and after 14 miles pass (right) the footpath to Smoo Cave.

SMOO CAVE, Highland

One of the most dramatic natural features in northern Scotland, Smoo Cave, is approached from a clifftop path which begins near the little settlement of Lerinmore. Its entrance is over 30ft high and 130ft wide, and the main chamber is 200ft long. Beyond is a second chamber into which the Allt Smoo stream plummets 80ft down a sheer rock face into a deep pool. Beyond this again is yet another chamber. The first cave is easily accessible, but the 2 further caves can only be reached by experts. The name Smoo is probably derived from the old Norse word, smjuga, which means cleft.

Continue to Durness.

DURNESS, Highland

Set on the hillsides above Sango Bay, Durness is the most north-western village in Britain. It is a neat and well-ordered community that has preserved its crofting traditions in the face of increasingly heavy odds. The name of Durness is thought to be derived from the Viking for Cape of the Wild Beasts — after the wolves which once plagued the area. Limestone cliffs, pocked by small caves and inlets, enclose the white sands of Sango Bay. Away to the north-west are the desolate lands which culminate in Cape Wrath, the extreme north-western point of the Scottish mainland. Although no public road leads to the cape, mini-buses carry visitors to it from the Kyle of Durness Ferry in the summer months. On this wild coast are the cliffs of Clo Mor, at 900ft the highest in Britain.

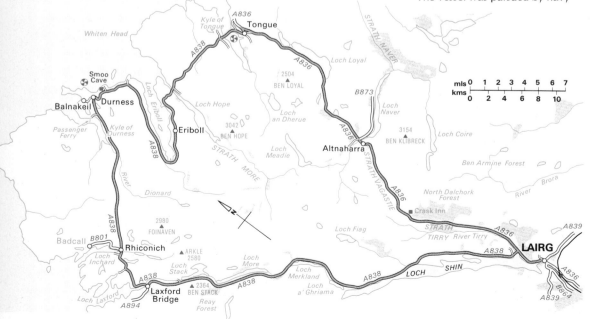

Above: looking westwards from Ard Neackie across Loch Eriboll towards 2,537ft-high Beinn Spionnaidh

Left: the entrance to Smoo Cave — a limestone cavern created by sea erosion and an underground river bed

A short detour to the north-west of Durness can be made to visit Balnakeil.

BALNAKEIL, Highland
On the road to this remote hamlet is Balnakeil Craft Village, a community of artists and craftsmen who established themselves in disused service-buildings during 1964. Visitors are made welcome at the pottery and art gallery. Balnakeil itself has roots which go back to the very beginning of British Christianity, but tangible remains, in the shape of a ruined monastery, date back only to 1619. The headland beyond Balnakeil has spectacular cliff scenery, especially at Flirium, where the strangely-contorted rock formations are a haven for puffins.

From Durness the main tour heads southwards along the Scourie road and after 1¾ miles passes the turning for the Kyle of Durness Ferry (right). Continue through barren, mountainous countryside to Rhiconich.

RHICONICH, Highland
A coaching inn once stood in this tiny hamlet at the head of Loch Inchard. It is surrounded by an extrordinary landscape of stark rocks littered with innumerable lochs and lochans. This almost lunar scene is formed from some of the most ancient rocks in the world. Views to the south-east encompass the bleak expanses of the Forest of Reay, a largely uninhabited land of bogs and craggy hills that was once the hunting ground of the chiefs of the Clan MacKay. Foinaven, whose highest peak reaches to 2,980ft, dominates this awesome scene.

Remain on the A838 to Laxford Bridge.

LAXFORD BRIDGE, Highland
This scattering of cottages at the head of Loch Laxford is at the heart of what has been called a fisherman's paradise; indeed, lax is the Norse for salmon. To the east, beneath the conical peak of 2,346ft Ben Stack, is Loch Stach, one of the finest fishing lochs in Scotland. Wildlife of many other kinds, including black-throated divers, otters, pine martens and red deer, can often be seen in and around the loch.

Turn left on to the Lairg road. Later pass beneath Ben Stack and follow the waters of Loch Stack. Pass a further succession of lochs before the long run alongside Loch Shin.

LOCH SHIN, Highland
Desolate Highland scenery surrounds this rather featureless loch. It is 17 miles long and its waters are used to produce hydro-electricity. A large dam near Lairg has raised the water level more than 30ft. Major engineering works needed to make the system work efficiently included the construction of a 2½ mile-long tunnel to bring water into the loch from Glen Cassley, and another tunnel, 5 miles long, which carries water to a generating station at Inveran. The highest mountain in the old county of Sutherland, 3,273ft Ben More Assynt, rises to the north-west.

Near the far end of the loch turn right on to the A836 for the return to Lairg.

INDEX

Continued overleaf

W

Y

Langdale and the Langdale Pikes, Cumbria